Developmental Education

Readings on Its Past, Present, and Future

EDITED BY

Hunter R. Boylan

Appalachian State University

Barbara S. Bonham

Appalachian State University

Bedford/St. Martin's　　　　Boston ◆ New York

For Bedford/St. Martin's

Publisher for Composition: Leasa Burton
Developmental Editor: Jonathan Douglas
Publishing Services Manager: Andrea Cava
Production Supervisor: Steven Dowling
Senior Market Development Manager: Karita France dos Santos
Project Management: DeMasi Design and Publishing Services
Text Design: Claire Seng-Niemoeller
Cover Design: Donna Lee Dennison
Composition: Jeff Miller Book Design
Printing and Binding: RR Donnelley & Sons

President, Bedford/St. Martin's: Denise B. Wydra
Editorial Director, English and Music: Karen S. Henry
Director of Marketing: Karen R. Soeltz
Production Director: Susan W. Brown
Director of Rights and Permissions: Hilary Newman

Manufactured in the United States of America.

9 8 7 6 5 4
f e d c b a

For information, write: Bedford/St. Martin's, 75 Arlington Street, Boston, MA 02116
(617-399-4000)

ISBN 978-1-4576-3081-1

Acknowledgments

This book is dedicated to our students, who have inspired our desire to study developmental education and to teach them using what we've learned.

Acknowledgments

Developmental Education is the result of input and support from many people and we would like to acknowledge several of them here. We begin by thanking Alan Craig, who shared freely from his doctoral dissertation research on the history of learning assistance and developmental education. Thanks also go to Norm Stahl and Sonya Armstrong, who provided the opportunity to experience the actual process of editing a book by including us as co-authors of previous Bedford/St. Martin's publications.

The good folks at Bedford/St. Martin's, Jonathan Douglas, Alexis Walker, and Linda DeMasi, provided a great deal of assistance, without which we could not have completed this task. In addition, there is a long list of mentors such as Frank Christ, Gene Kerstein, Martha Maxwell, and Bill White, who are no longer with us but whose advice, counsel, and occasional scolding inspired both of us during our careers.

Finally, we would like to thank those who teach developmental courses or work in learning centers at colleges and universities throughout the world. Your efforts to encourage and support our underprepared, disadvantaged, and underrepresented citizens in attaining their educational goals have been an inspiration to our work. We hope this book will not only provide readers with some guidance for their important efforts, but also contribute to the scholarship of the field.

Introduction

The students leaving our high schools and entering today's colleges and universities represent greater diversity than at any time in the history of our nation's postsecondary education, and the population of developmental students reflects this diversity. Developmental students come from the full range of socioeconomic and ethnic backgrounds. They have been subjected to racism and favoritism, prejudice and preference, disadvantage and advantage. Some are recent immigrants who have lived in poverty all their lives and had little schooling from their home country. Some come from backgrounds of wealth and power in their own countries but have received schooling that translates imperfectly to the requirements of postsecondary institutions in the United States.

No matter how K–12 standards are changed, expanded, or raised, there will always be students who, for a plethora of reasons, go on to higher education underprepared for college-level work. No matter what courses or programs are set up for underprepared students, some will be successful and some will not. But all of these students will still be part of our college and university population. It is time (perhaps past time) we stop viewing underpreparedness as a problem to be solved and start viewing it as an accepted fact in U.S. higher education. If it is a fact of life, then we need to continue exploring the best, most efficacious, and most cost-effective ways of responding. We also need to ensure that our teaching and our practices reflect these realities.

This is what the book you are about to read attempts to do. The material collected in it summarizes what we know about past efforts to serve underprepared students; it explains what we know about responses to underpreparedness today; and it suggests promising practices for the future.

The good news is that we now have a great deal of research and literature to guide us in addressing the needs of underprepared learners and increasing their chances for success. Thirty years ago, there were only two or three books and a handful of articles that discussed underprepared students and ways to serve them. In preparing this book, it has been a distinct pleasure and a tremendous benefit to have thousands of books, articles, and reports on these topics available to review, from which we have selected what we regard as both representative and exemplary works.

The resulting text is intended primarily to support and guide the professionals who actually do the work in the field. Not all of the material included here translates directly into an answer for "What do I do on Monday?" however. Much of it addresses the history of the field, as well as policy and research issues. It is the authors' view that professionals in the field need to be just as aware of research and policy issues as they are of teaching and learning issues. If we are unable to understand and communicate our history to others, we allow the myth to continue that developmental education is a recent phenomenon in higher education that will simply go away if we come up with the right policies. Similarly, if we do not understand the policy issues surrounding contemporary developmental education, we will be unable to influence them or even carry out policies properly.

We should perhaps clarify here what we mean when we refer to remediation and developmental education. The term *remediation* refers specifically to courses that teach the basic academic skills necessary for college-level work. The term *developmental education* refers to a range of integrated courses and services governed by the principles of adult learning and development. They help students improve their personal and academic skills in ways that lead to success in college. Although the vast majority of time, energy, and money spent on developmental education addresses underprepared undergraduate students, developmental education also takes place at the upper division and graduate levels. A student who needs to read better in order to pass an introductory sociology course can profit from developmental education. So, also, can an entering medical school student profit from learning to read and comprehend faster in order to master all the new material he or she will face while pursuing a medical degree. As the motto of the National Association for Developmental Education points out, developmental education is designed to help "underprepared students prepare, prepared students advance, and advanced students excel."

The key to implementing developmental education at any level is that coursework and support services must be integrated and must be guided by what we know about adult development and learning. Many of the models presented in this book represent the integration of remedial courses and various forms of academic support. All of them are grounded in what we know about how adults learn and how they develop their cognitive and affective skills and characteristics.

It is vitally important that we use the information in this book as well as other sources of research that can improve the quality of our practice. The field of developmental education faces tougher criticism from legislators, policy makers, and researchers than at any other time in its history. Some of this criticism is justified. We are not doing nearly as much to prepare students to be successful in college as we need to. At a time when we need to produce more college graduates, and do so more rapidly, developmental education at some institutions contributes little to graduation and extends the amount of time required for a degree. Developmental education on some campuses is serving as a barrier rather than a path to completion. (In some places, only one in ten of those placed in developmental education ever completes a college degree or certificate.)

Much of the criticism of developmental education, however, is ill-founded, based on misinterpretations of the data or the failure to understand the goals of developmental education. Some of this criticism is also based on results from aggregate data which obscures the successes of individual programs and institutions. The bottom line is that developmental education is working in some places, preparing students to complete gateway courses and graduate from college. This is despite the fact that developmental educators are working with some of the most at-risk students in higher education. All of the factors that contribute to high drop-out rates among college students — poverty, first-generation status, nonnative language, and underpreparedness — are well represented among those students participating in developmental education. In addition, most developmental programs have inadequate resources. A recent Ohio study, for instance, reported that although developmental education serves 38 percent of the state's first-time, full-time students, it is allocated only 3.6 percent of the instructional resources (Wellman & Vandal, 2011).

At a time when we face greater criticism, higher expectations, and reduced resources, it is imperative that we use the best of what we know to guide our program development and implementation as well as our instruction. We can do more with less if we truly understand the lessons from research and practice. We can help more students be successful in college if we evaluate what we are doing, determine where we need to change, and make revisions accordingly. We can prove that what we do represents a pathway to success if our professional practice reflects the best of what we know from thirty years of research. It is the authors' hope that this work will serve in some small way to help those who wish to accept the challenge of making developmental education a pathway to success for those who aspire to improve their lives through higher education.

References

Wellman, J., & Vandal, B. (2011, July 21). 5 myths of remedial education. *Inside Higher Education*. Retrieved from http://www.insidehighered.com/views/2011/07/21/wellman_vandal_5_myths_about_remedial_education

Contents

Historical Programs and Theories in Developmental Education

Georges Santayana, the famed Spanish-American philosopher, is credited with saying, "Those who fail to learn the lessons of history are doomed to repeat them." This comment is certainly true when it comes to developmental education. Some of us appear to have forgotten many of the lessons we learned about developmental education throughout its history in the United States.

Some of us have forgotten, for instance, that we have had developmental education programs in one form or another since the beginnings of American higher education. The existence of programs for underprepared students may have recently been discovered by legislators, policy makers, and researchers but their discovery of developmental education is much like Columbus's "discovery" of America. As soon as the nation's first higher education institution, Harvard College, was founded in 1636, it was determined that applicants needed to have a working knowledge of Greek and Latin. Those aspiring to be admitted to Harvard College without such knowledge obtained tutoring in Greek and Latin from local clergy in order to qualify for admission. Although this tutoring was not a "program" in the modern sense, it did represent an organized intervention responding to underpreparedness or a lack of college readiness.

When the University of North Carolina was founded in 1795, "vast numbers of its students, it was discovered, had come unprepared" (Snider, 1992, p. 29). As a result the university established a preparatory school where underprepared students were taught basic grammar, writing, and arithmetic. Those who mastered these subjects to the satisfaction of their professors were permitted to enter as regular university students (Knight, 1952). We have thus had formal programs to serve underprepared students in American higher education, with countless students, faculty, and staff working to improve students' skills, for over 200 years.

Such preparatory programs were common in U.S. colleges and universities throughout the nineteenth century. They were offered at institutions as diverse as Purdue University, the University of Minnesota, the University of Georgia, Yale University, the University of North Carolina, Cornell University, Harvard University, Vassar College, and the University of Nebraska (Arendale, p. 28 in this book; Brier, p. 11 in this book; Maxwell, 1997; and White, Martirosyan, & Wanjohi, p. 18 in this book). Not only were these programs offered but large numbers of students participated in them. According to Martha Maxwell (1997) more than half of the students enrolled at Ivy League universities in 1913 had failed the college entrance examination and were placed in preparatory courses.

It is important for practitioners in the field to understand this lesson. Each of us needs to be able to communicate to our colleagues that remediation is not a new phenomenon and remedial students have not suddenly descended on higher education. They have been with us since the very beginning of American higher education and are likely to be with us for the foreseeable future.

This leads to a second lesson: as our nation's postsecondary education system has become more egalitarian, every new group to attain entry has entered without being deemed fully college ready. In the 1800s when women were first admitted to postsecondary education, they were considered unready for college. In the latter part of the nineteenth century, the sons and a few daughters of the working class began to be admitted to college. They, too, were considered underprepared. In fact, the student newspaper at Cornell University referred to these new students as a "vandal horde" of "unconventionalities" (Brier, p. 13 in this book). In the mid-1900s when African Americans began to attend institutions other than historically black colleges and universities, they too were regarded as unready for college. By the beginning of the 1970s, a combination of educational opportunity, affirmative action, and federal financial aid brought a wave of what K. Patricia Cross (1971) referred to as the "new college student." These were students who, heretofore, had never been considered college material. They included the poor of every minority ethnic group in the nation, single parents, displaced workers, and older adults. They were to become the new underprepared. In the twenty-first century, the ranks of the underprepared have been joined by immigrants, both legal and illegal.

Those developmental educators who feel that they and their students are not valued at their institutions should recognize that this is part of a historical institutional bias against students considered to be underprepared and those who serve them. In choosing to become a developmental educator one also chooses to accept this bias at many institutions. This does not mean, however, that we are powerless to change it through affirming our history and demonstrating the quality of our professionalism. It should also be noted that each cycle of new underprepared students has somehow managed to produce many success stories (Merisotis & Phipps, p. 63 in this book). The number of these stories may not be as large as we would like, but the fact that there *are* successes suggests that developmental education can, indeed, serve whatever cycle of new underprepared students may be introduced to postsecondary education today and in the future.

A third lesson to learn from the history of developmental education is that although underpreparedness is still with us, it has actually decreased. To a substantial degree, efforts to increase the availability of free public schooling during the early 1900s contributed to the preparedness of many students during the last century. Brubacher and Rudy have estimated that more than half of the students enrolled in universities at the turn of the twentieth century were enrolled in developmental or preparatory departments (1976). According to the National Center for Education statistics, participation in developmental education had by 2003 declined to 28 percent at universities and 43 percent in community colleges (National Center for Education Statistics, 2004). Thus, taking the long view, the percentage of underprepared students in the entire college-going population has declined even while their absolute number has increased, thanks to increased access to postsecondary education.[1]

A final important lesson we might take away from examination of this history of developmental education is that reform efforts take time. In 1983, according to the National Center for Education Statistics, 29 percent of students were placed in one or more developmental courses (U.S. Department of Education, 1984). It is worth noting that 1983 was the publication year of *A Nation at Risk*, a report that described a number of weaknesses in American public education and stimulated an ongoing reform movement that continues to this day. Yet according to a National Center for Education Statistics report twenty years later, the percentage of students placing into one or more developmental courses stood at 28 percent, only a 1 percent decrease in two decades (U.S. Department of Education, 2004). Although twenty years of reform efforts may have improved public schools, they did not have an impact on the college readiness of those who graduated from public schools. One concludes that, in the short term, no amount of public school reform is going to substantially reduce the number of underprepared students entering American postsecondary education. Underprepared students have been with us for a very long time and they are likely to continue to be with us for a very long time.

The articles presented in this chapter address the history of underprepared students and the programs that have served them. The articles by Hunter Boylan and William White and by William White with Nara Martirosyan and Reubenson Wanjohi make it clear that institutions were dealing with underpreparedness in a programmatic manner in the early nineteenth century. Ellen Brier's article discusses the historical reception of underprepared students at the institutions they attended. Finally, the chapter concludes with a selection from David Arendale's 2010 book *Access at the Crossroads*, which is the only source to date to trace the entire history of developmental education from the 1600s to present.

Note

1. More recently, according to Merisotis and Phipps (p. 63 in this book), the percentage of underprepared students enrolling in U.S. colleges and universities between 1989 and 1995 remained relatively stable even though the size of the American college and universities population increased by half a million students.

References

Brubacher, J., & Rudy, W. (1976). *Higher education in transition: A history of American colleges and universities, 1636–1976*. New York, NY: Harper & Row.

Cross, K. P. (1971). *Beyond the open door*. San Francisco, CA: Jossey-Bass.

Knight, E. W. (Ed.). (1952). *A documentary history of education in the South before 1860: Vol. 3. The rise of the state university*. Chapel Hill, NC: University of North Carolina Press.

Maxwell, M. (1997). *Improving student learning skills*. Clearwater, FL: H & H Publishing.

Snider, W. D. (1992). *A history of the University of North Carolina at Chapel Hill*. Chapel Hill, NC: University of North Carolina Press.

U.S. Department of Education. (1984). *The condition of education 1984*. Washington, DC: National Center for Education Statistics.

U.S. Department of Education. (2004). *The condition of education 2004*. Washington, DC: National Center for Education Statistics.

Additional Readings

Casazza, M., & Silverman, S. (1996). *Learning assistance and developmental education*. San Francisco, CA: Jossey-Bass.

Parker, T. (2007, October). Ending college remediation: Consequences for access and opportunity. *ASHE/Lumina Policy Briefs and Critical Essays #2*. Ames, IA: Iowa State University, Department of Educational Leadership and Policy Studies.

Stanley, J. (2010). *The rhetoric of remediation*. Pittsburgh, PA: University of Pittsburgh Press.

Educating All the Nation's People: The Historical Roots of Developmental Education

Hunter R. Boylan and William G. White, Jr.

This article, published in 1986, was one of the first to address the history of developmental education and where it fits into the evolving history of American higher education. The authors argue that developmental education has been present throughout the history of American higher education and that developmental education has facilitated the enrollment of new groups of students in colleges and universities. As such it has been a force for egalitarianism in higher education.

On most American college and university campuses developmental educators are regarded as the "newest kids on the block." To most professionals in academe, developmental programs and the students they serve are of relatively recent vintage—a phenomenon that resulted from 1960's egalitarianism and the subsequent "open door" admissions policies of public colleges and universities. College administrators, legislators, and the public believe that the problem of underpreparedness that developmental programs are designed to resolve is a recent one—one that results from all the shortcomings of American public education that a spate of recent reports has so eloquently pointed out. Unfortunately, most developmental educators would probably agree with those views even though they are, for the most part, inaccurate.

A more accurate view would be that developmental education programs, and the students they serve, are not new to higher education. They have been present on college and university campuses in one form or another since the very beginnings of American higher education.

Underpreparedness is not a new problem in American higher education. Large numbers of students have been unprepared for the institutions they attended since the first American college admitted its first students.

Like many fields of endeavor in education, developmental education is not particularly new. The field of developmental education is simply the modern version of past efforts to respond to the fact that, at their point of entry, many college students are unable to succeed without some sort of special assistance. It also represents the most recent version of American higher education's long-standing commitment to providing access to college for all the nation's citizens who might profit from it.

This issue of *Research in Developmental Education* is devoted to an initial discussion of the historical antecedents of developmental education. It will summarize efforts to make access to college more equal and to serve those who are underprepared for college success. It is the first in a series of issues of *Research in Developmental Education* to be devoted to this topic. Future issues will deal with the role of historically Black colleges in developmental education as well as more recent legislation and events with an impact of the field of developmental education. It is hoped that discussion of the historical roots of the field will help developmental educators and others understand the past, present, and future significance of developmental education as a field of endeavor within higher education.

17th Century Precedents for Developmental Education

America's first college was founded as a result of an act passed by the leaders of the Massachusetts Bay Colony. This act provided for the establishment of a college that would train clergymen for the colony "... once our present generation of ministers has passed from this Earth" ("Old Deluder Satan Act" of 1624).

The institution that was founded as a result of this act, Harvard College, did not open its doors until several years later—1636, to be exact. When it did open, it was immediately confronted with a need for remediation among its students. This need for remediation resulted from the fact that the language in which most learned books were written was Latin. Furthermore, following the European model of the time, Latin was also the language of instruction for most courses. It is worth noting that the King James Version of the Bible was one of the first books written in common English so that all the citizens of England might be able to read it. And the King James Version of the Bible was not published until the early seventeenth century. Few books, particularly scholarly works, were available in any language other than Latin. Unfortunately, the learning of an academic language was not a high priority for colonists attempting to carve a homeland out of the wilderness.

Consequently, it was necessary for those who wished to attend Harvard College to study Latin before they could be successful in their studies. Harvard, therefore, provided tutors in Latin for incoming students (Brubacher and Rudy, 1976). The provision of such tutorial assistance may rightly be regarded as the first remedial education effort in North America—the earliest antecedent of developmental education in American higher education. The use of books written in Latin and the use of Latin as a language of instruction persisted well into the 18th century in American colleges. It was not until after the American Revolution that English language texts and English language instruction became available on a widespread basis (Brubacher and Rudy, 1976). Until this happened, tutorials in Latin were a predominant feature of American colleges.

Developmental Education in the 19th Century

One of the major political and philosophical forces in the United States from the early- to mid-nineteenth century was "Jacksonian Democracy." One of its hallmarks was an appreciation of the common man combined with an effort to serve his needs and aspirations through government. The "Jacksonian Period" is generally regarded as falling between 1824 and 1848, the period between the election of Andrew Jackson to the presidency and the election of Zachary Taylor—the latter marking the decline of Jacksonian ideals.

Spanning more than two decades, Jacksonian Democracy had a considerable impact on all facets of American life. During this period, suffrage was extended, the lot of workers was improved, the middle class of merchants and tradesmen grew rapidly, and education at all levels was provided to an increasing number of citizens.

One area in which educational access was expanded during this period was in higher education. In an effort to improve the lot of the common man, to provide training for merchants and tradesmen, and to expand the pool of engineering, agricultural, and scientific talent in the developing nation, new colleges were established in practically every state in the union (Van Deusen, 1986). But because education had, heretofore, been neither mandatory nor universal, there were few people available who had much prior preparation for college. Yet, if the new colleges were to remain open, they would have to collect fees from students.

It should be noted that the colleges of this period were largely self-sustaining operations. While they were sometimes funded by land sales such as those provided for by the Ohio Land Grant Act of 1802, more often than not, they were funded by private donations and student fees. This being the case, a major criterion for admission to college was the student's ability to pay his own way (the masculine gender is used here purposefully since women were not generally admitted to college in the early 19th century). In essence, this meant that anyone who had the money to attend college was able to do so without regard to prior learning or preparation (Brubacher and Rudy, 1976).

As a result, the colleges of the time were confronted with substantial numbers of students who were unprepared to do college level work. Most efforts to respond to this problem consisted of individual tutoring of students. As enrollments grew, however, the number of individual tutors became insufficient to meet the demand. As Brier (p. 11 in this book) points out, many colleges had more people involved in giving and receiving tutoring than were involved in delivering and taking classes.

At the University of Wisconsin, the problem became so severe that the institution established the nation's first college preparatory department in 1849 (Brier, p. 11). This department functioned in much the same way as a modern developmental education program. It provided remedial courses in reading, writing, and arithmetic to students who lacked sufficient background to succeed in more advanced college courses. The college preparatory department model was soon adopted by other institutions across the country. In fact, by 1889, more than 80 percent of the colleges and universities in the United States offered college preparatory programs (Brier, p. 11).

The growth of college preparatory programs was stimulated not only by an influx of underprepared students but also by a further expansion in the number of colleges and universities. While a combination of economic and political conditions stifled the growth of higher education in America in the years immediately preceding the Civil War, the Morrill Act of 1862 was to stimulate another period of growth for higher education institutions following the Civil War. Furthermore, the Morrill Act (1862), or the Land Grant Act as it is commonly known, also made it clear that institutions established as a result of this act should serve "the industrial classes" of America. The act was designed not only to expand the number of qualified engineers, agricultural, military, and business specialists, it was also designed to promote access to higher education for a greater variety of citizens.

During the latter part of the 19th century, an unprecedented period of growth took place in the number and variety of higher education institutions. State land grant colleges were not the only institutions that expanded in number following the Civil War. Colleges for women, agricultural colleges, technical colleges, and colleges for Blacks also expanded. And, as the number and variety of institutions grew, so did the number of college students who were underprepared for college.

Women's colleges, which first appeared in the late 1830's, were an outgrowth of a great reform movement that sought legal, political, and social and educational equality for women and which was, in many ways, linked with Jacksonian Democracy. With every college of the early 19th century except Oberlin refusing to accept women, a number of institutions were established to cater solely to them.

Those opposed to admitting women to college argued that they were mentally unsuited for higher education. While that certainly was untrue, it was true that most women were underprepared for college because they were unable to obtain an adequate secondary education. The early women's colleges were thus forced to keep the age of admission low, and the curriculum provided was understandably more akin to secondary than higher education. The baccalaureate degrees they granted were not recognized as equal to those granted by other institutions.

The Civil War, in addition to settling a number of constitutional issues, also settled a number of social ones, including the question of whether women should attend college. Following the war, the question changed from "if" to "where?"

In the northeastern states the dominant pattern became superior, but separate, women's colleges with independent institutions such as

Vassar, Wellesley, Smith, and Bryn Mawr and coordinated women's colleges affiliated with several "Ivy League" schools. But even in these efforts, preparatory schools were still necessary.

One of the earliest women's colleges, Vassar, had a college preparatory program from its very beginnings. But in spite of the fact that Vassar was founded for the purpose of including those who had previously been denied access to higher education there were those who questioned the presence of underprepared students. In fact, the question of whether or not underprepared women should be admitted at all to the institution was a major issue for the college during the late 1800's (Report to the Trustees of Vassar College, 1890). Nevertheless, Vassar continued then and continues now to admit women who have inadequate secondary preparation (Boylan, 1986).

The trend to establish separate colleges for women was not, however, a universal one. In the newer universities of the East and in colleges throughout the Western states, where coeducational secondary schools were preparing young people for college, coeducation became the pattern (Brubacher and Rudy, 1976).

The increase in the number of students going to college following the Civil War was not only the result of a democratic movement but also of a greater demand by men and women for higher training to prepare them for an increasing number of professions, trades, industries, and businesses that required specialized preparation.

Two other efforts to provide postsecondary education for students who were either uninterested in or underprepared to pursue the traditional classical/liberal arts curriculum centered in technical institutes and scientific schools. Technical institutes had first appeared in the 1820's and were the first to offer extension programs and evening courses which made higher education accessible to non-traditional students. These efforts were the precursors of the modern adult education programs.

Technical institutes were soon followed by scientific schools, established alongside a number of leading colleges, to care for "practical minded students" who in many cases were not prepared to complete the classical curriculum. And, like higher education for women, scientific schools and technical institutes faced strenuous opposition from those who wanted to preserve the integrity of the classical college curriculum (Butts, 1939). In many respects, the early technical and scientific schools faced challenges and opposition analogous to that faced by junior and community colleges in the twentieth century.

Another major precedent for developmental education was the establishment of colleges for Blacks during the latter part of the 19th and the early part of the 20th century. Following the Civil War, it was apparent that Black Americans would become part of the social, political, and economic systems of the nation. Yet the institution of slavery had systematically denied most of these citizens access to all but the most rudimentary forms of education.

In response to this, postsecondary institutions for Black Americans were established through a number of channels. The American Missionary Society set up a number of institutions in the South for the purpose of educating freed slaves (Brubacher and Rudy, 1976). The Second Morrill Act (1890) also provided for the establishment of land grant colleges for Black Americans. In addition to these, Black Americans also established several colleges through their own efforts.

All of these institutions were confronted with the enormous problem of providing the training necessary to prosper in a modern industrial society to a generation of people who had been denied access to education in any form. In fact the contribution of historically Black colleges in delivering a massive remedial and developmental education effort has been largely ignored in the field of developmental education. For many of these institutions, their entire mission might be defined as remedial and developmental. And it should be noted that the early Black institutions were extraordinarily successful in the face of overwhelming odds. The fact that so many of the Black leaders, scientists, legislators, doctors, and attorneys of the late 19th and early 20th centuries, as well as today, were trained at these institutions attests to their effectiveness. It could well be argued that some of the most amazing feats of developmental education were accomplished at historically Black institutions in the United States.

References

Boylan, H. R., "Developmental Education: A Hundred Years of Promise . . . a Decade of Crisis," Address before the National Conference on Exemplary Programs in Developmental Education, October, 1986.

Brubacher, J. S., and Rudy, W., *Higher Education in Transition*, New York: Harper and Row, 1976.

Butts, R. F., *The College Charts its Course*, New York: McGraw-Hill, 1939.

Massachusetts Bay Colony, "The Old Deluder Satan Act," An Act of the General Assembly of the Colony of Massachusetts Bay, September, 1624.

Vassar College, "Report to the Trustees," as cited in Brier, E., "The Controversy of the Underprepared Student at Vassar College and Cornell University, 1865–1890," Paper presented at the Annual Meeting of the Association for the Study of Higher Education, Chicago, IL, 1984.

Van Deusen, G. G., *The Jackson Era: 1828–1848*, New York: Harper and Row, 1986.

Bridging the Academic Preparation Gap: An Historical View

Ellen Brier

This article addresses efforts to assist underprepared students in nineteenth-century universities in the United States. It describes the rise of preparatory departments at some of the nation's most elite institutions and discusses the politics surrounding this growth. It also points out that the programs and the students they served were often far from welcome at the universities which had admitted them, a trend that appears to continue at some institutions to this day.

The American college is obliged to supplement the American school. Whatever elementary instruction the schools fail to give, the college must supply" (Eliot, 1869). With this statement, Charles William Eliot presented a clear challenge to American higher education in his inaugural address as president of Harvard College in 1869. Despite the early date of Eliot's call for action, developmental education within the context of American higher education has an untold history.

It can be asserted accurately that bridging the academic preparation gap has been a constant in the history of American higher education and that the controversy surrounding it is an American educational tradition. Indeed, the issues involving underprepared college students and higher education's responsibility to provide appropriate educational opportunities for these students have been an integral part of the development of higher education in the United States. The popular belief that the academically underprepared student and developmental education efforts are by-products of the open admissions of the 1960s is no more than a widely believed myth. In order to debunk this myth, a close look at the nineteenth century movement to bridge the academic preparation gap is necessary.

The Presence of Underprepared Students

First, it is essential to establish the presence of underprepared students in American colleges during the nineteenth century. Although student recordkeeping as it is now known was nonexistent in the nineteenth century, conclusions about students can be drawn from numerous other sources. Among the most useful sources are institutional records and archives, student publications, alumni collections, institutional histories, and faculty papers.

These sources indicate unequivocally that nineteenth century American colleges and universities admitted students considered by faculty and administrators to be far below acceptable "college level" standards. Throughout the nineteenth century the cry for "more adequately prepared" students went out. As early as 1828, the *Yale Report* called for an end to the admission of students with "defective preparation." This cry to stop the admission of underprepared students was countered, however, by the ever-growing movement toward educational egalitarianism. As the new nation moved into what educational historian Lawrence Cremin (1980) has called the "National" period (1783–1876), American higher education increasingly embraced the principles of Jacksonian democracy. Colleges multiplied almost exponentially, and more and more of them opened their doors to growing numbers of individuals unfamiliar with academe (Allmendinger, 1975; Burke, 1982). Many of these newly founded colleges served local educational needs and local students as a result of their being locally controlled (Potts, 1977).

After the Civil War, however, the demand for an improved caliber of entering students as well as improvement in American higher education increased in intensity. The nineteenth century college growth movement greatly expanded the meaning of institutional and student diversity. At the beginning of the nineteenth century, church-related colleges for men served as the sole model of American higher education. By the last quarter of the century, institutional types included scientific and technical institutions, state colleges, professional and graduate schools, colleges for women and for blacks, and coeducational institutions. New and developing institutions brought what K. Patricia Cross (1976) eventually referred to as "new students"—students with developmental educational needs—into higher education. Repeatedly, college reformers such as Charles William Eliot, Noah Porter, William Rainey Harper, and Andrew Dickson White appealed for the admission of students who were adequately prepared to meet the demands of elevated college curricula; but within the colleges themselves, faculties confronted the educational problems presented by academically weak students.

Cornell University, for example, firmly stated in its registers that only adequately prepared, scholastically qualified applicants would be admitted to the university. However, a popular anecdote about founder, Ezra Cornell, a faculty member, and a group of underprepared students illustrates an extreme example of the problem faced by faculty during the nineteenth century. Mr. Cornell, at the request of a group of students who did not pass the entrance examinations, approached the professor in charge of admissions. When he asked why the students were not passed, the admissions professor answered that they did not know enough. Cornell then asked the professor why he did not teach the students what they did not know, and the professor retorted that he was unable to teach them the alphabet. Not about to drop the matter, Cornell then asked if the students could not read. The professor suggested to Mr. Cornell that if he wanted the faculty to teach spelling, he ought to have "founded a primary school and not a university" (Boyesen, 1889). The professor, however, yielded and allowed students to take a second entrance examination. Additional evidence of the presence of underprepared students at Cornell was the existence of a faculty committee on "Doubtful Cases" (Cornell University, "Faculty Minutes," 1864). Its purpose was to make decisions about academically marginal applicants and students. Thus, although Cornell University promoted itself as an academically selective institution with no preparatory programs for the unqualified, it did in truth have a group of underprepared students, and it did respond to them and their needs.

While Cornell represents an extreme on the side of maintaining an image of academic selectivity, there were many colleges throughout the United States which made no such claims. Open-admissions colleges abounded in every region and were restricted to no particular type of institution. Most established preparatory departments to serve inadequately prepared students. This abundance of collegiate preparatory departments provides ample proof of the presence of underprepared students in American colleges during the last century. In 1889, James H. Canfield reported to the National Council of Education meeting in Nashville, Tennessee, that of the nearly four hundred institutions of higher education in the United States, only sixty-five "have freed themselves from the embarrassment of preparatory departments." At many institutions preparatory enrollments matched or exceeded the "regular" college enrollments. If accurately represented, many of these institutions were preparatory schools with college departments rather than colleges with preparatory departments.

Student Inadequacies

After establishing the early presence of an underprepared student population, it is important to consider the nature of the students' academic inadequacies. As with today's underprepared students, nineteenth century students ran the full gamut of academic deficiencies. Faculty and administrators complained frequently about students' inabilities in the basic skills areas. Spelling, writing, geography, and mathematics often were identified as areas in which college students needed to develop skills. Faculty complaints about students' inabilities to spell and to write repeatedly appeared in nineteenth century faculty papers. At Cornell, in his annual report to the Board of Trustees in 1869, President Andrew Dickson White reported that the "utter ignorance" of many students in the "common English branches" was "astounding" (Cornell University, *President's Report*, 1869); apparently professors a century ago were no less frustrated by students' lack of basic skills than we are today. Students who did not know how to study also were common (Orton, 1871), as were students who were not prepared for the level of socialization expected in academe. College histories are filled with examples of what might be classified as "sub-collegiate" behavior. *The Vassar Miscellany* referred to some of the underprepared students as "a vandal horde" and a group of "unconventionalities" (1882). Thus, colleges not only had to face the problem of finding appropriate academic remedies for the less qualified students, but some also had to provide an educational structure aimed at helping students develop social skills as well.

Developmental Education

Faced with underprepared applicants and a strong need for enrollment, nineteenth century colleges, like many of their twentieth century descendants, admitted students whether they were prepared or not. Dealing with these underprepared students varied from institution to institution; however, several basic approaches formed the models for developmental/remedial education during the nineteenth century.

First and foremost among nineteenth century remedial education efforts were the preparatory departments, which varied greatly in terms of organizational and instructional specifics. Most, however, fell into the category of academies and were located within academe as secondary schools within colleges. Preparatory departments of this type were separate programs operated under the name and auspices of the colleges. They shared college facilities and faculties, and students were identified as college students, although they were in what today would be termed six-year programs. At many of these colleges, preparatory students often took college courses as well as preparatory courses; and by the last quarter of the century, examinations sometimes accompanied by faculty and/or presidential recommendations were used to place and promote these students.

The University of Wisconsin provided an excellent example of the typical "preparatory department" experience. Begun in 1849 "to bridge the gap" between the common schools or academies and the university, Wisconsin's preparatory department persisted for thirty-one years. It was sometimes disguised under other names and endured constant attack from the faculty and the Board of Trustees (Curti and Carstensen, 1949).

Preparatory education at Vassar College also followed the "preparatory department" model (Brier, 1983). While the tuition of the "preparatory" or "sub-freshmen" students was welcomed, the presence of the students often was not and frequently served as a source of institutional embarrassment. Indeed, at Vassar the preparatory students were referred to in *The Vassar Miscellany* as "inferior forms" as well as a "reproach to be wiped away" (July, 1872). Vassar also acknowledged, however, that preparatory education and its students were viewed as a financial necessity for the life of the developing college (Vassar College, *Annual Report*, 1866).

Though colleges did not operate specific preparatory departments, they did offer pre-college courses to remedy students' academic deficiencies. While these courses and the students enrolled in them were frowned upon, the drive for enrollment and the paucity of adequately prepared students made the courses necessary for institutional survival. Colleges which offered preparatory courses only and avoided supporting whole preparatory departments could boast of being strictly colleges and not hybrid college-secondary institutions. Given, however, the nature and scope of course titles and the diverse methods of reporting such information, it is difficult or impossible to identify any consistency in colleges' efforts to offer preparatory courses.

Some institutions which outwardly refused to offer any type of preparatory course work did, however, provide tutoring for students with academic gaps. The tutors came from the ranks of students as well as faculty and offered extra class sessions to students with academic difficulties. Students who had scholastic deficiencies frequently were "conditioned" (assigned certain criteria to fulfill); underprepared students frequently were admitted "on condition." These conditions varied but the most widely recorded conditions were assignment to preparatory courses, tutoring, and/or extra class sessions. Cornell University was in this category of institution. Cornell records abound with references to "conditioning" students and providing special class sessions for students in academic need (Cornell University, *President's Report*, 1869; *The Cornell Era*, 1871); Cornell University, "Faculty Minutes," 1869).

The least known of the preparatory education efforts aimed at addressing the academic inadequacies of nineteenth century college students was the "tutoring school." Although the particulars of these schools differed, the basic offerings included tutoring in college as well as in college-preparatory subjects. In some instances, as in the case of the Cascadilla School in Ithaca, New York, intensive courses designed to prepare students for college entrance examinations were offered (*Cornell University Register*, 1875–1876). Tutoring schools represented an educational/business enterprise which were stimulated and supported by the presence of underprepared students. In addition, tutoring schools frequently provided college faculty opportunities to earn extra income, as was the case with the Cascadilla School founded by Cornell Professors Wait and MacKoon. These schools were the precursors of today's examination prep schools such as the Kaplan schools. Along with the models cited, there were numerous other practices idiosyncratic to particular colleges and universities throughout the country. What is critical to note is that few institutions of higher education during the nineteenth century were not faced in some way with the issue of underprepared students and with providing educational opportunities for them.

The Causes for Admission of Underprepared Students

What initially led to the admission of underprepared students, and what effect did their presence have on American higher education? The answers to these questions are as complex and interrelated as nineteenth century American history itself.

First among the reasons for admitting inadequately prepared students to higher education was the financial structure of the colleges. Colleges needed enrollment to generate the revenue required to operate.

Second, the number of colleges far exceeded the required number of adequately prepared students. In this sense, higher education was over-expanded *vis a vis* secondary education. Nineteenth century college development rivaled nineteenth century canal and church building, and higher education's development often preceded secondary education's development or at best paralleled it. The development of widespread secondary education was strongly influenced by leaders in higher education, and the eventual emergence of secondary education diminished the need for higher education's preparatory programs. Throughout much of the nineteenth century, however, opportunities for secondary education were inadequate. Outside the Northeast, where the academy movement was strong, preparatory schools were far less numerous. Thus, many students interested in getting an adequate preparatory education had no opportunity to do so.

Third, many in higher education believed in providing educational opportunity. This philosophy reflected the national faith in democratic principles, Jacksonian democracy.

Finally, as college curricula changed, so too did the prerequisite skills for admission. Throughout the entire century these remained idiosyncratic to institutions, so preparation for college was also idiosyncratic. Students needed academic preparation which was custom-tailored to a particular college. Since colleges and curricula changed with some degree of frequency, especially at the end of the century, students found it difficult or impossible to get appropriate preparation.

Effects of Colleges' Admitting Underprepared Students

The admission of scholastically deficient students was a source of institutional as well as public controversy during the nineteenth century, as it is now. Numerous policy questions surrounded the admission of unqualified students. For example, should the college curriculum be modified to accommodate the skills level of the students? Should preparatory (developmental) education be offered by the college? Should college credit be granted for "sub-collegiate" course work? In addition to these policy questions, a number of questions regarding procedure emerged. For example, who should be in charge of preparatory students? Where should pre-college courses be held—in the same area or in a separate facility from the college courses? Should the same rules apply to both collegiate and "sub-collegiate" students? Institutional records are filled with examples of discussions of questions of policy and procedure. Vassar College and Cornell University provide excellent case studies of these issues (Brier, 1983).

Embarrassment on the part of the faculty, alumni, and students resulted from the presence of underprepared students, as institutional records and alumni papers record. Again, Vassar College and Cornell University abound with examples of expressions of institutional embarrassment about the dismal state of student preparation.

On the positive side, however, efforts to achieve articulation and cooperation with the developing secondary schools grew out of the colleges' frustration and embarrassment with the underprepared students. Both Cornell and Vassar, as well as numerous other institutions, initiated formal efforts to improve college/secondary school relationships (Brier, 1983). In addition, the participation of leaders of higher education on the Committee of Ten was significant (Cremin, 1955).

More standardized admission requirements also resulted from these same frustrations and embarrassments. The movement toward standardized admission requirements led to the development of the College Board (Feuss, 1950). However, dissatisfaction with the underprepared student did not end with the advent of the College Board.

Academically underprepared students have not disappeared from American higher education; neither have contingent educational programs and the traditional controversy surrounding the presence of these students and programs designed to serve them. Although the particulars have changed, the substance remains the same. Underprepared students have been and continue to be an integral part of American higher education. Further, efforts to bridge the academic preparation gap are part of the traditional, if not formal, mission of higher education.

If what we now call developmental education is to gain recognition as a credible, legitimate, and valuable dimension of postsecondary education, those in the field must examine its history with scholarly attention and thus develop an historical perspective as part of the process of achieving professional status for the field. History holds the truth; developmental education has a traditional place in American higher education. It is by no means a new arrival.

References

Allmendinger, D. F. *Paupers and scholars: The transformation of student life in nineteenth century New England.* New York: St. Martin's Press, 1975.

Annual report, 1866. Poughkeepsie, NY: Vassar College, 1866.

Boyesen, H. H. *Cosmopolitan.* Ithaca, NY: Cornell University, 1889.

Brier, E. M. *Bridging the academic preparation gap at Vassar College and Cornell University, 1865 to 1890.* Unpublished doctoral dissertation, Columbia University, New York, 1983.

Burke, C. B. *American collegiate populations: A test of the traditional view.* New York: New York University Press, 1982.

Canfield, J. H. *The opportunities of the rural population for higher education.* Nashville: National Council on Education, 1889.

The Cornell Era. Ithaca, NY: Cornell University, 1871.

Cornell University Register, 1875–1876. Ithaca, NY: Cornell University, 1876.

Cremin, L. A. *American education: The national experience 1783–1876.* New York: Harper & Row, 1980.

Cremin, L. A. The revolution in American secondary education, 1893–1918. *Teachers College Record,* 1955, *56,* 295–308.

Cross, K. P. *Accent on learning.* San Francisco: Jossey-Bass, 1976.

Curti, M., & Carstensen, V. *The University of Wisconsin, 1848–1925.* Madison: University of Wisconsin Press, 1949.

Eliot, C. W. *A turning point in higher education: The inaugural address of Charles William Eliot as president of Harvard College, October 19, 1869.* Cambridge: Harvard University Press, 1969.

Faculty minutes. Ithaca, NY: Cornell University, 1869.

Feuss, C. *The College Board: Its first fifty years.* New York: Columbia University Press, 1950.

Orton, J. *Old and New,* 1871, *4,* 257–264. Poughkeepsie, NY: Vassar College, 1871.

Potts, D. B. College enthusiasm as public response, 1800–1860. *Harvard Educational Review,* 1977, *47,* 28–42.

Vassar Miscellany. July. Poughkeepsie, NY: Vassar College, 1872.

Vassar Miscellany. March. Poughkeepsie, NY: Vassar College, 1882.

Yale Report. New Haven: Yale College, 1828.

Preparatory Programs in Nineteenth Century Midwest Land Grant Colleges (Part 1)

William G. White, Nara Martirosyan, and Reubenson Wanjohi

The selection that follows is the first of a three-part series describing the growth and development of preparatory departments at Midwestern land grant colleges in the nineteenth century. It discusses admission requirements that led to the need for preparatory departments, as well as the development of these departments and their curricula. The article suggests that nineteenth century preparatory programs were the precursors to modern developmental education programs. Because of Dr. White's untimely death, this represents his seminal work.

The advent of contemporary remedial and developmental education programs in the late 1960s and 1970s elicited grave concern on the part of many academics who lamented the admission of underprepared students and the provision of precollegiate studies on college campuses. Concern over the assumption of an apparent new collegiate mission is an illustration of the ignorance of most college and university faculty about the history of American higher education. Harcleroad and Ostar (1987) sought to dispel such ignorance more than 20 years ago:

A few very significant themes recur through these various time periods [of American higher education history]. For the entire three centuries, at least three stand out. First the need for higher education institutions to offer preparatory programs has been constant. As new additional groups of students have been accommodated, for whatever reason, special programs for makeup or preparatory work have been absolutely necessary and offered continuously. Whether they are called remedial work, developmental programs, or preparatory divisions, they have been established, often with considerable faculty complaint and sometimes concern by the college's constituents. (p. 10)

Early Preparatory and Remedial Efforts

Harvard College, the first college established in British North America in 1636, provided a pattern for future colleges in several respects (Brubacher & Rudy, 1997; Rudolph, 1990). The Massachusetts Bay Colony established the college without obtaining a charter (the right to confer academic degrees) from the Crown, a privilege that had been granted only to Oxford and Cambridge. When neither the universities nor the Crown objected, a pattern was established of American colleges chartered by legislative acts, controlled by boards of trustees, and subjected to little legal regulation.

Massachusetts established Harvard before it established any common (i.e., elementary) schools (Brubacher & Rudy, 1997; Rudolph, 1990). To preserve their English culture, colonial leaders first needed to educate clergy, civic leaders, and teachers for the soon to be established common schools. This practice of creating colleges before common schools became the norm in the American colonies and then in the United States. In the interim, the young men who enrolled at Harvard had to be prepared by private tutors hired by their families or by ministers schooled in Latin and Greek, fluency in which—especially Latin—was the principal admission requirement because all instruction and textbooks were in Latin (Rudolph, 1977). In spite of the entrance examinations, some students were admitted with insufficient Latin skills, and the college provided tutors to remediate them (Lucas, 2006). This practice spread to other colonial colleges and later to American colleges.

American Higher Education in the Nineteenth Century

The nineteenth century brought substantial change and chaos to American higher education. Despite their European and English heritage, American colleges and universities were shaped by North American geographic, political, social, and religious conditions (Selden, 1960). The U.S. Constitution made education a state rather than federal power, and state legislatures willingly granted college charters to almost anyone requesting them (Brubacher & Rudy, 1997; Rudolph, 1990). Fueled by Jacksonian democratic ideals, denominational sectarianism, geographic separation, and local pride, the United States had more than 50 degree-granting colleges by the 1830s. Tewksbury (1932) chronicled the creation of more than 900 colleges—and the demise of 700 of them—by 1861.

The one common factor among colleges in the first half of the nineteenth century was the curriculum, an amalgam of the medieval arts and sciences and classical languages and literature. Except for the introduction of additional mathematics and science in the late eighteenth and early nineteenth centuries, the curriculum looked remarkably like that on which it had been modeled in 1636—the curriculum of Emmanuel College, Cambridge University (Brubacher & Rudy, 1997; Rudolph, 1977, 1990).

The latter half of the nineteenth century witnessed major changes in American life. The Civil War fueled an explosion in manufacturing and technology, creating a need for more specialized collegiate education and leading most faculty and students to regard the classical curriculum as outmoded. Public colleges and universities that emerged in the 1840s and thereafter broadened the curriculum to include more science and mathematics along with the liberal arts. With the Morrill Act of 1862, Congress used land grants to enhance the new state universities and to endow agricultural and mechanical colleges that would provide, in addition to the normal classical and liberal arts studies, education in agriculture and the mechanic arts including disciplines such as engineering, business, and military science. These land grant colleges were designed to provide greater access to higher education for the working and industrial classes (Brubacher & Rudy, 1997; Hofstadter & Hardy, 1952; Lucas, 2006; Nevins, 1962; Rudolph, 1977, 1990). Increasingly diverse types of postsecondary institutions (e.g., scientific/technical institutes, colleges for women and Blacks, denominational colleges, and state colleges) had been attracting growing numbers of academically underprepared and nontraditional students beginning in the 1820s; the land grant colleges produced a surge of such new students in the last third of the century.

College curricula and admission requirements varied greatly and presented a major problem to public secondary school systems, most still in their infancy. Growing numbers of applicants unprepared for real collegiate study forced most institutions to offer preparatory programs to prepare them to enter the freshman class. During the last third of the century, college enrollments rose significantly, with especially rapid growth in the 1890s and in the Midwest (Brubacher & Rudy, 1997; Lucas, 2006; Rudolph, 1990). Preparatory enrollment grew along with collegiate enrollment. Geiger (2000) reported that in the 1880s, collegiate enrollment in American colleges increased by 31% while preparatory enrollment increased 51%. In 1890 preparatory enrollment was only 5,000 less than the 39,000 regular collegiate students.

Underprepared Students in Midwest Land Grant Colleges

The challenge of underprepared students was particularly acute in the Midwest where there were few public secondary schools and a growing number of private and public colleges, including land grant colleges. In the Midwest there were more colleges than needed for the number of high school graduates, and land grant colleges "were compelled to adjust their entrance requirements . . . to the program and standards of the public schools. The college curriculum had to be built on this very elemental and often unsubstantial foundation" (Ross, 1942, p. 120).

As Geiger (1963) noted, in the process of democratizing higher education, the new subjects, lack of qualified instructors to teach them, unsuitable texts, and the admission of poorly prepared students resulted in lower standards. Low admission standards were necessary because enough students were needed to keep the new land grant colleges open. However, low admission standards and preparatory departments were not limited to land grant colleges and preceded their creation. As the Board of Regents of the University of Wisconsin (1853) acknowledged, "In common with all collegiate institutions in the new states, it has been necessary for the University to create its own material . . . before the college classes could be formed" (p. 13).

This study of preparatory programs in Midwest land grant colleges focused on eight institutions (see Table 1). Some of the institutions predate the 1862 Morrill Act, some were created after passage of the act and were later designated as official land grant institutions, and some were actually established as land grant institutions.

Table 1. Midwest Land Grant Institutions Included in the Study

Institution	Date Opened	Name Changes in 19th Century	Date
Illinois Industrial University	1868	University of Illinois	1885
Purdue University	1874		
Iowa State Agricultural College	1869	Iowa State College of Agriculture and Mechanic Arts	1886
Kansas State Agricultural College	1863		
University of Minnesota	1867		
University of the State of Missouri	1841		
University of Nebraska	1871		
University of Wisconsin	1849		

Midwest College Preparatory Programs in the Nineteenth Century

The Decades of the 1840s through the 1860s

COLLEGIATE ADMISSION REQUIREMENTS.   The post–Civil War industrial revolution was accompanied by the increasing importance of science and technology. Significantly influenced by the German universities, state universities, land grant institutions, and prominent private colleges and universities abandoned the old prescribed, undergraduate, classical liberal arts curriculum. Instead, they adopted elective curricula that required varying amounts of work in the liberal arts and sciences, and permitted students to select a number of elective courses and specialize in an academic discipline. These changes resulted in a slow but steady transformation of the undergraduate curriculum into one of increasing variety and rigor (Brubacher & Rudy, 1997; Hofstadter & Hardy, 1952; Nevins, 1962; Rudolph, 1977, 1990).

Admission to Midwest land grant colleges in the mid-nineteenth century was, like admission to most colleges in the nation, by entrance examination. Early exams covered a few academic areas at rather elementary levels. Over time they reflected the increasing diversity of the freshman curriculum. For example, the University of the State of Missouri (UMO) (1859, 1861, 1865) examined new students to determine their scholastic attainments and to assign them to the classes (e.g., preparatory, freshman, sophomore) for which they were qualified. Early entrance exams were rather general, as evidenced in 1866–67 when applicants for the freshman class in the classical and scientific courses were examined in English grammar and analysis, U.S. history, and general history (UMO, 1867). Applicants for the freshman class in the department of ancient languages, however, faced much more focused and rigorous exams on specific Latin and Greek textbooks and classical works or their equivalents.

Early entrance exams at University of Wisconsin (UW) illustrate the same trend and also clearly demonstrate the relationship among freshman entrance examinations, the freshman curriculum, and the preparatory curriculum. In 1852 applicants for the freshman class had to pass an examination in all the studies of the preparatory school or their equivalents (UW, 1853). By 1864 applicants to the freshman class continued to be examined in all of the studies of the preparatory course—common aspects of English, algebra, plane geometry, Greek and Latin—with applicants to the scientific course exempted from the ancient languages (UW, 1864).

CREATION OF PREPARATORY PROGRAMS.   All eight institutions were immediately confronted with underprepared students and the need to provide preparatory studies. It has been often repeated that the UW created the first college preparatory department in 1849. Although it did create a preparatory department in 1849, it was not the first institution to do so. When UMO opened in 1841, the majority of its students were preparatory (Lowry, 1898). As early as 1844 the university had organized a formal preparatory department (UMO, 1845). In 1855 the General Assembly established by statute the Primary (preparatory) Department "to meet the wants of such students as are too young or too little advanced to enter the University" (UMO, 1859, p. 28).

Although UMO was the first institution of those in this study to operate a preparatory department, other colleges did so earlier. For example, when Methodists opened Indiana Asbury University (now DePauw University) in 1837, a preparatory department was part of the institution (Goodrich & Tuttle, 1875). Indiana College, the forerunner of Indiana Asbury University, opened in 1825 and may have had a formal preparatory department earlier than 1837. The same could be true for many other colleges throughout the country.

At their first meeting in October 1848, the UW Regents elected John H. Lathrop (chancellor of UMO) as chancellor of the new university and, among other things, established a preparatory school. According to Butterfield (1879), establishing "a preparatory school within the department of science, literature, and the arts, was deemed by the regents to be in accordance with the usage of similar institutions elsewhere" (p. 35). It was necessary because there were in 1849 "very few academic institutions in the state where proper instruction could be obtained to qualify students to enter the regular classes" (p. 35). Butterfield's comments add further evidence that preparatory departments were already a well-known phenomenon in 1849.

The preparatory school was the only part of UW that opened in the Winter 1849 term, with the entire faculty of one—Professor John W. Sterling—teaching the 20 or so preparatory students. He was joined in that effort by Chancellor Lathrop who arrived in Fall 1849. Two students were finally considered qualified for collegiate work in Fall 1850 (Butterfield, 1879; Pyre, 1920). "This provision for preparatory instruction in the University," said Lathrop, "must be continued until the academic or union schools, one in each township" (Butterfield, p. 47) were able to prepare students adequately for university studies.

The Board of Trustees of Illinois Industrial University (IIU) believed the university should not "do the work already provided for in the public high schools," because it would "create a gigantic and expensive high school" (Committee on Courses, 1867, p. 14) and fail to become a real university. "It is absolutely essential . . . that it shall leave the preparatory work mainly, if not entirely, to the public high schools and academies of the State" (p. 14). Unfortunately, by 1862 there were only about 55 public high schools in the state (Walker, 1964). When IIU opened in Spring 1868, it had 50 students, three faculty members (including the president), a meager curriculum, and elementary standards (Foerster, 1937). None of the 75 students who were eventually enrolled that spring were able to pass the entrance exams for collegiate work and exhibited a "lamentable lack of true scholarship, even in the ordinary common school branches" (IIU, 1871, p. 36). All of the students studied preparatory subjects (Powell, 1918). By the autumn term there were 12 students sufficiently prepared to take collegiate courses. The problem continued, and IIU finally relented and established a preparatory school in 1875. The trustees explained,

> A needful advance in the standard for admission to the College comes and the necessity of providing temporarily at least for those who will come from places where no good High Schools exist, now induce the Trustees to provide for preparatory classes in the studies lying between the common School Studies and the College courses [*sic*]. (IIU, 1876, p. 24)

Throughout IIU's infancy, "the great majority of the students were engaged in preparatory work" (Powell, p. 287).

The University of Minnesota (UMN) had operated from 1851–61. When the legislature reorganized the university in February 1868, the act required the Board of Regents to include a preparatory department (UMN, 1871). The regents explained in the university's 1869–70 catalog that "to supply in some measure the present and temporary lack of preparatory schools in our young State, this [preparatory] Department has been organized and put into successful operation" (UMN, 1870, p. 6). A few years later the university explained,

> In common with all Colleges or Universities of the newer states, the institution has been obliged to carry a large amount of preparatory work. . . . The elementary [preparatory] work of the University will begin at the point where the schools of the State leave off. (UMN, 1875, p. 34)

PREPARATORY CURRICULA.   Curricular and instructional changes previously described resulted not only in steadily increasing college entrance requirements but also concomitant growth in the breadth and depth of preparatory curricula. For example, in 1844–45 UMO's preparatory curriculum consisted of English grammar, geography, Greek, Latin, and arithmetic (UMO, 1845). By 1861, UMO's (1861) preparatory program had become a primary department and a subfreshman class; students unable to pass the entrance exams for the subfreshman class were assigned first to the primary department. The primary department curriculum included English grammar, rhetoric/composition, reading, spelling, and penmanship; geography, U.S. geography, and U.S. history; Greek and Latin; arithmetic, algebra, and geometry; and natural philosophy (physical sciences). The entrance exams for the subfreshman class included all of these areas. The subfreshman curriculum then focused on preparing students to enter the freshman class by preparing them with further study in English grammar and rhetoric/composition, Greek, Latin, algebra, and geometry. By the mid-1860s, UW (1865) had expanded its preparatory curriculum to three years; students were enrolled for varying lengths of time based on their level of academic preparation. The curriculum included English (elocution, rhetoric/composition, reading, and spelling); geography; Greek; Latin; arithmetic, algebra, and geometry; and science.

COLLEGIATE AND PREPARATORY ENROLLMENTS. Determining early collegiate and preparatory enrollments is difficult because of the manner in which they were reported in annual college catalogs and the way in which the catalogs were published. Today, a college catalog for 2009–10 reflects what will be true during that academic year. That, however, was not the case until the early twentieth century. In mid-nineteenth century, a college catalog might indicate only one calendar year, for example, 1848, and references in that catalog to the first term could mean the winter, spring, or autumn term. By the 1860s, colleges had generally settled on an academic year that ran from fall through spring, and most catalogs were published bearing dates such as 1868–69. However, catalogs were largely historic records. For example, a catalog for 1885–86 would normally be published in 1886. Near the end of the century, some catalogs contained a circular or supplement of the year in progress when the catalog was published or, in some cases, announcements regarding the coming year. Thus, a catalog for 1892–93 would be published in 1893 (perhaps during the spring term but more likely in the summer or fall), would contain information on entrance exams, degree requirements, courses of instruction, students' names, faculty, and so forth for the 1892–93 academic year; and might contain a circular with limited information about the 1893–94 year. This information may include administration and faculty rosters, new academic policies and, if published in the fall, enrollment figures for the Fall 1893 semester already under way.

College catalogs throughout the nineteenth century contained lists of students by class (including preparatory students by whatever name they were known) and normally reported enrollment by classes and a total for the college. However, in many cases these enrollment figures were not for the fall term, as they would be reported today, but included all students who were enrolled for one or more terms or during the academic year, thus inflating the enrollment. Only after the U.S. Commissioner of Education began publishing annual reports on education in 1870 can collegiate and preparatory enrollments in the nation's colleges be reported with some confidence. Even then the enrollments reported by institutions in this study to the U.S. Bureau of Education and the information published in their catalogs never exactly matched.

Summary

The 1840s through the 1860s was a significant period in the history of Midwest college preparatory programs. The need of preparatory studies for underprepared students entering land grant colleges led to the creation of preparatory departments, which became an integral part of

American Higher Education for the upcoming years. Part II of this study will continue presenting the history and evolution of preparatory programs in nineteenth century institutions, focusing on the 1870s decade.

References

Brubacher, J. S., & Rudy, W. (1997). *Higher education in transition: A history of American colleges and universities* (4th ed.). Edison, NJ: Transaction Publishers.

Butterfield, C. W. (1879). *History of the University of Wisconsin, from the first organization to 1879, with biographical sketches of its chancellors, presidents, and professors.* Madison, WI: University Press Co.

Committee on Courses of Study and Faculty for the Illinois Industrial University. (1867). *Report of Committee on Courses of Study and Faculty for the Illinois Industrial University. Published by order of the Board of Trustees.* Springfield, IL: Baker, Bailhache & Co.

Foerster, N. (1937). *The American state university: Its relation to democracy.* Chapel Hill, NC: University of North Carolina Press.

Geiger, L. G. (1963). *Higher education in a maturing democracy.* Lincoln, NE: University of Nebraska Press.

Geiger, R. L. (2000). The era of multipurpose colleges in American higher education. In R. L. Geiger (Ed.), *The American college in the nineteenth century* (pp. 127–152). Nashville, TN: Vanderbilt University Press.

Goodrich, D. C., & Tuttle, C. R. (1875). *An illustrated history of the State of Indiana.* Indianapolis, IN: Richard S. Peale & Co.

Harcleroad, F. F., & Ostar, A. W. (1987). *Colleges and universities for change: America's comprehensive public state colleges and universities.* Lanham, MD: University Press of America.

Hofstadter, R., & Hardy, C. D. (1952). *The development and scope of higher education in the United States.* New York, NY: Columbia University Press.

Illinois Industrial University. (1871). *Fourth annual circular of the Illinois Industrial University, Urbana, Champaign County, Ills. 1870–71.* Urbana, IL: Author.

Illinois Industrial University. (1876). *Catalog and circular, Illinois Industrial University. 1875–76.* Champaign, IL: Author.

Lowry, T. J. (1898). The University of the State of Missouri. In M. S. Snow (Ed.), *Higher education in Missouri* (U.S. Bureau of Education Circular of Information No. 2; Contributions to American Educational History No. 21, H. B. Adams [Ed.]; pp. 9–48). Washington, DC: Government Printing Office.

Lucas, C. J. (2006). *American higher education: A history* (2nd ed.). New York, NY: Palgrave Macmillan.

Nevins, A. (1962). *The state universities and democracy.* Urbana, IL: University of Illinois Press.

Powell, B. E. (1918). *Semi-centennial history of the University of Illinois. Volume 1: The movement for industrial education and the establishment of the university, 1840–1870.* Urbana, IL: University of Illinois Press.

Pyre, J. F. A. (1920). *Wisconsin.* New York, NY: Oxford University Press.

Ross, E. D. (1942). *A history of the Iowa State College of Agriculture and Mechanic Arts.* Ames, IA: The Iowa State College Press.

Rudolph, F. (1977). *Curriculum: A history of the American undergraduate course of study since 1636*. San Francisco. CA: Jossey-Bass.

Rudolph, F. (1990). *The American college and university: A history*. Athens, GA: University of Georgia Press.

Selden, W. K. (1960). *Accreditation: A struggle over standards in higher education*. New York, NY: Harper & Brothers.

Tewksbury, D. (1932). *Founding of colleges and universities before the Civil War*. New York, NY: Teachers College, Columbia University.

University of Minnesota. (1870). *The University of Minnesota. Announcement for 1869–70*. St. Anthony, MN: Author.

University of Minnesota. (1871). *The University of Minnesota. Announcement for 1870–71*. St. Anthony, MN: Author.

University of Minnesota. (1875). *The University of Minnesota. The calendar for the year 1874–75*. Minneapolis, MN: Author.

University of the State of Missouri. (1845). *Third annual catalogue of the officers and students of the University of the State of Missouri, for the year ending July 31, 1845*. Columbia, MO: William F. Switzler.

University of the State of Missouri. (1859). *Seventeenth annual catalogue of the officers and students at the University of the State of Missouri, for the year ending July 4th, 1859: Together with a list of graduates and of persons who have held office in connection with the institution*. Jefferson City, MO: W. G. Cheeney, Printer.

University of the State of Missouri. (1861). *Nineteenth annual catalogue of the officers and students of the University of the State of Missouri, for the year ending July 4th, 1861: Together with a list of former officers*. Columbia, MO: Statesman Office.

University of the State of Missouri. (1865). *Catalogue of the officers and students of the University of the State of Missouri for the years ending June 1862, -3, -4, and 5. Together with a list of former officers of the university and of the graduates of the institutions*. Columbia, MO: *Missouri Statesman*.

University of the State of Missouri. (1867). *Announcement of the University of the State of Missouri, containing catalogue of officers and students, for the year ending June, 1867*. Columbia, MO: William F. Switzler.

University of Wisconsin. (1853). *Catalogue of the faculty and students of Wisconsin University. For the year ending July 27th, 1853*. Madison, WI: Author.

University of Wisconsin. (1864). *Annual catalogue of the officers and students of the University of Wisconsin, for the year closing June 22, 1864*. Madison, WI: William J. Park & Co.

University of Wisconsin. (1865). *Annual catalogue of the officers and students of the University of Wisconsin for the academic year closing June 28, 1865*. Madison, WI: William J. Park & Co.

Walker, W. G. (1964). The development of the free public high school in Illinois during the nineteenth century. *History of Education Quarterly, 4*, 264–279.

History of Learning Assistance in U.S. Postsecondary Education

David R. Arendale

This is a chapter from Arendale's book Access at the Crossroads, *which is the only source to date to trace the entire history of developmental education from the 1600s to present. It divides that history into six phases characterized by the types of students served by programs during that particular phase. It also describes the organization of developmental programs as well as the strategies used throughout their history to support different groups of students. In addition, Arendale addresses the emerging role of community colleges as major providers of developmental education.*

E xamining the long history of approaches and programs of learning assistance frames the field and provides context for better understanding of the profession today. This chapter explores phases and forms of learning assistance since the 1600s to today through six distinct phases.

The history of learning assistance begins with the founding of the first college in the United States (Arendale, 2002b). This field has grown in complexity over time. Careful analysis results in the identification of six chronological phases. Names used to describe the field, activities and approaches employed, integration of the field with the core of the institution, and types of students served are compared throughout each phase (Arendale, 2001). Table 1 provides a roadmap for this journey through history.

Phase One: 1600s to 1820s

The first phase began with the founding of U.S. colleges in the 1600s and concluded in the early 1800s. During that time, learning assistance only provided individual tutors, and no remedial or developmental courses were offered. The majority of students involved in postsecondary education were white males from privileged cultural and economic backgrounds. Tutoring was used in many classes and involved nearly all these affluent students. Therefore, little or no stigma was attached to receiving tutoring services.

Origins of Learning Assistance

Learning assistance emerged in response to college admission requirements. Admission was denied to nearly all applicants as a result of deficiencies in foreign language requirements (Latin and Greek) and other academic areas such as mathematics. This situation is not sur-

Table 1. Six Phases of Learning Assistance History

Time Phase	Name(s) Commonly Used with Activities	People Served Predominantly during This Time Period
Phase One: 1600s to 1820s	Tutoring	Privileged white male students
Phase Two: 1830s to 1860s	Precollegiate preparatory academy and tutoring	Privileged white male students
Phase Three: 1870s to Mid-1940s	Remedial education classes in college preparatory programs and tutoring	Mostly white male students
Phase Four: Mid-1940s to 1970s	Compensatory education, counseling center, opportunity program, reading clinic, remedial education classes integrated in the institution, tutoring	Traditional white male students, nontraditional males and females such as war veterans, and federal legislative priority groups: first-generation college students, economically disadvantaged students, and students of color
Phase Five: Early 1970s to Mid-1990s	Access program, developmental education, learning assistance, opportunity program, tutoring	Groups listed above, with an increase in older students who return to education or attend postsecondary education for the first time, and some general students who want to deepen mastery of academic content
Phase Six: Mid-1990s to the Present	Access program, developmental education, learning assistance, learning/teaching center, learning enrichment, opportunity program	Groups listed above, with an increase in general students, students with disabilities, and faculty members who seek professional development in learning and teaching skills

Source: Arendale, 2001.

prising, considering the dismal or nonexistent status of public elementary and secondary education for most citizens at the time.

Students seeking admission to Eaton or Oxford in England sometimes attended a "dame school" to prepare them for the rigorous college admission test. These boarding schools were small tutorial centers run by educated women of high social standing and education. In colonial times, some Virginia aristocratic families sent their children to such schools in England to prepare for college admission tests. Some U.S. clergymen modified this practice by assuming this role and eliminated the need for students to leave the country for academic preparation programs (Gordon and Gordon, 1990).

Prevalence of Tutoring Programs

Precollegiate academic assistance for most students at Harvard and Yale consisted of private tutors who prepared them for college entrance examinations in Greek and Latin and provided evidence of good moral character that was also required for admission. In the mid-1700s, Yale required proficiency in arithmetic in addition to the already stringent requirements. Other postsecondary institutions soon followed. Students who did not attend Latin grammar schools had few options for entering college. One option for gaining admittance to Yale was for a minister to place students in his home for private tutoring until they were ready for the college entrance exam (Cowie, 1936). This option was similar to the dame schools in England.

Once admitted to Harvard, most students continued to receive tutoring, as assigned readings and textbooks were written in Latin. Many college professors delivered lectures in the same language. Even in the most privileged families, verbal and written competency in Latin was unusual. Therefore, Harvard was the first postsecondary institution in the United States to require remedial studies for most of its first-year class of students (Boylan and White, p. 5 in this book). After admission to prestigious colleges such as Harvard and Yale, students entered a cohort. Each week they met with the same tutor for group sessions. The tutors' primary role was reading aloud the lesson material and then conducting a recitation session to detect whether students had correctly memorized the text. This practice failed to meet the needs for the most gifted and the struggling students, as it focused on the average student's mastery level of the academic content material. The literature contains no evidence of the efficacy of this crude form of academic assistance.

Impact of Economics

Economics intervened in academic admission policies during the late 1700s. Because of the social norm of considering only white male students from highly prestigious families, most postsecondary institutions found it in their financial interest to admit students less prepared academically but possessing resources to pay college tuition and thus generate more revenue. By the time of the American Revolution, institutions began to differentiate themselves from one another by academic preparation levels of incoming college students and their official mission statements. Amherst and Williams admitted students unable to attend Harvard and Yale as a result of lower academic preparation or inadequate finances (Casazza and Silverman, 1996). Students experienced unofficial segregation policies and procedures. Stereotypes of perceived academic inabilities and discrimination against females and students of color fueled this discrimination. Nathaniel Hawthorne described the students at Williams as "a rough, brown featured, schoolmaster-looking, half-bumpkin, half-scholar, in black, ill-cut broadcloth" (Rudolph, 1956, p. 47). These assumptions, based on ethnic and class prejudices, reflected social norms and prejudices shared by many in society, including key college policymakers. Admission criteria and procedures influenced by these stereotypes contributed to differentiation and stratification among postsecondary institutions.

Phase Two: 1830s to 1860s

Academic preparation academies emerged during the mid-1800s. These new postsecondary education units provided education equivalent to public high schools, which were not common in most of the United States at the time. Colleges recognized that tutoring as it was being practiced was insufficient to serve the needs of the expanding college student population. Often academies operated in the local community rather than on the college campus. In addition to tutoring, the academies enrolled students in remedial classes in reading, writing, and mathematics. This phase was a short one, as the expansion of public education across the United States replaced the need for many of the new academies. The composition of the student body changed little during this phase. Most students were white males from privileged families. Because most students were involved with learning assistance and from the upper class, little stigma was attached, as it was perceived as a natural part of the education process, a process that was available to so few at the time.

Impact of Jacksonian Democracy

Some historians identified several elements of Jacksonian democracy as affecting U.S. society in the mid-1800s. Whites benefited from the extension of voting privileges, middle-class workers and small shop owners received financial support, and education was extended to more of the population. One application of Jacksonian democracy was expansion of postsecondary education through common schools, public education, and an expanded curriculum for more people in the middle class rather than only the most privileged.

During this time, expansion of postsecondary education was essential to support development of the economic middle class of merchants, tradesmen, engineers, agriculturalists, and scientists needed to meet the needs of the growing nation and to support its economic development. This intersection of interests among political progressives and economic forces indirectly supported learning assistance as a means to ensure higher productivity of colleges to graduate sufficient numbers of skilled workers and leaders.

With poor or nonexistent secondary education and even inadequate primary education in some cases, however, many college aspirants could barely read and write (Craig, 1997). The number of those who tutored and the number who received tutorial assistance were nearly identical to the number of teaching faculty and their enrolled students (Brier, p. 11 in this book), documenting the extensive involvement of learning assistance in postsecondary education. Since the early years, debate has continued about how to meet the needs of admitted college students. Providing tutoring for students was insufficient to meet their needs during this time. More services would emerge.

One option for meeting students' academic preparation needs was to provide remedial and developmental courses in the institution's curriculum. Proponents of elitism in postsecondary education prevailed temporarily against that option, however. The fixed college curriculum prescribed the same slate of classical courses for all students, without regard to individual needs for development of improved learning strategies and mastery of fundamental academic content material in mathematics and writing. Thus, academic preparatory academies continued to house remedial and developmental courses.

Academic Preparatory Academies

In 1830, New York University created an early prototype of an academic preparatory academy. It provided instruction in mathematics, physical science, philosophy, and English literature (Dempsey, 1985). The focus, however, was acquiring basic academic content knowledge, not the cognitive learning strategies that are often prerequisite for mastery of new academic material. These academies were a necessary bridge for many college aspirants as a result of the lack of formal secondary education for many. The U.S. education movement started from the top down. First, colleges and universities were established and then public elementary and secondary schools were developed. Some colleges functioned essentially as both high schools and rigorous colleges. The academic preparatory academies supported the rising academic rigor of postsecondary institutions and provided an access conduit for those seeking a college education. The academies expanded with surprising speed in a short time. By 1894, 40 percent of first-year college students had enrolled in college preparatory courses (Ignash, 1997).

Since the beginning, tutorial programs were the most common form of academic enrichment and support at most prestigious institutions such as Harvard and Yale. Many college administrators responded to the high number of students academically underprepared by creating a special academic department that was essential to meet their academic needs. In less selective institutions, the number of underprepared students outnumbered those not requiring additional support. For example, the University of Wisconsin in 1865 could place only forty-one of 331 admitted students in "regular" graduation credit courses. The majority of the new students admitted were restricted to remedial courses (Shedd, 1932). Quality of primary and secondary education was uneven or missing in most of the United States. Most colleges provided instruction in basic skills of spelling, writing, geography, and mathematics, as they were the only venue for such instruction (Brier, p. 11 in this book). Instruction in basic content areas lengthened the undergraduate bachelor's academic degree to six years or more (Casazza and Silverman, 1996).

In 1849, the University of Wisconsin established the first modern learning assistance program. Instead of offering remedial courses through an external academic preparatory academy, Wisconsin created an academic department for these courses and hired a separate faculty to teach them. The Department of Preparatory Studies instructed students through remedial courses in reading, writing, and arithmetic. Because of an insufficient number of tutors to meet the academic needs of most admitted students, the institution quickly responded by establishing the new academic department. Of the 331 admitted students, 290 enrolled in one or more remedial courses in the preparatory studies department. These courses were similar to those offered at a public high school (Brubacher and Rudy, 1976). Many institutions across the United States implemented the Wisconsin model of learning assistance (Brier, p. 11 in this book). The department persisted until 1880. Continuous internal political battles among the department, campus administrators, and the rest of the university faculty served as a catalyst for its demise. Faculty members from outside the department demanded its elimination because of the fear of stigma for the university. College administrators tried to appease critics through strategies such as renaming the department. New campus administrators finally closed the department after its short and contentious history (Curti and Carstensen, 1949).

Academic preparatory departments emerged at more than 80 percent of all postsecondary institutions (Canfield, 1889). These departments bridged the gap between inadequate academic preparation of high school graduates and college-level curricular expectations (Clemont, 1899). Review of college admission documents indicated that the farther west the college was located, the lower the entrance requirements for the institution as a result of insufficient preparation in high school. As the public school movement spread from the Northeast farther south and west, college entrance requirements of the institutions eventually rose. After a half century of use, however, remedial college credit courses were entrenched in most colleges.

Recruitment of Academically Underprepared Students

After the U.S. Civil War, students who were considered academically underprepared were aggressively recruited. Economic and social changes throughout the United States fueled by the Civil War significantly influenced expansion of learning assistance at more colleges. Many male students did not seek admission or left college to join their respective armies. Many colleges in the North and South replaced them and their tuition payments through expanded academic preparatory departments that supported underage students who were too young to enlist. Examples from the North include Valparaiso University in Indiana, which replaced college students through a rapid expansion of the academic preparatory department. Although the liberal arts college and theology school at Bucknell University closed temporarily in 1865, the academic preparatory school at the same college significantly increased its enrollment. Offsetting enrollment decreases saved many institutions from closing. Southern colleges followed the same pattern of Northern institutions through extended academic preparatory departments and acceptance of applicants formerly denied admission. In 1861 the University of Alabama created an academic preparatory department for boys twelve years and older. In 1863 the University of Georgia created University High School and suspended rules prohibiting admission of boys younger than fourteen to the university. The Faculty Senate of South Carolina College in 1862 voted to admit young students to replace revenue lost by former students who had left the institution to join the Confederate Army (Rudy, 1996).

Phase Three: 1870s to Mid-1940s

The third phase of postsecondary education history began during the late 1800s and continued until World War II. The major activities during this era were expansion of tutoring and incorporation of remedial courses in the college curriculum. Academic preparatory academies had been the temporary home for this curriculum earlier in the 1800s. The most frequent service continued to be individual and group tutoring. White male students from privileged cultural and economic backgrounds still dominated college campuses. Women and students of color attended newly established institutions reserved for them. These institutions also embraced remedial courses.

Relationship of the Federal Government and Learning Assistance

The federal government increased direct involvement with postsecondary education during this time. The First Morrill Act (1862) established land-grant colleges, which was the federal government's first significant financial involvement with postsecondary education. The mission of these new colleges fostered new degree programs in applied education such as agriculture and the mechanical arts. Established denominational private institutions had not previously offered this curriculum. This action broadened the curriculum and increased access for students of modest academic preparation and lower socioeconomic backgrounds.

Although colleges offered wider access through the 1862 Morrill Act, academic preparation of potential students remained uneven. Many new college students had not attended public high school, as few were in operation in the expanding West of the United States. The dramatic widening of access to postsecondary education accelerated development of academic departments that offered remedial courses and tutoring deemed essential for the new students. "Iowa State College simply required that entering freshmen be fourteen years old and able to read, write, and do arithmetic. However, when they lacked these skills, students were placed in the college's preparatory department" (Maxwell, 1997, p. 11). College enrollments soared and many of these new students enrolled in remedial courses. Offering remedial courses and other learning assistance services in a college department addressed many of the problems experienced by external academic preparatory academies such as lack of coordinated curriculum, poor teaching facilities, lack of proper administrative control, and increased stigma for participating students. These problems were the result of the very nature of these academies, as they were clearly separate and seen just as a prerequisite to the college experience.

Remedial Education

The need for academic preparatory departments increased with admission of more students that were academically underprepared. Eighty-four percent of land-grant institutions offered remedial courses by the late 1880s (Craig, 1997). The most frequent term used to describe learning assistance from the 1860s through the early 1960s was "remedial education." Remedial education targeted students' specific skill deficits and employed new educational approaches. Clowes (1980) applied an analogy of the traditional medical model for remedial education. Academic weakness was detected through assessment. The problem was hoped to be cured through prescribed treatment. Clowes categorized students enrolled in remedial education as "academically backward or less able students" (p. 8). Repeated academic treatment persisted until students achieved the desired outcomes or "cures." Students possessed many academic deficits needing prescriptive remediation. Remedial education focused on cognitive deficits and not on improvements in the affective domain. An early glossary developed by the College Reading and Learning Association defined remedial as "instruction designed to remove a student's deficiencies in the basic entry or exit level skills at a prescribed level of proficiency in order to make him/her competitive with peers" (Rubin, 1991, p. 9). Remedial students were identified as "students who are required to participate in specific academic improvement courses/programs as a condition of entry to college" (p. 9).

Remedial education was a prerequisite to enrolling in college-level courses. Remedial courses focused on acquiring skills and knowledge at the secondary school level. Developmental courses, on the other hand, developed skills above the exit level from high school that were needed for success in college. These courses entered the college curriculum during the next historical phase.

In 1879 Harvard admitted 50 percent of applicants "on condition" because they failed the entrance examination. Tutorial programs initially designed for success with college entrance exams were expanded to assist these provisionally admitted students to succeed in their college courses (Weidner, 1990). The Harvard Reports of 1892, 1895, and 1897 documented poor academic preparation of admitted students. University administrators were surprised to discover that students who suffered academic difficulty were not only those from poor or nonexistent high school education. Instead, it was also the "picked boys" (Goodwin, 1895, p. 292), students from the upper class of U.S. society (Hill, 1885). Provision of tutoring and remedial credit courses demonstrated academic rigor at Harvard and exceeded the academic preparation level even for students with formal preparation for postsecondary education. The gap between academic preparation and college performance placed many of the elite students in need of learning assistance (Brier, p. 11 in this book).

Remedial Courses in the Curriculum

By 1874 Harvard was first to offer a first-year remedial English course in response to faculty complaints that too many students lacked competency for formal writing activities. Harvard was the first institution that permitted elective courses in response to changing needs of the curriculum. Without flexibility with course options, remedial courses would have been available only as a precollege option. Academic conditions remained unchanged at Harvard, Yale, Princeton, and Columbia by 1907 when half the students failed to earn the minimum composite entrance exam score. Harvard offered a remedial reading course beginning in the early 1900s (Brubacher and Rudy, 1976).

One of the earliest manifestations of college-level learning assistance was the remedial course. The most frequent remedial courses were reading and study skills. More than 350 colleges in 1909 offered "how to study" classes for academically underprepared students. The U.S. Commissioner for Education reported in 1913 that approximately 80 percent of postsecondary institutions offered college preparatory programs with a wide variety of services, including tutoring and remedial courses (Maxwell, 1979). This rate was nearly the same as the mid-1800s. Sensitive to perceptions by students, professors, and others, many colleges began to redefine remedial activities to make them more acceptable by students and campus administrators. When the director of Harvard's Bureau of Study Counsel renamed Remedial Reading to the Reading Class, enrollment increased from thirty to four hundred annually in 1938 (Wyatt, 1992). Through the introduction of the first developmental course, provision of noncredit academic support, and careful use of language to describe its services and course offerings, the learning assistance field owes much to the leadership and innovations of Harvard University.

Junior colleges (later renamed community colleges) extended the new secondary school movement in the early 1900s. Among the broad mission of many junior colleges was college academic preparation. An analogy for this focus on serving academically underprepared students is calling them "the Ellis Island of higher education" (Vaughan, 1983, p. 9). Many four-year institutions transferred their academic preparatory programs to junior colleges in the early 1900s. As described earlier, standardized admissions test scores permitted colleges to refer students to different types of institutions that maintained varying levels of admission selectivity. As four-year institutions received more state and federal appropriations, the institutional financial profile improved. The need to admit high numbers of students who needed academic help to generate tuition revenue and meet institutional expenses lessened (Richardson, Martens, and Fisk, 1981).

A national survey in 1929 of institutions revealed about one-fourth of survey respondents confirmed that their college assessed reading with the admission examination. Nearly half of all students were enrolled in remedial courses (Parr, 1930). These courses often focused heavily on reading skills. Nearly 90 percent of respondents stated they had not conducted research studies regarding the effectiveness of their learning assistance program (Parr, 1930). Societal changes in the middle of the twentieth century required a major expansion of learning assistance to meet a rapidly growing student body—growing in its diversity and level of academic preparation for college-level work.

Phase Four: Mid-1940s to 1970s

The fourth phase of learning assistance history occurred throughout the middle of the twentieth century. Learning assistance dramatically expanded to meet increased needs resulting from escalating college enrollment. Building on past practices of tutoring and remedial courses, learning assistance expanded services to more students through compensatory education and learning assistance centers. Stigma heightened for learning assistance participants because of increased stratification of academic preparation among entering students. Although previously enrollment in remedial classes was common for most college students (Brubacher and Rudy, 1976; Maxwell, 1979), it was no longer the case. Entering students from privileged backgrounds were better prepared academically than the new first-generation college and economically disadvantaged students who were entering postsecondary education for the first time. Stigma began to attach to the students who enrolled in the remedial and subsequent developmental courses by those who did not need to do so. Well-prepared privileged students did not need extensive learning assistance during college as had the previous generation of college students. The new students, especially those from rural communities and urban centers and many historically underrepresented students of color, had uneven access to such education. This dichotomy of experiences created a perception that developmental courses were needed primarily for students of color. Actually, two-thirds of students enrolled in these courses were white, but it is true that students of color are twice as likely at two-year colleges and three times more likely at four-year institutions to enroll in the courses in relationship to their proportion of the overall population of all college students (Boylan, Bonham, and Bliss, 1994).

Increased Federal Involvement

Federal involvement intensified during this time with increased financial support, legislative oversight, and creation of new college access programs. Significant events occurred: the GI bill, expansion of civil rights, and equal opportunity legislation. The National Center for Education Statistics (1993) tracks a variety of educational activities, including rates of college enrollment. A retrospective in trends over a period of 120 years revealed an increase in college enrollment. College enrollment increased significantly during the 1950s, as the college enrollment rate rose from 15 to 24 percent among eighteen- to twenty-four-year-olds over that decade. During the 1960s, the rate increased to 35 percent, finally reaching 45 percent in the 1970s. Much of this later growth was the result of increased enrollment by adult and part-time students, who required learning assistance support different from their peers (National Center for Education Statistics, 1993).

Colleges were increasingly asked to provide services for older students who often faced concurrent challenges of failure to enroll in college-bound curriculum while in high school and the interruption of education between high school and college as a result of entering the workforce, raising a family, or enlisting in the military. Academic skills often atrophied during the intervening years. These students often brought multiple needs that required academic support and enrichment. Many college preparatory programs expanded as a result. A national survey (Barbe, 1951) documented the growth of reading clinics created to meet the increased number of students academically underprepared for college-level work. Another resource introduced beginning in the 1950s was counseling services in remedial programs (Kulik and Kulik, 1991).

Another catalyst for change was the civil rights movement, manifested in the early 1960s in various forms that resulted in major societal changes of infrastructure—including in learning assistance programs (Chazan, 1973; Clowes, 1980). The Civil Rights Act of 1964 and other programs of President Lyndon Johnson's Great Society focused on increasing opportunities for people of color as well as those people historically excluded from many of society's benefits. Learning assistance services, especially remedial and developmental courses, took on additional tasks. Their responsibility expanded beyond preparation of students for college-level courses, and the learning assistance field received an indirect mandate to serve as a major resource to enable post-secondary institutions to increase dramatically their enrollments by students who had been excluded before—the poor, students of color, and students from families that had never completed college. This informal social responsibility by the learning assistance community would overwhelm its capacity to meet the need as a result of insufficient funding and a lack of trained personnel to provide the services. Although not formally stated in official documents, college learning assistance programs were expected to compensate for inadequate secondary schools, especially in rural and urban centers, and assist students to quickly develop college-level skills in an academic term or two. Overcoming an inadequate elementary and secondary education with limited time, resources, and personnel was a nearly impossible task. The field is still informally held to these expectations today and contributes to criticism for not achieving desired student outcomes.

Compensatory Education

Deep-rooted social problems influencing many students of color and those from low socioeconomic backgrounds created the need for a new type of education program. During the early 1960s, national civil rights legislation established the Office of Compensatory Education in the U.S. Office of Education (Chazan, 1973). The civil rights movement chose a different perspective of learning assistance. "Compensatory education" remedied a previous state of discrimination: "Compensatory education in higher education would take the form of remediation activities such as preparatory and supplementary work . . . all with a program to provide an enriching experience beyond the academic environment to counterbalance a nonsupportive home environment" (Clowes, 1980, p. 8).

Some believed environmental conditions, often induced by poverty, were responsible for students' poor academic achievement. Compensatory education defined itself as "those efforts designed to make up for the debilitating consequences of discrimination and poverty" (Frost and Rowland, 1971, p. vii). President Johnson's War on Poverty also targeted the negative outcomes caused by these environmental conditions. Compensatory education provided an improved home environment that had been identified as a significant factor for future academic achievement (Maxwell, 1997; Ntuk-Iden, 1978). This paradigm shift from remediating deficits of individual students to remedying deficits of the learning environment and the community required different learning assistance interventions. The response was systemic and involved interventions beyond the provision of tutorial programs and remedial credit courses. Such compensatory programs required significant federal oversight, funding, and management.

New compensatory education programs such as TRIO and other Equal Opportunity programs originated in the 1969 civil rights legislation. According to federal legislation, student eligibility for these new programs required them to meet one or more of the following criteria: (1) neither parent completed college; (2) an economically disadvantaged background; or (3) an eligible disability. The TRIO college access programs became an official entitlement for a federally defined population based on historical underrepresentation in postsecondary education or physical disability (Kerstiens, 1997).

Compensatory education also included traditional approaches to learning assistance—tutoring, counseling, and remedial credit courses—along with a new package of activities including educational enrichment and cultural experiences (Clowes, 1980). Compensatory education leaders distanced themselves from traditional learning assistance activities, however, to avoid the stigma associated with those programs. They positioned compensatory education as creating a new learning culture for students who had suffered historic discrimination and had been underserved by their previous education (Clowes, 1980).

Compensatory education was based on the public health model rather than the medical model (Clowes, 1980). The model expanded beyond the individual to the surrounding academic and economic environment that affected students. Identifying student deficits, providing remedial assistance, and adding supplemental enrichment activities were essential for compensatory education. In addition to a curriculum that included remedial courses, compensatory education also sought to immerse students in a new learning culture that included enrichment activities.

Therefore, compensatory education is not identical to traditional learning assistance approaches. It provides a specific response to a new student population in postsecondary education. Added to its mission was the cultural enrichment of students whose impoverished backgrounds mandated a different approach. Rather than changing the physical surroundings in which students lived and attended school, compensatory education sought to create a separate and enriched learning community for these students. Another approach to create a supportive learning environment for historically underrepresented college students took place in the junior and community colleges.

Federally funded compensatory education programs were a response by the national government to historic injustices. These new programs were accountable, monitored, and funded by the federal government. They were a direct intervention into individual postsecondary institutions. Only approved students could be served through the programs to ensure that the local institution did not divert funds for other purposes. This direct and narrow focus met the needs of many who were served (Grout, 2003). It also became an enormous missed opportunity that not only marginalized the students served and the compensatory programs but also failed to meet the larger issue.

The campus environment and allocation of resources also contributed to lower performance by historically excluded students of color, poor students, and first-generation students. The federal response could have been to hold postsecondary institutions accountable for outcomes of all students. Instead, the response was to create small communities that operated in the larger institutions that could only serve about 10 percent of eligible students (Nealy, 2009; Swail and Roth, 2000). States could also have joined this demand for accountability and made college funding contingent on improved student outcomes, including persistence toward graduation, not only for the overall student population but also for demographic groups such as those from low socioeconomic status, students of color, and first-generation students.

The British provide a model for this type of accountability for higher education. Their "widening participation" initiative holds colleges accountable for student outcomes, among them graduation rates for all students, including those historically neglected (Higher Education Funding Council for England, 2006). Rather than national funds provided for narrowly targeted populations and accompanying services, the funds are for initiatives that result in changes in the campus culture and are critical elements of the campus strategic goals (Higher Education Funding Council for England, 2006). The demographics of the entering student body are to be reflected in the graduating students, or part of the annual appropriation by the national government is subject to withholding. This type of financial accountability as well as supplemental funding from the government for efforts at widening participation could have been implemented in the United States as well.

Instead, the federal government informally endorsed the marginalization of first-generation, economically disadvantaged, and disabled students by providing programs for only a small portion of those who were eligible. These students were identified as different from the others and provided separate programs to serve them, and the participants as well as the service providers suffered from the ensuing stigma while the institutional culture remained essentially unchanged.

Role of the Junior and Community Colleges

When junior and community colleges expanded in the early 1900s, the entry-level test scores for college applicants were moderately lower than those for four-year institutions (Koos, 1924). This situation dramatically changed in the 1960s as open-door admissions policies at two-year colleges brought many students to postsecondary education that formerly entered the workforce immediately after high school. Junior colleges expanded their mission beyond only preparing students for successful transfer to senior institutions. Community colleges retrained their transfer function and expanded their mission to serve students who were academically underprepared and those enrolled in new certificate vocational programs that served the local community. This shift in focus led the majority of these junior colleges to rename themselves community colleges because of their expanded vision and mission of service (Cohen and Brawer, 2002).

Increased pressure was placed on community colleges in the 1970s and 1980s as four-year institutions recruited more college-bound students to replace ballooning enrollments from returning war veterans (who used the federal GI bill) and the subsequent postwar baby boom. Senior institutions recruited more academically able students and left community colleges to seek more students who were academically underprepared, dramatically increasing the need for comprehensive learning assistance centers and remedial or developmental community college courses. An unanticipated result of this shift in the academic profile of students enrolled at senior institutions created a false perception that little need existed for learning assistance. The opposite occurred at four-year institutions as faculty perceived, wrongly, that new student admits were more academically able to master difficult course material (Hankin, 1996). The gap between student preparation and faculty expectations required a different form of learning assistance, leading to the creation of noncredit learning assistance centers and the decline of remedial credit courses.

New populations of nontraditional students joined traditional-aged students. Expanded federal financial aid through the GI bill and federal civil rights legislation that created compensatory programs such as TRIO fueled an increase in enrollments. The rapidly growing community colleges became the primary offerors of credit-bearing remedial and developmental courses. The core mission of two-year colleges often included providing services for students who had been identified as academically underprepared, but no corresponding statement was made about serving these students in most public four-year colleges and universities. This lack of official institutional priority for serving students that were academically underprepared in one or more academic content areas served as a catalyst for the shift in credit-bearing remedial and developmental offerings from four-year to two-year institutions. This shift contributed to the attachment of further stigma to remedial and developmental courses.

Before this shift occurred in the 1990s, however, many college academic preparatory services at four-year and two-year institutions had responded to the new influx of students by increasing the comprehensiveness of their learning services (Boylan, 1988; Boylan, 1995a). In the mid-1970s, nearly 80 percent of all postsecondary institutions provided academic enrichment and support programs (Roueche and Snow, 1977). Although this rate was nearly the same as the late 1880s, services provided by these programs were more comprehensive, extensive, and coordinated than earlier ones.

Almost half of first-time community college students in the late 1960s and 1970s were underprepared for college-level courses in one or more academic areas. Students often enrolled in one or more developmental courses (Roueche and Roueche, 1999; McCabe and Day, 1998). Although college-bound students in high school enrolled in college preparatory courses, they may have selected the wrong ones or the quality of them may have been insufficient for success in first-year, graduation-credit college courses (Horn, Chen, and MPR Associates, 1998). Frustration with the inability to predict student success created great frustration for all stakeholders involved in the academic enterprise: "The open door often turned into a revolving door, with students dropping out and stopping out regularly. This led to a highly charged debate about the lowering of standards, often followed by the call to raise admission standards and close the doors of opportunity to the thousands of prospective new students" (Casazza and Silverman, 1996, p. 28).

Sometimes change occurs because of intentional choices and visionary leadership by a few individuals. Other times it occurs through reaction to the surrounding environment. Learning assistance during this phase changed because of the latter reason. A major variable that affected U.S. postsecondary education in the mid-1900s was rapid expansion of the student body and failure by many institutions to provide sufficient learning assistance services to support their academic success. As a major influx of new students came into college, the previous learning assistance activities were unable to meet the need. For example, only a fixed number of counseling appointments were available weekly, as few colleges were able or willing to hire more staff. The same was true for faculty teaching remedial courses. Newer, more flexible and scalable learning assistance systems were created. These new services employed student and paraprofessional staff along with the professional staff, prompting creation of new learning assistance approaches in the fifth phase of higher education history.

Phase Five: 1970s to Mid-1990s

The fifth phase of postsecondary education history introduced new learning assistance non-credit-bearing activities and approaches, especially among public four-year institutions. A second feature of this phase was curtailment of remedial instruction that focused on high school students' development of skills. Corresponding with that decrease, developmental courses that focused on the skill development required for college-level courses rapidly increased. Learning assistance built on past activities of tutoring and credit-bearing courses was replaced by learning assistance centers that served students from a wider range of academic ability.

New forms of learning assistance emerged to serve students with low academic preparation or those who had previously earned low grades in a college course. Previously, nearly all students experienced learning assistance. As the learning assistance model and student body changed, some participated and some did not. The college student body became more diverse with regard to economic, cultural, and academic preparation. Learning assistance grew more quickly at community colleges because they enrolled the largest numbers of underprepared students. Those who participated, especially those forced to participate because of mandatory placement in remedial or developmental courses, were more stigmatized.

Learning Assistance

In the early 1970s, learning assistance centers (LACs) were introduced: (Arendale, 2004; Christ, 1971). Frank Christ at California State University–Long Beach developed the first LAC (then called the learning assistance support system) and was the first to use the technical term in the professional literature (Arendale, 2004). White and Schnuth (1990) identified a distinguishing characteristic of LACs: their comprehensive nature and mission in the institution. Rather than an exclusive focus on underprepared students, LACs extended services for all students and even faculty members. The center naturally extended the classroom with enrichment activities for all students.

LACs, according to Christ, were comprehensive in their theoretical underpinnings and services provided, compared with earlier reading labs and other forms of academic assistance. LACs shared a common mission: to meet the needs of students facing academic difficulty in a course and to provide supplemental and enrichment learning opportunities for any students at the institution. The reading labs worked only for students dealing with severe difficulty in reading. Students went to counseling centers only when they were having extreme academic and emotional difficulties. The LACs served these students and the general student population as well. Therefore, no stigma was attached to the LACs. "[LACs] differed significantly from previous academic support services by introducing concepts and strategies from human development, the psychology of learning, educational technology, and corporate management into an operational rationale specific to higher education; by functioning as a campus-wide support system in a centralized operational facility; by vigorously opposing any stigma that it was 'remedial' and only for inadequately prepared, provisionally admitted, or probationary students; and by emphasizing 'management by objectives' and a cybernetic subsystem of ongoing evaluation to elicit and use feedback from users for constant program modification" (Christ, 1997, pp. 1–2). Learning centers avoided the remedial label that had stigmatized other forms of learning assistance. Although some institutions did not offer developmental courses, especially public four-year institutions, nearly all institutions accepted the challenge to offer learning assistance and enrichment services to all students.

Various factors encouraged the rapid development of learning centers, which (1) applied technology for individualized learning; (2) responded to lowered admission standards; (3) focused on cognitive learning strategies; (4) increased student retention; and (5) were perceived to enrich learning for all students, regardless of their previous level of academic performance (Enright, 1975). The LAC was a catalyst for improved learning across the campus. Rather than continuing the previous practice of preparatory programs and remedial courses that were often outside the heart of the college, these centers contributed to the core institutional mission (Hultgren, 1970; Kerstiens, 1972). Faculty members often recognized these centers as extensions of the classroom and encouraged their use for deeper mastery of college-level material. "The resource center does not define the goals of the learning it supports; it accepts the goals of the faculty and the students" (Henderson, Melloni, and Sherman, 1971, p. 5). LACs were consolidated, and centralized operations were housed in a single location on campus. All students—not just those experiencing academic difficulty—benefited from a LAC's services. LACs provided a model for learning and teaching centers established at some U.S. colleges beginning in the 1980s that assisted students and faculty members. Those centers supported students' mastery of rigorous academic content material and faculty professional development.

As mentioned, LACs were sometimes integrated into campuswide student retention initiatives. Organizations such as the Noel-Levitz centers have acknowledged a variety of learning assistance programs by recognizing increased student persistence (Noel-Levitz Center, 2010). A LAC that includes this objective as part of its mission is at Lees-McRae College (Banner Elk, North Carolina). The Division of Student Success (http://www.lmc.edu/sites/Academics/StudentSuccess/) hosts traditional learning assistance services. It also provides additional services supporting student retention by housing the Office of Students with Disabilities, the First Year Experience Program, summer orientation, and student retention services for students placed on academic probation. Learning assistance is bundled with other campus services and guided by the campus student retention plan. Sometimes these bundled efforts also support persistence in college majors in academically challenging areas such as science, technology, engineering, and mathematics (Seymour and Hewitt, 1997).

Developmental Education

Beginning in the 1970s, "developmental education" emerged as another term used to describe the field of learning assistance. This term borrowed concepts from the field of college student personnel. An underlying assumption was that all college students were developing throughout their college career. "The notion of developmental sequence is the kingpin of developmental theory. . . . A goal of education is to stimulate the individual to move to the next stage in the sequence" (Cross, 1976, p. 158). This perspective returned learning assistance to its historic roots by focusing on the entire student population.

Proponents of developmental education viewed it as a more comprehensive model because it focused on personal development of the academic and affective domains (Boylan, 1995b; Casazza and Silverman, 1996; Hashway; 1988; Higbee, 2005; Higbee and Dwinell, 1998). This value-added or talent development perspective assumed each student possessed skills or knowledge that could be further developed. Cross expressed the differences between remedial and developmental education in the following way: "If the purpose of the program is to overcome academic deficiencies, I would term the program remedial, in the standard dictionary sense in which remediation is concerned with correcting weaknesses. If, however, the purpose of the program is to develop the diverse talents of students, whether academic or not, I would term the program developmental. Its mission is to give attention to the fullest possible development of talent and to develop strengths as well as to correct weaknesses" (Cross, 1976, p. 31).

Access Programs

Thus far this review of learning assistance has focused on its use in the United States. Tutorial programs and the earlier dame schools were common learning assistance approaches in Europe. During this period, the United Kingdom developed a new approach for learning assistance called "access programs."

Unlike the system in the United States, higher education in most other countries was coordinated, funded, and evaluated by the national government. The United Kingdom employed a different approach and terminology to meet the needs of students who were academically underprepared during the late 1970s. Two organizations in particular provided leadership—the European Access Network (http://www.ean-edu.org/) and the Institute for Access Studies (http://www.staffs.ac.uk/institutes/access/). Most postsecondary institutions in the United Kingdom offered student services similar to those in the United States, including advising, counseling, disability services, orientation, mentoring, and tutoring (Thomas, Quinn, Slack, and Casey, 2003). Students with additional needs for developmental courses were required to complete a prerequisite certificate offered through the access program.

One noticeable difference between the United States and the United Kingdom was length of academic terms of remedial or developmental courses. The United Kingdom organized these courses into a unit called an "access program." These programs were located in a postsecondary institution or an adult education center operated independently in the local community. Admission to a college or university depended on successful completion of the one-year program, which also resulted in a certificate of completion. Although some similarities existed between access programs in the United Kingdom and academic preparatory programs in the United States, an important difference between the two countries was that U.S. colleges were more likely to admit students who had less academic preparation than were those in the United Kingdom. U.S. institutions were more willing to admit students to determine whether they could benefit from the college experience, while U.K. institutions demanded a greater likelihood of academic success before admission (Burke, 2002; Fulton and others, 1981).

The U.K. national government first initiated access programs in 1978. In addition to the proactive stance by the national government to require this prerequisite learning venue for some college aspirants, several distinctive features of access programs contrasted with learning assistance in the United States:

> They were recognized as an official route into further higher education.

> They met minimum standards set by the national government before access programs students were admitted to college.

> They targeted underrepresented students such as disabled learners, the unemployed, female returnees, minority ethnic groups, and those from lower socioeconomic backgrounds.

> They were evaluated by the Quality Assurance Agency, a national government agency similar to the U.S. Government Accounting Office (Universities and Colleges Admission Service, 2003a, 2003b).

The British government created and provides ongoing evaluation for access programs, while in the United States they are generally under local institutional review. In the United States, the federal government is not a partner with learning assistance except for some competitive funds allocated through grant programs such as Title III, Title VI, and TRIO. It has been a missed opportunity for the national learning assistance professional associations to develop a formal, ongoing relationship with the U.S. Department of Education that could have led to more legitimacy, improvement, and perhaps more funding support.

Pilot Experiments with Outsourcing Developmental Courses

Forces coincided during the late 1980s through the 1990s to experiment with commercial companies' provision of developmental college courses. Nationwide, budget priorities shifted during the 1980s as state revenues previously devoted to public higher education began to erode because of escalating costs for state health care, transportation systems, prison facilities, and public K–12 education. With stagnant revenue growth and escalating operating costs, many colleges identified cost savings perceived to have little negative impact. A popular approach was outsourcing services traditionally performed by college staff. Requiring highly competitive service bids and shifting escalating health insurance and other benefits (the fastest-growing component of labor costs) to subcontractors would save significant costs for institutions. Numerous services were successfully outsourced: bookstores, food service, building maintenance, housing, and transportation services (Lyall and Sell, 2006). Another area for outsourcing was the delivery of developmental courses (Johnsrud, 2000).

A small handful of colleges contracted with Kaplan, Inc. (http:// kaplan.com) and Sylvan Learning Systems (http://reportcard.sylvan .info/) in the mid-1990s to provide instruction in remedial and developmental mathematics, reading, and writing. Colleges that participated in the pilot program included Greenville Technical College (South Carolina), Columbia College Chicago (Illinois), Howard Community College and Towson University (Maryland), and several other unnamed proprietary schools. National interest and debate were generated through the pilot projects (Blumenstyk, 2006; Gose, 1997). Initial reports were mixed in Maryland's pilot program with Sylvan (Maryland Higher Education Commission, 1997). Students paid a surcharge between two and four times the regular tuition rate to cover instructional and administrative expenses and allow the companies to turn a profit.

Both Kaplan and Sylvan ended the pilot programs in agreement with the hosting institutions in the late 1990s. The reasons for their failure were primarily economic. The initial hope was to contain instructional costs and deliver improved student achievement and subsequent higher student retention rates that would justify the annual contract cost, but it was unrealistic for a for-profit company to market a program for a lower cost than the ones that could be provided by the institution with the use of modestly paid adjunct instructors who could be assigned large classes (Blumenstyk, 2006; Boylan, 2002a). The same economic forces that were the catalyst for the experiment ultimately became the cause for this first wave of outsourcing to end. A second wave of outsourcing was expected to be more effective during the first decade of the twenty-first century as the focus changed from onsite developmental courses to online tutoring.

Rise of the Professional Associations

The 1980s witnessed the birth of several national associations serving professionals in the field of learning assistance, coinciding with the explosive growth in college enrollment and number of public postsecondary institutions, especially community colleges. Institutions expanded their teaching staff for remedial and developmental courses. The exponential growth of learning assistance centers required a new category of college employees. These new professionals needed organizations that met needs for postsecondary education rather than older organizations devoted to serving educators in elementary and secondary education. They needed to increase their professionalism and provide venues for conversation with colleagues and experienced leaders in learning assistance. The new organizations provided a supportive community for new professionals who might be isolated on campus and were sometimes stigmatized because of their association with learning assistance programs.

Established in 1952, the Southwest Reading Conference, later renamed the National Reading Conference, was first to serve postsecondary educators in this field. The College Reading and Learning Association (CRLA, previously named the Western College Reading Association and later the Western College Reading and Learning Association) was founded in 1966. The CRLA publishes a quarterly newsletter, annual conference proceedings, and the biannual *Journal of College Reading and Learning*. Conferences are held annually at national venues and at CRLA-affiliated chapters throughout the United States. The focus of the CRLA was clearly postsecondary education. Previously, learning assistance personnel had few options for professional development other than from other organizations with a predominately elementary and secondary education focus such as the International Reading Association. The CRLA and the other learning assistance associations that followed it provided an identity and a place for postsecondary learning assistance professionals to gather and exchange information.

Following passage of national legislation creating the federal TRIO programs for first-generation and economically disadvantaged students, political advocacy was essential to expand financial and stable support for these programs. During the early 1970s, regional professional associations created by TRIO staff members represented their interests for increased national funding and provided professional development services for themselves. Clark Chipman, a regional USDOE higher education administrator for the Upper Midwest, was a key leader for development of the first TRIO association. It was called the Mid-American Association of Educational Opportunity Program Personnel. Afterwards, nine additional regional associations formed across the United States. In 1981 Clark Chipman and Arnold Mitchem coordinated efforts of preceding regional associations to influence national policy through creation of the National Council of Educational Opportunity Associations. In 1988 the association changed its name to the Council on Opportunity in Education (Grout, 2003).

The National Association for Developmental Education (NADE, initially named the National Association for Remedial/Developmental Studies in Postsecondary Education) was founded in 1976. Because of uncertainty about what would become the more widely adopted term, both "remedial" and "developmental" were included in the association's original name. In 1981 the NADE contracted with the National Center for Developmental Education to provide the *Journal of Developmental Education* as a membership benefit and official journal of the association. The NARDSPE changed its name to the NADE in 1984.

A variety of other professional associations were born in the 1990s. The National College Learning Center Association provided professional development for learning center directors. The National Tutoring

Association served educators from higher education, secondary education, and private individuals engaged in tutoring. The Association for the Tutoring Profession was created for similar purposes. The Council for Learning Assistance and Developmental Education Associations (initially named the American Council of Developmental Education Associations) began in 1996 to serve as a forum for these professional associations to meet and engage in cooperative activities, information sharing, and networking.

The growth of these organizations signified historically that learning assistance was becoming more complex, employing more professionals, and needed professional associations focused on their special needs in higher education. Large established organizations such as the International Reading Association, Conference on College Composition and Communication, and American Mathematical Society generally provided special interest groups for postsecondary learning assistance professionals. They missed the opportunity, however, to fully meet the needs of the professionals who preferred the smaller and more narrowly focused learning assistance associations. This situation led to duplication of services among the larger content-focused organizations and the smaller learning assistance associations. It also may have led to increased stigma for the learning assistance professionals, as they did not become members and attend the conferences of the larger organizations that attracted membership of mainstream college faculty and staff members. It was another way that some learning assistance professionals stood apart from the mainstream in higher education.

Support Systems for Leaders and Practitioners

Several other national organizations, graduate education programs, and publications have contributed to the history of the learning assistance community. A three-year grant from the Kellogg Foundation established the National Center for Developmental Education (NCDE) in 1976. Two years later NCDE began publishing *The Journal of Developmental Education* (initially named *Journal of Developmental and Remedial Education*). *Review of Research in Developmental Education* was another NCDE publication; created in 1983, it focused on current research in the field. Since 1980 the center has also hosted the Kellogg Institute for the Training and Certification of Developmental Educators.

During this period, a variety of formal and informal systems of professional development for learning assistance were established. Practitioners in the field previously relied on degree programs for elementary and secondary education. Secondary educators teaching reading, English, and mathematics staffed many of the learning assistance centers and taught developmental courses in post-secondary institutions.

New graduate programs also emerged to equip learning center professionals at the college level rather than relying on preparation for secondary schools. The first graduate programs in developmental education (M.A. and Ed.S.) began at Appalachian State University in 1972. Grambling State University (Louisiana) in 1986 offered the nation's first doctoral program (Ed.D.). National Louis University (Chicago), Texas State University at San Marcos, and the University of Minnesota–Twin Cities (Minneapolis) also established learning assistance graduate certificate or degree programs during this period. Collectively these advanced degrees contributed to the professionalization and ability to meet student needs by learning assistance faculty and staff members. A major challenge with the national impact of these programs is that they are few in number and many current learning assistance professionals find it difficult to relocate them to meet residency requirements and to secure funds for tuition. An expansion of distance learning pedagogies for the degree programs would permit easier access for graduate students who are place bound and unable to participate in long required residency stays at the degree-granting institutions.

Phase Six: Mid-1990s to the Present

Turbulence in postsecondary education defines the current phase of history. Learning assistance activities and services have been curtailed at a growing number of four-year institutions, especially large public universities. This change is concurrent with increased diversity of the student population, increased college enrollments, increased competition for institutional funds, and decreased percentage of operating funds from state governments for public institutions. Although the need for learning assistance has expanded, its resources have become scarcer.

In the late 1990s, the perception of learning assistance changed for some—and not for the better. Critics have been particularly harsh toward programs that used the term "developmental education" to describe themselves. Large, public four-year institutions are engaged in intense dialogue about this topic. The terms *developmental education*, *compensatory education*, and *remedial education* suffer from stigma. In 1998 Martha Maxwell noted, "Developmental education has become a euphemism for remedial with all the negative connotations that word implies. . . . Today, students taking developmental courses are stigmatized. . . . In primary and secondary schools the term developmental education applies to programs for the mentally retarded" (Piper, 1998, p. 35). As remedial education engendered negative reactions from some policymakers, so did developmental education.

Several publications have prompted considerable conversation about improving the campus learning environment (Barr and Tagg, 1995; Lazerson, Wagener, and Shumanis, 2000). A number of learning assistance professionals have reinvented themselves as resources for the entire campus—students and faculty alike—by aligning with this paradigm of learning.

A result of the paradigm shift from teaching to learning led to creation of learning and teaching centers at some institutions. Although the name of these centers was the same, two variations were apparent. One type of learning and teaching center provides professional development for the teaching staff. Services include resource libraries, training programs for new instructors, ongoing mentoring programs, classroom observations with subsequent private consultations, and the like. A second type of learning and teaching center extends the professional development services for faculty by providing learning assistance services for students such as tutoring, learning skill workshops, drop-in learning centers, and credit courses.

Methods for operating these teaching and learning centers vary widely. An online search for these centers suggests that most were established at four-year institutions (Center for Teaching Excellence, 2009). Reviewing the Web sites for the centers suggests that they have been expressed differently based on administrative location under academic or student affairs. Those in student affairs tend to have a higher focus on delivery of learning assistance services for students. Those located under academic affairs more commonly focus on teaching faculty development activities. Another factor that has affected these centers is whether a faculty or staff member leads it. Those led by faculty members tend to be under academic affairs, those led by staff members most often under student affairs. Unlike the aforementioned learning assistance professional associations, no clear national organization represents these teaching and learning centers.

The teaching and learning center model has emerged to meet the broad needs that exist to assist student learning and faculty development. An online search for postsecondary teaching and learning centers identified several examples among prestigious institutions. Cornell University (Ithaca, New York), through its Center for Learning and Teaching (http://www.clt.cornell.edu), serves students through the learning strategies center (tutoring, workshops, supplemental classes), student disability services, and international teaching assistance development program (workshops to improve communication and pedagogical skills). Instructors can access teaching assistance services (individual consultations and workshops to improve teaching skills) and faculty services (individual consultations to improve teaching effectiveness). At Stanford University (Palo Alto, California), the Center for Teaching and Learning (http://ctl.stanford.edu/) provides faculty development opportunities and tutoring, learning skills workshops, and academic coaching for students.

As these examples illustrate, common practices of these expanded centers include providing academic assistance to all students enrolled in identified courses, publishing teaching effectiveness newsletters, conducting learning effectiveness workshops, providing teaching mentors, and consulting on innovative instructional delivery. Both illustrate how learning assistance appears very differently at these prestigious institutions in comparison with open access community colleges. Developmental courses are not provided at these institutions; instead, services for students focus on tutoring and noncredit learning strategies workshops.

Summary

Learning assistance serves a pivotal role in the history of U.S. postsecondary education. It developed a variety of approaches, and the language used to describe it has evolved. Regardless of the expressions, learning assistance bridges the gap between students' academic preparation and expectations of college courses. It began as an embedded service by providing tutoring for all students enrolled in college during the first century of the United States. Later, the services became less embedded in the curriculum—with some students participating in learning assistance and others not. At times it has been essential for supporting student enrollment and persistence to graduation, and at other times it has been rejected and stigmatized. Sometimes these different perspectives on learning assistance have existed at the same time in different types of postsecondary institutions.

As learning assistance approaches permitted voluntary participation or required mandatory placement, stigma sometimes emerged for those using the services. The student body can become divided: students required to participate, students choosing to participate, and those who elect not to participate. The stigma issue is most pronounced for students enrolled in remedial or developmental credit courses, but credit courses are only one approach to learning assistance. Other students who did not enroll in such courses often accessed other forms of learning assistance such as tutoring, learning assistance centers, or other services. Students who use these services, however, especially those from more advantaged backgrounds, do not suffer from the same stigma. These learning assistance activities and services are perceived as supplemental or enrichment and have escaped negative stereotyping.

A balanced review of the history places learning assistance in its proper position, operating at the crossroads of three major components of higher education: academic affairs, student affairs, and enrollment management. The next chapter explores the scope and expression of learning assistance today. The expression of learning assistance is often quite different among different institutional types based on admissions selectivity and degrees conferred.

References

Arendale, D. R. (2001). Effect of administrative placement and fidelity of implementation of the model on effectiveness of supplemental instruction programs. Doctoral dissertation, University of Missouri–Kansas City, 2000.

Dissertation Abstracts International, 62, 93. ERIC Document Reproduction Service ED 480 590.

Arendale, D. R. (2002b). Then and now: The early history of developmental education. *Research & Teaching in Developmental Education, 18*(2), 3–26.

Arendale, D. R. (2004). Mainstreamed academic assistance and enrichment for all students: The historical origins of learning assistance centers. *Research for Education Reform, 9*(4), 3–21.

Barbe, W. (1951). Reading-improvement services in colleges and universities. *School and Society, 74*(1907), 6–7.

Barr, R. B., and Tagg, J. (1995). From teaching to learning: A new paradigm for undergraduate education. *Change Magazine, 27*(6), 13–25.

Blumenstyk, G. (2006, March 10). Businesses have remedies for sale, but a cure is not guaranteed: Companies have mixed results in the sale of remedial education. *Chronicle of Higher Education,* B30.

Boylan, H. R. (1988). The historical roots of developmental education. Part III. *Review of Research in Developmental Education, 5*(3), 1–3.

Boylan, H. R. (1995a). Making the case for developmental education. *Research in Developmental Education, 12*(2), 1–4.

Boylan, H. R. (1995b). A review of national surveys on developmental education programs. *Research in Developmental Education, 12*(5), 1–6.

Boylan, H. R. (2002a). A brief history of the American Council of Developmental Education Associations. In D. B. Lundell and J. L. Higbee (Eds.), *Histories of developmental education* (pp. 11–14). Minneapolis: Center for Research on Developmental Education and Urban Literacy, General College, University of Minnesota.

Boylan, H. R., Bonham, B. S., and Bliss, L. B. (1994). Who are the developmental students? *Research in Developmental Education, 11*(2), 1–4.

Boylan, H. R., and White, W. G., Jr. (1987). Educating all the nation's people: The historical roots of developmental education. Part I. *Review of Research in Developmental Education, 4*(4), 1–4.

Brier, E. (1984). Bridging the academic preparation gap: An historical view. *Journal of Developmental Education, 8*(1), 2–5.

Brubacher, J. S., and Rudy, W. (1976). *Higher education in transition: A history of American colleges and universities, 1636–1976* (3rd ed.). New York: Harper & Row.

Burke, P. J. (2002). *Accessing education: Effectively widening participation.* Sterling, VA: Trentham Books.

Canfield, J. H. (1889). *The opportunities of the rural population for higher education.* Nashville: National Council on Education.

Casazza, M. E., and Silverman, S. L. (1996). *Learning assistance and developmental education: A guide for effective practice.* San Francisco: Jossey-Bass.

Center for Teaching Excellence. (2009). *Database and web links to teaching and learning centers in the U.S. and in other countries.* Lawrence, KS: Center for Teaching Excellence. Retrieved December 15, 2009, from http://www.cte.ku.edu/cteInfo/resources/websites.shtml.

Chazan, M. (1973). *Compensatory education.* London: Butterworth.

Christ, F. L. (1971). Systems for learning assistance: Learners, learning facilitators, and learning centers. In *Fourth annual proceedings of the Western College Reading Association. Volume IV: Interdisciplinary aspects of reading instruction* (pp. 32–41). Los Angeles: Western College Reading Association.

Christ, F. L. (1997). The learning assistance center as I lived it. In S. Mioduski and G. Enright (Eds.), *Proceedings of the 15th and 16th annual institutes for learning assistance professionals: 1994 and 1995* (pp. 1–14). Tucson: University Learning Center, University of Arizona.

Clemont, W. K. (1899, February). The Northwestern State University and its preparatory school. *Educational Review, 17*, 154–163.

Clowes, D. A. (1980). More than a definitional problem: Remedial, compensatory, and developmental education. *Journal of Developmental and Remedial Education, 4*(1), 8–10.

Cohen, A. M., and Brawer, F. B. (2002). *The American community college.* (4th ed.). San Francisco: Jossey-Bass.

Cowie, A. (1936). *Educational problems at Yale College in the eighteenth century.* New Haven, CN: Yale University Press.

Craig, C. M. (1997). *Developmental education: A historical perspective.* Paper presented at the National Association for Developmental Education Annual Conference, Atlanta, GA. Available from C. M. Craig, assistant professor of mathematics in learning support, Augusta State University, 2500 Walton Way, Augusta, GA 30904.

Cross, K. P. (1976). *Accent on learning.* San Francisco: Jossey-Bass.

Curti, M., and Carstensen, V. (1949). *The University of Wisconsin: A history 1848–1925* (Volume I). Madison: University of Wisconsin Press.

Dempsey, B. J. L. (1985). *An update on the organization and administration of learning assistance programs in U.S. senior institutions of higher education.* ERIC Document Reproduction Service ED 257 334.

Enright, G. (1975). College learning skills: Frontierland origins of the learning assistance center. In *Proceedings of the Eight Annual Conference of the Western College Reading Association: College Learning Skills Today and Tomorrow* (pp. 81–92). Las Cruces, NM: Western College Reading Association. ERIC Document Reproduction Service ED 105 204.

Frost, J., and Rowland, G. (1971). *Compensatory education: The acid test of American education.* Dubuque, IA: William C. Brown.

Fulton, O., and others. (1981). *Access to higher education: Programme of study into the future of higher education.* Surrey, England: Society for Research into Higher Education. ERIC Document Reproduction Service ED 215 603.

Goodwin, W. W. (1895). School English. *Nation, 61*, 291–293.

Gordon, E. E., and Gordon, E. H. (1990). *Centuries of tutoring: A history of alternative education in America and Western Europe.* Lanham, MD: University Press of America.

Gose, B. (1997, September 19). Tutoring companies take over remedial teaching at some colleges. *Chronicle of Higher Education*, A44.

Grout, J. (2003, January). Milestones of TRIO history, Part 1. *Opportunity Outlook*, 21–27.

Hankin, J. N. (Ed.). (1996). *The community college: Opportunity and access for America's first-year students.* Monograph Series No. 19. Columbia: National Resource Center for the First-Year Experience and Students in Transition, University of South Carolina.

Hashway, R. M. (1988). *Foundations of developmental education.* New York: Praeger.

Henderson, D. D., Melloni, B. J., and Sherman, J. G. (1971). *What a learning resource center (LRC) could mean for Georgetown University.* Unpublished manuscript. ERIC Document Reproduction Service ED 055 417.

Higbee, J. L. (2005). Developmental Education. In M. L. Upcraft, J. N. Gardner, and B. O. Barefoot (Eds.). *Challenging and supporting the first-year student: A handbook for improving the first year of college* (pp. 292–307). San Francisco: Jossey-Bass.

Higbee, J. L., and Dwinell, P. L. (Eds.). (1998). *Developmental education: Preparing successful college students.* Monograph Series No. 24. Columbia: National Resource Center for the First-Year Experience and Students in Transition, University of South Carolina.

Higher Education Funding Council for England. (2006). *Widening participation: A review.* London: Higher Education Funding Council for England.

Hill, A. S. (1885, June). English in our schools. *Harper's Magazine,* 123–133.

Horn, L. J., Chen, X., and MPR Associates. (1998). *Toward resiliency: At-risk students who make it to college.* Washington, DC: Office of Educational Research and Improvement, U.S. Department of Education.

Hultgren, D. D. (1970). The role of the individual learning center in effecting educational change. In G. B. Schick and M. M. May (Eds.), *Reading: Process and pedagogy.* 19th National Conference Yearbook (Volume 2, pp. 89–94). Milwaukee: National Reading Conference.

Ignash, J. M. (Ed.). (1997). *Implementing effective policies for remedial and developmental education.* New Directions for Community Colleges, no. 100. San Francisco: Jossey-Bass.

Johnsrud, L. K. (2000). Higher education staff: Bearing the brunt of cost containment. In *NEA 2000 almanac of higher education* (pp. 101–118). Washington, DC: National Education Association.

Kerstiens, G. (1972). The ombudsman function of the college learning center. In F. Greene (Ed.). *College reading: Problems and programs of junior and senior colleges. 21st National Reading Conference Yearbook* (Volume 2, pp. 221–227). Milwaukee: National Reading Conference.

Kerstiens, G. (1997). Taxonomy of learning support services. In S. Mioduski and G. Enright (Eds.), *Proceedings of the 15th and 16th annual institutes for learning assistance professionals: 1994 and 1995* (pp. 48–51). Tucson: University Learning Center, University of Arizona.

Koos, L. V. (1924). *The junior college.* Minneapolis: University of Minnesota.

Kulik, J. A., and Kulik, C.-L. C. (1991). *Developmental instruction: An analysis of the research.* Boone, NC: National Center for Developmental Education, Appalachian State University.

Lazerson, M., Wagener, U., and Shumanis, N. (2000). Teaching and learning in higher education, 1980–2000. *Change, 32*(3), 12–19.

Lyall, K. D., and Sell, K. R. (2006). The de facto privatization of American public higher education. *Change Magazine, 38*(1), 4–13.

Maryland Higher Education Commission. (1997). *Study of the effectiveness of "privatizing" remedial services.* Annapolis: Maryland Higher Education Commission. Retrieved February 9, 2007, from http://www.mhec.state.md.us/publications/research/1997Studies/StudyofTheEffectivenessofPrivatizingRemedialServices.pdf.

Maxwell, M. (1979). *Improving student learning skills: A comprehensive guide to successful practices and programs for increasing the performance of underprepared students.* San Francisco: Jossey-Bass.

Maxwell, M. (1997). *Improving student learning skills: A new edition.* Clearwater, FL: H&H Publishing Company.

McCabe, R. H., and Day, P. R. (Eds.). (1998). *Developmental education: A twenty-first-century social and economic imperative.* Washington, DC: League for Innovation in the Community College and The College Board. ERIC Document Reproduction Service ED 421 176.

National Center for Education Statistics. (1993). *120 years of American education: A statistical portrait.* Washington, DC: Office of Educational Research and Improvement, U.S. Department of Education.

Nealy, M. (2009, June 10). Students rally at U.S. Capitol to urge increased support of TRIO and GEAR UP programs. *Issues in Higher Education.* Retrieved December 20, 2009, from http://diverseeducation.com/artman/publish/article_12627.shtml.

Noel-Levitz Center. (2010). *Database of past national award winners of exemplary student retention programs.* Retrieved January 5, 2010, from https://www.noellevitz.com/Papers+and+Research/Retention+Excellence+Awards/.

Ntuk-Iden, M. (1978). *Compensatory education.* Westmead, England: Teakfield Limited.

Parr, E. W. (1930, April). The extent of remedial reading work in state universities in the United States. *School and Society, 31*(799), 547–548.

Piper, J. (1998). An interview with Martha Maxwell. *Learning Assistance Review, 3*(1), 32–39.

Richardson, R., Martens, K., and Fisk, E. (1981). *Functional literacy in the college setting.* AAHE/ERIC Higher Education Research Report, no. 3. Washington, DC: American Association for Higher Education.

Roueche, J. E., and Roueche, S. D. (1999). *High stakes, high performance: Making remedial education work.* Washington, DC: American Association of Community Colleges, Community College Press.

Roueche, J. E., and Snow, J. G. (1977). *Overcoming learning problems.* San Francisco: Jossey-Bass.

Rubin, M. (1991). A glossary of developmental education terms compiled by the CRLA Task Force on Professional Language for College Reading and Learning. *Journal of College Reading and Learning, 23*(2), 1–14.

Rudolph, F. (1956). *Mark Hopkins and the log.* New Haven, CN: Yale University Press.

Rudy, W. (1996). *The campus and a nation in crisis: From the American revolution to Vietnam.* Cranbury, NJ: Associated University Press.

Seymour, E., and Hewitt, N. M. (1997). *Talking about leaving: Why undergraduates leave the sciences.* Boulder, CO: Westview Press.

Shedd, C. (1932). Higher education in the United States. In W. M. Kotschnig and E. Prys (Eds.), *The university in a changing world: A symposium* (pp. 125–162). London: Oxford University Press.

Swail, W. S., and Roth, D. (2000). The role of early intervention in education reform. *ERIC Review, 8*(1), 3–18. Retrieved December 20, 2009, from http://www.educationalpolicy.org/pdf/ERIC%20Review.pdf.

Thomas, L., Quinn, J., Slack, K., and Casey, L. (2003). *Effective approaches to retaining students in higher education: Directory of practice.* Stoke-on-Trent, U.K.: Institute for Access Studies, Staffordshire University. Retrieved January 31, 2005, from http://www.staffs.ac.uk/institutes/access/docs/Directory1.pdf.

Universities and Colleges Admission Service. (2003a). *Homepage.* Retrieved January 31, 2005, from http://www.ucas.com/access/.

Universities and Colleges Admission Service. (2003b). *Questions asked by higher education admissions staff.* Retrieved January 31, 2005, from http://www.ucas.com/ucc/access/ewni/staff.html.

Vaughan, G. B. (Ed.). (1983). *Issues for community college leaders in a new era.* San Francisco: Jossey-Bass.

Weidner, H. Z. (1990). *Back to the future.* Paper presented at the annual meeting of the Conference on College Composition and Communication, Chicago. ERIC Document Reproduction Service ED 319 045.

White, W. G., Jr., and Schnuth, M. L. (1990). College learning assistance centers: Places for learning. In R. M. Hashway (Ed.), *Handbook of developmental education* (pp. 155–177). New York: Praeger.

Wyatt, M. (1992). The past, present, and future need for college reading courses in the U.S. *Journal of Reading, 36*(1), 10–20.

Chapter 1 Questions for Further Reflection

1. Developmental education in one form or another has been a fixture of higher education for hundreds of years. Why do so few people outside the field realize this? What can we do about it?

2. At one point, underprepared students represented the majority in universities, and even today they represent a considerable percentage of the population at community colleges. In spite of their numbers, they are often unwelcome. Why is this? What can we do to change it?

3. Developmental education has evolved from one-to-one tutoring in the 1600s to multifaceted programs featuring courses and support services in the twenty-first century. What are the themes that have consistently characterized the field as it has undergone this evolution?

4. The introduction to this chapter describes some of the lessons that many college and university officials have failed to learn from the history of developmental education. What lessons have you learned from this chapter?

5. It has often been said that the history of higher education represents a struggle between elitism and egalitarianism. How does developmental education fit into this struggle?

6. Apparently, many people have assumed that the problem of underpreparedness will simply go away when enough reforms have been implemented. We have been reforming education for a hundred years. Why has the "problem" not gone away?

2

Developmental Education and the Present

In the 1970s, when we first began to talk about *developmental* as opposed to *remedial* education, we were looking for a new tool to support social justice and educational opportunity for nontraditional students. It was clear to many of us that remedial courses designed to simply reteach what had been taught in high school, using more or less the same methodology and without providing academic support, were not working. The concept of developmental education grew from the realization that remedial courses needed to be accompanied by a variety of student support services if colleges and universities were to effectively provide true educational opportunity. Otherwise, the newly available open door would become a revolving door (Cross, 1971).

At the same time, developmental psychology was emerging as a model for understanding human interaction and behavior. The work of authors such as Art Chickering (1969), Erik Erikson (1968), and William Perry (1970) suggested that intellectual development and personal development were connected in such a way that as one was enhanced, so was the other. This not only reinforced the argument for integration of academic and student support services but also provided a theoretical model to guide both. Consequently, the term *developmental education* entered into the lexicon of higher education. It was meant to describe the integration of remedial courses and academic support services governed by the principles of adult development and learning. It was also meant to be a more effective model for meeting the needs of nontraditional and underprepared students.

Perhaps the most useful description of this model was provided by Ruth Keimig in 1983. She argued that the most effective way to improve student learning was through a comprehensive approach in which campus instructional and support services were integrated in a systematic manner and focused on improving student performance. She also described varying degrees of integration and systemization that a college or university campus might strive to attain, with the lowest level being remediation and the highest level being what she refers to as "comprehensive learning systems" (Keimig, 1983, p. 21).

If this is the model for developmental education, one might argue that we do not know whether developmental education works. We have yet to try it. We provide a large number of remedial courses and we provide a variety of support services; but these are usually provided in a random manner and are seldom fully coordinated or integrated in a systematic way with each other.

Today there is a great deal of debate about the effectiveness of what many researchers, writers, and policy makers refer to as developmental education. Large sample quantitative studies have reported mixed results. Using a sample from the Ohio Board of Regents database of students enrolled in developmental courses at Ohio colleges and universities, Bettinger and Long (2007) found that these courses had a modest positive effect on the graduation rates of underprepared students. Calcagno and Long (2008) studied the progress of nearly 100,000 community college students in Florida and found that although remedial courses contributed to student persistence through their first year in college, such courses had little long-term effect on graduation rates. Matorell and McFarlin (2007), using a database from the Texas Higher Education Coordinating Board, were able to track more than 400,000 students over a six-year period. They found that participation in remediation does not increase the amount of time necessary for students to complete a degree; they also found no evidence that remediation contributes to improving the graduation rates of underprepared students. Bahr (2008), studying math remediation at 107 California community colleges, reported that participation in remedial mathematics does improve students' mathematics skill and increases their likelihood of passing college-level mathematics courses. An ACT research report (Perkhounkova, Noble, & Sawyer, 2006) studied students enrolled in remedial courses at several community colleges and found that students who earned at least a B in these courses were more likely to be retained and to pass gatekeeper courses than students with similar levels of academic preparation. Bailey, Jeong, and Cho (p. 125 in this book), using the Achieving the Dream database of over 250,000 students in 57 different colleges, concluded that, although remedial courses are beneficial for some students, the developmental education system as a whole is ineffective. Given this range of results, it comes as no surprise that there are those who review the studies and conclude that remediation works and there are those who look at the same studies and conclude that remediation does not work.

Nevertheless, the remediation debate does not really reflect what developmental education is supposed to be. As Boylan, Carringer, Saxon, and Shiles (2009) point out, many newspaper reporters have written that "developmental education" is simply a politically correct term for "remediation." Many researchers use the term *developmental education* but are, in fact, studying only remedial courses. Many policy makers discuss reforms in developmental education, but when they describe the reforms they are talking about changing the way remedial courses are taught.

Certainly reforms in remedial instruction are necessary. But if the potential of developmental education is to be realized, reforms must also include improved integration of remedial courses with student support services. Furthermore, this integration must be accompanied by a focus on student success and be in accordance with the principles of adult development and learning as initially articulated by Malcom Knowles and later by Casazza and Silverman. It must also be accompanied by teaching faculty who understand and can apply these principles.

Fortunately, a number of researchers are rediscovering the original developmental education model. In a discussion of high-performance institutions, Jenkins (2011) asserts the importance of "coordinating instruction and student support services" (p. 8) to promote student completion. Following a review of the literature on techniques for improving student outcomes, Karp (2011) argues for better coordinated and more intrusive academic support services to complement the instruction received by underprepared students. Such services might include dedicated counseling, required mentoring and academic advising, or mandatory tutoring. In describing research-based models that contributed to the success of developmental students, Rutschow and Schneider advocate "developing more extensive support services for students who have remedial needs, in an effort to better support their progress in college" (p. 213 in this book). In one of the most extensive reviews of the developmental education literature ever undertaken, Boroch and colleagues (2010) found consistent evidence for collaboration between instructional and academic support services as a means of improving the effectiveness of developmental education.

The readings in this chapter create a picture of where developmental education stands at the beginning of the twenty-first century, beginning with a summary by Jamie Merisotis and Ronald Phipps of the national developmental education effort. Although this article was written in 2000, the issues it addresses remain part of the developmental education landscape today. It is followed by a 2010 discussion by Robert Frost and his colleagues emphasizing campus partnerships between academic and student affairs programs and demonstrating how they contribute to student success. Deloris Perin then describes how learning assistance can support student success in remedial courses. This selection is followed with an article by Susan Scrivener and Erin

Coghlan who synthesize promising practices based on a recent study of six community colleges. A report from Thomas Bailey, Dong Wook Jeong, and Sung-Woo Cho provides data on how students actually progress through sequences of remedial courses. Then Paul Attewell, David Lavin, Thurston Domina, and Tania Levey describe how various types of underprepared students fare in developmental courses and reach some conclusions that, while informative, are rarely reported. Finally, Elizabeth Rutschow and Emily Schneider conclude the chapter with one of the most extensive discussions of promising practices available in current literature.

This chapter attempts to describe efforts to serve undereprepared college students, how successful they are, and the most current methods used to do so. Most of these efforts involve either remedial courses or support services but many involve the integration of the two. Consequently, they reflect an integrated, systematic, and theory-based model that was originally intended to define developmental education.

References

Bahr, P. (2008). Does mathematics remediation work? A comparative analysis of academic attainment among community college students. *Research in Higher Education*, 49(5), 420–450.

Bettinger, E. P. & Long, B. T. (2007). Institutional responses to reduce inequalities in college outcomes. In S. Dickert-Conlin & R. Rubinstein (Eds.), *Economic inequalities in higher education: Access, persistence, and success* (pp. 69–100). New York, NY: Russell Sage Foundation Press.

Boroch, D., Hope, L., Gabriner, R., Smith, B., Mery, P., Asera, R., & Johnstone, R. (2010). *Student success in community colleges: A practical guide to developmental education*. San Francisco, CA: Jossey-Bass.

Boylan, H. R., Carringer, C., Saxon, D. P., & Shiles, C. (2009). Developmental education: A study of print news reporting. *Research in Developmental Education*, 22(3).

Calcagno, J. C. & Long, B. T. (2008, April). *The impact of postsecondary remediation using a regression-discontinuity approach: Addressing endogenous sorting and noncompliance* (NCPR Working Paper). New York, NY: National Center for Postsecondary Research.

Casazza, M. & Silverman, S. (1996). *Learning assistance and developmental education: A guide for effective practice*. San Francisco: Jossey-Bass.

Chickering, A. W. (1969). *Education and identity*. San Francisco, CA: Jossey-Bass.

Cross, K. P. (1971). *Beyond the open door: New students to higher education*. San Francisco, CA: Jossey-Bass.

Erikson, E. H. (1968). *Identity: Youth and crisis*. New York, NY: Norton.

Jenkins, D. (2011, January). *Redesigning community colleges for completion: Lessons from high-performance organizations* (CCRC Working Paper No. 24). New York, NY: Community College Research Center, Teachers College, Columbia University.

Karp, M. M. (2011, April). *How nonacademic supports work: Four mechanisms for improving student outcomes* (CCRC Brief No. 54). New York, NY: Community College Research Center, Teachers College, Columbia University.

Knowles, M. S. (1970). *The modern practice of adult education: Andragogy versus pedagogy.* Englewood Cliffs, NJ: Prentice Hall/Cambridge.

Keimig, R. T. (1983). *Raising academic standards: A guide to learning improvement.* Washington, DC: Association for the Study of Higher Education/Educational Resources Information Center.

Martorell, P., & McFarlin, I. (2007, July). *Help or hindrance? The effect of college remediation on academic and labor market outcomes.* Washington, DC: Rand Corporation.

Perkhounkova, Y., Noble, J., & Sawyer, R. (2006, August). *Modeling the effectiveness of developmental instruction.* Iowa City, IA: ACT.

Perry, W. G. (1970). *Forms of intellectual and ethical development in the college years.* Troy, MO: Holt, Rinehart, and Winston.

Remedial Education in Colleges and Universities: What's Really Going On?

Jamie P. Merisotis and Ronald A. Phipps

Although this article is more than a decade old, it remains relevant to current discussions of developmental education because the purposes of developmental education have not changed, nor have many of the issues confronting the field. In fact, this selection addresses questions that are being raised today by policy makers and administrators. Merisotis and Phipps do an excellent job of analyzing the purposes of remediation, describing who participates, and discussing some of the policy issues surrounding developmental education. Perhaps most important, they also accurately describe the social and economic consequences of failing to provide developmental education, thus offering practitioners some useful arguments in support of their efforts.

Offering coursework below college level in higher education institutions is coming under increased scrutiny. Variously referred to as "remedial education," "developmental education," "college prep," or "basic skills," it constitutes a field about which policy makers are asking: Why are so many students in institutions of higher learning taking basic reading, writing, and arithmetic—subjects that should have been learned in high school, if not junior high school?

Over the past several years, some states—including Arkansas, Louisiana, Oklahoma, Tennessee, and Virginia—are attempting to limit remedial education. In 1998, the trustees of the City University of New York (CUNY) voted to phase out most remedial education in the system's 11 four-year institutions, and the CUNY plan has moved ahead steadily since its implementation in September 1999. Following similar patterns, some states such as Florida have moved virtually all remediation to community colleges. Legislators in Texas and other states are expressing concern that tax dollars are being used in colleges to teach high school courses. In response, the legislatures in the states of New Jersey, Montana, Florida, and Oregon, among others, are considering proposals that would require public school systems to pay for any remedial work that a public school graduate must take in college.

A survey of state legislators showed that they were split three ways on the topic. In response to the statement that colleges and universities should give remedial education more attention, 34% disagreed, 32% agreed, and 32% were neutral. While state legislators agree that the problem is inherited from the K–12 sector, they are less clear about who to hold responsible (Ruppert, 1996). Educators mirror this ambivalence. Proponents and opponents alike point to the effects of remedial education on the quality, accountability, and efficiency of higher education institutions. The quality of discussions on the effect of remediation on diversity, educational opportunity, and enrollment is diminished by the lack of agreement on the nature of remediation. There is little consensus and understanding about what remedial education is, whom it serves, who should provide it, and how much it costs. Consequently, this lack of fundamental information and imprecision of language often renders public policy discussions ill informed at best.

This article, which is adapted from a recent publication on remediation by the Institute for Higher Education Policy (1998a), seeks to bring some clarity to the policy discussions. It includes an analysis of remediation's core function in the higher education enterprise, a review of the current status of remedial education at the college level, a discussion of financing remedial education, an argument about the costs of not providing remedial education, and a set of recommendations intended to reduce the need for remediation while also enhancing its effectiveness.

Remediation's Core Function in Higher Education

Given the increased attention to remedial education, it may be easy to conclude that efforts providing compensatory education to under-prepared students in colleges and universities are recent events that somehow reflect the present condition of U.S. postsecondary education. Although some individuals may argue that the quality of the higher educational enterprise has decreased over the years, the fact remains that remedial education has been part of higher education since early colonial days. Dating back to the 17th century, Harvard College provided tutors in Greek and Latin for those underprepared students who did not want to study for the ministry. The middle of the 18th century saw the establishment of land-grant colleges, which instituted preparatory programs or departments for students below average in reading, writing, and arithmetic skills (Payne & Lyman, 1998). In 1849, the first remedial education programs in reading, writing, and arithmetic were offered at the University of Wisconsin (Breneman & Haarlow, 1998). By the end of the 19th century, when only 238,000 students were enrolled in all of higher education, more than 40% of first-year college students participated in precollegiate programs (Ignash, 1997).

Due to increased competition for students among higher education institutions at the beginning of the 20th century, underprepared students continued to be accepted at growing rates. For instance, over half of the students enrolled in Harvard, Princeton, Yale, and Columbia did not meet entrance requirements and were placed in remedial courses. The vast influx of World War II veterans taking advantage of the G.I. Bill created another surge in the need for remedial education. Then thousands of underprepared students enrolled in colleges and universities from the 1960s to the 1980s in response to open admissions policies and government funding following the passage of the Civil Rights Act of 1964 and the Higher Education Act of 1965 (Payne & Lyman, 1998).

In short, those halcyon days when all students who enrolled in college were adequately prepared, all courses offered at higher education institutions were "college level," and students smoothly made the transition from high school and college simply never existed. And they do not exist now. A comprehensive survey of remediation in higher education, conducted by the National Center for Education Statistics (NCES) for fall 1995, provides evidence of this reality. Remedial courses were defined as courses in reading, writing, and mathematics for college students lacking skills necessary to perform college-level work at the level required by the institution. Thus, what constituted remedial courses varied from institution to institution. Here are NCES's major findings (U.S. Department of Education, 1996):

- Over three-quarters (78%) of higher education institutions that enrolled first-year students in fall 1995 offered at least one remedial reading, writing, or mathematics course. All public two-year institutions and almost all (94%) institutions with high minority enrollments offered remedial courses.

- Twenty-nine percent of first-time first-year students enrolled in at least one remedial reading, writing, or mathematics course in fall 1995. First-year students were more likely to enroll in a remedial mathematics course than in a remedial reading or writing course, irrespective of institution attended.

- At most institutions, students do not take remedial courses for extended periods of time. Two-thirds of the institutions indicated that the average time a student takes remedial courses was less than one year, 28% one year, and 5% more than one year.

Because NCES conducted similar surveys for the academic year 1983–1984 and for fall 1989, it is possible to compare the intensity of remedial education course offerings over the past decade. The consistency is striking. In 1983–1984, 82% of the institutions offered remedial education in all three areas (reading, writing, and mathematics), compared to 78% in fall 1995. Sixty-six percent provided remedial reading courses in 1983–1984 compared to 57% in fall 1995; for remedial writing, 73% and 71%; and remedial mathematics, 71% and 72%, respectively.

Statistics for first-year students enrolled in remedial courses were not estimated for the academic year 1983–1984; however, comparisons can be made between fall 1989 and fall 1995. Thirty percent of first-year students enrolled in all three remedial courses in fall 1989 compared to 29% in fall 1995. Thirteen percent of first-year students enrolled in remedial reading for both years. Remedial writing courses were taken by 16% of the first-year students in fall 1989 compared to 17% in fall 1995. In remedial mathematics, the percentages were 21% and 24%, respectively. Interestingly, although little change resulted in the percentage of students enrolling in remedial courses from fall 1989 to fall 1995, college and university enrollment increased by approximately a half million students.

Institutions That Do Not Offer Remediation

Twenty-two percent of the institutions in the NCES survey indicated that they did not offer remedial education courses. Of that percentage, two-thirds noted that their students did not need remediation. Approximately a quarter reported that those students needing remediation take such courses at another institution and/or that institutional policy prohibits the offering of remedial courses on their campus.

There is some reason to believe that the percentage of institutions not offering remedial courses is much lower than reported and, conversely, that the percentage of students requiring remedial courses is higher. This conclusion, based on the nature of the higher education enterprise, is supported by anecdotal evidence. For example, many institutions do not find it in their best interests to acknowledge that they enroll students who require remediation. In a paper presented to the American Council on Education, Astin (1998) posits that an institution's "excellence" is defined primarily by resources and reputation. A major boost to an institution's reputation is the enrollment rates of students with the highest GPAs, the top test scores, and the strongest recommendations. Astin states:

> It goes without saying that the underprepared student is a kind of pariah in American higher education, and some of the reasons are obvious: since most of us believe that the excellence of our departments and of our institutions depends on enrolling the very best-prepared students that we can, to admit underprepared students would pose a real threat to our excellence. (1998, p. 11)

However, there is a disproportionate emphasis on the credentials and the abilities of the *applicants* compared to the knowledge and skills of the *graduates*—as evidenced by virtually every national ranking publication (Astin, 1998, p. 11).

Steinberg, as cited in Breneman and Haarlow, refers to the National Assessment of Educational Progress and the Third International Math and Science Study to suggest that more high school students than we would like to admit are unprepared for college-level work (Breneman & Haarlow, 1998). Even in high-performing states, only one-third of American high school students meet or exceed levels of grade-appropriate proficiency in mathematics, science, reading, and writing. The country's 12th graders perform as poorly on standardized math and science tests as their counterparts from the worst-performing industrialized countries in the world. Steinberg states:

> Even if we assume that none of these sub-proficient students graduating from American high schools goes on to postsecondary education (surely an untenable assumption), the fact that somewhere close to 60% of U.S. high school graduates do attend college suggests that a fairly significant number of college-bound young people cannot do, and do not know, the things that educators agree that high school graduates ought to know and be able to do. (Qtd. in Breneman & Haarlow, 1998, p. 46)

The purpose of this analysis is not to place blame or point fingers at the nation's K–12 system or the higher education community. It is merely to suggest that there is validity behind the hypothesis that more remedial activities are occurring than meet the eye. Therefore, it is reasonable to say that a portion of the 22% of institutions reporting that they do not offer remedial education courses enroll underprepared students and provide some sort of remedial service. Also, it is likely that *at least* 78% of higher education institutions enroll underprepared students and that, in all probability, more than 30% of the students require remediation.

The Many Faces of Remedial Education

The discussion of remedial education evokes the image of courses in reading, writing, and mathematics whose content is below "college-level." The term "college-level" suggests that agreed-upon standards exist, or at least enjoy a consensus by educators. A reasonable assumption would be that the academic community has identified specific knowledge and skills that are required of students to be successful in a college or university. Conversely, if students do not possess the specified knowledge and skills, remedial education is needed for academic success.

The fact is that remedial education is in the eye of the beholder. Rather than being based on some immutable set of college-level standards, remedial education, more often than not, is determined by the admissions requirements of the particular institution. Obviously, remediation at a community college with open admissions is not the same as remediation at a doctoral research institution. As Astin points out: "Most remedial students turn out to be simply those who have the lowest scores on some sort of normative measurement—standardized tests, school grades, and the like. But where we draw the line is completely arbitrary: lowest quarter, lowest fifth, lowest 5%, or what? Nobody knows. Second, the 'norms' that define a 'low' score are highly variable from one setting to another" (Astin, 1998, p. 13). A case in point is the 21-campus California State University (CSU) System. Although state policy in California mandates that students entering CSU are supposed to be in the top third of their high school graduating class, the *Los Angeles Times* reported that 47% of the fall 1997 first-year class required remedial work in English and 54% needed remedial work in mathematics (National Center, 1998).

Furthermore, remediation standards vary even for institutions with similar missions. A 1996 study by the Maryland Higher Education Commission found that policies, instruments, and standards used by Maryland colleges and universities to identify and place remedial students differed, even within the community college sector. Institutions employ various approaches toward the particular subject areas of remediation, including locally developed norms, nationally developed norms, grade-level equivalences, and specific deficiencies and/or competencies.

Another study conducted in 1998 by the Maryland Higher Education Commission illuminates the relationship between high school preparation and the need for remediation in college. The conventional wisdom is that students who complete college-preparatory courses in high school will not need remedial education in college, while students who have not taken a college-preparatory curriculum in high school will probably need remediation. This particular study measured the college success rates of recent high school graduates. The basic findings of the report agree with common sense. Students who completed college-preparatory courses in high school performed better in college than students who did not complete college-preparatory courses in high school. College-preparatory students earned higher grades in their initial math and English courses and had higher grade point averages after their first year in college than students who did not complete the college-preparatory curriculum. Also, fewer college-preparatory students required assistance in math, English, and reading.

It is helpful, however, to examine these data further. First, a significant number of students who took college-preparatory courses in high school needed remediation in college. For students who completed college-preparatory courses in high school and immediately attended a community college, 40% needed math remediation, one out of five required English remediation, and one out of four needed remedial reading. At one community college, 73% of college-preparatory students needed math remediation, 79% English remediation, and 76% reading remediation. At the public four-year institutions, 14% of college-preparatory students needed math remediation, 7% English remediation, and 6% reading remediation.

Some disconnect exists between what high schools consider college-preparatory, particularly in mathematics and English, and what colleges are requiring of their entering students. But a more interesting question emerges from these data. The percentages of *college-preparatory* students requiring remediation at the community colleges is dramatically higher than the percentage of *college-preparatory* students at the public four-year institutions. How can that be? Conventional wisdom would suggest that the percentages would be approximately the same for both higher education sectors because all of the students have completed a state-mandated college-preparatory curriculum. Or, for those who contend that community colleges are less academically rigorous than four-year institutions with selective admissions (a debatable argument), the expectation would be that the percentages would be reversed. That is, since all students have enjoyed the benefit of a college-preparatory curriculum, those enrolling in community colleges would be quite prepared for the easier curriculum compared to those enrolling in four-year institutions with the more academically rigorous curriculum.

There can be many explanations for this intriguing issue. One could argue that the college-preparatory students admitted by the four-year institutions are academically superior to the college-preparatory students admitted by the community colleges and therefore need less remediation. Also, it could be that community colleges, because of their open-door mission, have more structured procedures than four-year colleges for determining which students require remedial courses. Critics of the quality of high schools may posit that college-preparatory students from high schools that lack academic rigor, in spite of the college-preparatory label, choose to attend a community college because they are concerned about their academic preparation. Whatever the explanation, this example helps to affirm the essential point made by Astin and others: remedial education in colleges and universities is relative and arbitrary.

Remedial Education's Diverse Client Population

The examination of remedial education is incomplete if it focuses only on recent high school graduates. According to several studies, a substantial proportion of postsecondary education students are 25 years of age or older, and many of these adult students are enrolled in remedial courses. The exact proportion or number of older students requiring remedial education, however, is difficult to discern and the data on age distribution of remedial students vary widely from state to state.

One important source of national data in the composition of students in remedial courses is provided by the National Center for

Developmental Education (NCDE). NCDE data indicated that approximately 80% of remedial students in the country's colleges and universities are age 21 or younger (Breneman & Haarlow, 1998). However, other data suggest that a much higher proportion of older students is taking remedial courses and that the remediation population is bipolar in terms of age and time elapsed between secondary and postsecondary experiences. According to NCES, 31% of entering first-year students who took a remedial education class in 1992–1993 were 19 or younger. In contrast, 45% of the entering first-year students who took a remedial course were over 22 years of age, the traditional age of the baccalaureate degree graduate. Another study found that one-quarter (27%) of entering first-year students in remedial courses were 30 or older (Ignash, 1997).

Data from individual states support the NCES findings. For instance, Maryland found that more than three-fourths of remedial students in the community colleges in 1994–1995 were 20 years of age or older (Maryland Higher Education Commission, 1996). In Florida, a reported 80% of the students in remedial classes were not recent high school graduates but older students who needed to brush up their skills, usually in mathematics, before entering the higher education mainstream (National Center, 1998). First-year students also are not the only students who take remediation. NCES data show that 56% of students enrolled in remedial courses were first-year students, 24% were sophomores, 9% were juniors, and 9% were seniors (Ignash, 1997).

The policy debate about remediation in higher education must address not only first-year students who recently graduated from high school but also students of all ages and levels of undergraduate progress. In fact, it appears that, in the future, older students will attend colleges and universities in record numbers and will require remedial education. According to a recent report, between 1970 and 1993, the participation in higher education by students age 40 and over increased from 5.5% of total enrollment to 11.2%—the largest jump of any age cohort (Institute for Higher Education Policy, 1996). Policies addressing remediation must recognize that the demand for remedial education is being fueled in part by older students who need refresher courses in mathematics or writing.

How Successful Is Remedial Education?

Research about the effectiveness of remedial education programs has typically been sporadic, underfunded, and inconclusive. For instance, a study of 116 two- and four-year colleges and universities revealed that only a small percentage conducted any systematic evaluation of their remedial education programs (Weissman, Bulakowski, & Jumisco, 1997). The Southern Regional Education Board has observed that, because few states have exit standards for remedial courses, it is unclear whether many states know whether their programs work (Crowe,

1998). Adelman (1998) examined college transcripts from the national high school class of 1982 and, not surprisingly, found an inverse relationship between the extent of students' need for remedial courses and their eventual completion of a degree. Of the 1982 high school graduates who had earned more than a semester of college credit by age 30, 60% of those who took no remedial courses, and 55% of those who took only one remedial course, had either earned a bachelor's or associate's degree. In contrast, only 35% of the students who participated in five or more remedial courses attained either a bachelor's or associate's degree.

Focusing upon reading remediation reveals another perspective. Sixty-six percent of students required to take remedial reading were in three or more other remedial courses, and only 12% of this group earned bachelor's degrees. Among students who were required to take more than one remedial reading course, nearly 80% were in two or more other remedial courses, and less than 9% earned bachelor's degrees. When reading is at the core of the problem, the probability of success in college appears to be very low.

According to Adelman, the need to take remedial education courses reduces the probability of achieving a degree. Yet it is also instructive to look at the ratio of students who did not need remedial education and those who did. Students who did not take remediation courses had a graduation rate of 60%. But even the least academically prepared students — those who took five or more remedial education courses — had a 35% graduation rate. Therefore, remediation allowed the academically weakest students to perform almost three-fifths as well as the students who did not need any remediation. Further, students who needed two remedial courses performed almost three-quarters as well as the academically strongest students. These data seem to indicate that remediation is, in fact, quite effective at improving the chances of collegiate success for underprepared students.

Financial Costs

Hard evidence regarding the costs of remediation nationwide is elusive. The most recent analysis of the cost, authored by Breneman and Haarlow (1998), suggests that nationally remedial education absorbs about $1 billion annually in a public higher education budget of $115 billion — less than 1% of expenditures. This estimate, derived by conducting a survey of all 50 states along with individual site visits to five states, includes the costs associated with remediation for both traditional age first-year students and returning adult students.

Among states and between higher education segments, the percentage of remedial education expenditures to the total budget showed wide variance. In FY1996, 1.1% of the direct salary budget of public universities in Illinois was dedicated to remediation, while it took 6.5% of the community college direct salary budget. In FY1995, the percentage of expenditures for remediation in Maryland was 1.2% of the total expenditures for the public campuses. In Washington, 7% of total expenditures was earmarked for remedial education in 1995–1996. Focusing on the appropriation per full-time equivalent (FTE) student for individual states, the cost to California for remediation is about $2,950 per FTE student and the cost to Florida is about $2,409.

It is important to note what the total national cost estimate of $1 billion does *not* entail. First, this estimate does not include the remediation budget of private colleges and universities. Second, costs borne by students through foregone earnings and diminished labor productivity were not calculated. Third, there was no effort to figure the costs to society as a whole by failing to develop the nation's human capital to its fullest potential. These limitations notwithstanding, the Breneman and Haarlow report compiles the most comprehensive, accurate information to date.

There are several impediments to collecting reliable data about the costs of remediation:

- There is no universally accepted definition of what constitutes remedial education within the academic community.

- How "costs" are distributed among the several activities within a college or university can, and do, vary widely.

- Even if the functions to be included in determining the cost of remediation were understood, higher education institutions have difficulty supplying precise breakdowns of remediation costs.

- It is not always clear whether reported cost figures include expenditures or appropriations. As Breneman and Haarlow point out, "These are two different measures of cost, and ideally, one would want all the figures on both bases, but what one gets is a mix of the two" (1998, pp. 12–13).

- Because states do not compute remediation education costs regularly, financial data can either be relatively current or several years old.

Perhaps the most intractable barrier to collecting valid and reliable data on remediation is that noted by commentators like Astin and Steinberg: Official estimates of the extent and cost of remediation are often understated for a variety of reasons—not the least of which is the perceived damage to the "reputation" of a college or university. Unfortunately, there are many incentives for agencies and institutions to underreport remediation. Thus, we can reasonably conclude that the costs of remediation are higher than reported. Our estimate is that the figure is probably closer to $2 billion. However, if $2 billion—which amounts to 2% of higher education expenditures—is the actual cost of remediation, it is still a relatively modest amount to be spent on an activity of such importance to the nation. If remedial education were terminated at every college and university, it is unlikely that the money would be put to better use.

A useful case study is the Arkansas Department of Higher Education's comprehensive study over several years that compares direct and indirect instructional costs of academic programs for the state's public colleges and universities. In 1996–1997, the total cost of remediation in Arkansas colleges and universities was $27 million—approximately 3% of the total expenditures. At community colleges, 9% of the total expenditures went to remedial education compared to 2% at four-year institutions. The total state subsidy for remedial education was almost $14 million. The state subsidy for community colleges was 59% of the total expenditures compared to 40% at four-year institutions. These data show that, although remediation is provided at both four-year and two-year institutions, community colleges commit substantially more resources toward remedial education—which is not surprising given their open admissions policies.

The Arkansas cost study shows that the cost per FTE student for remedial education at the four-year institutions was $7,381. The average program costs per FTE student at four-year institutions ranged from $7,919 for psychology, to $8,804 for English, to $9,320 for mathematics, to $12,369 in music. The cost per FTE student for remedial education at the community colleges was $6,709. The average program costs per FTE student at the community colleges ranged from $6,163 for general studies, to $7,730 for business, to $8,235 in nursing.

These data illustrate that remediation costs per FTE student generally are lower than the costs per FTE student for core academic programs—English, mathematics, etc.—that lead to an associate or bachelor's degree. Knowing the cost per FTE student for remediation vis-à-vis the cost per FTE student for academic programs provides another viewpoint in the remediation debate. One issue that most institutions grapple with is resource reallocation: How can the institution use limited resources to the greatest benefit? What is the cost/benefit of providing remediation? Many institutions are targeting "low-demand programs"—programs with few graduates—for elimination. How does the cost of low-demand programs compare to remedial education costs, and can resources be better used elsewhere? How is the cost per FTE student in academic programs affected by remedial students who are successful and who participate in college-level courses? These and other questions can frame the public policy debate regarding the cost of remediation.

In addition to examining the financial cost of providing remedial education in higher education, it is helpful to look at the other side of the coin. More explicitly, what are the financial gains of a successful remedial education program for a specific institution? A remedial education program that enables a significant proportion of remedial students to continue their education after completing remedial courses is beneficial for the institutional bottom line since it enhances revenue that can partially offset costs associated with providing remediation.

Social and Economic Costs of Not Providing Remediation

What does the nation get for its $1 to $2 billion investment in remedial education? There is considerable evidence that the nation cannot afford to disfranchise even a small portion of the population who has the potential of succeeding in college from participating in some form of postsecondary education. Therefore, the costs and benefits associated with providing access to underprepared students and helping them succeed in higher education must be measured accurately.

Ponitz, as cited in Breneman and Haarlow, points out that 80% of sustainable jobs today require some education beyond high school (Breneman & Haarlow, 1998). Currently, 65% of the nation's workers need the skills of a generalist/technician, including advanced reading, writing, mathematical, critical thinking, and interpersonal group skills. Twenty years ago, that figure was only 15% (Breneman & Haarlow, 1998).

According to a Lehman Brothers report (citing Bureau of Labor Statistics data), the growth rate in jobs between 1994 and 2005 will be the greatest for categories that require at least an associate's degree (Ghazi & Irani, 1997). Jobs requiring a master's degree will grow the fastest (at a rate of 28%), followed closely by those requiring a bachelor's degree (27%), and an associate's degree (24%). "All jobs requiring postsecondary education and training of an associate's degree or better are projected to grow significantly higher than the average, and all those with lesser levels of training are expected to grow below the average," summarizes the Lehman Brothers' report. "In our opinion, this is a clear indication that the transformation to a knowledge-based economy will require a more highly skilled, more adept, and more knowledgeable work force" (Ghazi & Irani, 1997, p. 71).

A report from the Institute for Higher Education Policy (1998b) summarizes four types of benefits of going to college: private economic benefits, private social benefits, public economic benefits, and public social benefits. While much of the recent public policy focus has been on the private benefits, the public benefits of going to college are extensive. Since going to college results in greater benefits to the public as a whole—increased tax revenues, greater productivity, reduced crime rates, increased quality of civic life, etc.—then students who benefit from the remedial instruction provided by higher education also must be contributing to the public good.

However, not all agree with these findings. Rubenstein (1998) argues that the economic return of higher education to the graduate is an illusion. Significant factors relating to higher wages of college graduates when compared to high school graduates include the higher socioeconomic background of college graduates, in addition to their higher motivation and, probably, higher IQs. He further notes that too many colleges are chasing many marginal students and that the United States has an abundance of college graduates, not a deficit. As a consequence, in 1995 approximately 40% of people with some college education—and 10% of those with a college degree—worked at jobs requiring only high school skills. In 1971, the figures were 30% and 6% respectively. Rubenstein concludes that functionally literate graduates are in short supply. College graduates who do not have the functional literacy traditionally associated with college degrees are taking jobs that had previously gone to employees with high school diplomas.

Rubenstein's argument is alarming and, if accurate, poses a challenge to educators in both the K–12 and higher education sectors. The obvious challenge is to ensure that college graduates are functionally literate and possess the skills necessary to compete in a global society. Few would argue, it seems to us, that there can be too many functionally literate people, whether they are college graduates or not. As a society, we have little choice about providing remediation in higher education, with the goal of increasing functional literacy. Abandoning remedial efforts in higher education and therefore reducing the number of people gaining the skills and knowledge associated with postsecondary education is unwise public policy. Thus, it is appropriate to confront the causes of underpreparation and try to reduce the necessity for remediation as much as possible. In addition, policies should be explored to improve the effectiveness of remediation programs, and cost efficiencies should be implemented wherever needed

Recommendations

The evidence is compelling that remediation in colleges and universities is not an appendage with little connection to the mission of the institution but rather represents a core function of the higher education community that it has performed for hundreds of years. Although the financial data are not as reliable as some would like, there is sufficient reason to assume that the cost is minimal when compared to the total higher education budget. Also, the case has been made that attempts to eliminate remediation completely from higher education are both unrealistic and unwise public policy. Realizing this, where do we go from here?

It is important to recognize that not all remediation is delivered effectively or efficiently. Like any educational process, remedial education must be continuously examined and revised to meet prevailing conditions and needs. Therefore, good public policy must focus upon two mutually reinforcing goals: (1) implementing multiple strategies that help to reduce the need for remediation in higher education, and (2) improving the effectiveness of remedial education in higher education. It is evident that a piecemeal approach to addressing the problem of remediation in higher education has not worked. Intermittent schemes to "correct" remedial education are stop-gap solutions at best. Only a systemic design at the state level comprised of a set of interrelated strategies will succeed.

The discussion below presents a set of strategies that states and institutions can use to achieve the public policy goals outlined here. We emphasize that there is a positive relationship between the number of implemented strategies and the probability of meeting the public policy goals. Implementing one or two of the strategies may be helpful, but fundamentally addressing the issue requires using the entire range of strategic options.

The importance of collaboration cannot be understated. Borrowing the realtor's mantra—location, location, location—reducing the need for remediation in higher education will require collaboration between and among: colleges and universities and high schools; states and their colleges and universities, as well as state departments of education, K–12 public and private schools, public and private two- and four-year colleges and universities, businesses, and philanthropies. We have no illusions that the various players in the educational enterprise will welcome cooperation and abandon their traditional turf. We simply state that a lack of a true, invested collaborative effort among the parties will doom any effort to fully address the issue of remediation.

Reducing the Need for Remediation in Higher Education

Strategies for reducing the need for college remediation include: (a) aligning high school requirements and course content with college competency and content expectations; (b) offering early intervention and financial aid programs that target K–12 students by linking mentoring, tutoring, and academic guidance with a guarantee of college financial aid; (3) tracking students and providing high school feedback systems; and (4) improving teacher preparation. Many of these approaches are found in the K–16 movement occurring in many states.

1. *Aligning High School Requirements with College Content and Competency Expectations.* Several state initiatives are under way to define specifically what a first-year college student needs to know and be able to do. These initiatives often are identified in terms of content and competency levels rather than Carnegie units or high school class rank. College entry-level content standards and competencies apply across the curriculum to all first-year students who are recent high school graduates. They do not target students enrolling in a specific course or a specific major. The competency categories parallel college general education categories and align with the content standards being adopted in school districts.

2. *Early Intervention and Financial Aid Programs.* Some states have developed, or are considering developing, early intervention strat-

egies in the high schools, often beginning in the ninth grade. These techniques are designed to correct student academic deficiencies before the students reach college. Also, a number of states have established early intervention financial aid programs modeled after the Taylor Plan in Louisiana, which in addition to enhancing access, contain provisions to increase the ability of students to succeed in college. Although details vary from state to state, the programs guarantee low-income K–12 students admission to college if they meet certain criteria, including completion of a college-preparatory curriculum, achieving a minimum grade point average, and participating in a counseling program. The federal government has enacted the Gaining Early Awareness and Readiness for Undergraduate Programs (GEAR UP) for low-income students. This program encourages states and university-school partnerships to provide support services to students who are at risk of dropping out of school by offering them information, encouragement, and the means to pursue postsecondary study.

3. *Student Tracking and High School Feedback Systems.* An effective tool for enhancing collaboration between high schools and colleges, in addition to identifying areas of mutual concern, is to provide feedback to high schools regarding the success of their students in college. Several states provide high schools with information on student admission exemptions; remedial course work in mathematics, English, and reading; performance in the first college-level courses in English and mathematics; cumulative grade point averages; and persistence (Wallhaus, 1998).

4. *Improved Teacher Preparation.* Teacher education reform is now on the national agenda, as evidenced by the 1998 reauthorization of the Higher Education Act of 1965. The legislation replaces several small teacher education programs—which were not funded—with a three-part grant: 45% of the funding will go to states to improve the quality of its teachers; 45% will go to partnerships between colleges and secondary schools; and 10% will go to recruiting more students to teach in low-income school districts (Burd, 1998).

Initiatives in several states include: (a) reexamining teacher certification and licensure requirements based on specific standards of what teachers should know and be able to do, (b) emphasizing academic disciplines in the teacher education curricula, and (c) establishing performance-based career advancement opportunities for veteran teachers.

Improving the Effectiveness of Remediation in Higher Education

What can be done to improve the effectiveness of remediation in higher education? We have identified three core strategies: (a) creating interinstitutional collaborations, (b) making remediation a comprehensive program, and (c) utilizing technology.

1. *Interinstitutional Collaboration.* Astin makes a strong case for interinstitutional collaboration between institutions of higher education in a region or state. The opportunities for collaborative research—given that there are hundreds of remedial programs of all types and perhaps thousands of individual courses—are remarkable. Research on programs for underprepared students and faculty preparation to teach such students should be a collaborative effort among colleges and universities in a system or state. Although admitting that such collaboration would be difficult to achieve because of threats to institutional "reputation," interinstitutional conversations hopefully would be successful in leading the participants to agree that (a) "developing effective programs for lower-performing students at *all levels of education* is of vital importance not only to our education system, but also to the state and the society at large" and (b) "finding and implementing more effective programs for underprepared students is a 'systems' challenge that must be accepted and shared by all institutions at all levels of education" (Astin, 1998, pp. 29–30; emphasis ours).

2. *Making Remediation a Comprehensive Program.* Substantial research has been conducted to identify essential components of an effective remedial education program. One recent study by the Massachusetts community colleges provides an excellent overview of best practices in remedial education (Massachusetts, 1998). These practices include:

- *Assessment and Placement.* All incoming students are evaluated and, where necessary, placed in remediation according to a mandatory comprehensive instrument for assessing reading, writing, and mathematics.

- *Curriculum Design and Delivery.* The goals and objectives of the remedial program must be defined clearly so that all students understand them.

- *Support Services.* Underprepared students require individualized help. Effective programs use "intrusive" advising to identify and solve problems early.

- *Evaluation.* The remedial education program's effectiveness is assessed according to how many students complete remedial education programs, how many excel [and] continue on to college-level courses, how many complete college-level courses, and how many reach their academic goals.

3. *Utilizing Technology.* In the past decade or so, computers have enhanced the teaching-learning process, particularly in remedial courses that are hierarchical, linear, and stable in their structure and content. Many private companies have developed, or are developing, remedial software. One such company, Academic Systems Corporation, has generated computer-assisted remedial courses in mathematics and writing that are being used in hundreds of colleges and universities

Enhancing Student Learning with Academic and Student Affairs Collaboration

Robert A. Frost, Stephen L. Strom, JoAnna Downey, Deanna D. Schultz, and Teresa A. Holland

This article articulates the need for partnerships between academic and student affairs programs on college and university campuses and discusses why such partnerships have, until recently, been relatively rare. Frost, Strom, Downey, Schultz, and Holland also describe a number of programs exemplifying the sorts of partnerships that are possible and how these programs contribute to student success.

Introduction

During the early years of postsecondary education, student affairs work was accomplished by academic faculty and administrators (Colwell, 2006). However, as the student affairs profession developed, expanded, and specialized over the last century, a disconnect between it and academics appeared (Kezar, 2003). Despite the separation, the literature on student affairs in higher education (Bourassa & Kruger, 2001; Dale & Drake, 2005; Kezar, 2001; Martin & Samels, 2001) shows movement towards collaboration and integration of academic affairs and student affairs—the curricular and the co-curricular. The major focus of the collaboration is to integrate the academic, experiential, and practical, then ultimately, retain students through to completion of their educational goals (Blake, 2007). Schuh (1999) aptly stated "the failure of colleges to establish links between students' out-of-classroom experiences and their academic endeavors has impeded not only students' overall personal development but also the quality of their academic experience" (p. 85).

Several obstacles to successful academic and student affairs partnerships include cultural distinctions in administration, faculty, and services staff; the historical separation between curricular and co-curricular instruction; the perceived second-class status of student affairs in relation to the academic mission; and differing views on student learning (Bourassa & Kruger, 2001). To overcome these barriers and increase student success, student affairs professionals, academic faculty, and administrators must develop collaborative partnerships that share values, goals, and a commitment to comprehensive and seamless educational environments.

Discussion

With its emphasis on blended learning experiences, "the community college sector is leading the way in the formation of strong, vibrant student and academic affairs partnerships as well as collaborative efforts with external constituencies in the development and advancement of educational outcomes" (Bourassa & Kruger, 2001, p. 15). These positive partnerships lead to several benefits. The institutional culture becomes one of shared mission and values (Colwell, 2006), student learning becomes more personal (Jacoby, 1999), the institution itself becomes more collegial and accountable for student learning outcomes (Kezar, 2001), and student success and student learning become the primary foci of the entire institution (Dale & Drake, 2005).

Collaborative academic and student affairs partnerships that effectively support student learning produce a variety of models with common and unique outcomes. Proven partnerships include first-year experience programs, learning communities, student life, and service learning (Bourassa & Kruger, 2001; Dale & Drake, 2005; Jacoby, 1999). But, what exactly do these partnerships look like? What are the essential ingredients? The following sections of the article will add practical examples and refine the proven partnerships so that college staff can make more informed decisions about their relevance and application to the community college.

First-Year Experience Programs

Nevitt Sanford initially introduced the first-year student education program nearly fifty years ago, arguing students needed to be challenged and supported to succeed in college (Upcraft, Gardner, Barefoot, & Associates, 2005). Prior to 1960, the attitude toward student success was one of sink-or-swim, but since then, "higher education has engaged in a massive social experiment of providing access to higher education that at its worst included anyone who could fog a mirror and had a demonstrable pulse" (Upcraft et al., 2005, pp. 1–2). Decades later, first-year students still are more likely to fail, or be low achievers, than any other student group (Keup, 2006; Swing & Skipper, 2007).

First-year experience (FYE) programs were developed to address the lack of academic success of students in the first year of college (Crissman Ishler & Upcraft, 2005; Hunter & Murray, 2007; Keup, 2006). However, it was not until the 1980s that a concerted effort was made to involve all institutional stakeholders and tie specific initiatives to the retention of first-year college students (Barefoot, 2005; Upcraft et al., 2005). The initiatives include orientations, first-year seminars, and supplemental instruction (Rhodes & Carifio, 1999).

ORIENTATION PROGRAMS

Offered by over 95% of American colleges and universities, orientation serves as a primary foundational component of FYE programs (Barefoot, 2005; Crissman Ishler & Upcraft, 2005), allowing new students to make critical connections to a variety of institutional offerings from academic to student support services. In addition, focusing orientation design on the changing community college demographics and including more academic activities—testing, advising, and scheduling—ensure quality delivery to students (Barefoot, 2005; Benjamin, Earnest, Gruenewald, & Arthur, 2007).

FIRST-YEAR SEMINARS

As part of American higher education for over a hundred years, first-year seminars are one of the most researched environmental influences affecting new students (Crissman Ishler & Upcraft, 2005). The first-year seminar, offered by over 60% of community colleges, is the most commonly used curricular initiative directed at new students (Barefoot, 2005). Regardless of the seminar topic—study skills, time management, or critical thinking—the goal is to provide students with the skills to navigate successfully the higher education system (Hunter & Linder, 2005; Siegel, 2005).

SUPPLEMENTAL INSTRUCTION

Also known as peer mentoring or peer-assisted study, supplemental instruction "is a validated initiative that targets traditionally difficult introductory classes—those with high failure or withdrawal rates" (Hunter & Murray, 2007, p. 33). Such a program—used in higher education for over 25 years (Martin & Hurley, 2005)—is found at over 30% of community colleges (Barefoot, 2005). By thinking in terms of high-risk courses versus high-risk students, supplemental instruction helps most students succeed without individually identifying those most in need of assistance. Furthermore, because the efforts often are ad hoc—where faculty and advisors identify and team around paired classes or a specific gateway course—the need to develop a formal program or budget line is not a hindrance to action.

AN FYE PROGRAM IN ACTION

Academic Peer Instruction (API)—LaGuardia Community College's proven supplemental instruction program—began in 1993. *Four Pillars* serves as the foundation of this successful collaboration between academic and student affairs:

- supervisors—leadership, oversight, and support for the other three pillars;

- student leaders—the critical processes for hiring and training instructional leaders;

- faculty—well-versed on and supportive of the program; and

- college administration—necessary for overall institutional support and funding for the program (Zaritsky & Toce, 2006).

From the LaGuardia Community College (2010) website, it is easy to see the positive effect on community college student success for those participating in the program. Between 1993 and 2008, API served nearly 8,500 students in 706 classes with an average annual grade differential of 1.02—one letter grade higher than those students not participating.

Learning Communities

One of the earliest learning communities was established by Alexander Meiklejohn at the University of Wisconsin in 1927, integrating general education and the first two years of undergraduate studies into a single curricular program (Gabelnick, MacGregor, Matthews, & Smith, 1990; Meiklejohn, 1932; Shapiro & Levine, 1999). Due to controversy and a declining economy, the University of Wisconsin Experimental College closed in 1931 (Smith, MacGregor, Matthews, & Gabelnick, 2004). The concept of learning communities lay dormant until the 1960s and 1970s when universities and community colleges expanded rapidly, and innovations in education were widespread (O'Banion, 1997; Smith et al., 2004). Meiklejohn's curricular structure and John Dewey's theories of teaching were the foundations for the new learning communities (Shapiro & Levine, 1999).

The goal of learning communities is to provide students with curriculum that is connected and relevant, allowing intellectual interaction with faculty and fellow students, and typically involving the restructuring of student time, credit, and learning experiences (Gabelnick et al., 1990). Researchers (Levine & Shapiro, 2000; Smith et al., 2004) have identified three models of student learning communities: subgroups within unmodified courses, linked or clustered courses, and team-taught learning communities.

SUBGROUPS WITHIN UNMODIFIED COURSES

Two or three courses, taught without modification, become learning communities when subgroups of students in them enroll in an additional course focused on making connections between the courses. As the simplest and most efficient form of learning communities, models of this type include freshman interest groups and federated learning communities (Shapiro & Levine, 1999; Smith et al., 2004).

LINKED OR CLUSTERED COURSES

Linked courses consist of two discrete courses, typically a combination of skills-based and content-based courses, in which a small number of students enroll as a cohort (Lenning & Ebbers, 1999; Smith et al., 2004). Clustered courses, an expanded form of linked ones, consist of three or more discrete courses which may be common freshman- or sophomore-level classes with large and small enrollments (Smith et al.,

2004). Students enroll by choice as part of the cohort, and the learning community courses often make up most of the course load for the term (Lenning & Ebbers, 1999).

TEAM-TAUGHT LEARNING COMMUNITIES

Team-taught learning communities are the most complex because the model completely integrates two or more courses around a theme, using a single syllabus and extended class time (Shapiro & Levine, 1999). Referred to as coordinated or integrated studies programs, students register for the program rather than individual courses. In addition to the class sessions, students attend seminars to delve more deeply into textbooks or additional readings (Smith et al., 2004). Faculty teaching in a team-taught learning community requires an exceptional commitment to collaboration, team teaching, and providing an intellectually stimulating experience for students (Shapiro & Levine, 1999).

A LEARNING COMMUNITY IN ACTION

Lane Community College in Eugene, Oregon, offers several learning communities in which students take common courses as members of a cohort. These linked or clustered courses may be centered on a theme, such as politics and the environment, or a career goal such as health occupations. Learning communities at Lane have also grown to include cohorts for first-year student athletes and women in transition (McGrail, 2010). Students have responded positively to the linked courses and additional support, indicating the learning community helped them connect with other students (3.27 on a 4.0 scale) and inspired them to learn (3.18 on a 4.0 scale) (Lane Community College, 2009). Overall, 88% of learning community students would recommend a learning community experience to other new college students (Lane Community College, 2009).

Student Life

Increasing student engagement in *and* out of the classroom, *student life* has long been shown to foster more effective student learning (Nesheim et al., 2007; Schroeder, 1999); but only recently has research focused on how effective partnership programs between student and academic affairs enhance student learning at community colleges. "A whole new mindset is needed to capitalize on the interrelatedness of the in-and-out-of-class influences on student learning and the functional interconnectedness of academic and student affairs" (Terenzini and Pascarelli, 1994, as cited in Nesheim et al., 2007, p. 32).

Both the 2009 Community College Survey of Student Engagement (CCSSE) and the Survey of Entering Student Engagement (SENSE) emphasized the importance of engaging students within the first semester. Successfully completing the first semester improves student retention and attainment of personal and academic goals such as grad-uation and employment. But retention is only a part of the solution. Improving student success requires effective collaboration between student affairs and academic faculty so that students "feel engaged, supported and challenged by their courses" (Bueschel, 2009, p. 5). Part-nership programs allow for enhanced interaction between students and faculty (Nesheim et al., 2007). Three areas address the importance of student life and, in turn, facilitate student learning and retention: campus involvement, academic engagement, and interactions with fac-ulty and other students.

CAMPUS INVOLVEMENT

Programs providing curricular and non-curricular opportunities create a "seamless learning environment and foster student engagement" (Nesheim et al., 2007, p. 437). Cornell and Mosley (2006) noted that successful programs build relationships with the community, while Schroeder (1999) noted that campus involvement "fostered higher lev-els of educational attainment for students in historically underrepre-sented groups" (p. 13).

ACADEMIC ENGAGEMENT

High-impact learning has been championed as a best practice for edu-cators seeking to improve student engagement (Kuh, 2008; Schroeder, 1999). Students receiving frequent feedback from an instructor or advi-sor develop new ways of thinking. Internships, field study, and learn-ing opportunities that respond to the learning styles of new students (Schroeder, 1999) all promote engagement that increases the odds stu-dents will connect with the learning environment (Kuh, 2008).

INTERACTIONS WITH FACULTY AND OTHER STUDENTS

When academics and student services work to influence how students learn, rather than focusing only on what they learn, the result can be powerful and long lasting (Nesheim et al., 2007). Access to instructors increases student confidence and the likelihood students will receive the necessary advising so essential to maintaining their access to cam-pus services and assistance. Peer support also increases when assigned collaborative projects encourage contact with other students outside the classroom (Upcraft et al., 2005).

STUDENT LIFE IN ACTION

Research shows that student life programs are active on community college campuses across the country, but three programs in particular exhibit great promise for benchmarking. Community colleges as diverse as Delgado Community College (2010) in Louisiana, Erie Community College (2010) in New York, and Edmonds Community College (2010) in Washington, understand the connection between academic success and student engagement. Student Life Centers have opened on these campuses, providing opportunities to expand classroom learning by linking students with co-curricular activities, leadership programs, lectures, and support services—all geared to encourage students to stay involved, engage with peers, and discover new ways to define learning.

Service Learning

The concept of civic engagement and community service has a long history in higher education (Hutchison, 2001). In the early 1900s, John Dewey and Jane Addams recognized that civic responsibility and community involvement were necessary parts of a true democracy (Longo, 1974). In the early 1960s, civic engagement and community service became more broadly recognized as service learning. According to the National Service Learning Clearinghouse (2009), there are many different interpretations of service learning as well as varying objectives and contexts. However, a core concept within multiple interpretations is that service learning combines service objectives with learning objectives, changing both the recipient and the provider of the service (Hutchison, 2001; Weglarz & Seybert, 2004). Service learning is accomplished by combining service tasks with structured opportunities, linking the task to self-reflection, self-discovery, and the acquisition and comprehension of values, skills, and knowledge content (National Service Learning Clearinghouse, 2009).

Service learning is the collaboration between organizations, students, and faculty members. Community-based organizations, service organizations, and private businesses partner with educational institutions and individual faculty members to develop an educational curriculum for the student. Faculty have the responsibility to construct a meaningful educational experience and provide students with ample opportunity for critical thinking and reflection through discussion and writing (Eyler & Giles, 1999; Moser & Rogers, 2005).

Critical thinking and reflection are key learning requirements of service learning. Learning in a broader context provides students with the opportunity to use developing skills and knowledge in real-life situations and promotes a sense of community awareness that leads to better citizenship and an enhanced awareness of civic responsibility (Cohen & Brawer, 2008; Hutchison, 2001).

Service learning promotes greater academic learning and social justice awareness (Prentice, 2007). Participation in service learning also leads to better retention and graduation rates. In a study performed by Brevard Community College in Florida, students participating in service learning programs had higher graduation rates than those not participating (Robinson, 2007; Moser & Rogers, 2005). On campuses where students actively participate in the organization and promotion of service learning, the program flourishes (Schneider, 1998).

SERVICE LEARNING IN ACTION

Service learning has a substantial presence in community colleges across the nation. According to Prentice (2001), participation in such programs at community colleges increased from 31% in 1995 to nearly 50% in 2000. By 2010, the American Association of Community Colleges (AACC) found over 60% of community colleges have some level of service learning in the curriculum, and an additional 30% are interested in exploring service learning opportunities. The AACC is an avid supporter of service learning initiatives and—in partnership with the Corporation for National and Community Service and its Learn and Serve America program—established the Community Colleges Broadening Horizons through Service Learning initiative. Every three years since 1994, community colleges across the nation have competed through a grant process for funding to initiate service learning activities on their campuses. Currently, 47 colleges have participated in the initiative and successfully implemented service learning opportunities (AACC, 2010a, 2010b).

Conclusions

Isolation and fragmentation, resulting from rapid growth in higher education during the last half-century, are the greatest threats to successful student learning. "Specialization often results in what is popularly described as functional silos or mine shafts . . . which effectively curtails communication and collaboration between areas" (Schroeder, 1999, p. 9). There are also cultural differences between student affairs professionals and academics that inhibit partnerships. According to Love and Estanek (2004), faculty tend to focus on the classroom, collegiality, reflection, and self-governance; whereas student affairs professionals value teamwork and activity over reflection. Getting both areas to recognize the commonalities and benefits of their respective priorities continues to be a challenge for these groups as well as the administrators who lead integration efforts between the two. Effective integration occurs when academic and student affairs professionals articulate a shared vision and identify outcomes that can result from collaborative implementation (Schroeder, 1999).

While the above programs can happen through inspiration from faculty or services staff, the efforts to reduce and eliminate silos, thus creating a common purpose, require additional effort beyond the program and student outcomes. Administrators and supervisors need to develop a common vocabulary, achieve strong majority buy-in for integration, and do so through various small opportunities to bring faculty and staff together in productive activities beyond "programming" and classroom models referenced above.

An adviser speakers bureau available to classrooms; collaborations in e-advising or online success communities; ongoing classroom partnerships that mix course content with advising on career, society, and post-graduation connections; attacking campus problems through connecting faculty, library staff, counselors, veterans services staff (and any other diverse grouping) around the same table to work on a problem not connected with a program or academic grouping are also extremely important to achieving a cultural shift toward integrated learning.

Some colleges, like West Shore Community College in Michigan, are in discussions to reimagine faculty advising, including it as part of a full-time load and structuring the work through scheduled hours in the student services area, especially during peak enrollment periods. It will not be easy or automatic since contract language, the contemporary role of faculty, and already busy schedules are major hurdles to consider. By reintroducing faculty to the services area, though, and doing the same for services staff in instruction, administrators can promote integration of purpose, work, and schedules to move effectively toward cultural integration.

Even as some colleges have enjoyed success with learning communities, and others with one of the other three programs discussed, community colleges clearly offer the right ingredients to combine into integrated programs. While personalities and specializations will produce unique strengths and variations, the research is nearly unanimous in the benefits achieved through linking formal instruction with success strategies, career and life focus, experiential application, and the act of "giving back" through service opportunities. Furthermore, students benefit from participating in the active dialogue that happens between instructional and service "learning cultures" in the classroom. The benefits of the programs were less certain prior to the advent of learning organization concepts. Now, over twenty years later, we can truly celebrate the rooting of such enhanced learning opportunities into the community college landscape.

References

American Association of Community Colleges. (2010a). *Grantee colleges.* Retrieved from http://www.aacc.nche.edu/Resources/aaccprograms/horizons/Pages/colleges.aspx

American Association of Community Colleges. (2010b). *Service learning.* Retrieved from http://www.aacc.nche.edu/Resources/aaccprograms/horizons/Pages/default.aspx

Barefoot, B. O. (2005). Current institutional practices in the first college year. In M. Upcraft, J. Gardner, B. Barefoot, & Associates (Eds.), *Challenging and supporting the first-year student: A handbook for improving the first year of college* (pp. 47–63). San Francisco, CA: Jossey-Bass.

Benjamin, M., Earnest, K., Gruenewald, D., & Arthur, G. (2007). The first weeks of the first year. *New Directions for Student Services, 117*, 13–24. doi:10.1002/ss.229

Blake, J. H. (2007). The crucial role of student affairs professionals in the learning process. *New Directions for Student Services, 117*, 65–72. doi:10.1002/ss.234

Bourassa, D. M., & Kruger, K. (2001). The national dialogue on academic and student affairs collaboration. *New Directions for Higher Education, 116*, 9–38. doi:10.1002/he.31

Bueschel, A. C. (2009). The landscape of politics and practices that support student preparation and success. *New Directions in Community Colleges, 145*, 1–10. doi:10.1002/cc.351

Cohen, A. M., & Brawer, F. B. (2008). *The American community college* (5th ed.). San Francisco, CA: Jossey-Bass.

Colwell, B. W. (2006). Partners in a community of learners: Student and academic affairs at small colleges. *New Directions for Student Services, 116*, 53–66. doi:10.1002/ss.225

Cornell, R., & Mosley, M. L. (2006). Intertwining college with real life: The community college first-year experience. *Peer Review, 8*(3), 23–25.

Crissman Ishler, J. L., & Upcraft, M. L. (2005). The keys to first-year student persistence. In M. Upcraft, J. Gardner, B. Barefoot, & Associates (Eds.), *Challenging and supporting the first-year student: A handbook for improving the first year of college* (pp. 27–46). San Francisco, CA: Jossey-Bass.

Dale, P. A., & Drake, T. M. (2005). Connecting academic and student affairs to enhance student learning and success. *New Directions for Community Colleges, 131*, 51–64. doi:10.1002/cc.205

Delgado Community College. (2010). Student life center. In *Auxiliary services.* Retrieved from http://www.dcc.edu/division/auxiliary/studentcenter

Edmonds Community College. (2010). *Office of student life.* Retrieved from http://www.edcc.edu/stulife

Erie Community College. (2010). *Student life.* Retrieved from http:/www.ecc.edu/studentlife

Eyler, J., & Giles, D. E., Jr. (1999). *Where's the learning in service learning?* San Francisco, CA: Jossey-Bass.

Gabelnick, F., MacGregor, J., Matthews, R. S., & Smith, B. L. (1990). Learning communities: Creating connections among students, faculty, and disciplines. *New Directions for Teaching and Learning, 41.*

Hunter, M. S., & Linder, C. W. (2005). First-year seminars. In M. Upcraft, J. Gardner, B. Barefoot, & Associates (Eds.), *Challenging and supporting the first-year student: A handbook for improving the first year of college* (pp. 275–291). San Francisco, CA: Jossey-Bass.

Hunter, M. S., & Murray, K. A. (2007). New frontiers for student affairs professionals: Teaching and the first-year experience. *New Directions for Student Services, 117*, 25–34. doi:10.1002/ss.230

Hutchison, P. (2001). *Service learning: Challenges and opportunities.* Retrieved from http://www.newfoundations.com/OrgTheory/Hutchinson721.html

Jacoby, B. (1999). Partnerships for service learning. *New Directions for Student Services, 87*, 19–35. doi:10.1002/ss.8702

Keup, J. R. (2006). Promoting new-student success: Assessing academic development and achievement among first-year students. *New Directions for Student Services, 114*, 27–45. doi:10.1002/ss.205

Kezar, A. (2001). Documenting the landscape: Results of a national study on academic and student affairs collaboration. *New Directions for Higher Education, 116*, 39–51. doi:10.1002/he.32

Kezar, A. (2003). Enhancing innovative partnerships: Creating a change model for academic and student affairs collaboration. *Innovative Higher Education, 28*(2), 137–156. doi:10.1023/B:IHIE.0000006289.31227.25

Kuh, G. D. (2008). Why integration and engagement are essential to effective educational practice in the twenty-first century. *Peer Review, 10*(4), 27–28.

LaGuardia Community College. (2010). Statistics. In *Academic peer instruction (API)*. Retrieved from http://www.lagcc.cuny.edu/API/

Lane Community College. (2009). *Learning communities assessment.* Retrieved from http://www.lanecc.edu/lc/fresources/FacultyLCAssessment.htm

Lane Community College. (2010). *Learning communities at Lane.* Retrieved from http://www.lanecc.edu/lc/index.html

Lenning, O. T., & Ebbers, L. H. (1999). *The powerful potential of learning communities: Improving education for the future* (ASHE-ERIC Higher Education Report, Vol. 26, No. 6). Washington, DC: The George Washington University, Graduate School of Education and Human Development.

Levine, J. H., & Shapiro, N. S. (2000). Curricular learning communities. *New Directions for Higher Education, 109*, 13–22. doi:10.1002/he.10902

Longo, N. V. (1974). *Why community matters: Connecting education with civic life.* Albany, NY: State University of New York Press.

Love, Patrick G., & Estanek, Sandra M. (2004). *Rethinking student affairs practice.* San Francisco, CA: Jossey-Bass.

Martin, D. C., & Hurley, M. (2005). Supplemental instruction. In M. Upcraft, J. Gardner, B. Barefoot, & Associates (Eds.), *Challenging and supporting the first-year student: A handbook for improving the first year of college* (pp. 308–319). San Francisco, CA: Jossey-Bass.

Martin, J., & Samels, J. E. (2001). Lessons learned: Eight best practices for new partnerships. *New Directions for Higher Education, 116*, 89–100. doi:10.1002/he.36

McGrail, A. (2010, January). *Learning Communities News.* Retrieved from Lane Community College web site: http://www.lanecc.edu/lc/fresources/LearningCommunitiesNews.htm

Meiklejohn, A. (1932). *The experimental college.* New York: Harper. Retrieved from http://digital.library.wisc.edu/1711.dl/UW.MeikExpColl

Moser, J. M., & Rogers, G. E. (2005). The power of linking service to learning. *Tech Directions, 64*(7), 18–21.

National Service Learning Clearinghouse. (2009). *What service learning is.* Retrieved from http://www.servicelearning.org/what_is_service_learning/service-learning_is/index.php

Nesheim, B. E., Guentzel, M. J., Kellogg, A. H., McDonald, W. M., Wells, C. A., & Whitt, E. J. (2007). Outcomes for students of student affairs-academic affairs partnership programs. *Journal of College Student Development, 48*(4), 435–454. doi:10.1353/csd.2007.0041

O'Banion, T. (1997). *A learning college for the 21st century.* Phoenix, AZ: American Council on Education and Oryx Press.

Prentice, M. (2001). *Institutionalizing service learning in community colleges.* Retrieved from http://www.aacc.nche.edu/Publications/Briefs/Documents/02012002institutionalizingservice.pdf

Prentice, M. (2007). Social justice through service learning: community colleges as ground zero. *Equity & Excellence in Education, 40*(3), 266–273. doi:10.1080/10665680701396735

Rhodes, L., & Carifio, J. (1999). Community college students' opinions regarding the value of their freshman seminar experience. *Community College Journal of Research and Practice, 23*(5), 511–523. doi:10.1080/106689299264701

Robinson, G. (2007, January 5). Service learning. *Community College Times, 3.*

Schneider, M. K. (1998). Models of good practice for service learning programs: What can we learn from 1,000 faculty, 25,000 students, and 27 institutions involved in service? *Bulletin of the American Association for Higher Education, 50*(10), 9–12.

Schroeder, C. C. (1999). Partnerships: An imperative for enhancing student learning and institutional effectiveness. *New Directions for Student Services, 87,* 5–18. doi:10.1002/ss.8701

Schuh, J. H. (1999). Guiding principles for evaluating student and academic affairs partnerships. *New Directions for Student Services, 87,* 85–92. doi:10.1002/ss.8707

Shapiro, N. S., & Levine, J. H. (1999). *Creating learning communities: A practical guide to winning support, organizing for change, and implementing programs.* San Francisco, CA: Jossey-Bass.

Siegel, B. L. (2005). Inviting first-year student success. In M. Upcraft, J. Gardner, B. Barefoot, & Associates (Eds.), *Challenging and supporting the first-year student: A handbook for improving the first year of college* (pp. 176–190). San Francisco, CA: Jossey-Bass.

Smith, B. L., MacGregor, J., Matthews, R. S., & Gabelnick, F. (2004). *Learning communities: Reforming undergraduate education.* San Francisco, CA: Jossey-Bass.

Swing, R. L., & Skipper, T. L. (2007). Achieving student success in the first year of college. In G. Kramer & Associates (Eds.), *Fostering student success in the campus community* (pp. 369–391). San Francisco, CA: Jossey-Bass.

Upcraft, M. L., Gardner, J. N., Barefoot, B. O., & Associates (Eds.). (2005). *Challenging and supporting the first-year student: A handbook for improving the first year of college.* San Francisco, CA: Jossey-Bass.

Weglarz, S., & Seybert, J. (2004). Participant perceptions of a community college service-learning program. *Community College Journal of Research & Practice, 28*(2), 123–132. doi:10.1080/10668920490253618

Zaritsky, J. S., & Toce, A. (2006). Supplemental instruction at a community college: The four pillars. *New Directions for Teaching and Learning, 106,* 23–31. doi:10.1002/tl.230

Remediation beyond Developmental Education: The Use of Learning Assistance Centers to Increase Academic Preparedness in Community Colleges

Dolores Perin

Based on a qualitative study of fifteen campuses, Perin describes a variety of learning assistance services that support academic courses. Among the many research projects coming out of the Community College Research Center, this is the only one that not only articulates the ways in which learning assistance programs support instruction but also reports the positive outcomes associated with participation in learning center services.

Community colleges' commitment to open access brings with it the challenge of educating a heterogeneous population (Maxwell et al., 2003). Among this population are students whose academic history and personal lives have not prepared them for the reading, writing, or math demands of postsecondary study. Over the years, providing remediation[1] to prepare students for college-level work has become an important community college mission (Howard & Obetz, 1996; Raftery & VanWagoner, 2002). The most visible form of remediation is developmental education (Boylan, Bliss, & Bonham, 1997; Foote, 1999; Johnson, 1996; McCabe & Day, 1998; Roueche & Roueche, 1999), at the heart of which are sequences of reading, writing, and math courses. However, institutions may not require academically underprepared students to enroll in these courses (Jenkins & Boswell, 2002; Shults, 2000). Even when enrollment is mandated, developmental education is not always effective (Burley, Butner, & Cejda, 2001; Crowe, 1998; Grubb et al., 1999; Perin & Charron, forthcoming).[2] Although remedial and introductory college-level English and math courses are intended to prepare students for the academic demands of postsecondary content-area learning, only one-quarter or less of first-time community college students enroll in these courses (Maxwell et al., 2003). Consequently, the issue of academic preparedness extends beyond developmental education and may affect a significant portion of the college degree program as underprepared students enroll in college-credit courses. Besides developmental education, classroom approaches to academic difficulty include "hidden remediation" (Grubb et al., 1999) and writing across the curriculum (Lester et al., 2003). Another alternative, outside of the classroom, is the use of learning assistance centers.

Most community colleges have learning assistance centers designed to support students' learning in developmental education and college-credit courses. Learning assistance services include academic tutoring, computer-assisted learning, assessment, advisement, and counseling, for example, as listed by Stern (2001). In their scope and variety of services, college learning centers conform to one of O'Banion's (1997) six principles of the ideal "learning college," the availability of a variety of learning options.

A main function of academic support centers is to help students develop efficient learning processes, an especially important function in light of instructors' observations of academic difficulties that impede content learning in college-level courses (Grubb et al., 1999; Perin & Charron, forthcoming). The focus of learning assistance centers is compatible with that of developmental education, construed as remedial courses and ancillary advisement and counseling designed to improve college-readiness (Boylan, 2002; Casazza, 1999). In fact, colleges sometimes house their developmental education courses in the learning center (Roueche, Ely, & Roueche, 2001). Further, many developmental education courses have a required tutoring or lab component which may be undertaken in a college learning center (Boylan, 2002). However, the aims of developmental education and learning assistance centers do not overlap completely because the former is intended for students with identified reading, writing, or math weaknesses, and the latter is available to the college student body at large.

Typically, all the services of a college learning center are free and available to all enrolled students, who may be self-referred, sent by course instructors because they are displaying academic difficulty, or fulfilling a developmental education lab requirement.

Tutoring in learning assistance centers is provided by professional or peer tutors to individual students or groups who work at their own pace (Koski & Levin, 1998). When the tutoring is provided to support a college-level discipline course, help with reading, writing, or math skills is a means to the end of completing a subject-matter assignment. In this case, basic academic skills can be learned implicitly through exposure and practice. In contrast, the tutoring provided to support developmental education course work provides explicit instruction designed to strengthen specific literacy or math skills.

Despite the strong presence of learning centers in community colleges, there is little research into the ways in which they aid in the enhancement of the academic skills of either developmental education or college-credit students. The study reported in this paper explored the services of community college learning centers in order to learn more about their remedial function.[3] This investigation was part of the National Field Study of the Community College Research Center at Teachers College, Columbia University, a multi-topic case study of current issues in a national sample of 15 community colleges. The current research asked whether and how remedial functions were served by learning assistance centers[4] at the study sites, and what issues arose in the use of this instructional format.

Method

Participants

The 15 sites were located in six states, Washington, California, Texas, Illinois, Florida, and New York, selected because they had large, well-developed community college systems. Four of the states together accounted for approximately half of the national community college enrollments. Within each state, sites were selected based on urbanicity, size, and willingness to participate. The sample consisted of five urban, five suburban, one mixed (urban and suburban), and four rural community colleges, with enrollments ranging from 1,854 to 28,862 students. Minority participation ranged from 5–96%. College information is listed in Table 1; the (fictitious) names indicate urbanicity.

Data Collection and Analysis

This is a qualitative, instrumental case study (Stake, 1995) that aimed to understand ways in which learning assistance centers help increase academic preparedness. The methods of data collection and interpretation were based on Merriam (1988), Miles and Huberman (1994), Patton (1990), Stake (1995), and Yin (1994). The study was approved by the Institutional Review Board at Teachers College, Columbia University, and participants provided signed consent in advance of the data collection.

Each site was visited by a research team consisting of at least two senior researchers and three research assistants. The current author participated in several of the visits. Interviews were based on a protocol covering all of the topics being investigated in this multi-topic case study. The questions pertaining to the current study reflected issues discussed in previous research on academic preparedness and remediation including Boylan et al. (1997), Grubb et al. (1999), Jenkins and Boswell (2002), McCabe and Day (1998), and Roueche and Roueche (1999). A total of 630 people participated, individually or in groups, in 458 interviews that lasted approximately one hour each. Each interview was recorded and transcribed. The interview transcripts were the major source of data for this study, and were supplemented by college documents such as course catalogs and institutional reports, as well as examples of instructional materials furnished by the colleges.

Sixty-three percent ($n = 290$) of the 458 interview transcripts were selected for coding for this study based on a word search using 20 different terms relating to academic preparedness and developmental education. The transcripts were coded by the author and two research assistants using QSR-Nud*Ist version N5 software (www.qsrinternational.com). (Codes available from author.)

Table 1. Colleges and Learning Center Services

College	State	Fall 2000 Enrollment	Minority Participation	Learning Centers and Labs	Services Offered	Students Served
Northwest Suburban CC (NWSCC)	WA	11,234	30%	Learning center; separate reading, writing, and math labs	Computer-assisted instruction, tutoring	Both developmental education (reading) and college-credit students (writing and math)
Northwest Rural CC (NWRCC)	WA	1,854	25%	Learning center, writing lab, math-science lab	Tutoring, study skills workshops, computer-assisted instruction, study groups, special test-taking conditions	Both developmental education and college-credit students
Western Urban CC (WUCC)	CA	14,406	61%	3 learning centers: content-area; reading, writing, critical thinking; math center	Tutoring, self-paced math courses	Both developmental education and college-credit students
Western Suburban CC (WSCC)	CA	13,233	35%	Learning center, lab for nursing students planned	Short courses in academic skills, computer-assisted instruction; portion of math courses taught at learning center; tutors assist in subject-area classrooms; coordination of supplemental learning	

Institution	State	Enrollment	%	Center	Services	Students served
Western Rural CC (WRCC)	CA	4,344	59%	Learning center	Tutoring to support work in any course	Both developmental education and college-credit students
Southwest Urban CC (SWUCC)	TX	25,735	35%	Learning center	Tutoring in academic skills, science, foreign languages	75% college-credit students; 25% developmental education (required lab component)
Southwest Suburban CC (SWSCC)	TX	12,996	25%	Learning center, math lab	Tutoring in academic skills and subject areas	Both developmental education and college-credit students
Midwest Urban CC (MWUCC)	IL	8,147	81%	Learning center, tutoring in math department	Tutoring in academic skills and subject areas; specialized workshops in academic skills	Both developmental education and college-credit students, mostly older, returning, limited English proficiency females
Midwest Suburban CC (MWSCC)	IL	28,862	27%	General tutoring center, writing and math labs, specialized skill centers	Tutoring in academic skills and subject areas; self-paced computer-assisted courses and tutoring in specialized centers	Both developmental education and college-credit students
Midwest Rural CC (MWRCC)	IL	7,675	10%	Learning center, math center, career assistance center; writing center planned	Tutoring in academic skills and subject matter, computer-assisted instruction	Both developmental education and college-credit students

Table 1. (continued)

College	State	Fall 2000 Enrollment	Minority Participation	Learning Centers and Labs	Services Offered	Students Served
Southern Urban CC (SUCC)	FL	27,565	42%	Learning, writing, and math centers on each campus	Tutoring and computer-assisted instruction	Both developmental education (required lab component) and college-credit students
Southern Mixed CC (SMCC)	FL	13,186	20%	Several learning centers on each campus	Tutoring and computer-assisted instruction; lending of ancillary subject-area materials	Both developmental education and college-credit students
Northeast Urban CC (NEUCC)	NY	6,928	96%	Writing lab, learning center for disadvantaged students, discipline-specific tutoring in departments	Tutoring	Both developmental education and college-credit students
Northeast Suburban CC (NESCC)	NY	9,304	12%	Central learning center and several smaller specialized centers	Tutoring and computer-assisted instruction	Both developmental education and college-credit students
Northeast Rural CC (NERCC)	NY	4,521	5%	Learning center on main campus	Tutoring	Both developmental education and college-credit students, especially older, returning adults

Findings

All of the colleges in the sample contained at least one learning assistance center, as shown in Table 1 and described in the following vignettes. Table 2 summarizes the functions and operation of the learning centers across sites.

Table 2. Summary of Function and Operation of Learning Assistance Centers

Overview of Services	Details and Issues
	Characteristics of Facilities
• Learning centers serve both college-credit and developmental education students; tutoring or computer-assisted instruction in reading, writing, math, and academic subjects, including foreign languages, also study skills, writing skills, and conversation workshops, some specialized for subject-area; staff are professional tutors, college instructors, and/or peer tutors: all sites	• One or more learning centers, and specialized learning labs: NWSCC, NWRCC, WUCC, SWSCC, MWSCC, MWRCC, NESCC • Centralized writing lab; learning center limited to designated population; and discipline-specific tutoring in academic departments: NEUCC • One or more tutoring centers on each campus of a multi-campus college: SUCC, SMCC • Single learning center: WSCC, WRCC, SWUCC • Single learning center, some tutoring available in math department: MWUCC • Single learning center on main campus, no services at satellite sites: NERCC
	Nature of Services
• College-wide supplementary learning initiative directed by learning center staff: WUCC • Specialized reading, writing, and/or math labs provide tutoring, study groups, and services for students with disabilities; labs may be autonomous, connected to department, or part of college learning center: NWSCC, NWRCC, WSCC, SWUCC, SWSCC	• Tutors help students with assignments from college-credit courses: NWSCC, NWRCC, NEUCC, NESCC, MWUCC, SWUCC • Tutors help with developmental education assignments: SWUCC, NESCC • Retention rate in college English improves as result of help in writing lab: NEUCC • Self-paced remedial math course offered through learning center: NWSCC • Learning center offers short-duration remedial courses: WUCC • Individualized, short-duration courses to be eliminated because considered unproductive, to be replaced by peer tutoring and student study groups; strong student preference for tutoring over computer-assisted learning: WSCC • Specialized skills lab for nursing students: WSCC • Tutoring counted as a counseling service: NERCC

Table 2. (continued)	

Overview of Services	**Details and Issues**
	Source of Referral
	• Students referred by developmental and/or college course instructors, or self-referred: NWSCC, NWRCC, WUCC, WSCC
	• Tutoring and computer-assisted learning required by developmental education provided in learning center or specialized lab: SUCC, SMCC
	• Learning center services only at request of student, no connection to developmental education: WRCC
	Population Served
	• 75% of learning center visits by college-credit students, 25% by developmental education students: SWUCC
	• Reading services sought mainly by developmental education students, can take one-credit option: NWSCC
	• Multiple centers with different purposes and services, may be funded to serve different populations: MWSCC, MWRCC, NEUCC, NESCC
	• Many users foreign-born, some have learning disabilities but tutors do not have special training: MWUCC
	Funding and Demand
	• Funding for learning centers not secure: WUCC
	• Large demand for learning center services: MWRCC, NEUCC
	• Highest demand for reading assistance for developmental education students: NWSCC
	• Highest demand for reading assistance for college-credit students: SWUCC
	• Highest demand for math: SWSCC, NESCC
	• Under-utilized, decrease in demand and/or increase in need for recruitment: WSCC, MWSCC, NESCC, NERCC, WSCC, SWSCC (learning disabled students)
	Scheduling and Credit
	• 24 hours of tutoring in learning center in one semester bears .5 credit: WSCC
	• Learning centers and/or skills labs open most days, long hours, may allow walk-in appointments: NWSCC, WUCC, SWUCC
	• Every student entitled to 16 hours of tutoring in learning center per semester

Overview of Services	*Details and Issues*
	Connection to Learning Resource Centers
	• Resource center and learning center combined: SMCC
	• Resource center staff refer students to writing lab: NEUCC

Northwest Suburban Community College (NWSCC)

The main service provided by NWSCC's learning assistance center was computer-assisted instruction. In Fall 2000, 7,480 visits were made for reading assistance, 3,800 for writing, and 4,000 for math. Services were available for all enrolled students. Reading assistance was sought mainly by developmental education students (95% of visits), while 65% of the writing visits and 45% of the math visits were made by college-credit students. The college also had specialized reading, writing, and math labs in which students could enroll for a one-credit series of tutoring sessions in discipline-specific literacy or math skills. For example, tutors in the writing lab helped students with papers assigned in subject-matter courses:

> If you need help on essays you can go and get their help on grammar. They'll correct your essays and go over it with you and explain the rules of English. (Student, NWSCC)

The math lab was open seven days per week, with two tutors always present. Assistance was provided at all math levels but most of the demand was for pre-calculus. Most of the remedial math students used the lab, which was described as having "a very warm and relaxed atmosphere." A student described it as "our second home, basically."

Northwest Rural Community College (NWRCC)

At NWRCC, a learning center and a writing lab provided individualized tutoring and study skills workshops. Personnel at the writing lab assisted students with assignments in a range of disciplines:

> We don't proofread it for them. We sit down with them. And we consider that we do more instructing, you know, with the student. Oftentimes, the student will read the paper out loud to the tutor and they'll discuss the kinds of mistakes that, you know, that they're going through. . . . Even [an instructor], who has all in-class essays, when . . . when he hands [his first essay] back to the students, he'll . . . pinpoint people and say . . . "You've got to get into the English lab and do some practice essays." In fact, he'll bring people. . . . We have people that bring in research papers from other

> classes . . . social sciences, whatever. We have music students running papers past us. We have art students running their research papers past us. (Administrator, NWRCC)

NWRCC also had a math-science lab that offers computer-assisted instruction, tutoring, study groups, and customized test-taking conditions for students with special learning needs.

Western Urban Community College (WUCC)

There were three learning centers at WUCC: one offered tutoring by professional tutors and instructors in most content-area subjects, a second provided peer tutoring in reading, writing, and critical thinking, and the third was a math center open 60 hours per week for both tutoring and self-paced, open-entry, open-exit developmental math courses. The self-paced courses were a highly popular alternative to the traditional developmental math courses also available. The math center was supported by a patchwork of funding and its existence was not secure.

Western Suburban Community College (WSCC)

WSCC's learning center offered half-credit, short-duration courses in basic academic skills, as well as tutoring and computer-assisted instruction. In addition to the learning assistance center, the nursing program had plans to use grant funds to hire a nurse to run a separate, nursing-specific skills lab for at-risk students. Students were both referred to the learning assistance center by faculty, or self-referred:

> Most students know what they want. They either want help with tutoring, or they've been referred by a faculty member for assistance with writing, or they are just a little bit lost and have self-identified that this is a place that can provide some assistance. (Administrator, WSCC)

Demand for computer-assisted instruction was low because students preferred to work with instructors. However, math instructors taught their classes in the learning center 20 hours per week using the computers. Some of the learning center's tutors provided assistance in subject-area classrooms, and a learning center staff member directed the college's supplemental instruction effort (Hafer, 2001).

At the time of the site visit, there were plans to relocate the center in a new campus library, allowing the center to triple its space. Interviewees considered the facility to be understaffed, although demand for services had leveled off when the college abandoned the use of standardized placement tests several years earlier (Perin, 2003). However, the center provided key services such as assistance to non-native English speakers whose course instructors had difficulty helping them.

The short-duration courses were taught by faculty members. Instruction was increasingly done with groups rather than individual students because of a shortage of funds. There was more demand for tutoring than for these courses because the former required an even shorter time commitment. According to an administrator, "for a student who wants a quickie, they usually choose the tutoring." In fact, at the time of the site visit the short-duration courses were about to be eliminated because they were considered unproductive and "hard to orchestrate." A plan under discussion was to move the courses to the academic departments and substitute less costly peer tutoring, student study groups, and support services provided by personnel other than faculty.

Western Rural Community College (WRCC)

WRCC's learning center offered tutoring to support work across the curriculum. Services were provided at the request of the student and were not formally tied to any specific course.

Southwest Urban Community College (SWUCC)

SWUCC had a learning center that offered walk-in tutoring in math, reading, writing, science, and foreign languages. Approximately 75% of the students who used the center were enrolled in college-credit courses, the rest in developmental education. In Fall 2000 there were 7,087 visits for reading, 4,942 for writing, and 6,321 for math. The center was open seven days a week and held late evening hours four days a week. The tutors were 20 hour per week adjunct faculty, some of whom also taught college composition courses. Some of the students did their developmental English and math homework in the learning center with the help of a tutor. In addition, some of the tutoring was a required lab component of the developmental reading and writing courses.

Since it was assumed that many of the students would continue to need tutoring at the credit level, some students were familiarized with learning center services while they were in developmental education. Indeed, college composition instructors referred students to the learning center for tutoring to support their work in the course. However, because there was a question of the tutors' role in improving students' work, some instructors administered in-class assessments:

> [An English instructor] has all in-class essays. And for some of the students, that's a real chore, because they'll have an hour to write those essays . . . some people just can't do that. Some people just freeze up. . . . But there's a real advantage to the reason he does it. In part, is so that he knows they're the ones doing the writing. Because, so often, even we see that in the lab, they can get help from various tutors. I mean, you end up with a pretty good essay, once you run it past four different tutors, you know. (Developmental Education Faculty, SWUCC)

Southwest Suburban Community College (SWSCC)

SWSCC had a learning assistance center and a math lab. The learning center provided tutoring to all students, both in developmental education and college-credit courses. Only 21 students requested support in reading and writing in Fall 2000, smaller than the demand for assistance in math (185 students) and subject areas such as chemistry and biology (124 students).

Midwest Urban Community College (MWUCC)

MWUCC's learning center provided tutoring to approximately 300 students per semester in a range of subjects. Demand for math and English was heavier than for the subject areas. The majority of students seeking assistance were low-proficiency English speakers and older, returning female students. Students signed up for hourly appointments, and were entitled to 16 hours of tutoring per course per semester. Tutoring was available on weekdays and included evening hours on four of the days. The center was fully utilized, and received approximately 500 requests for tutoring in the Spring 2001 term.

Besides tutoring, the center conducted specialized workshops, such as writing for the humanities and English as a Second Language conversation. On staff at the learning center were 18 tutors, including both professional tutors and advanced students at the college. Some of the students who received tutoring appeared to have learning disabilities but the tutors, not having specialized training, confined their efforts to helping with course assignments and building confidence. A professional tutor described difficulties he had in working with a student with special learning needs:

> Some of the students are very challenged. And some aren't. Some just need support . . . my emphasis is English, speech, social science, when necessary philosophy, humanities. I like to teach people anything but math and science . . . the people who are especially challenged, just did not get to go to school early on. One young lady, I called her young, she's probably about 50 . . . has 16 brothers and sisters. And then working and raising those brothers and sisters since she was ten, really never went to high school. . . . She's learning . . . but she couldn't comprehend the difference in yesterday and tomorrow . . . [she was native-born and] I was totally unprepared for that. . . . [To help her] it's like when you get some sense that you are in deep water, you either are trying to touch the bottom and push yourself up or tread water and try to get to the top. And I started getting the sense of how deep her problems were. And decided that I really didn't want to find out how bad they were. I was more concerned about focusing on the assignment that she had, and mutually appreciating some success with respect to that specific assignment. And so by the time that was over, we both had a sense that we had made progress. . . .
> I need to say very candidly that other people on the staff primarily work with [students with severe needs]. That is not my forte. I do work with

them [sometimes], and it reminds me of why professionally I stayed out of grammar school and high school. My patience level is not consistent with that.... Their needs are just so deep ... first you have to encourage people to believe in themselves. That's part of the problem. And I can do that. But then when you have a student who may forget something that either you said or that they said ten minutes ago, then we have a real problem. (Tutor, MWUCC)

In addition to assistance in the learning center, students could schedule tutoring in the math department at certain times.

Midwest Suburban Community College (MWSCC)

MWSCC's had separate learning centers for math and writing, and a general tutoring center to provide support in the subject areas. An interviewee stated that the writing center was under-utilized because participation was voluntary. At the time of the site visit, a new reading center was scheduled to open in response to an instructor survey which revealed deep concern about students' reading skills. The math and writing centers were staffed by faculty, one of whom oversaw the developmental reading instruction.

In addition to the above centers, there were five Student Success Centers that offered developmental education as well as college-credit courses using self-paced, computer-assisted programs. For the developmental education courses, students signed up for a specified number of sessions per semester and received instruction from a staff member and/or computer. The Student Success Centers also offered a one-credit course in job-related spelling and writing.

Midwest Rural Community College (MWRCC)

There were three learning centers at MWRCC. First, there was an academic assistance center, funded through grants, that provided tutoring in reading, writing, math, and other subjects. The second was an office in the math department that was set up as a math center, staffed by a group of peer tutors and a professional tutor. The center was well attended, and math faculty, whose offices were nearby, also provided assistance as needed. The third learning center was a career assistance lab that had software packages such as "Wrong Sentences" to teach academic skills. The college also had plans to set up [a] writing center staffed by a full-time faculty member who would receive release time to oversee this effort.

Southwest Urban Community College (SUCC)

SUCC was a multi-campus college. There were several tutoring centers on each campus that provided assistance in reading, writing, and math. The math center provided tutoring as well as computer-assisted learning, and staff at the writing center helped students critique and proofread essays assigned in various courses.

Southwest Mixed Community College (SMCC)

SMCC, also a multi-campus college, served a mixed urban and suburban population. As with SUCC, there were learning centers on each campus providing assistance in reading, writing, and math. The centers were staffed by both full- and part-time instructors and tutors. Developmental education students fulfilled their lab requirement through computer-assisted practice in the learning centers. There were close connections between the learning centers and remedial classes since the developmental education instructors also provided some of the tutoring in the learning centers. One of the instructors customized part of a remedial English textbook so it could be used in tutoring in the learning center. While many other colleges have separate resource centers and learning centers, these two forms of assistance were combined at SMCC, where one of the learning centers had a library of materials to assist content-learning. For example, the nursing students could borrow manipulative materials to help them learn the names and functions of body parts.

Northeast Urban Community College (NEUCC)

NEUCC was part of a large municipal university system in an urban area in New York State. Minority participation was very high and many students were immigrants whose native language was not English. Although developmental education placement was strongly enforced for low-scoring students (Perin, 2003), there was heavy utilization of tutoring across the degree programs because students who placed in college-level courses continued to have difficulties with basic skills. Tutoring also was provided to support some of the developmental education courses.

> They have to . . . reach a certain a score on the ACT test. Now, does that mean that they can engage fully in challenging course work that's credit bearing towards a degree program? No, not necessarily. They still might need some extra support, particularly when we are talking about students who are using English as a second language and who come out of high school without the math skills that they really need, and if they are going into something that is a strong technological area where they need certain skills, they might not have them . . . a lot of the tutoring is after a remediation level. (Administrator, NEUCC)

There were numerous academic learning centers around the campus, mostly in the academic departments. Some specialized in assistance to ESL students, some were linked to the developmental education courses, and others were linked to various college credit courses in the discipline areas. A writing center that previously operated only in the English department recently expanded to be a campus-wide service and many students enrolled in college English received tutoring. This service appeared to improve the retention rate for these classes, in which dropout occurred as the work became harder. Also, there was a tax-levied Support Center that provided tutoring and mentoring for first-year students who were able to demonstrate that they came from disadvantaged backgrounds.

As with many other colleges across the country, NEUCC had a separate learning resource center where students could borrow ancillary audio-visual and print materials to reinforce their learning of course content. Students who were considered to need academic skills development were referred by learning resource staff for tutoring at one of the college's learning centers.

Northeast Suburban Community College (NESCC)

NESCC's learning assistance center was well-funded, well-staffed, and highly visible on campus, occupying ample and pleasant space in the college library. Since the facility stands out in the National Field Study sample for its strong support by college administration and its high-quality coordination, it is worth describing in detail.

The center, which was directed by an associate dean, was open from 7 a.m. to 10 p.m. on weekdays and also held hours on weekends. The college computer center was located in the same building. The learning assistance center provided individual and group tutoring to support both developmental education and college-credit courses. For example, a writing tutor helped students write papers for courses such as biology. The heaviest demand was for tutoring in math, science, and chemistry. The center also provided a lab component required by all developmental education courses (Boylan, 2002). Besides tutoring, the center provided freshman orientation sessions as well as stand-alone workshops on academic skills, strategies for handling test anxiety, and managing time.

According to college policy, remedial enrollment was voluntary for students who failed the placement test. Students who declined remediation could use tutoring as an alternative:

> To be honest with you, the majority of students when they find out it is a remedial course or I call it a refresher course, it has no credit, they will not take it because it will delay their degree progress. So what we've done is we rely heavily on the [learning center]. (Developmental Education Faculty, NESCC)

Students with borderline placement test scores were referred by advisors to the center:

> They end up down there not really on their own, but because they have a discussion with their advisor, they know that it's an option to a noncredit course, the advisor has said, "You're kind of [borderline] on the placement test" and given their high school grades and the way you feel about how many courses or what you're going to take, you may be able to complete this course if you work in the [center]. (Administrator, NESCC)

The center provided assistance to students who enrolled in remedial courses. A developmental education instructor noted that students who used the learning center had better persistence rates but sometimes received an inappropriate amount of help with course assignments:

> We have [a learning center], so many of them go there. The students that actually make it through the course and stick to it—because we have a very large dropout rate, as you can imagine—many of them use the [center] because it's a place where they can get help in their content areas, and they also need help with their writing . . . every once in a while, I'll have a few students who . . . knock themselves out trying to create strategies to avoid writing in front of me and then suddenly appear with polished papers. (Developmental Education Faculty, NESCC)

Two students spoke highly of the tutoring they had received in math and writing. Student 2's statement about improved grades lends weight to the concern of the developmental education instructor just quoted:

> *Student 1:* It's good because the one lady, in particular, she knows how to explain step by step by step, like in simple terms, and other ones will just skip steps, and I don't know where she got the answer from. As far as the learning center, I've told the one lady down there that I think they should have more room for math, because that's the only section that ever gets filled up, is the math. They have three full timers; they need another one down there, and stuff like that.
> *Student 2:* There are people in the [learning center] who know each teacher's way, method. The algebra. I mean you can have five different teachers and they ask you who is your teacher, so they show you what [your teacher] is showing you, and that's really helpful because if you don't ask questions you're not going to get the answers. And if you're asking somebody to show you something and you don't give them the information that you're in [a particular class] they'd be teaching you in a completely different way, then you have numbers and everything running all over your head that goes everywhere; you can't put them into place. And then with the reading, I bring my essays there, and they helped me go from a B to an A just by looking it over telling me [how to correct punctuation], they assist you in getting a better grade on the paper. They're really great over there, they really are. (Student group, NESCC)

An institutional study found a significant positive correlation between frequency of visits and GPA—grade point averages were one point higher for students who made six or more visits in one semester than students who used the center less frequently. In the 1998–1999 academic year, 19,233 visits were made by a total of 2,936 students (mean 6.6 visits per student), in both developmental education and college-credit courses.

The center was seen as vital to the education of NESCC students and although the administration ensured funding, the state was not as supportive:

> Consequently dollars have to come from other programs, and as an open-enrolled institution, we spend an inordinate amount of money on remediation [and] our [learning center]. I think I probably have about eight full-time people dedicated to that. And if I didn't do that, I don't know what would happen to some of these youngsters coming from inner-city schools. (Administrator, NESCC)

In addition to the learning assistance center, there were other, smaller support centers connected with the academic departments, some of which relied on tutors provided by the main learning center:

> Everybody wants a little space and everybody wants a little study center, and so chemistry has a little area and physics has a little area and early childhood has a little study center . . . [but] they don't have staffing, it's not staffed. There are faculty during their office hours or it's open and they can have the CDs and maybe they have a couple computers and the software that comes with their textbook, but it's not staffed. So what I'm doing is providing staff for these sites and . . . then traffic is down at the [main learning center] and there's pressure. I say you can't measure our success on numbers any more when we're sending people out all over. I don't want to compete with those areas. . . . And yet I have three full-time specialists sitting down there, sometimes waiting for business, you know, so I'm not sure. (Administrator, NESCC)

There were attempts to centralize the college's learning assistance services over the years. The interviewee just quoted also cited Boylan's (2002) work in support of the centralization of support services:

> [In] my opinion [the college] hasn't made up its mind whether it's better to offer support services in a centralized or decentralized manner, and although I can tell them that the research says centralized support services are more effective, and I can show them everything that I learned at Kellogg, you know, the Exxon Study and all that, supports that. [At NESCC], we're kind of between. Some years I think that we're centralizing, and then all of a sudden there are little study centers all over campus. (Administrator, NESCC)

The center had some spare capacity, and English and math specialists visited the English and math department meetings to recruit students for tutoring. Also, the college promoted the learning center's services through a weekly campus-wide "tutorial" event.

Northeast Rural Community College (NERCC)

NERCC was comprised of a main campus and several satellite sites. There was a learning center on the central campus that offered tutoring in reading, writing, and math. Although the satellite campuses served more academically lower-functioning students than the main campus, they have no learning centers and did not provide tutoring. Instructors on the main campus who observed academic difficulties in class could refer students for tutoring, especially older, returning adults. NERCC counted tutoring as a counseling service. The service seemed to be underutilized as students saw it as a punishment:

> I'm finding that a lot of times when the student is asked to come and see us that they're looking at it like being sent to the principal rather than viewing it as a support service or a place of opportunity. And you know truly it is support . . . but they don't understand that to begin with and so that's why they don't really show up. (Counselor, NERCC)

There was a disability specialist on staff in the learning center who advised students and faculty regarding educational accommodations and schedules.

Discussion and Conclusion

Every one of the 15 colleges in the National Field Study sample had at least one learning center, and seven sites had both learning centers and specialized skills labs. These facilities served either as a supplement or alternative to developmental education in preparing students for the academic demands of postsecondary education. Four of the sites had multiple centers with different services, and some of the funding targeted specific populations. All sites offered tutoring, and nine of the colleges also offered computer-assisted instruction. Several sites provided short-duration or self-paced courses, as well as specialized workshops in their learning centers.

Students in both college-credit and developmental education courses availed themselves of the assistance and, in some cases, the learning centers provided a lab component for developmental education. Different segments of the community college population showed different utilization of the services. For example, the heaviest use of learning assistance at SWUCC was by students in college-credit courses, and at MWUCC by low-proficiency English speakers. Demand within skills area also varied. For example, reading assistance was sought mostly by developmental education students at NWSCC and by college-credit students at SWUCC.

In cases where students decline remedial courses or where these classes are ineffective, assistance in learning centers can help fill in gaps in reading, writing, and math skills. Additional research is needed to compare the effectiveness of the learning of skills in developmental education versus learning assistance centers. For example, since students appear to approach tasks differently depending on subject matter (Jones, Reichard, & Mokhtari, 2003), a hypothesis that could be tested is that the generic instruction in developmental education courses may be less effective than the contextualized learning of skills that may occur when students are coached on reading, writing, or math skills while completing specific subject-matter assignments in learning centers or skills labs.

A determination of the outcomes of learning assistance was beyond the scope of the current research. However, NESCC reported that students who paid more than six visits to the learning center had a GPA of a point or more higher than those who paid fewer visits, and NEUCC reported an increase in retention in college English courses when students received learning assistance. This type of correlational information needs to be corroborated with controlled comparisons, for example to rule out the possibility that students with better skills (higher GPA) are more inclined to seek help than those with poorer skills (lower GPA). Similarly, the same students who tend to persevere rather than drop out of courses also may seek learning assistance. Thus, future research needs to determine whether characteristics of students or learning centers are responsible for the outcomes.

A good deal of the learning assistance at the study sites was focused on helping students complete course assignments. There was some concern that in some cases, tutors were providing too much help, leading instructors to question whether the resulting product was really the student's own. Another issue that arose concerned the utilization of learning assistance centers: Six of the sites reported that the services were under-utilized, that there had been a decrease in demand, or that there was a need to recruit participants. Since there appeared to be a proliferation of learning assistance services, future research could determine whether there was any duplication of services among the centers and specialized labs that led to an appearance of under-utilization.

Finally, the extended quote from the tutor at MWUCC suggests a need for professional development. If a portion of students seeking help in learning assistance centers have learning disabilities, orienting tutors to instructional strategies shown to be effective with special-needs populations may be beneficial. In any case, the ubiquity of learning assistance at community colleges reinforces the reputation of these institutions as places that prioritize instruction and care deeply about students.

Notes

1. Although the terms "remediation" and "developmental education" imply different philosophies of instruction, they are used interchangeably in this paper.
2. Fictitious names are used throughout this report to protect anonymity of sites, learning centers within sites, and personnel.
3. The study also investigated state and institutional policies for assessment and remedial placement, and the nature of developmental education in the study sites. The findings are reported in Perin (2003); and Perin & Charron (forthcoming).
4. Many of the sites also had learning resource centers from which students could borrow ancillary materials to support course work. Learning resource centers are different from learning assistance centers, and are beyond the scope of the current study.

References

Boylan, H. R. (2002). *What works: Research-based best practices in developmental education.* Boone, NC: Continuous Quality Improvement Network with the National Center for Developmental Education, Appalachian State University.

Boylan, H., Bliss, L., & Bonham, B. (1997). Program components and their relationship to student performance. *Journal of Developmental Education, 20*(3), 2–9.

Burley, H., Butner, B., & Cejda, B. (2001). Dropout and stopout patterns among developmental education students in Texas community colleges. *Community College Journal of Research and Practice, 25,* 767–782.

Casazza, M. E. (1999, Fall). Who are we and where did we come from? *Journal of Developmental Education, 23*(1), 6–8, 10, 12.

Crowe, E. (1998, September). Statewide remedial education policies: State strategies that support successful student transitions from secondary to postsecondary education. Technical report. Denver, CO: State Higher Education Executive Officers.

Foote, E. (1999, July–August). Remedial education policies in community colleges (ERIC report). *Community College Journal of Research and Practice, 23*(5), 539–542.

Grubb, W. N., and Associates. (1999). Honored but invisible: An inside look at teaching in community colleges. New York: Routledge.

Hafer, G. R. (2001). Ideas in practice: Supplemental instruction in freshman composition. *Journal of Developmental Education, 24,* 30–37.

Howard, J., & Obetz, W. S. (1996). Using the NALS to characterize the literacy of community college graduates. *Journal of Adolescent and Adult Literacy, 39*(6), 462–467.

Jenkins, D. & Boswell, K. (2002). State policies on community college remedial education: Findings from a national survey. Technical report no. CC-0201. Denver, CO: Education Commission of the States, Center for Community College Policy. Available: www.ecs.org

Johnson, L. F. (1996). Developmental performance as a predictor of academic success in entry-level mathematics. *Community College Journal of Research and Practice, 20,* 333–344.

Jones, C., Reichard, C., & Mokhtari, K. (2003). Are students' learning styles discipline-specific? *Community College Journal of Research and Practice, 27*, 363–375.

Koski, W. S., & Levin, H. M. (1998, March). Replacing remediation with acceleration in higher education: Preliminary report on literature review and initial findings. Draft Document. Stanford University, CA: National Center for Postsecondary Improvement.

Lester, N., Bertram, C., Erickson, G., Lee, E., Tchako, A., Wiggins, K. D., & Wilson, J. (2003). Writing across the curriculum: A college snapshot. *Urban Education, 38*, 5–34.

Maxwell, W., Hagedorn, L. S., Cypers, S., Moon, H. S., Brocato, P., Wahl, K., & Prather, G. (2003). Community and diversity in urban community colleges: Coursetaking among entering students. *Community College Review, 30*(4), 21–46.

McCabe, R. H., & Day, P. R., Jr. (Eds.) (1998). *Developmental education: A twenty-first century social and economic imperative.* Mission Viejo, CA: League for Innovation in the Community College.

Merriam, S. B. (1988). *Case study research in education: A qualitative approach.* San Francisco: Jossey-Bass.

Miles, M., & Huberman, M. (1994). *Qualitative data analysis* (2nd ed). Thousand Oaks, CA: Sage.

O'Banion, T. (1997). *A learning college for the 21st century.* Washington, DC: Oryx Press.

Patton, M. Q. (1990). *Qualitative evaluation and research methods* (2nd ed). Newbury Park, CA: Sage.

Perin, D. (2003, June). Is access winning over standards? A case study of community college remedial policy. Accepted for publication pending revisions.

Perin, D., & Charron, K. (2006). Lights just click on every day. In T. Bailey, & V. S. Morest (Eds.), *Defending the community college equity agenda* (pp. 155–194). Baltimore: The Johns Hopkins University Press.

Raftery, S., & VanWagoner, R. (2002). Using learning communities to develop basic skills. Phoenix, AZ: League for Innovation in the Community College. Available: www.league.org/publication/abstracts/learning/lelabs0902.htm

Roueche, J. E., Ely, E. E, & Roueche, S. D. (2001). *In pursuit of excellence: The Community College of Denver.* Washington, DC: Community College Press.

Roueche, J. E., & Roueche, S. D. (1999). *High stakes, high performance: Making remedial education work.* Washington, DC: Community College Press.

Shults, C. (2000, May). Institutional policies and practices in remedial education: A national study of community colleges. Technical report. Washington, DC: American Association of Community Colleges.

Stake, R. (1995). *The art of case study research.* Thousand Oaks, CA: Sage.

Stern, S. (2001, August). Learning assistance centers: Helping students through. ERIC Digest ED 455901. Los Angeles, CA: ERIC Clearinghouse for Community Colleges. Available: www.ed.gov/databases/ERIC_Digests/ed455901.htm

Yin, Robert K. (1994). *Case study research: Design and methods* (2nd ed). Thousand Oaks, CA: Sage.

Opening Doors to Student Success: A Synthesis of Findings from an Evaluation at Six Community Colleges

Susan Scrivener and Erin Coghlan

This study from MDRC, a nonprofit nonpartisan education and social policy research organization, is the first to provide rigorous scientific evidence supporting the efficacy of a range of interventions designed to improve student retention and completion. Among the relevant interventions discussed are reform of instructional techniques and enhancement of various student support services. In addition, Scrivener and Coghlan make recommendations to both policy makers and practitioners for improving student performance.

In today's economy, having a postsecondary credential means better jobs and wages. Community colleges, with their open access policies and low tuition, are an important pathway into postsecondary education for nearly half of all U.S. undergraduates. Yet only one-third of all students who enter these institutions with the intent to earn a degree or certificate actually meet this goal within six years. The reasons for this are many, including that community college students are typically underprepared for college-level work, face competing priorities outside of school, and lack adequate financial resources. Recent cuts to higher education spending along with insufficient financial aid and advising at colleges only add to the problem. Ultimately, these factors contribute to unacceptably low persistence and completion rates.

In response to these issues, MDRC launched the Opening Doors Demonstration in 2003—the first large-scale random assignment study in a community college setting. (Random assignment is widely recognized as the "gold standard" of program evaluation.) The demonstration pursued promising strategies that emerged from focus groups with low-income students, discussions with college administrators, and an extensive literature review. Partnering with six community colleges across the country, MDRC helped develop and evaluate four distinct programs based on the following approaches: financial incentives, reforms in instructional practices, and enhancements in student services. Colleges were encouraged to focus on one strategy but to think creatively about combining elements of the other strategies to design programs that would help students perform better academically and persist toward degree completion.

Opening Doors provides some of the first rigorous evidence that a range of interventions can, indeed, improve educational outcomes for community college students. The findings spurred some of the colleges to scale up their programs and led to additional large-scale demonstrations to test some of the most promising strategies. More work must be done, however, both to determine whether the early effects can last and to test even bolder reforms. This policy brief describes the different strategies tested, discusses what MDRC has learned from Opening Doors, and offers some suggestions to policymakers and practitioners for moving forward.

The Opening Doors Programs and Their Effects on Students

The Opening Doors Demonstration tested four distinct programs targeting four different groups of community college students. The initial positive findings provide a good starting point for building even better programs in the future: Financial incentives tied to academic performance helped students do better and stay in school; learning communities, an instructional reform, improved some academic outcomes for freshmen; and two different enhanced student services programs improved academic outcomes. The programs and their key effects are described below and summarized in Table 1. (For more information on the programs, see the full reports on MDRC's Web site, www.mdrc.org.)

Table 1. Summary of Opening Doors Programs and Effects

	Program	*Description*	*Effects*
Financial Incentives	Performance-Based Scholarship	Up to $1,000 for each of two semesters if students enrolled at least half time and maintained a "C" or better GPA. Counselors monitored students. Targeted low-income parents.	Students more likely to enroll full time, persist in college, and earn more credits.
Instructional Reform	Learning Communities	Program for incoming freshmen, most requiring developmental English. Linked courses; provided enhanced counseling, tutoring, and a text book voucher.	Increased number of courses passed and credits earned, and moved students more quickly through developmental English requirements.
Enhanced Student Services	Enhanced Academic Counseling	Tested enhanced academic counseling and a modest stipend.	Modest impact on registration during second semester and first semester after program ended.
	Enhanced Targeted Services	Program for students on probation linked student success course to Success Center visits.	Increased credits earned and GPA, and moved students off probation.

Financial Incentives

PERFORMANCE-BASED SCHOLARSHIPS IMPROVED STUDENTS'
ACADEMIC OUTCOMES

Inadequate financial aid is a barrier to academic progress and success for many college students. Common criticisms of financial aid include that government aid has not kept up with the rising costs of college attendance and that the various aid programs sometimes fail to direct support to the neediest students. Many students are misinformed about aid that is available to them, and end up working in low-paying jobs, detracting from their focus to complete their degree. Some experts say that the financial aid system does not do enough to promote high academic achievement, persistence, or completion.

Focusing on these issues, two colleges in the New Orleans area tested a program as part of the Opening Doors Demonstration that offered a *performance-based scholarship* in which students received money only if they met certain academic benchmarks. Students could choose to spend the funds on non-tuition expenses; this flexibility was an important feature and something that the program was explicitly designed to test. This model attempts to help address financial needs while providing an incentive for students to perform well in their courses.

The Louisiana program offered students up to $1,000 for each of two semesters for a total of $2,000. The scholarship was paid in three increments throughout the semester if students enrolled at least half time and maintained a "C" (2.0) or better grade point average (GPA). Program counselors monitored academic performance and disbursed the scholarship checks directly to students. Notably, the scholarships were paid in addition to federal Pell Grants and other financial aid. Because the program was funded with state welfare funds, eligibility was limited to low-income parents (though they did not need to be on welfare). The research sample was mostly African-American single mothers. Students in the study's control (or comparison) group in Louisiana could not receive the Opening Doors scholarship, but they had access to standard financial aid and the colleges' standard counseling.

The evaluation found that tying financial aid to academic performance can generate large positive effects—some of the largest MDRC has found in its higher education studies. The program substantially improved students' academic outcomes, and the positive effects continued through the third and fourth semesters of the study, when most students were no longer eligible for the scholarship. Students in the study's program group were more likely to attend college full time. They also earned better grades and more credits. As Figure 1 shows, the program group students registered at higher rates than the control group students throughout the study. For example, during the second program semester, the registration rate among students in the program group was 57 percent, compared with 39 percent of the students

Figure 1. Louisiana Performance-Based Scholarships (*Program Helped Keep More Students in School, Even After Program Ended*)

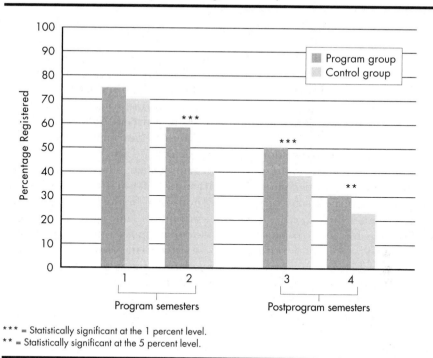

*** = Statistically significant at the 1 percent level.
** = Statistically significant at the 5 percent level.

in the control group—a statistically significant difference (meaning that the difference was not likely a result of chance). Making scholarship payments contingent on academic benchmarks succeeded on two important fronts: Low-income students received additional financial assistance *and* improved their academic performance.

Just after the Opening Doors program ended, Hurricane Katrina struck the Gulf Coast region; the colleges involved in the study shut down temporarily, and many students in the study moved away. As a result, MDRC was not able to study the long-term impacts of the program. However, the very promising findings from Louisiana spurred MDRC to launch the Performance-Based Scholarship Demonstration to test variations of the program.

Instructional Reforms

LEARNING COMMUNITIES PROVIDED INITIAL BOOST FOR FRESHMEN

Learning communities are operated by colleges across the nation to promote students' involvement and persistence in school. Learning communities typically place groups of students in two or more linked courses, often with mutually reinforcing themes and assignments. They seek to build peer relationships, intensify connections to faculty, and deepen understanding of coursework.

Learning communities commonly target students in developmental (or remedial) education, who enter community colleges underprepared for college-level work. Recent data indicate that 42 percent of community college freshmen enroll in at least one developmental reading, writing, or math course, designed to bring students' basic skills to college-level standards. Many developmental students drop out of those classes and only a minority ever receive a degree. Strategies to help developmental students succeed are critical in the overall effort to increase graduation rates.

Kingsborough Community College in Brooklyn, New York, launched a learning community for incoming freshmen. Groups of up to 25 students took three classes together during their first semester: an English class; a standard college course, such as health or psychology; and a student success course that covered topics such as time management, study skills, and college rules. Students' English classes were based on their proficiency: about 7 of every 10 students in the program took developmental English, and the rest took college-level English. Most learning community instructors met regularly to coordinate assignments and discuss student progress. The program provided enhanced academic counseling, tutoring, and a voucher for text books. Students in the study's control group could not participate in the learning community but had access to the college's standard courses and services. The students in the study were young (mostly 17 to 20 years old) and diverse in terms of race and ethnicity.

MDRC tracked students' outcomes for two years. The learning communities provided an initial boost for students, but most of the effects diminished over time. During the first semester, program group students passed more courses and earned more credits than control group students. They also moved more quickly through developmental English requirements: That semester, more program group members took and passed the English skills assessment tests that are required for graduation or transfer. Notably, the control group members had not "caught up" in terms of taking and passing these tests two years later. Program group students felt more integrated at school and more engaged in their courses and with their instructors and fellow students. Despite this improvement in performance, the program did not have an immediate effect on students' persistence in college. There was some indication, however, that program group students were more likely to be enrolled in college at the end of the two-year study period. MDRC is still following the Kingsborough students in order to examine their longer-term persistence and graduation and is managing the Learning Communities Demonstration to see whether other types of learning community programs will be effective.

Encouraged by the early findings from the study, Kingsborough scaled up its learning communities program. Today, the Opening Doors learning communities serve the vast majority of incoming freshmen at the college.

Enhanced Student Services

REFORMS CAN HELP IMPROVE STUDENTS' OUTCOMES

Student services—such as academic counseling, career counseling, tutoring, study skills training, and personal counseling—help students navigate through school and can play a critical role in helping them succeed. Unfortunately, resources for these services at community colleges are somewhat limited. For example, student-to-counselor ratios are often more than 1,000 to 1, restricting the assistance students receive. In the Opening Doors Demonstration, colleges tested two different enhanced student services programs intended to give more intensive and personalized assistance to students: one program provided enhanced academic counseling for students early in their college career, and another provided an array of enhanced services for students on academic probation.

ENHANCED ACADEMIC COUNSELING HAD MODEST SHORT-TERM EFFECTS. Two colleges in northern Ohio—Lorain County Community College and Owens Community College—ran an enhanced academic counseling program. Students in the program group at the colleges were assigned to one of a team of counselors, with whom they were expected to meet at least two times per semester for two semesters to discuss academic progress and resolve any issues that might affect their schooling. Each counselor worked with far fewer students than the regular college counselors—an average of fewer than 160 students, compared with more than 1,000 for the regular counselors. This facilitated more frequent, intensive, and personal contact. Students were also eligible for a $150 stipend for two semesters (totaling $300). The stipend, paid in two increments after meetings with a counselor, was designed to be an incentive to draw students into counseling. Students in the control group received standard college services and no Opening Doors stipend. The Ohio colleges targeted low-income students who were new to the college or who were continuing and had completed fewer than 13 credits. The students were "nontraditional"—most were in their mid-twenties, and many were working and had children.

MDRC tracked students' outcomes for three years. The enhanced academic counseling program generated modest positive effects that dissipated once the program ended. Specifically, compared with the control group, a somewhat higher proportion of the program group returned to school the second semester and they earned more credits.

Program group members were also slightly more likely to register for school during the first semester after the program ended. Beyond that point, the program did not meaningfully affect students' outcomes.

TARGETED SERVICES HELPED STUDENTS MOVE OFF ACADEMIC PROBATION. Chaffey College, about 40 miles east of Los Angeles, operated a program that provided enhanced student services to probationary students to help them do better in their classes and get off probation. Many community college students end up on academic probation because of poor grades or inadequate academic progress. When Chaffey's program began, about one of every five students at the college was on probation. Probation can prevent students from getting financial aid and can eventually lead to dismissal from college. Little is known about how to help probationary students get back on track and increase their chances of completing their studies.

Chaffey's Opening Doors program offered a student success course, taught by a college counselor, that covered topics such as personal motivation, time management, study skills, and college expectations. Students were expected to meet with their instructors outside of class for academic counseling and to visit the college's *Success Centers*, which provide supplementary individualized or group instruction in reading, writing, and math. Students in the control group at Chaffey were not targeted for any special services but had access to the college's standard student services and courses. Students in the study were relatively "traditional"—most were young, unmarried, and did not have any children.

Chaffey ran two versions of the program. The original version of the program lasted one semester and was voluntary. Only about half of the students in the study's program group enrolled in the student success course, and the program did not have any meaningful effect on students' academic outcomes. College administrators and staff then reformed the program, extending the student success course to two semesters. Program group students were told that they were *required* to attend the course, and about three-fourths did so. The requirement to participate was important in that it got students to take part in the program who would not have volunteered for services. Over two semesters, the revised program increased students' cumulative GPAs and, as Figure 2 shows, almost doubled the proportion that moved off probation. The program did not, however, increase persistence during the follow-up period. MDRC is still tracking students in order to look at the longer-term effects of the revised program.

After seeing the promising results from the study, Chaffey institutionalized the revised version of the program. The college has since provided targeted enhanced services to thousands of probationary students. Chaffey also developed a version of the program for new students identified through the college's assessment process as being at risk of experiencing difficulties.

Figure 2. Chaffey Enhanced Services (*Program Almost Doubled Proportion of Students Who Moved Off Probation Over Two Semesters*)

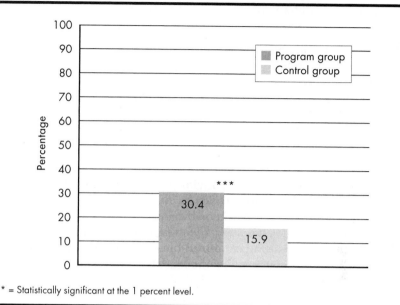

*** = Statistically significant at the 1 percent level.

Lessons from Opening Doors

The Opening Doors Demonstration was the first large-scale random assignment evaluation of areas clearly ripe for reform, and the initial findings provide a good starting point for building reliable knowledge. Although much is still unknown about the right combination of ingredients, the results show that something can be done to improve the dismal statistics on persistence and student success at many community colleges. The findings from Opening Doors suggest the following lessons:

- **Reforms in higher education practices and policies can help students succeed**—even nontraditional students. When MDRC's demonstration began, this was an open question. Encouragingly, all of the programs tested yielded at least some positive changes for students. It is notable that the programs helped groups that were facing substantial challenges: students in developmental education and probationary students as well as "nontraditional" students, including low-income parents and working adults.

- **Short-term enhancements can generate short-term effects but are not likely to generate longer-term gains.** The programs tested in Opening Doors lasted one or two semesters, and, for the most part, the positive effects for students dissipated after the enhancements ended. (The notable exception is the performance-based scholarship program in Louisiana.) This suggests that short-term interventions will likely not act as an "inoculation" against the challenges facing many community college students.

- **Single-focus, "light-touch" student service interventions can make a difference for students but may not be robust enough to substantially improve outcomes.** The enhanced academic counseling program in Ohio represents the "lightest touch" of the interventions tested as part of Opening Doors. The other programs offered more program components, more intensive services, or both, and generated more substantial changes in students' outcomes.

- **Financial incentives can influence students' behavior.** Much research has shown that financial work incentives can increase employment, and Opening Doors provides evidence that financial incentives can be effective in higher education settings, too. The performance-based scholarship in Louisiana was the largest financial incentive in Opening Doors, and it substantially improved students' academic outcomes. The modest stipend in Ohio served as an incentive to get students to see their counselors, and program group students did in fact complete more counselor visits than students in the study's control group. It's important to note that the financial incentives were given directly to students, who had the flexibility to spend the funds on non-tuition expenses.

- **Requirements can increase participation and improve student outcomes.** Chaffey's original program for probationary students was voluntary and had low participation rates and no meaningful effects on student outcomes. The revised program, in which students were told that the program was mandatory, generated much higher participation rates and moved many students off probation. Kingsborough's program, which moved students more quickly through developmental English, required most students to take a developmental English course as part of the learning community. The findings from these two sites suggest that requirements can play an important role in increasing students' engagement and success.

The Opening Doors Demonstration was only a first step in rigorously evaluating select strategies in community colleges, and much work remains to find programmatic solutions that will markedly improve students' persistence and graduation rates.

Looking Forward

Rates of persistence and graduation in community colleges remain stubbornly low, but the current national focus on increasing these rates is encouraging. The Obama Administration, state governments, higher education institutions, and foundations have made a strong push to increase the community college graduation rate. National movements, such as Achieving the Dream, and government agencies are encouraging colleges to use data on student outcomes to make better-informed institutional and programming decisions. And community colleges themselves are willing partners in developing and testing promising practices.

The Opening Doors Demonstration provides encouraging evidence that changes in community college practices can lead to improvements in student outcomes. Taken together, however, the studies also suggest that more work needs to be done to identify effective strategies that will lead to significant increases in college completion rates. MDRC is continuing to follow students in two of the Opening Doors colleges (Kingsborough and Chaffey) to understand their long-term trajectories and identify how many ultimately earn degrees. MDRC is also doing additional research on learning communities and performance-based scholarships to learn how these important interventions work in different settings and with other groups of students. Finally, MDRC is conducting research on the cost of the Kingsborough learning communities program, some other learning communities, Chaffey's enhanced services, and performance-based scholarships to help guide policymakers and college administrators who may want to adopt these reforms.

Although the results from Opening Doors are encouraging, the effects for students were for the most part modest and they often diminished once the services ended. Programs that last longer, are more comprehensive and multifaceted, or substantially change the way colleges do business may have more potential to markedly improve students' outcomes and lead to increased persistence and graduation. Some promising areas for exploration include:

- **New reforms in financial aid.** Financial aid remains a barrier for many community college students. Promising reforms include providing better information to students about financial aid, simplifying the application process, and restructuring the way aid is delivered so that it rewards student progress and helps students balance school and outside work obligations. Providing more aid and providing flexible aid that can be used on non-tuition expenses may substantially help low-income students who struggle to cover their expenses and end up dropping out of school. Finally, aid can be used to strengthen connections between college and careers, such as providing work-study jobs in students' fields of study.

- **Innovations in developmental education.** Much work is left to be done in improving developmental education. Contextualized approaches that integrate basic English and math instruction with occupational skills or subject matter that students want to learn — as Washington State is doing with its I-BEST program — show promise. Another idea is to provide instruction in short, focused modules, rather than in semester-long classes. Programs that accelerate students' progression through a sequence of developmental courses — getting them more quickly to credit-bearing classes — are promising reforms. Other innovations include reforming the skills assessment and placement of students in developmental education to better identify their true skills and needs.

- **Initiatives that aim to reduce the number of students who require developmental education.** Some states and colleges are developing interventions to identify and address problems of low basic skills before students even get to college. Early assessment programs, for example, test the skills of high school students with the same assessment instruments used at college entry. Students who are underprepared can strengthen their skills *before* they begin college. Dual enrollment or early college programs allow high school students to enroll in college courses and earn college credits. And summer bridge programs provide instruction during the weeks before college begins in the fall.

While building on promising programs and exploring new innovations, it is important that colleges continue to enhance their collection and analysis of student data. Through funding and policy reforms, state governments can incentivize innovation and reward colleges for improving student success. Many states have already begun to tie part of colleges' funding to student outcomes, including graduation rates and intermediate outcomes like moving from developmental-level to college-level courses. Government, foundations, and other organizations can support the expansion of practices already proven to be effective both through funding and by providing information on how to implement specific strategies.

The U.S. economy depends on a skilled, educated workforce. The nation's community colleges are central in preparing this workforce, but there is a crisis in completion rates at these institutions. According to the Georgetown University Center on Education and the Workforce, the U.S. economy will have 22 million new jobs for college-educated workers by 2018; if we continue at our current pace, we will be 3 million workers short of filling this capacity. The Opening Doors Demonstration offers a good start to building reliable evidence about what works to improve academic outcomes, but much more needs to be done to ensure that the right reforms are implemented at scale to open doors to better jobs and success for all students.

Referral, Enrollment, and Completion in Developmental Education Sequences in Community Colleges

Thomas Bailey, Dong Wook Jeong, and Sung-Woo Cho

This article is the first to rigorously study whether students actually take the entire developmental course sequence into which they place. Bailey, Jeong, and Cho find that many developmental students never complete their sequences, often because they did not register for all the courses required. The findings of this report have important ramifications for academic advisors, counselors, and mentors at colleges and universities.

D evelopmental education is designed to provide students who enter college with weak academic skills the opportunity to strengthen those skills enough to prepare them for college-level coursework.[1] The concept is simple enough—students who arrive unprepared for college are provided instruction to bring them up to an adequate level. But in practice, developmental education is complex and confusing. To begin with, experts do not agree on the meaning of being "college ready." Policies and regulations governing assessment, placement, pedagogy, staffing, completion, and eligibility for enrollment in college-level credit-bearing courses vary from state to state, college to college, and program to program. The developmental education process is confusing enough simply to describe, yet from the point of view of the student, especially the student with particularly weak academic skills who has not had much previous success in school, it must appear as a bewildering set of unanticipated obstacles involving several assessments, classes in more than one subject area, and sequences of courses that may require two, three, or more semesters of study before a student (often a high school graduate) is judged prepared for college-level work.

The policy deliberation and especially the research about developmental education give scant attention to this confusion and complexity. Discussions typically assume that the state of being "college ready" is well-defined, and they elide the distinction between students who need remediation and those who actually enroll in developmental courses. What is more, developmental education is often discussed without acknowledgment of the extensive diversity of services that bear that label. Any comprehensive understanding of developmental education and any successful strategy to improve its effectiveness cannot be built on such a simplistic view.

In this article, we broaden the discussion of developmental education by moving beyond consideration of the developmental course and focusing attention instead on the developmental *sequence*. In most colleges, students are, upon initial enrollment, assigned to different levels of developmental education on the basis of performance on placement tests.[2] Students with greater academic deficiencies are often referred to a sequence of two or more courses designed to prepare students in a step-by-step fashion for the first college-level course. For example, those with the greatest need for developmental math may be expected to enroll in and pass pre-collegiate math or arithmetic, basic algebra, and intermediate algebra, in order to prepare them for college-level algebra. We define the "sequence" as a process that begins with initial assessment and referral to remediation and ends with completion of the highest level developmental course—the course that in principle completes the student's preparation for college-level studies. Although a majority of students do proceed (or fail to proceed) through their sequences in order, some students skip steps and others enroll in lower level courses than the ones to which they were referred, so the actual pattern of student participation is even more complicated than the structure of courses suggests. (We will discuss this in more detail later.) At times we extend the notion of "sequence" into the first-level college course in the relevant subject area, since in the end the short-term purpose of remediation is to prepare the student to be successful in that first college-level course.

We examine the relationship between referral to developmental education and actual enrollment, and we track students as they progress or fail to progress through their referred sequences of remedial courses, analyzing the points at which they exit those sequences. We also analyze the demographic and institutional characteristics that are related to the completion of sequences and exits at different points along them.

We carry out this analysis using data collected as part of the Achieving the Dream: Community Colleges Count initiative, a multi-state, multi-institution initiative designed to improve outcomes for community college students. The sample includes over 250,000 students from 57 colleges in seven states. The sample is not representative of all community college students, so we check our results against an analysis using the National Education Longitudinal Study of 1988 (henceforth, NELS:88).[3] Results of that analysis are consistent with results derived from the Achieving the Dream database.

An exploration of the distinction between *the course* and *the sequence* reveals some startling conclusions. While the majority of individual course enrollments do result in a course completion, between 33 and 46 percent of students, depending on the subject area, referred to developmental education actually complete their entire developmental sequence. And between 60 and 70 percent of students who fail to complete the sequence to which they were referred do so even while having passed all of the developmental courses in which they enrolled.

This collection of articles is dedicated to Henry Levin and our article relates particularly to his influential Accelerated Schools Project (ASP). Remediation in college is necessary because students arrive at the end of high school without adequate academic skills. The ASP was of course designed to avoid just this type of problem. Many of the students who arrive at community college with weak academic skills fell behind their classmates early in elementary school. ASP is a strategy to strengthen the academic skills of elementary and secondary students more effectively than traditional approaches to "remediation." Thus widespread use of ASP would reduce the need for developmental education in college. Moreover, we will argue that the ASP approach makes sense for remediation at the postsecondary level as well.

The remainder of this paper is organized in the following manner: in Section 2 we provide some general background on the characteristics and outcomes of remediation; in Section 3 we describe the Achieving the Dream and the NELS:88 databases; Section 4 presents the results of the analyses on student placement and progression in developmental education; Section 5 shows the results of multivariate analyses of the student and college characteristics that are related to an individual's likelihood of progressing through developmental education; Section 6 summarizes the results and presents conclusions and recommendations.

Developmental Education Basics

More than one half of community college students enroll in at least one developmental education course during their tenure in college. In the National Postsecondary Student Aid Study of 2003–04 (NPSAS:04), 43 percent of first- and second-year students enrolled in public two-year colleges took at least one remedial course during that year (Horn & Nevill, 2006). Longitudinal data that allow a measure for the incidence of developmental education over multiple years of enrollment show even higher levels of enrollment. Attewell, Lavin, Domina, and Levey (p. 153 in this book) found that in the NELS:88 sample, 58 percent of community college students took at least one remedial course, 44 percent took between one and three remedial courses, and 14 percent took more than three such courses. In the Achieving the Dream database, which will be described in detail below, about 59 percent of the sample enrolled in at least one developmental course.

Developmental programs absorb sizable public resources. More than ten years ago, Breneman and Haarlow (1998) estimated that remediation cost more than one billion dollars a year. A more recent study calculated the annual cost of remediation at $1.9–2.3 billion dollars at community colleges and another $500 million at four-year colleges (Strong American Schools, 2008). State reports cite expenditures in the tens of millions of dollars (Arkansas Department of Higher Education, n.d.; Florida Office of Program Policy Analysis and Government Accountability, 2006; Ohio Board of Regents, 2006).

The costs of remediation to the taxpayer are substantial, but the financial, psychological, and opportunity costs borne by the students themselves may be even more significant. While they are enrolled in remediation, students accumulate debt, spend time and money, and bear the opportunity cost of lost earnings. In some states, they deplete their eligibility for financial aid. Moreover, many students referred to developmental classes, most of whom are high school graduates, are surprised and discouraged when they learn that they must delay their college education and in effect return to high school. A recent survey of remedial students found that a majority believed that they were prepared for college (Strong American Schools, 2008). This can cause students to become frustrated and to give up and leave college (Deil-Amen & Rosenbaum, 2002; Rosenbaum, 2001). Many students referred to remediation try to avoid it by using loopholes and exceptions that can be found in many regulations and guidelines (Perin & Charron, 2006).

Although remediation has high costs, clearly some provision must be made for students who enter college unprepared. Proponents argue that it can be an effective tool to improve access to higher education, particularly for underprivileged populations (McCabe, 2006), while others argue that the costs of remediation, for both society and student, outweigh the benefits. The controversy about remediation has prompted some research on the effectiveness of remedial programs in preparing students for college-level courses, but, given the size and significance of the developmental education function, that research is surprisingly sparse. Some descriptive studies have compared different approaches to remediation (Boylan, 2002). But only a handful of studies have compared the success of students who enroll in developmental courses to the success of similar students who enroll directly in college courses. Bettinger and Long (2005) used different remediation assignment cutoff scores among community colleges in Ohio to compare similar students who were and were not referred to developmental education to measure the effect of the remedial instruction. They used the distance from the student's home to the college as an instrument. Their sample was restricted to students who had taken the SAT or ACT. They found that students placed in math remediation were 15 percent more likely to transfer to a four-year college and took ten more credit hours than similar students not placed in remediation. They found no positive effect for reading developmental placement. Calcagno and Long (2008) and Martorell and McFarlin (2007) analyzed the effects of remediation on subsequent outcomes in Florida and Texas, respectively, where statewide remedial assignment cutoff scores allowed regression discontinuity analyses. These studies find no positive effect of remediation on college credit accumulation, completion, or degree attainment. Calcagno and Long found a small positive effect on year-to-year persistence in Florida, but Martorell and McFarlin found no effect on any outcome variable. The Florida and Texas studies in particular provide reliable but discouraging results; nevertheless, these results are only relevant to students scoring near the remediation assignment cutoff scores. In terms of the concept of a sequence, these are the students referred to developmental classes only one level below college-level.[4]

What accounts for these discouraging results? Certainly one fundamental problem is that most students referred to remediation, even those referred to only one level below college-level, do not complete their sequences. In the rest of this article, we analyze the patterns and determinants of that problem.

Achieving the Dream Initiative: Data Description

Achieving the Dream: Community Colleges Count is a multiyear, national initiative designed to improve outcomes for community college students. As of early 2009, 19 funders and over 80 colleges in 15 states participated in the initiative. One of its most important goals is helping participating colleges and state agencies to build "a culture of evidence"—to gather, analyze, and make better use of data to foster fundamental change in the education practices and operations of community colleges for the purpose of improving student outcomes. The Achieving the Dream initiative collects longitudinal records for all first-time credential-seeking students in specified cohorts at all of the colleges participating in the initiative, including data on cohorts starting two years before the college entered the initiative. These cohorts will be tracked for the life of the initiative (at least six years for participating colleges) and possibly beyond. The dataset includes student demographics, enrollment information, the number of credits accumulated, and the receipt of any degrees or certificates. It also includes detailed information on referral to developmental education; enrollment and completion of remedial courses in reading, writing, and mathematics; and enrollment and completion of "gatekeeper" courses—the first college-level courses corresponding to the developmental subject fields.[5] The initiative started in 2004 with five participating states: Florida, New Mexico, North Carolina, Texas, and Virginia. Twenty-seven colleges were chosen from those states. Each had student populations that were at least 38 percent Pell Grant recipients or 54 percent African American, Hispanic, or Native American. In 2005 and 2006, 31 colleges from Connecticut, Ohio, Pennsylvania, Washington, and Texas joined the initiative.[6] Although subsequently 26 colleges in eight states joined the initiative, we use data only from those who joined in 2004, 2005, or 2006, because we have at least three years of post-enrollment data on students from those colleges.

Table 1 describes institutional characteristics of 57 Achieving the Dream colleges in fall 2004.[7] We retrieved the data from the Integrated Postsecondary Education Data System (IPEDS) to compare Achieving the Dream colleges with national and state public two-year institutions. The first column represents national public two-year colleges, the second column represents public two-year colleges in Achieving the Dream states, and the third represents the colleges included in

Table 1. Characteristics of Achieving the Dream Colleges

Variables	Public two-year (Nation)	Public two-year (Achieving the Dream states[a])	Achieving the Dream colleges[b]
Percent of Black students	14.22 (17.02)	14.13 (13.31)	16.56 (11.84)
Percent of Hispanic students	8.54 (13.67)	12.07 (17.07)	22.39 (20.71)
Full-time equivalent enrollments (FTE)	2114.2 (2142.2)	2150.7 (2216.8)	6609.5 (3350.6)
Percent of students receiving federal financial aid	43.94 (18.71)	41.41 (17.34)	38.45 (14.52)
Average amount of federal financial aid received per FTE (in dollars)	2708.2 (637.5)	2646.3 (633.4)	2878.98 (465.61)
Instructional expenditures per FTE (in dollars)	5261.5 (20,987)	5025.6 (12,675)	3339.47 (848.90)
Location			
Urban	39.47%	48.99%	80.94%
Suburban	23.72%	21.14%	14.77%
Rural	36.81%	29.87%	4.29%
Full-time retention rate (fall 2003–fall 2004)	57.73% (13.85)	56.30% (13.56)	57.61% (6.50)
Observations (N)	1169	307	57

Note: Standard deviations for continuous variables are in parentheses.
[a]Achieving the Dream states include Connecticut, Florida, Ohio, New Mexico, North Carolina, Pennsylvania, Texas, Virginia, and Washington.
[b]For the purpose of comparison, we excluded three four-year institutions from the Achieving the Dream colleges.

the sample. Compared to the national and state samples, Achieving the Dream colleges serve substantially higher proportions of African American and Hispanic students. Achieving the Dream colleges also enroll a larger number of students per college, and they make noticeably smaller instructional expenditures per full-time equivalent enrollment (FTE). They are also more likely to be located in urban areas. Thus the Achieving the Dream sample more closely represents an urban, low-income, and minority student population than do community colleges in the country as a whole. The sample therefore characterizes an important sub-group of community colleges, but when possible we check our results against the national NELS:88 sample.

The Achieving the Dream database we used for this study was derived from 256,672 first-time credential-seeking students who began their enrollment in fall 2003 to fall 2004 in 57 colleges that provided detailed information on developmental education. We followed their enrollments in remediation through the summers of 2006 and 2007 — three academic years. For simplicity, we focused on two common developmental education subjects: math and reading. The database contains information on student gender, race/ethnicity, age at entry, full- or part-time enrollment, major, all remedial courses taken, and the grades earned in those courses. One unique aspect of this dataset, particularly important for our purposes, is that it includes a variable indicating whether students were referred to developmental education and, for those who were referred, the level to which they were referred.[8]

Student Progression through Developmental Education

Student Placement in Developmental Education

Most Achieving the Dream colleges use a placement test and/or academic records to place beginning students into developmental education. Based on their performance on the test/records, many individuals are referred to a sequence of developmental courses. The Achieving the Dream database classifies all beginning students into four groups for each type of developmental education: students referred to (1) no developmental education, (2) developmental education one level below the entry-level college course (henceforth we will refer to this as Level I), (3) two levels below (henceforth Level II), and (4) three or more levels below (henceforth Level III). Some students are thus expected to finish three or more developmental courses before enrolling in college-level classes. Fifty-nine percent of students were referred to developmental math: 24 percent to Level I, 16 percent to Level II, and 19 percent to Level III. Far fewer students — only 33 percent — were referred to reading remediation: 23 percent, 7 percent, and 3 percent into the respective three levels.[9]

Different colleges provide different numbers of levels of developmental education. In fall 2000, public two-year colleges reported to offer, on average, 3.6 remedial courses in math while offering 2.7 courses in reading. Among the 53 Achieving the Dream colleges in the sample that provided information on remedial math offerings, 35 offer three or more levels of remedial math, 9 offer two levels, and 9 offer one level. Among the 51 such colleges that provided information on remedial reading offerings, 20 offer three or more levels of remedial reading, 20 offer two levels, and 11 offer one level (see Table 2).

Student Progression Through Developmental Education

In colleges with multiple levels of developmental education, in principle, only those who passed the course into which they were originally referred can pursue a higher level developmental course. In reality,

Table 2. Developmental Course Offerings and Student Referrals of Achieving the Dream Colleges

| Developmental course offerings | Number of colleges | Level of developmental education referral | | | | Number of students (N) |
		3+ levels below	2 levels below	1 level below	Not referred	
Math						
One level	9			51%	49%	29,714
Two levels	9		30%	17%	53%	22,381
Three or more levels	35	33%	18%	16%	33%	89,495
Reading						
One level	11			39%	61%	22,361
Two levels	20		11%	20%	69%	28,015
Three or more levels	20	8%	9%	17%	66%	27,773

Note: Among 57 Achieving the Dream colleges, four and six provided no information on developmental education in math and reading, respectively.

many students enroll in higher and even lower level courses than those to which they are referred or skip courses in the sequence. Some referred students skip remediation entirely and enroll directly in the first college-level course in the relevant subject area.

Overall, 46 percent of students referred to reading remediation and 33 percent of those referred to math remediation completed their sequence of developmental education. Students who passed the highest level developmental course in their referred sequence are defined as sequence completers (see Table 3). Not surprisingly, developmental education completion rates are negatively related to the number of levels to which a student is referred. Of those students in our Achieving the Dream sample who were referred to Level I remediation (Table 3), 45 percent and 50 percent completed developmental math and reading, respectively.[10] The corresponding figures are 17 percent and 29 percent for those referred to Level III.

Many of the students who failed to complete their remediation sequence did so because they never even enrolled in a developmental course to begin with. Just under one-third of all students referred to remediation in this sample did not enroll in any developmental course in the relevant subject area within three years.

Of those students who did enroll in a remediation course, many— 29 percent of all students referred to math and 16 percent of those referred to reading—exited their sequences after failing or withdrawing from one of their courses. But a substantial number—11 percent for math and 8 percent for reading—exited their sequence never having failed a course. That is, they successfully completed one or more

Table 3. Student Progression among Those Referred
to Developmental Education

| Developmental course referral | Student progression | | | | |
	Never enrolled in developmental education	Did not complete — never failed a course[a]	Did not complete — failed a course	Completed sequence[b]	Total (N)
Math					
Level I	37%	2%	17%	45%	59,551
Level II	24%	13%	32%	32%	38,153
Level III	17%	23%	44%	17%	43,886
Total	27%	11%	29%	33%	141,590
Reading					
Level I	33%	5%	12%	50%	54,341
Level II	21%	13%	24%	42%	16,983
Level III	27%	19%	25%	29%	6,825
Total	30%	8%	16%	46%	78,149

[a] The small percentage of those who were referred to Level I and never failed a course are likely to have enrolled in a lower level of remediation, passed that course, and left the system.
[b] Sequence completion refers to the completion of Level I.

developmental courses and failed to show up for the next course in their sequence. Thus if one combines the number of students who never enrolled with those who exited between courses, more students did not complete their sequence because they did not enroll in the first or a subsequent course than because they failed a course. For example, for reading, 30 percent never enrolled, and 8 percent left between courses, while only 16 percent failed or withdrew from a course.

The goal of developmental education is to prepare students for college-level courses. How did sequence completers fare in those college-level courses? In the Achieving the Dream dataset, the first college-level courses are referred to as gatekeeper courses (see note 5 for a definition). Data displayed in Table 4 indicate that between 50 and 55 percent of sequence completers also completed a gatekeeper course. But to complete the gatekeeper course, students must first enroll and then pass the course. About two thirds of the sequence completers enroll and three quarters of those who enroll pass, so once again, as was the case with developmental education completion, failure to enroll is a greater barrier than course failure or withdrawal.

The high pass rate is encouraging, but developmental education completers are already a selected group of students who have successfully navigated their often complicated sequences. When considered from the beginning of the sequence, only 20 percent of students referred to math remediation and 37 percent of those referred to reading

Table 4. Enrollment and Completion Rates among
Developmental Enrollees

| | Students who enrolled in developmental education | | | | |
| | | | Among developmental education completers | | |
Developmental course referral	Remediation enrollment among those referred	Gatekeeper pass rate among those referred	Gatekeeper pass rate	Gatekeeper enrollment	Pass rate among those who enrolled in gatekeeper
Math					
Level I	76%	27%	48%	61%	78%
Level II	78%	20%	53%	66%	81%
Level III	83%	10%	53%	68%	78%
Total	79%	20%	50%	63%	79%
Reading					
Level I	64%	42%	56%	73%	75%
Level II	78%	29%	52%	68%	75%
Level III	70%	24%	55%	71%	78%
Total	67%	37%	55%	72%	75%

complete a gatekeeper course in the relevant subject area within three years.

As we have seen, many of those referred to developmental education fail to complete a college course because they never even enroll in their first remedial course: between one quarter and one-third of referred students never enroll in developmental education (see Table 3). Table 5 presents data on what happened to those students. These students do not necessarily leave college. In some colleges or states, remediation is not mandatory and in most colleges, students can take courses in subjects for which the remedial course to which they were referred is not a prerequisite.[11] It may be that students, perhaps with the collaboration of some faculty or counselors, simply do not comply with the regulations (Perin & Charron, 2006).

Many students ignored the advice (or instructions) of the placement and referral system and skipped their developmental sequence, enrolling directly in a gatekeeper course in the subject area for which they were presumably in need of remediation (see Table 5). Among those students who never enrolled in remediation, about 17 percent of students referred to math remediation and 45 percent of those referred to reading remediation enrolled directly in a gatekeeper course. These students passed their gatekeeper courses at a slightly lower rate than those students who enrolled in a gatekeeper course after they completed their sequences. But many students who comply with their placement

Table 5. Enrollment and Completion Rates among Developmental Non-Enrollees

	Students who did not enroll in developmental education					
Developmental course referral	Never enrolled in remediation in that subject	Gatekeeper enrollment	Gatekeeper pass rate	Enrolled in another course within three years	No credits obtained after first term	Number of students who did not enroll (N)
Math						
Level I	24%	24%	18%	64%	38%	14,045
Level II	22%	14%	10%	62%	42%	8,338
Level III	17%	6%	4%	54%	51%	7,439
Total	21%	17%	12%	61%	42%	29,822
Reading						
Level I	36%	50%	36%	71%	36%	19,375
Level II	22%	29%	21%	61%	44%	3,800
Level III	30%	26%	17%	59%	49%	2,059
Total	33%	45%	32%	68%	38%	25,234

never reach a gatekeeper course. Perhaps a more revealing analysis would compare the probability of completing a gatekeeper course for referred students who enter that college-level course directly to that probability for those who follow the recommendations of the counseling system and enroll in the course to which they are referred. About 72 percent of those who went directly to the college-level course passed that course, while only about 27 percent of those who complied with their referral completed the college-level course.

It appears that the students in this sample who ignored the advice of their counselors and proceeded directly to college-level courses made wise decisions. One interpretation is that the developmental education obstacle course creates barriers to student progress that outweigh the benefits of the additional learning that might accrue to those who enroll in remediation. This is at least consistent with the research cited earlier that suggested that remedial services do little to increase the chances that a student will be successful in their first college-level course. An alternative explanation is that these students have a better understanding of their skills than the counselors, armed with widely used assessments.

For other students, especially for those referred to math remediation, non-enrollment had a more negative effect. Of those students referred to math remediation who never enrolled, only 61 percent enrolled in another course and 42 percent never earned a college credit in three years after their first term.

Any multiple-step sequence of courses presents many possibilities for pathways through that sequence. Students can skip courses and of course they can pass or fail and they can move on or fail to move on to subsequent courses. For example, taking the 43,000 students in our sample who were referred to Level III math remediation, we counted 75 different pathways used by at least one student through (or more likely not through) the developmental maze.

National Education Longitudinal Study of 1988

In the remainder of this section, we provide a comparison to the Achieving the Dream data by using a national micro-level dataset taken from NELS:88. One of the key advantages that NELS provides is the inclusion of more extensive information than the Achieving the Dream database on student characteristics. But there are disadvantages: the data refer to a period about ten years before the Achieving the Dream data era, NELS does not indicate whether a student was referred to developmental education, and the sample is much smaller. In 2000, the National Center for Education Statistics (NCES) collected the NELS:88 fourth follow-up survey respondents' college transcripts from approximately 3200 postsecondary institutions. This set of transcripts is referred to as the Postsecondary Transcript Study (PETS) of 2000.[12] Our analytic sample consists of 3410 students who started postsecondary education at community college and whose transcripts are available.[13] Table 6 contrasts demographic characteristics of the NELS and Achieving the Dream samples. Summary statistics indicate that African American and Hispanic populations are significantly over-represented in the Achieving the Dream sample.[14] This overrepresentation may reflect the selection process under which colleges serving

Table 6. Demographic Characteristics of Achieving the Dream and NELS Students

Characteristics	Achieving the Dream college students	NELS students[a]
Female	56%	55%
White	50%	68%
Black	17%	7%
Hispanic	22%	16%
Other	8%	9%
Age at college entry	23.6 (8.48)	19.1 (1.75)
Observations	256,672	3410

Note: Standard deviations for continuous variables are in parentheses.
[a] The sample consists of individuals who were enrolled in community college soon after high school and whose college transcripts are provided by their institutions. The sample does not include older students.

a high proportion of minority students were chosen to participate in Achieving the Dream. But it also reflects general changes in the demographic characteristics of community college students. In the past decade, there has been a significant increase in the proportion of minority populations attending community colleges: from 10 percent in 1990 to 14 percent in 2003 for African Americans, and from 8 percent to 14 percent for Hispanics over the same period (Snyder, Tan, & Hoffman, 2006). The table also shows that the NELS students are on average four years younger at college entry than the Achieving the Dream students. In contrast to NELS, the Achieving the Dream sample includes older students who entered college perhaps many years after high school.

College transcript records taken from PETS contain information on student enrollment and performance in developmental education courses. From these course-by-course and term-by-term records, we were able to identify a set of developmental math courses[15] that students ever enrolled in: (1) pre-collegiate math or arithmetic, (2) basic algebra, and (3) intermediate algebra.[16] Table 7 presents NELS students' first-time math course enrollment, whether developmental or college-level.[17] Among the 3410 NELS students, 25, 16, and 12 percent enrolled for their first math course in pre-collegiate math, basic algebra, and intermediate algebra, respectively. Almost 26 percent enrolled in a college-level course. The remaining 20 percent did not enroll in any math course during their college career.

NELS does not indicate whether a student was referred to developmental education. In order to compare the present analysis to our analysis of the Achieving the Dream data, we estimated the need for developmental education among NELS students using 12th grade standardized math test scores. . . .

Table 7. Type of First Enrollment in a Math Course for NELS Students

Enrollment/ assignment	All students	First enrolled math course				
		Never enrolled in a math course	Pre-collegiate math	Basic algebra, plane geometry	Intermediate algebra[a]	College-level math course
Enrollment	3400[b] [100%]	690 [20%]	860 [25%]	550 [16%]	420 [12%]	880 [26%]
Assignment	3400 [100%]	–	1100 [32%]	720 [21%]	520 [15%]	1060 [31%]

Notes: To be consistent with the Achieving the Dream sample, only student transcripts that captured three years or less of a student's academic performance were used. For the purposes of assignment, a student's 12th grade math scores were used for imputation.
[a] In this paper we consider intermediate algebra to be a developmental course.
[b] Ten observations were dropped from the original sample of 3410 due to missing data.

Table 8 describes the NELS students' progression through developmental education in math. We first observe that few students who we estimate to be in need of remediation actually completed their full sequences. For example, only 10 percent of those with test scores indicating that they needed pre-collegiate math enrolled in and passed all three courses in the sequence: pre-collegiate math, basic algebra, and intermediate algebra. The corresponding figures are only 24 percent for individuals in need of basic algebra and 65 for those in need of intermediate algebra. When aggregating the data across the course levels, we see that only one-third of developmental students completed all of their necessary courses in math. This is very close to the same percentage as the corresponding Achieving the Dream students (33 percent). Among those completers, two out of three are reported to have enrolled in and passed at least one college-level math course. As was the case with the Achieving the Dream developmental education completers, the percent of NELS completers who passed a college-level course is similar across the three levels of developmental need: 51, 58, and 59 percent for those with a demonstrated need for pre-collegiate math, basic algebra, and intermediate algebra, respectively. Approximately 28 percent of all developmental education completers (regardless of first enrollment) did not even attempt to take any college-level math courses.

Table 8. Developmental Math Progression among NELS Students

	Referred to		
Course level	Pre-collegiate math	Basic algebra, plane geometry	Intermediate algebra
Pre-collegiate math			
Not enrolled	22%		
Not passed	15%		
[Sub-total]	[37%]		
Basic algebra, plane geometry			
Not enrolled	34%	23%	
Not passed	7%	18%	
[Sub-total]	[41%]	[41%]	
Intermediate algebra			
Not enrolled	10%	26%	19%
Not passed	3%	10%	16%
[Sub-total]	[13%]	[36%]	[35%]
Completed	10%	24%	65%
Observations[a]	1100	720	520

[a]NELS observations are rounded to the nearest 10 to protect the confidentiality of individually identifiable respondents.

As was the case with the Achieving the Dream students, many developmental students in the NELS sample did not finish the first course in their sequence. More than a third of individuals estimated to be in need of pre-collegiate math failed to pass that course. The equivalent numbers are 41 percent for students in need of basic algebra and 35 percent for those in need of intermediate algebra. More than half of those non-completers never enrolled in the first course of their sequence throughout all of their tracked college years. This is very similar to analogous results from the Achieving the Dream data: 56 percent of the students who did not complete their developmental math sequence failed to do so because they did not enroll, often in the very first course to which they were referred, not because they tried and failed or dropped out of a course. Even for those who finished the first course in their sequence, many never enrolled in the next level. For example, of those with the greatest developmental need, 63 percent enrolled in and passed pre-collegiate math, but almost half of those who passed did not show up for the next course in the sequence, basic algebra. Two out of three of those developmental students who did not complete their full sequence of math courses never actually failed one of those courses.

In summary, the NELS data confirm the basic story that emerges from the Achieving the Dream analysis: (1) only a minority of students who need developmental education complete their full sequence of developmental courses, (2) many never pass their first developmental course in their sequence, and (3) a majority of those students who do not complete their full sequence of courses fail to do so because they do not enroll in their initial course or a subsequent course, not because they fail or drop out of any of the courses they attempt.

The Determinants of Developmental Progression: Multivariate Analysis

In this section, we use the concept of a developmental sequence to analyze the determinants of educational outcomes for remedial students. Our analysis so far has shown that many students drop out of their developmental education sequences. But there is considerable variation in these outcomes among students who are referred to the same remedial level. Can we identify student or institutional characteristics that are related to a higher likelihood of reaching intermediate points in the sequence, of completing the sequence, and of moving successfully into college-level courses?

In the following analysis we supplement the individual-level data from Achieving the Dream with institution-level data from the Achieving the Dream and the IPEDS databases to conduct a multivariate analysis that allows us to differentiate the relationships between individual and institutional factors and student progress through developmental education.

Empirical Model

To simplify our analysis, we focus on the step-by-step character of the remedial sequence. Developmental students are expected to enroll in and pass single or multiple developmental courses depending upon their placement. For those who are referred to the lowest level (three or more levels below college-level) of developmental education, their achieved outcome can be categorized into one of the following four types: (1) $Y = 0$, those who did not pass the third-level course (three or more levels below college-level); (2) $Y = 1$, those who passed the third-level course but did not progress any further; (3) $Y = 2$, those who passed the second-level course, but not the first-level; and (4) $Y = 3$, those who completed the entire sequence. The last three outcomes ($Y = 1, 2, 3$) are observed for those referred to two levels below while the last two ($Y = 2, 3$) are observed for those referred to one level below.

Compared to a binary definition of developmental education completion, the concept of a sequence allows us to treat non-completers differently depending on where they stop. For example, among individuals referred to three levels below college-level, those who finished the first course but not the next-level course ($Y = 1$) are presumed to be more successful in developmental education than those who did not even finish the first course ($Y = 0$). Consequently, we use an ordered logit regression. In this approach the ordinal variable is conceived of as the discrete realizations of an underlying continuous random variable, Y^*, indicating the degree to which the student completed developmental education. The unobservable Y^* can be expressed as a linear function of covariates X: $Y^* = \beta'X + \varepsilon$. The observed categorical variable, Y, is derived from unknown cutoff points ($\alpha_0, \alpha_1, \ldots, \alpha_j$) in the distribution of Y^*: $Y = j$ if $\alpha_{j-1} \leq Y^* < \alpha_j$. Let the probability of $Y = j$ be Prob($Y = j$). Then, the proportional odds model is

$$\frac{\text{Prob}(Y \leq j)}{\text{Prob}(Y > j)} = \exp(\alpha_j - \beta'X)$$

where Prob($Y \leq j$) denotes the probability of having at most jth level of developmental completion and Prob($Y > j$) denotes the probability of having above the level j. The parameter β represents the relationship between the covariate and the dependent variable. In this model, the association is assumed not to be the same for every category j. The regression coefficient β_l for a particular explanatory variable is the logarithm of the odds ratio for the dependent variable, holding others constant. To simplify the interpretation of the results, we transformed the raw coefficients into odds ratios.

Empirical Specifications

We hypothesized that success in developmental education depends on student demographics, college characteristics, and state-specific effects.

Student demographics include gender, race/ethnicity, age at entry, cohort year, intensity of first-term enrollment, major studied, developmental need in other subjects, and socioeconomic background. Gender, race/ethnicity, age, and cohort differences are commonly identified as determinants of postsecondary outcomes (Choy, 2002; Pascarella & Terenzini, 2005). Working while enrolled and attending part-time are also associated with a lower probability of retention and graduation. Students who major in academic areas including liberal arts are expected to succeed in developmental education at a higher rate than those studying in vocational areas. As a measure of pre-college ability, we added a dummy variable indicating whether the student was in need of remediation in other subjects.

We also used college-level variables from IPEDS to account for the influence of institutional characteristics on a student's likelihood of progressing through developmental education. College characteristics include school location, size, proportion of full-time students and minority students, tuition, average amount of federal aid received per FTE enrollment, instructional expenditure per FTE enrollment, and certificate orientation. College location, size, and student body demographics are commonly entered as covariates in the literature on student success in college (Bailey, Calcagno, Jenkins, Leinbach, & Kienzl, 2006). For example, students at large and urban colleges serving mainly minorities and economically disadvantaged populations are found to persist and/or graduate at lower rates than their counterparts. We included tuition as a cost of college attendance that is presumed to have a negative relationship with course completion. As a proxy for students' financial need, we entered the amount of financial aid received by students in the college per FTE enrollment. College resources devoted to instruction are expected to help students succeed in developmental education. In addition, certificate-oriented colleges may not stress developmental education as much as degree-oriented colleges. To control for certificate orientation, we included a dummy indicating whether the college awarded more certificates than associate degrees. Finally, we introduced into the analysis state-specific fixed effects to control for differences in state policy or funding systems that might influence outcomes for developmental students.

Results

Table 9 presents summary statistics of the Achieving the Dream college sample by level of developmental education to which they were referred. Regardless of the subject, female, young, Black, and Hispanic students tended to need more levels of developmental education. Full-timers were determined to have less need for developmental education than part-timers. Individuals studying in vocational areas tended to have more need for remediation than those studying in nonvocational areas. It is not surprising that students with a demonstrated

Table 9. Summary Characteristics of Achieving the Dream Students

Variables	Developmental math referred to				Developmental reading referred to			
	Not referred	1 level below	2 levels below	3+ levels below	Not referred	1 level below	2 levels below	3+ levels below
Student demographics								
Cohort 2004	0.516	0.503	0.488	0.496	0.501	0.507	0.517	0.531
Female	0.530	0.555	0.580	0.615	0.550	0.576	0.604	0.567
Age	24.98 (9.78)	21.82 (6.57)	22.42 (7.12)	23.34 (7.74)	24.44 (9.15)	21.40 (6.17)	22.26 (7.23)	22.37 (7.13)
White	0.548	0.473	0.473	0.335	0.550	0.374	0.263	0.145
Black	0.141	0.190	0.222	0.179	0.135	0.228	0.309	0.141
Hispanic	0.185	0.244	0.203	0.426	0.215	0.295	0.314	0.588
Other race/ethnicity	0.125	0.093	0.102	0.06	0.101	0.103	0.113	0.126
Full-time study in the 1st term	0.505	0.589	0.577	0.504	0.529	0.576	0.525	0.497
Major studied: vocational	0.349	0.327	0.349	0.312	0.327	0.307	0.343	0.357
Referred to math dev. ed.	0	1	1	1	0.440	0.838	0.871	0.891
Referred to reading dev. ed.	0.123	0.493	0.421	0.59	0	1	1	1
College characteristics								
Urban (=1)	0.760	0.760	0.853	0.884	0.790	0.758	0.843	0.865
Suburban (=1)	0.184	0.206	0.091	0.075	0.159	0.199	0.096	0.105
Rural (=1)	0.056	0.034	0.056	0.041	0.051	0.043	0.062	0.029
Small: 5000 or less (=1)	0.259	0.221	0.258	0.245	0.277	0.208	0.264	0.264
Medium: 5001–10,000 (=1)	0.138	0.112	0.089	0.107	0.133	0.102	0.088	0.173
Large: 10,000 or more (=1)	0.603	0.667	0.653	0.648	0.590	0.690	0.648	0.563
Offer 1 level of dev. ed. (=1)	0.294	0.499	0	0	0.227	0.411	0	0
Offer 2 levels of dev. ed. (=1)	0.258	0.139	0.369	0	0.411	0.337	0.571	0
Offer 3 levels of dev. ed. (=1)	0.448	0.362	0.631	1	0.362	0.252	0.429	1
Percentage of full-time students	22.71 (17.95)	24.49 (17.75)	22.72 (17.99)	26.73 (18.33)	23.72 (17.93)	23.19 (18.31)	21.36 (18.56)	35.55 (10.12)
Percentage of Black students	18.28 (12.77)	17.69 (11.85)	18.36 (11.83)	11.89 (9.36)	16.44 (11.64)	17.16 (11.55)	19.51 (16.28)	9.28 (9.53)
Percentage of Hispanic students	19.47 (18.39)	22.08 (19.60)	17.45 (17.91)	35.71 (26.59)	22.09 (20.40)	23.57 (20.79)	24.33 (24.84)	49.89 (24.14)
Tuition ($1000)	1.70 (0.67)	1.60 (0.55)	1.66 (0.66)	1.28 (0.43)	1.59 (0.61)	1.58 (0.58)	1.73 (0.81)	1.24 (0.25)
Average federal aid received/FTE	2.78 (0.62)	2.64 (0.79)	2.95 (0.40)	3.03 (0.40)	2.82 (0.57)	2.66 (0.80)	2.99 (0.41)	3.01 (0.45)
Instructional expenditure/FTE	3.53 (5.17)	3.21 (2.17)	3.87 (4.99)	3.84 (6.06)	3.55 (4.11)	3.58 (6.78)	3.86 (5.56)	3.57 (0.92)
Certificate orientation (=1)	0.024	0.029	0.030	0.059	0.033	0.025	0.052	0.084
Observations (N)	97,678	59,551	38,153	43,886	151,597	54,341	16,983	6825

Note: Standard deviations for continuous variables are in parentheses. Of the 256,672 Achieving the Dream students in the sample, data on developmental math are missing for 42,088 students and on developmental reading for 45,452 students.

developmental need for a particular subject tended to be referred to developmental education in the other subject. Finally, developmental students with greater need were more likely to enroll in colleges that were urban, large, certificate-oriented, and serving high proportions of minority students, particularly Hispanic and economically disadvantaged populations.

Now let us turn to the question of what determines developmental progression. Table 10 shows the results from the ordered logit regression for each group of students referred to a particular level of remediation. We first observe that there are substantial individual-specific differences in developmental progression. Female students tended to have significantly higher odds of progressing through developmental math education than their male counterparts. The results indicate that the odds of females passing to a higher level of developmental education were 1.53–1.56 times (depending on the level) as large as the odds for males, holding other factors constant. The corresponding figures for developmental reading range from 1.52 to 1.77. Older students tended to have lower odds of passing to a higher developmental level than their younger counterparts. It is noteworthy that the odds of African American students passing to a higher level of developmental math were 0.67–0.91 times the odds of their White peers. The equivalent numbers vary from 0.86 to 1.11 for developmental reading. In contrast, there is no indication that Hispanic students had lower odds of developmental progression than their White peers. We also observe that both the intensity of first-term enrollment (whether the student attends full-time or part-time) and the type of major are related to the odds of developmental progression. The odds of passing to a higher level of developmental math were 1.50–1.68 times as large when individuals studied on a full-time basis. These numbers are very similar to those for reading. The results also indicate that the odds of passing to a higher level in developmental math were lower (0.61–0.77) when studying in vocational areas. Individuals with a demonstrated developmental need for reading seem to have had lower odds of progressing through developmental math. In sum, men, Black students, and those attending part-time or studying in a vocational area had lower odds of progressing through their developmental sequences. Black students had particularly low odds when they were referred to developmental math at two or three or more levels below college-level. The gender effect is strong throughout the entire sequence for both math and reading, but the negative effect of age applies mostly to reading.

The table also shows that institution-level variables—in particular, college size, student composition, and certificate orientation—are important for developmental progression even after adjusting for individual demographics. The results indicate that the odds of passing to a higher level of math remediation were 0.71–0.77 times as large when students attended small colleges. The corresponding figures range from

Table 10. Odds Ratios Estimated from Ordered Logit Regressions for Achieving the Dream Students

Variables	Developmental math referred to			Developmental reading referred to		
	3+ levels below	2 levels below	1 level below	3+ levels below	2 levels below	1 level below
Cohort 2004	0.966 (0.034)	1.044 (0.051)	0.949 (0.056)	1.297 (0.230)	1.019 (0.084)	1.051 (0.086)
Female	1.561** (0.063)	1.535** (0.088)	1.527** (0.069)	1.768** (0.176)	1.706** (0.057)	1.519** (0.071)
Age	0.995 (0.003)	0.996 (0.003)	0.988** (0.003)	0.976** (0.006)	0.990* (0.005)	0.978** (0.004)
Black	0.669** (0.027)	0.753** (0.050)	0.906 (0.059)	0.864 (0.118)	0.866* (0.058)	1.105 (0.068)
Hispanic	1.125 (0.092)	1.196 (0.155)	1.108** (0.039)	1.048 (0.070)	1.167 (0.127)	1.094 (0.121)
Other race/ethnicity	1.258** (0.078)	1.172* (0.093)	1.277** (0.099)	1.130 (0.186)	1.249 (0.172)	1.359* (0.207)
Full-time study in the 1st term	1.502** (0.096)	1.684** (0.112)	1.681** (0.062)	1.531** (0.179)	1.744** (0.126)	1.672** (0.081)
Major studied: vocational	0.609** (0.043)	0.668** (0.028)	0.771** (0.067)	0.710** (0.076)	0.776** (0.053)	0.885 (0.067)
Referred to math/reading dev.	0.764** (0.041)	0.947 (0.085)	0.921 (0.074)	1.273 (0.308)	0.878 (0.089)	1.094 (0.165)
Suburban (=1)	0.786 (0.121)	0.550 (0.169)	0.656 (0.272)	0.313 (0.198)	0.778 (0.221)	0.870 (0.440)
Rural (=1)	0.831 (0.128)	0.989 (0.256)	0.974 (0.232)	0.633 (0.162)	0.607 (0.187)	1.025 (0.289)
Small: 5000 or less (=1)	0.768 (0.142)	0.770 (0.191)	0.709 (0.141)	0.697 (0.129)	0.697 (0.129)	0.783 (0.191)
Medium: 5001–10,000 (=1)	0.474** (0.067)	1.060 (0.249)	1.358 (0.429)	0.518 (0.273)	0.637* (0.131)	1.163 (0.381)
Percentage full-time students	0.990 (0.006)	0.980** (0.005)	0.989 (0.009)	1.012 (0.007)	0.996 (0.005)	0.996 (0.009)
Percentage Black students	1.010 (0.011)	0.987* (0.006)	0.990 (0.008)	0.955 (0.025)	0.998 (0.005)	0.974 (0.016)
Percentage Hispanic students	1.013 (0.005)	1.008* (0.004)	1.005 (0.007)	0.990 (0.012)	1.009* (0.004)	0.991 (0.008)
Tuition (in $1000 units)	0.530* (0.124)	0.985 (0.199)	0.854 (0.185)	0.395 (0.241)	1.270 (0.224)	0.764 (0.218)
Average federal aid received/FTE	0.977 (0.159)	0.938 (0.104)	0.954 (0.091)	1.022 (0.173)	0.813 (0.093)	0.822 (0.098)
Instructional expenditure/FTE	0.997 (0.004)	0.999 (0.003)	1.000 (0.007)	0.746 (0.113)	0.996 (0.002)	1.001 (0.003)
Certificate orientation (=1)	0.576 (0.201)	0.470* (0.168)	0.538 (0.183)	0.736 (0.119)	0.659 (0.189)	0.384** (0.137)
Offer 2 levels of dev. ed.		0.721 (0.185)	1.282 (0.460)		0.720 (0.141)	1.710 (0.688)
Offer 3 levels of dev. ed.			1.089 (0.262)			1.627 (0.717)
Log likelihood	−42,727.39	−36,238.18	−47,398.89	−8020.23	−15,942.93	−32,079.64
Chi-Squared	40,241.93	6,186.68	2,918.56	1694.61	10,110.64	3,790.55
Observations	35,189	32,151	49,865	6762	15,504	44,749

Note: Standard errors adjusted for college clusters are in parentheses. State dummies are commonly included in the regressions.

* Significant at 5 percent.

** Significant at 1 percent.

0.43 to 0.78 for reading. There seem to be similar associations among students at mid-size and large colleges. We also observe that student composition has some influence on the odds of progressing through developmental education. Individuals at institutions serving high proportions of Black and economically disadvantaged students (measured by receipt of federal aid) generally have lower odds of passing to a higher level of remediation than their peers at colleges serving low proportions of these populations. Tuition level seems to matter as well, particularly for individuals referred to the lowest levels of developmental education. Lastly, the results indicate that the odds of passing to a higher level of developmental education were lower when students enrolled in certificate-oriented colleges.

Robustness of the Results and Limitations of the Analysis

Potential analytic problems may derive from the fact that our analysis depends on crude measures of individuals and institutions available in the Achieving the Dream and IPEDS databases. For example, we did not include any measures of individual-level socioeconomic background that are presumed to be important determinants of developmental progression. Fortunately, the Achieving the Dream database includes students' residential ZIP codes according to which we can derive socioeconomic measures from outside sources. Specifically, we exploited the 2000 Census to obtain two ZIP code-level measures of socioeconomic background: neighbors' income and educational attainment. But more than 20 percent of the Achieving the Dream sample had no or incomplete ZIP code information. These observations were therefore dropped from the sample for this analysis. Nonetheless, the results from the ordered logit regressions with the two socioeconomic measures are very similar to those presented in Table 10. As expected, neighborhood income and educational attainment were positively related to the odds of developmental progression.

Another possible problem is related to the assumption that the associations between the independent variables and the dependent variable are constant across the transitions through developmental levels. This assumption is required for the use of the ordered logit model. A particular covariate may have different relations with developmental progression depending on the transition, category j. In order to address this issue, we ran a set of generalized ordered logit regressions, the so-called generalized threshold model (Maddala, 1983), where the odds ratios are allowed to vary across the ordinal categories. We observed some differences in the odds ratios for several variables across the categories; nevertheless, the results for each category are qualitatively similar to those presented in Table 10.

A final specific concern is that the ordered logit model does not take full advantage of the sequential nature of developmental progression. A student's progression toward a higher level of remediation is predicated on the student's success in the previous level. We used a sequential response model (Amemiya, 1985; Maddala, 1983) that estimates probabilities of passing different transitions. At each transition, individuals determine whether to drop out or continue developmental education. Basically, the sequential model is analogous to a discrete time hazard rate model in duration analysis that estimates the probability of exit at a particular time conditional on survival. For simplicity, we assumed that the probability of passing a given transition is conditionally independent of passing previous transitions; in other words, all transitions are considered a conditionally independent series of binary processes. The results from the sequential logit regressions suggest that there are some differences in the estimated odds ratios across the transitions, but they are also qualitatively similar to those presented in Table 10.

Lastly, we point out that our multivariate analysis is exploratory, not definitive. It shows the relationships between the covariates and the developmental outcome. It is difficult to make causal inferences from the results due to multiple sample selections at transitions. There may be unobserved individual-specific heterogeneity that is correlated with student success in the previous and current transitions.

Conclusion

In this article we have focused attention on the sequence of developmental courses. What does the concept of a sequence help us learn?

First of all, a focus on the sequence makes immediately clear the daunting task confronting many of the nearly two thirds of all community college students who are referred to developmental education in at least one area. Students arriving with weak academic skills can face semesters of work before they can in effect start college—at least in relevant areas. This developmental "obstacle course" presents students with many opportunities to step out of their sequences, and students in large numbers take those opportunities. Fewer than one half of students complete their sequences, and only 20 percent of those referred to math and 40 percent of those referred to reading complete a gatekeeper course within three years of initial enrollment.

Should we be concerned about these low completion rates? Given the circumstances, what is the optimal developmental education completion rate? Research does suggest that there is economic value in college education even if it does not end in a degree (Grubb, 1993; Kane & Rouse, 1995). Students who complete one or two developmental courses have probably learned valuable skills even though they have not learned enough to be eligible for college-level work. Even very early exit may not necessarily indicate a problem. Manski (1989) argued that initial college attendance can be seen as an experiment in which students gather information about their aptitude and taste for college. Many students have little concrete knowledge about college before they start.

During the early months of college, students learn whether they like college and how much work and effort they will have to exert in order to be successful. They can evaluate that against the likely benefits of persisting and perhaps completing college. Certainly the costs in time and money of a college education will be higher for students who must start in developmental courses. Thus their early exit may suggest that they had gathered enough information about the barriers that they faced to decide that the cost would be too high.

Without more information on these students and their motivations, it is difficult to make a judgment about this. Whether the low completion rates are in some sense optimal for individuals, we should remember that many of these students who exit the developmental sequence are high school graduates. Most high school graduates who enroll in remediation believe that they are prepared for college, so it seems reasonable that if high schools fail to carry out that preparation, some services ought to be available to do what the high schools should have done. Another problem with the optimal withdrawal argument is that withdrawals are still closely related to race and income. It is problematic from a social point of view to argue that the optimal withdrawal rate is higher for African American and low-income students than it is for middle-class White students. Finally, if there is a national goal to increase college success and graduation rates, that increase is going to have to come from among these types of students. The goal of educators therefore must be to try to lower the cost in time and resources to the student of successfully navigating the developmental sequence. If that can be done, then any cost benefit calculation would create incentives for a higher completion rate.

In addition to evidence on the overall completion rates, this article has presented information about the nature of the sequences and the places where students tend to exit the sequence. Analysis of developmental sequences makes clear that many students who exit their sequence do so even though they have never failed or withdrawn from a developmental course. This pattern extends into the first college-level course: among developmental completers in the sample, those who enrolled in a gatekeeper course had a good chance of passing it, but about 30 percent did not enroll in such a course within the three-year period of the study.

This article has also revealed the confusion and disarray that underlies the apparent orderliness of the developmental sequence. In theory, the system consists of an ordered set of courses into which students are placed with the assistance of assessments used by hundreds of thousands of students. But barely a majority of students actually follow their referral recommendations. For some students, deviation from the referral appears to be a wise decision, but others ignore the recommendations and disappear from the college altogether. And those who do enroll in remedial courses take a bewildering variety of pathways as they try to make progress toward college-level courses.

Given the confusion and ineffectiveness of the developmental system, one possible objective would be to reduce the length of time before a student can start college courses—to accelerate the remediation process. A system that used more accurate assessment that identifies the specific needs of students and focuses instruction on addressing those particular needs would be one way to minimize the time a student spends in remediation. It may be possible to provide that supplemental instruction, through tutoring for example, while the student is enrolled in an introductory college-level course. We have seen that students who choose to skip remediation do reasonably well. It might make sense to provide appropriate support so that more students could follow that path.

We have emphasized that more students fail to complete developmental sequences because they never enroll in their first or a subsequent course than because they drop out of or fail to pass a course in which they are enrolled. This insight suggests a wide variety of possible approaches. Perhaps colleges should combine two or three levels of instruction into one longer, more intensive, accelerated course. At the very least, concerted efforts should be made to encourage students who complete one course in their sequence to go on to the next. This might involve abandoning the semester schedule to prevent gaps between courses, or registering and scheduling students for the next course in a sequence while they are still in the previous course.

Returning to the link between our work and Henry Levin's Accelerated Schools Project (ASP), like Levin we have focused on the poor outcomes for students in remediation, although our focus has been on postsecondary remediation. Here is what Levin (2007, pp. 1410–1411) states:

> *Webster's New Collegiate Dictionary* describes *remediation* as the "act or process of remedying" where *remedy* is defined as "treatment that relieves or cures a disease" or "something that corrects or counteracts an evil." Although such meanings may appear far-fetched from education, they are accurate metaphors for what happens in the educational remediation of low-income and minority students. Presumably, children who are put into remedial programs are children who arrive at school with "defects" in their development that require repair of their educational faults. But, even this metaphor falls short of its own meaning because the typical child is never repaired, but remains in the repair shop for many years in enclaves labeled as Title I, or special education, or other categorical programs. And, contrary to gaining needed academic prowess, this approach stigmatizes the child with a label of inferiority and constrains academic development to the limitations of the remedial pedagogy. Low-income children fall farther behind the academic mainstream the longer they are in school.

Of course postsecondary students are young adults, so rather than stay in school for years, they more often simply leave, but for many students, like its K–12 counterpart, remediation does little to help them "catch up." Levin argued that the remedy for this is a program of accelerated learning. He argued that students with weak academic skills do not need a different type of education, but rather one that looks very much like the type of education that we as a matter of course provide to more advanced students. He states that "a better strategy for success is not to slow down their development and learning through repetition of the lowest level skills, but to incorporate those skills into more meaningful educational experiences that will accelerate their growth and development to bring them into the academic mainstream."

When students with weak academic skills arrive at college they are directed toward a complicated and time-consuming set of services that have uncertain value. Certainly the needs of these students should be addressed, but college staff have something to learn from Levin's experience with ASP. He suggested that educators working with students with weak academic skills, should "accelerate, do not remediate." This is apt advice for remediation in college as well.

Notes

1. Most practitioners use the term "developmental" rather than "remedial" education. In general, developmental education is taken to refer to the broad array of services provided to students with weak skills, while remediation is taken to refer specifically to courses given to such students. Moreover, the term "remedial" is often considered to carry a negative connotation. This paper discusses primarily developmental classes. To simplify the exposition and to avoid the overuse of either of these two words, we use "developmental" and "remedial" interchangeably. No positive or negative connotation is intended.

2. In fall 2000, 92 percent of public two-year colleges utilized placement tests in the selection process for remediation (Parsad, Lewis, & Greene, 2003).

3. A nationally representative sample of eighth-graders was first surveyed in the spring of 1988. A sample of these respondents was then resurveyed in four follow-ups in 1990, 1992, 1994, and 2000. On the questionnaire, students self-reported on a range of topics including: school, work, and home experiences; educational resources and support; the role in education of their parents and peers; neighborhood characteristics; educational and occupational aspirations; and other student perceptions. For the three in-school waves of data collection (when most were eighth-graders, sophomores, or seniors), achievement tests in reading, social studies, mathematics, and science were administered in addition to the student questionnaire (National Center for Education Statistics, 2003).

4. For critical analysis of the research on remediation, see Grubb (2001), Bailey and Alfonso (2005), Perin and Charron (2006), Levin and Calcagno (2008), and Bailey (2009).

5. Colleges are asked to choose their own "gatekeeper" courses. Gatekeeper courses are formally defined in the data gathering instructions to the colleges as the first college-level courses the student must take after remediation. These may be different for students enrolled in different programs within one institution. For example, a student enrolled in a medical

program may have a different college-level math requirement than a student in a business program.

6. These second- and third-round colleges include three open-admission, four-year institutions in Texas. However, these institutions were not included in our analysis.

7. One of the first 27 colleges dropped out of the initiative, so the sample consists of 26 colleges from the initial group, and 31 that joined in 2005 and 2006.

8. Participating institutions were given the following instructions on how to determine whether a student should be considered referred to remedial math or reading: "Student was referred for remedial needs in mathematics [reading]. Remedial courses are instructional courses designed for students deficient in the general competencies necessary for a regular post-secondary curriculum and educational setting. The student can be referred through a counselor, a developmental office, etc." Institutions with multiple levels of remedial education were asked to report the level to which the student was initially referred.

9. A sequence of developmental reading courses might include precollege reading, textbook mastery, and college textbook material.

10. For simplicity, throughout the paper, individuals in need of remediation at colleges having only one level are treated the same as those in need of remediation one level below college-level at institutions having two or three or more developmental levels. Of course, there may be differences in student characteristics among these groups, but for analytic purposes, all the individuals in these groups have only a single transition to pass through. Similarly, individuals referred to remediation two levels below college-level are treated the same regardless of the number of developmental levels offered by the college.

11. In most colleges, students are required to take the sequence of courses to which they are referred before they are eligible for college-level courses, but in some states and colleges, remediation is voluntary. In 75 percent of public two-year colleges, students are in principle required to take remedial courses to which they are referred while in the remaining 25 percent students are only recommended by colleges to take those courses (Parsad et al., 2003).

12. In 1988, 24,599 eighth-graders were selected for the NELS sample that was followed up four times (in 1990, 1992, 1994, and 2000). In the end, 12,144 individuals survived the base-year and four follow-up surveys. Attewell et al. (2006) provide a detailed description of the NELS data for their analysis on developmental education.

13. Given the fact that transcript data were retrieved from a restricted-use source, all sample size numbers are rounded to the nearest ten throughout the paper in accordance with the NCES policy regarding confidentiality. Transcripts are limited to a three-year period of observation in an effort to be consistent with the Achieving the Dream sample.

14. Even the NELS sample does not represent the entire community college student population at that time because of individuals who delayed post-secondary education after high school.

15. The NELS transcripts only identify one reading/English course as remedial, so we were not able to use NELS to analyze progression through a sequence of developmental reading courses.

16. NCES considers intermediate algebra a pre-college course even though in a small number of cases, students are granted additive credits for the course (Snyder et al., 2006). In this paper, we consider intermediate algebra to be a developmental course.

17. The length of time for transcript observation for each student is three years from the start of postsecondary education.

References

Amemiya, T. (1985). *Advanced econometrics*. Cambridge: Harvard University Press.

Arkansas Department of Higher Education. (n.d.). *2003–04 Arkansas academic cost accounting system: A strategic management tool for higher education planning and campus decision-making*. AR: Author.

Bailey, T. (2009). Challenge and opportunity: Rethinking the role and function of developmental education in community college. *New Directions for Community Colleges, 145*, 11–30.

Bailey, T., & Alfonso, M. (2005). *Paths to persistence: An analysis of research on program effectiveness at community colleges*. Indianapolis: Lumina Foundation for Education.

Bailey, T., Calcagno, J. C., Jenkins, D., Leinbach, T., & Kienzl, G. (2006). Is student-right-to-know all you should know? An analysis of community college graduation rates. *Research in Higher Education, 47*(5), 491–519.

Bettinger, E., & Long, B. (2005). *Addressing the needs of under-prepared college students: Does college remediation work?* Cambridge, MA: National Bureau of Economic Research. (NBER Working Paper No. 11325).

Boylan, H. (2002). *What works: A guide to research-based best practices in developmental education*. Boone, NC: Appalachian State University, Continuous Quality Improvement Network with the National Center for Developmental Education.

Breneman, D. W., & Haarlow, W. N. (1998). Remedial education: Costs and consequences. *Fordham Report, 2*(9), 1–22.

Calcagno, J. C., & Long, B. (2008). *The impact of postsecondary remediation using a regression discontinuity approach: Addressing endogenous sorting and noncompliance*. New York: National Center for Postsecondary Research. (NCPR Working Paper).

Choy, S. P. (2002). *Access and persistence: Findings from 10 years of longitudinal research on students*. Washington, DC: American Council on Education, Center for Policy Analysis.

Deil-Amen, R., & Rosenbaum, J. (2002). The unintended consequences of stigma-free remediation. *Sociology of Education, 75*(3), 249–268.

Florida Office of Program Policy Analysis and Government Accountability. (2006). *Steps can be taken to reduce remediation rates; 78% of community college students, 10% of university students need remediation*. FL: Author. (OPPAGA Report No. 06-40).

Grubb, N. (1993). The varied economic returns to postsecondary education: New evidence from the class of 1972. *Journal of Human Resources, 28*(2), 365–382.

Grubb, N. (2001). *From black box to Pandora's box: Evaluating remedial/developmental education*. New York: Columbia University, Teachers College, Community College Research Center.

Horn, L., & Nevill, S. (2006). *Profile of undergraduates in U.S, postsecondary education institutions: 2003–04: With a special analysis of community college students.* Washington, DC: U.S. Department of Education, National Center for Education Statistics. (NCES 2006-184).

Kane, T., & Rouse, C. (1995). Labor-market returns to two- and four-year college. *American Economic Review, 85*(3), 600–614.

Levin, H. (2007). On the relationship between poverty and curriculum. *The University of North Carolina Law Review, 85*(5), 1381–1418.

Levin, H., & Calcagno, J. C. (2008). Remediation in the community college: An evaluator's perspective. *Community College Review, 35*(3), 181–207.

Maddala, G. (1983). *Limited dependent and qualitative variables in econometrics.* Cambridge, MA: Cambridge University Press.

Manski, C. F. (1989). Schooling as experimentation: A reappraisal of the postsecondary dropout phenomenon. *Economics of Education Review, 8*(4), 305–312.

Martorell, P., & McFarlin, I. (2007). *Help or hindrance? The effects of college remediation on academic and labor market outcomes.* Unpublished manuscript.

McCabe, R. (2006). *No one to waste: A report to public decision makers and community college leaders.* Washington, DC: American Association of Community Colleges.

National Center for Education Statistics. (2003). *National Education Longitudinal Study: 1988–2000 Data Files and Electronic Codebook System. Base year through fourth follow-up.* Washington, DC: U.S. Department of Education, Institute of Education Sciences. ECB/CD-ROM (2003-348).

Ohio Board of Regents. (2006). *Costs and consequences of remedial course enrollment in Ohio public higher education: Six-year outcomes for fall 1998 cohort.* OH: Author.

Parsad, B., Lewis, L., & Greene, B. (2003). *Remedial education at degree-granting postsecondary institutions in fall 2000.* Washington, DC: U.S. Department of Education, National Center for Education Statistics. (NCES 2004-010).

Pascarella, E. T., & Terenzini, P. T. (2005). *How college affects students: A third decade of research.* San Francisco: Jossey-Bass.

Perin, D., & Charron, K. (2006). Lights just click on every day. In T. Bailey, & V. S. Morest (Eds.), *Defending the community college equity agenda* (pp. 155–194). Baltimore: The Johns Hopkins University Press.

Rosenbaum, J. (2001). *Beyond college for all.* New York: Russell Sage Foundation.

Royston, P. (2004). Multiple imputation of missing values. *Stata Journal, 4*(3), 227–241.

Snyder, T. D., Tan, A. G., & Hoffman, C. M. (2006). *Digest of education statistics 2005.* Washington, DC: U.S. Department of Education, National Center for Education Statistics. (NCES 2006-030).

Strong American Schools. (2008). *Diploma to Nowhere.* Retrieved October 8, 2008, from http://www.edin08.com/.

New Evidence on College Remediation

Paul Attewell, David Lavin, Thurston Domina, and Tania Levey

This article represents one of the more rigorous and comprehensive studies of developmental education available. Attewell, Lavin, Domina, and Levey discuss some of the major policy issues in developmental education, describe who takes developmental courses, and use multiple methodologies to explore the outcomes for those who participate in developmental courses. The authors conclude that participating in developmental education has differing effects for different students, courses, and institutions.

Most American colleges and universities offer special courses for students who lack some of the reading, writing, and mathematics skills that are critical for college-level work (Roueche & Roueche, 1999). This phenomenon is known popularly as remedial education, although many educators avoid that label, preferring terms such as developmental education, skills courses, or college preparation courses. Developmental or remedial education is widespread: Our analyses indicate that about 40% of traditional undergraduates take at least one such course, and remediation is even more common among older nontraditional students (Woodham, 1998).

Remedial coursework has become a politically contentious issue in the last decade or so (Kozeracki, 2002; Soliday, 2002). Some commentators view the existence of remedial or developmental courses as evidence that many of today's college students are not academically strong enough to manage college-level work and should not have been admitted into college in the first place (Harwood, 1997; Marcus, 2000; Trombley, 1998). From this perspective, the existence of remediation suggests that some institutions have lowered their standards for admission, and have subsequently "dumbed down" courses so that unprepared students can make their way through college (Bennett, 1994; MacDonald, 1997, 1998, 1999; Traub, 1995). Other critics argue that students get bogged down taking multiple remedial courses, leading many to give up and drop out. Remedial education, in this view, is a hoax perpetrated upon academically weak students who will be unlikely to graduate (Deil-Amen & Rosenbaum, 2002; Rosenbaum, 2001).

In recent years, such arguments have encouraged several states to remove developmental or remedial courses from their public four-year universities and to redirect students in need of remediation into community colleges (Bettinger & Long, 2004; Kozeracki, 2002; Soliday, 2002).

The opposite view maintains that developmental education is a necessary component of higher education, one with deep historical roots. Proponents note that many promising students combine strengths in certain subject areas with weaknesses in others, which can be addressed by skills courses. Moreover, many students enter college years after graduating high school and need to rebuild certain skills. Most importantly, proponents stress that most students who take remedial/developmental coursework subsequently complete their degrees successfully (McCabe, 2000; Merisotis & Phipps, p. 63 in this book).

Supporters of college remediation draw attention to the fact that students of color, students from less affluent families, and students for whom English is a second language are greatly overrepresented in remedial courses. Consequently, policies that prevent students who need remedial/developmental work from enrolling in four-year colleges could greatly reduce the likelihood that such students would ever obtain bachelor's degrees (Lavin & Weininger, 1998). Supporters of developmental education therefore construe the controversy over remediation as an attack on access to college.

Although much has been written about this controversy, there are large gaps in the empirical record. One review noted, "Research about the effectiveness of remedial education programs has typically been sporadic, underfunded, and inconclusive" (Merisotis & Phipps, p. 70 in this book). Another added, "Unfortunately, while debates for and against have been vociferous, the effectiveness of these programs has not been visible as an issue. Relatively few evaluations of remedial programs have been conducted, and many existing evaluations are useless" (Grubb, 2001, p. 1).

Exactly what constitutes "college-level work" is by no means clear. Institutions differ on this, and there are different expectations even within single institutions. Consequently, there is no objective or generally agreed upon cut-off below which college students require remediation. Each college follows its own set of practices, and this leads to the considerable variability in remediation we document below.

The recent availability of college transcript data from the National Educational Longitudinal Study (NELS:88) provides us with high-quality data describing a nationally representative cohort of students. This study provides a detailed picture of the remedial/developmental coursework that each student undertook, based on a coding of college transcripts undertaken with the advice of college and community college registrars and institutional research officers. It also includes detailed assessments of students' academic skills and coursework prior to college entry, plus measures of family background. This allows us to separate preexisting academic skills and weaknesses from the effects of taking remedial coursework during college.

The development of a statistical technique known as "the counterfactual model of causal inference" provides a superior methodological tool to separate the effects of remedial coursework from those of background variables. By applying counterfactual models to the NELS:88 transcript data, this article casts new light on the empirical facts underlying the controversy over college remediation.

This essay first documents how much remediation occurs in college and describes what kinds of students take remedial coursework. We then examine the effects of taking remedial courses on graduation rates and time to degree, including the consequences of taking many remedial courses. We explore whether some kinds of remediation are more consequential than others are, and we assess the effects of successful completion of remedial coursework on degree completion. Finally, we draw out the implications of our findings for recent policy controversies about remediation in higher education.

Previous Research

Merisotis and Phipps (1998, and p. 63 in this book) reviewed the controversy over remedial/developmental coursework in college, providing a historical context (see also Kozeracki, 2002; Roueche & Roueche, 1999). They noted that remedial courses have been a regular part of the curriculum at Ivy League universities and other colleges from the Colonial period to the present (cf. Breneman & Haarlow, 1998; Ignash, 1997; Payne & Lyman, 1996). The political movement against remediation that flourished in the 1990s and that led to important policy shifts was not triggered by any increase in remedial coursework on college campuses at that time, according to Merisotis and Phipps. On the contrary, the proportion of institutions offering such courses, and the proportion of students taking them, remained stable until after the new policies removed remedial coursework from many state universities.

Merisotis and Phipps (1998, and p. 63 in this book) summarized studies indicating that the bulk of remedial students are 20 years old or older, or returnees or delayed entrants to college. They also noted that remediation is considerably cheaper per student than regular college coursework, and in most institutions, it consumes a quite modest part of the budget. They concluded that the case for offering remediation in higher education is compelling: "[Remediation] is not an appendage with little connection to the mission of the institution but represents a core function of the higher education community that it has performed for hundreds of years" (Merisotis & Phipps, p. 75 in this book).

Clifford Adelman has studied the factors that affect college graduation rates and time to degree, and he has examined remediation in this context. His analyses of the "High School and Beyond" data set, which followed a cohort of students who graduated high school in 1982, documented that students who took remedial courses in college had markedly lower graduation rates: 39% earned bachelor's degrees, compared to 69% of students who took no remediation (Adelman, 1999, p. 74). He replicated this pattern for a later cohort, the high school class of 1992 (Adelman, 2004, p. 94). These studies indicate that students who need remedial courses are much less likely to graduate.

Less well-known than these figures on remediation and noncompletion is Adelman's finding that *college remediation ceases to predict graduation*, once a measure of secondary school academic performance and preparation is added to the model (1999, p. 75). This implies that poor high school preparation, rather than taking remedial coursework, is what reduces students' chances of graduating from college.

In analyses comparing the high school class of 1982 with the class of 1992, Adelman (2004, pp. 87–94) found that the number of students taking remediation had declined somewhat over time. He also documented that students who undertake many remedial courses in college, and those whose *reading* skills require remediation, are least likely to graduate from college, but that many other students do improve their skills and complete college despite academic weak spots. He concluded:

> The bottom line . . . is that "remediation" in higher education is not some monolithic plague that can be cured by a single prescription. Determined students and faculty can overcome at least mild deficiencies in preparation. . . . But when reading is the core of the problem, the odds of success in college environments are so low that other approaches are called for. (1998, p. 11)

One lesson of Adelman's work for our current study is that researchers should test whether remediation for reading has more deleterious consequences than remedial work in other subjects, and whether students taking multiple remedial courses decrease their likelihood of graduating. A second lesson is that research should distinguish between effects of remediation on chances of graduation and effects of remediation on time to degree.

Deil-Amen and Rosenbaum (2002) examined remediation in community colleges, locating their research in an earlier tradition that suggested that two-year institutions were places where students' educational aspirations were "cooled out." That is, many students are socialized at community college to accept a less desirable option than a bachelor's degree. Deil-Amen and Rosenbaum studied two community colleges. Both of these colleges emphasized students transferring to a four-year program and provided courses "that are intended to preserve standards and move remedial students into the college level courses that are accepted for transfer credit by senior institutions" (Deil-Amen & Rosenbaum, 2002, p. 254). Some of these courses were remedial and did not carry credit towards a degree. However, colleges obscured this fact in catalogues and in the ways they counseled students into taking the courses. "Students often go for several months, a full semester, or even a full year without knowing that their remedial courses are not counting toward a degree" (Deil-Amen & Rosenbaum, 2002, p. 260).

Deil-Amen and Rosenbaum judged these "lengthy delays" to be detrimental, concluding "This process looks a lot like the swindles that Goffman . . . described" and "the delayed recognition caused by a stigma-free approach may be contributing to students dropping out of college altogether and hence accumulating no credentials rather than a lesser degree" (2002, p. 264). They suggested that academically weak students would benefit more from taking occupational courses or the more vocational AAS degree rather than from attempting an AA degree with the goal of transferring to a four-year degree (cf. Rosenbaum, 2001).

In our analyses of the NELS:88, we will test whether remedial coursework leads students to accumulate few credits or results in delays in time to degree among two-year college students.

Lavin and Weininger (1998) examined a recent cohort of students who enrolled in bachelor's degree programs at the City University of New York (CUNY). Consistent with prior research, they found that graduation rates were inversely related to the number of academic skills tests failed. Nonetheless, about a quarter of those who initially failed all of the tests subsequently graduated. One finding was particularly instructive. Among African American, Hispanic, and Asian bachelor's degree recipients, the number who initially failed skills tests exceeded the number who passed all of their skills tests. *Well over half of minority students who ultimately graduated initially failed academic skills tests.* If higher education systems adopted a policy of not admitting students needing remedial coursework into four-year institutions, then the impact on minority students would be especially heavy. Lavin and Weininger's analyses also established that remedial placement is far from an academic death sentence: After taking remedial courses, many students do graduate.

Largely because of the failure to control for important selection biases, there has been little firm evidence that remediation improves a student's chances of graduation. Lavin, Alba, and Silberstein (1981) introduced controls for selection and found that remediation did make a positive contribution. After CUNY adopted a system of open admissions, it tested incoming students to determine their academic skill levels and provided remedial courses. However, many students who appeared to need remedial work were not placed in such courses, because mandatory placement was not a part of university policy at that time. So, among students who did *not* take remedial work were quite a few who were comparable to the students who were in remedial courses, in terms of high school background (high school grades, college preparatory courses taken, and percentile rank in high school graduating class) and level of need for remediation as measured by tests of reading and arithmetic skills. With these variables controlled, students who entered CUNY and were placed in remediation were compared with other low-skill students who were not placed in remedial courses.

While placement in remedial courses *per se* did nothing to enhance students' subsequent academic achievements, success in remedial courses did make a significant difference. Among students in bachelor's degree programs, those who passed at least one of their remedial courses were more likely to persist in college than were comparable low-skill nonremedial students, and they earned more credits. After

5 years, the former were slightly more likely to graduate (Lavin, Alba, & Silberstein, 1981). Among two-year college entrants, there were similar results. Students who passed at least one of their remedial courses (85% of takers were in this category) were more likely to stay in college, and were more likely to graduate or to transfer into a bachelor's degree program than were otherwise similar students who did not take remedial coursework. This suggested a positive influence of remedial courses, at least for the large majority of students who successfully complete them.

Bettinger and Long (2004) analyzed a longitudinal data set that followed 8,000 first-time freshmen enrolled in nonselective four-year public colleges in Ohio from 1998 to 2002, in order to assess the consequences of taking remedial coursework in mathematics. Their data set had extensive information on students' academic preparation and achievement in high school, so the analyses assessed the effects of remediation after controlling for prior academic skills. Bettinger and Long found that students placed in remedial college courses in mathematics were somewhat more likely to drop out or transfer to a two-year college, compared to academically equivalent students not in remediation. Surprisingly, however, remediation did not lower the likelihood of obtaining a bachelor's degree. In addition, when Bettinger and Long distinguished students in four-year colleges who *completed* their college remedial courses, they found that those remedial students were *more likely* to complete a bachelor's degree than were otherwise equivalent students who did not complete remedial math. Thus, they concluded that success at remedial mathematics improves a student's chances of graduation. This was balanced by the fact that students who completed remedial mathematics coursework took more time to graduate than nonremedial students took.

The import of the studies by Bettinger and Long and by Lavin et al. is that completion of remedial courses may have positive consequences that are not evident when looking at all students who enroll in remedial courses. Many students do fail to complete remedial courses: Some withdraw, others take incompletes, and some drop out of college altogether (Adelman, 2004, pp. vii–viii, 84). However, those students who do complete some remedial coursework may have superior prospects of graduating. We will test that hypothesis below using the NELS:88 data.

Data and Methods

The NELS:88 Study

The National Educational Longitudinal Study, known as the NELS:88, is a project of the U.S. Department of Education's National Center on Educational Statistics. In 1988, a representative sample of the nation's eighth-grade students was assembled, and detailed baseline information was collected about their family and academic background. The Educational Testing Service developed pencil-and-paper tests of each student's skills in reading and mathematics for the NELS:88, a sort of mini-SAT. These tests were repeated in eighth, 10th, and 12th grades. Additional data were collected from parents, teachers, and the students themselves during each follow-up survey. Later, NELS:88 students who entered college provided researchers with detailed information about the institutions they attended and the degrees they obtained. The most recent survey update was undertaken in 2000.

The NELS cohort was scheduled to graduate from high school in the spring of 1992. Later that year, high school transcripts were obtained from approximately 85% of the cohort. For those students who participated in the final survey of the NELS in 2000 and whose high school transcripts were complete, a measure of the intensity of high school curriculum was constructed. This measure along with high school GPA and class rank and score on a 12th-grade test of general learned abilities constitute the three core indicators of a student's academic achievement or preparation prior to entering postsecondary education.

More recently, the NELS:88 obtained college transcripts for those students who went to college, and coded the coursework, credits, grades, and degrees obtained. Researchers developed a taxonomy of college remedial courses in consultation with panels of registrars and institutional research officers, and this taxonomy was used in the process of coding the NELS postsecondary transcripts (Adelman, 2004). We use the NELS:88's assessments of the number and kinds of remedial courses taken. Adelman (1999, p. 7) has shown that student self-reporting about taking remedial courses, and reports by college officials of enrollment in remedial courses, both greatly understate the amount of remedial coursework undertaken, compared to the information provided by student transcripts. He has argued that the transcript studies are more reliable.

As a longitudinal panel survey, the NELS:88 experiences sample attrition and encounters issues of nonresponse bias. On occasion, the sample has been "refreshed" with additional respondents. The NCES contractor calculated different respondent weights for each combination of waves in the data collection, along with special characteristics of student records, so that, whichever subjects and topics a researcher chooses to study, the analysis will remain representative of the national 1988 cohort despite attrition and nonresponse bias. Our analyses included only respondents who participated in each of the NELS survey waves and who provided high school and college transcript data. We used a longitudinal weight provided by the NELS:88 for this combination, known as F4PHP3WT. This yields an unweighted N of 6,879 students, and a weighted N of 2,004,732, such that the weighted sample is representative of the national cohort. The case weight used in our regression models divided each person's value on F4PHP3WT by the mean value of that variable, to yield a total sample size of 6,879. Because the NELS provides several alternative weights, the findings reported below may differ slightly from other published analyses.

The resulting sample *is not* representative of the entire universe of U.S. undergraduates, for it excludes the kinds of students who enter college many years after leaving high school. The sample *is* representative of a single nationwide cohort of high school students who went on to college during the roughly 8 years following high school. That sample includes students who entered the full range of two- and four-year, private and public, selective and nonselective colleges, students who pursued postsecondary vocational credentials, as well as associate's and bachelor's degrees.

Missing Data

We deliberately excluded persons who had no high school or college transcript data; however, this leaves in the sample individuals who are missing particular pieces of transcript information. We did not wish to impute central dependent variables—namely, the numbers and kinds of remedial courses taken, degrees obtained, and time to college graduation. Anyone missing one of those variables was excluded from the particular regression model analyzing that individual outcome. For all other variables, which included family background, high school tests, and academic intensity measures, we used a multiple imputation method, using Amelia software developed and described by King, Honaker, Joseph, and Scheve (2001). The software and the mathematical algorithm used for imputation are described at: http://gking.harvard.edu/amelia/.

Variables

The central variables in our analyses describe whether or not a student took remedial coursework during college. We utilized variables provided by the NELS:88, based on their judgment as to which courses on college transcripts were remedial courses. "Any remediation" is a dummy variable we created that is coded 1 if a student took one or more remedial courses in college, or 0 otherwise, no matter whether the student passed, failed, or withdrew from that remedial course. "Many remedial courses" is a dummy variable that takes a value of 1 if a transcript includes *three or more* remedial courses, and 0 otherwise. Those courses could be in one subject (such as three remedial reading courses) or any combination of subjects (e.g., one remedial course in reading, one in mathematics, and one in writing).

The NELS:88 classified each remedial course by its subject matter. Using those codes, we created separate dummy variables for remedial reading, for remedial math, and for what we will refer to as "remedial writing, etc." This last category contains mainly remedial courses in writing plus some courses in "comprehensive language arts." This category excludes languages courses in reading or in speech, however. If a student took any remedial courses in the respective subject, that student was given a value of 1 for that dummy variable.

Finally, using the NELS course-level transcript data, we generated dummy variables indicating students who passed all of the remedial courses they took in each of these areas. For each course that a student takes, the NELS provides a flag indicating whether it was completed successfully. Students who passed each remedial course they took in a given subject are coded 1, and 0 otherwise.

The main outcome variables in this study are also derived from NELS:88's college transcript variables. Three are dichotomous variables: whether a student graduated with a degree, whether a student interrupted his or her college studies for a period of more than one semester; and whether or not a student earned more than 10 credits. Time to bachelor's degree (for those who did complete one) was a continuous variable, measured in years.

The NELS provided rich measures of students' academic skills and achievement during high school, which functioned primarily as control variables, as we sought to separate the effects of college remediation itself from competencies brought from high school. These included 12th-grade math and reading test levels; eighth-grade achievement test scores; middle school grades; class rank as of 12th grade (which correlated very highly with GPA); high school curricular intensity; and highest math course taken in high school.

We also used as controls several indicators of student orientation towards academic work, measured during high school: the student's behavioral history in school, school engagement, self-directedness, and self-esteem. A student's higher education plans in the senior year of high school was used as another control.

Several ecological variables about the student's middle and high schools were included as controls: proportion of schoolmates who were African American or Hispanic, measured in eighth grade; proportion of school that qualified for free lunch, measured in eighth grade; whether the student attended an urban, suburban, or rural high school; and whether that school was public or private.

Finally, two NELS:88 variables indicated whether a student enrolled in a public or private college, or a two- or four-year college. Because some students move from one college to another, we coded these for the first college that a student entered after high school.

Descriptive statistics for the variables used are provided in Appendix A, both for the sample as a whole and for the subset of students who took any remediation in college.

The Counterfactual Model of Causal Inference

Researchers have known for some time about problems in conventional regression models that estimate the causal effect of one particular variable (termed a treatment variable) on an outcome while controlling for other potentially confounding variables (Lieberson, 1985). Conventional regression models do not adequately control for selection bias:

On average, subjects with one value on the treatment variable may differ on numerous background variables from those with a different value on the treatment variable. The effects of these background differences become incorporated into the estimated coefficient for the treatment variable, creating an upward or downward bias and undermining causal inference (Winship & Morgan, 1999).

Statisticians have developed a theoretical framework known as the counterfactual model of causal inference to address this problem (Heckman & Hotz, 1989; Heckman, Ichimura, Smith, & Todd, 1998; Rosenbaum & Rubin, 1983, 1985). The approach may be understood by analogy to an experimental design with random assignment of subjects into treatment and control groups. In an experiment, the random assignment of individuals to treatment and control groups assures that both groups are identical on background characteristics, so that any difference subsequently observed between the two groups on a dependent variable is attributable to the treatment alone. Something analogous is achieved in a counterfactual model by first building a model that predicts the dichotomous treatment variable. This yields a propensity score (explained below). A sample is then constructed using this propensity score, such that the treatment and control groups are close to identical on background characteristics, thus removing or drastically reducing any selection bias.

In some of the analyses reported below, the "treatment" is whether a student takes remedial coursework; in other cases, remediation serves instead as the dependent variable that we are trying to predict, while the "treatment" becomes a possible causal factor such as two-year college versus four-year college entrant. In either case, a logistic regression model is first constructed to predict the treatment. That model includes all available variables that might distinguish students who receive the treatment from those who do not (e.g., who enters a four-year rather than a two-year college). Nonlinear versions of predictors, as well as linear ones, are included in this model, and interaction terms between predictors are added. The resulting logistic regression equation predicts for each respondent the probability of that student having the treatment. This statistic is known as a propensity score, and it takes values between 0 and 1.

A second step, known as caliper matching, matches or pairs each person with a given propensity score who *did* receive the treatment (e.g., entered a four-year college) with a person who has a nearly identical propensity score (likelihood of receiving treatment), but who actually *did not* receive the treatment (did *not* enter a four-year institution). The second person in each pair functions like a member of a control group, providing a "counterfactual" estimate of what the outcome for the treated individual would have been if that person had not received the treatment. A computer algorithm in the STATA statistical package generated matched pairs of respondents, selecting at random from those treated and untreated individuals whose propensity scores were within .01 of each other. It is possible to require an exact match on additional criteria beyond the propensity score; this may yield better standard biases (see Appendix B).

Statisticians argue that for propensity matching to approximate an experiment with random assignment, it is not necessary that the treatment group be identical to the control group on every predictor, so long as the two groups are correctly matched on the propensity for treatment (Rosenbaum & Rubin, 1983). Nevertheless, practitioners examine the balance between the treatment and control group on predictors (e.g., Harding, 2002). For each predictor, we calculated a standard bias that equals the difference between the mean value of a given predictor for the treatment group and the mean value of that predictor for the controls, divided by the standard deviation of the predictor (Rosenbaum & Rubin, 1985). Tables of standard biases for our analyses are reported in Appendix B. Although the propensity score is calculated using measured variables ("observables"), researchers have demonstrated that selection bias due to unobserved variables is also reduced by propensity-score matching (DiPrete & Engelhardt, 2000).

The last step in a counterfactual analysis employs the matched sample to compare the treatment group with the controls on a dependent or outcome variable. OLS or logistic regression may be used to estimate the effect of the treatment on the outcome for the matched sample. The resulting coefficient for the treatment dummy indicates the estimated average effect of treatment for those who receive the treatment. In our case, it might be the effect of entering a four-year college rather than a two-year college on the likelihood of taking remedial coursework; or the effect of taking remedial coursework in mathematics upon one's likelihood of college graduation, after minimizing selection bias and controlling for the effects of various background variables.

Findings

How Much Remediation Occurs in College and of What Type?

Among the traditional college students covered by the NELS:88 survey, 40% took at least one remedial course in college. Mathematics was the most common remedial subject, with 28% of students taking courses in that area. Nine percent of all students took some remediation in reading, 18% in writing and comprehensive language arts, and 9% in some other academic area.

Remediation was much more widespread among NELS:88 students at two-year colleges than among those at four-year institutions, and remediation was also less frequent at selective colleges: 58% of NELS students at two-year colleges enrolled in a remedial course, compared to 31% of students at nonselective four-year colleges, 14% of students at selective four-year colleges, and only 2% of students in highly selective four-year institutions. Given the contrast between two-year colleges and four-year institutions on this issue, we decided to undertake separate analyses for the two types of institution in several sections that follow. As we shall see, the effects of remediation are very different at two- and four-year institutions.

One theme in the controversy around remediation portrays students taking many remedial courses. Our analyses show that such students exist, but they are a numerical minority among students who take remedial courses. For example, at two-year colleges, 42% of students took no remediation, 44% took between one and three courses, and only 14% enrolled in more than three remedial courses. At nonselective four-year colleges, 69% took no remediation, 26% enrolled in between one and three courses, and 5% took more than three. At selective four-year colleges, 2% of NELS:88 students took more than three remedial courses, and at highly selective four-year institutions almost no one attempted multiple remediation courses.

In terms of policy debates, we emphasize that the NELS:88 cohort represents the situation that existed *before* many states adopted new policies that moved remediation out of four-year public colleges, reducing or eliminating its presence there. Most of these students entered college in 1992. Media commentary gave the impression that large proportions of students were immersed or bogged down in remedial courses in four-year colleges. The NELS:88 data indicate, however, that students who were taking more than three remedial courses (and were allegedly bogged down) constituted at most 5% of traditional undergraduates at nonselective four-year colleges.

Who Took Remedial Coursework in College?

Conventional wisdom suggests that colleges instituted remedial courses to cope with the consequences of poorly functioning high schools, especially inner-city high schools. Adelman (1998) demonstrated that this stereotype understates the geographical diversity of students who enroll in remedial courses in college, and his point is confirmed by the NELS:88 data. Forty percent of NELS:88 students who previously attended a rural high school took remediation in college, as did 38% of students from suburban high schools and 52% of students from urban high schools.

Although students from families in the lowest quartile of socioeconomic status (SES) were more likely to undertake remedial coursework (52% did so), nearly a quarter (24%) of the students from the highest quartile SES families also enrolled in remedial courses in college. Taking remedial or developmental courses in college is by no means limited to economically disadvantaged students.

Readers may expect that remedial coursework in college is restricted to students who leave high school having taken a less rigorous curriculum or whose academic skill levels are low. In reality, remedial/

developmental education encompasses a much broader swath of students and many ability levels. The NELS tested high-school seniors on their math and reading skills before they went to college. We can classify students according to how they scored on that combined math/ reading assessment in 12th grade, from the highest first quartile to the lowest-scoring fourth quartile. We find that many skilled students took some remedial coursework in college: 10% of those who scored in the top quartile on skills tests and 25% of students in the second quartile took remedial coursework.

Similarly, the NELS:88 used transcripts to classify 12th graders in terms of the academic rigor or curricular intensity of the program they took in high school. We divided this measure into quartiles, from first (most demanding) to fourth (least demanding). The NELS:88 data indicate that among students who took the most advanced curriculum in high school (the top or first quartile), 14% took some remedial coursework in college. In addition, 32% of students in the second quartile, who took fairly demanding courses in high school, enrolled in some remedial classes in college.

These numbers indicate that enrollment in remedial classes in college is *not* limited to NELS:88 students with low academic skills in 12th grade, or to students who have had a weak curricular preparation in high school. Many relatively skilled students take remedial coursework. Conversely, many of those students who left high school with low academic skills did not take remedial courses in college: 32% of students in the lowest skills test quartile took no remedial coursework. Likewise, 42% of students in the lowest quartile on high school curricular intensity avoided remedial courses in college, according to transcript data. In sum, while college remediation is correlated with weak academic skills or preparation in high school, there is only a partial overlap. Based on the NELS:88 assessments of student academic skills, there appears to be considerable variability or arbitrariness in the assignment of students to college remediation. (Older reentry students needing remediation do not cause this pattern; such students aren't in this sample.)

Researchers have observed a higher proportion of students enrolled in remedial courses in two-year colleges than in four-year colleges, and they have assumed that this was due to different skill levels of the students in both types of institution. We tested this with multivariate models. We also determined whether attending a public versus a private sector college affects one's likelihood of remediation, and whether African American students are more likely to take remediation than academically equivalent Whites are, and whether lower SES students are more likely to enroll in remedial courses.

In Table 1, we present two kinds of multivariate models, one employing conventional logistic regression and the other using propensity matching to minimize selection effects. The dependent variable in this table is whether a student took *any* remedial courses during college.

Table 1. Student Probability of Remedial Course Placement, by Type of College and Student Background

	Bivariate	Logistic Regression	Propensity Matched
Treatment: Level of entry			
Logistic Coefficient	1.367***	0.529***	0.425***
Predicted probabilities for:			
Two-year college entrants	0.5824	0.3826	0.5236
Four-year college entrants	0.2622	0.2675	0.4181
	N = 6724	N = 6724	N = 3246
Treatment: Public or private college (Four-year entrants only)			
Logistic Coefficient	0.545***	0.516***	0.353***
Predicted probabilities for:			
Public college entrants	0.2940	0.1965	0.2468
Private college entrants	0.1945	0.1273	0.1871
	N = 4154	N = 4154	N = 2456
Treatment: Student race (Black vs. White)			
Logistic Coefficient	1.082***	0.697***	0.443***
Predicted probabilities for:			
White students	0.3493	0.2696	0.4731
Black students	0.6129	0.4257	0.5831
	N = 5490	N = 5490	N = 606
Treatment: Student family SES (split at median)			
Logistic Coefficient	−0.762***	−0.159	0.088
Predicted probabilities for:			
High SES students	0.3167	0.2894	0.4250
Low SES students	0.4982	0.3232	0.4037
	N = 6879	N = 6879	N = 1852

Source: NELS:88

Logistic regression models control for student race; 12th-grade math and reading competency level; 8th-grade standardized achievement test scores; elementary school grades; class rank as of 12th grade; proportion of 8th grade Black or Hispanic; proportion of 8th grade qualifies for free lunch; parent's highest degree earned; family income; students' high school curricular intensity: highest math course; behavioral history; school engagement and higher education plans; self-esteem and self-directedness: urban, suburban, or rural high school; high school sector; college sector, level of entry.

The findings reported in the propensity matched column represent the effect of the treatment on matched pairs of students with equal probabilities to receive the treatment. Probabilities to receive the treatment are calculated using all of the controls utilized in the logistic regression models, as well as a series of interaction terms and multinominal terms to allow for nonlinear effects. As an additional constraint, we required that both students in the matched pairs be in the same quartile on the 12th grade achievement test.

* $p < 0.05$ ** $p < 0.01$ *** $p < 0.001$

The top row in Table 1 examines how two-year college entrants differ from four-year college entrants in terms of their log odds of taking remediation. Thus, the "treatment" is entry to a two-year versus a four-year college, while the outcome is taking any remedial coursework in college. Because log odds estimates are not easy to interpret, we have also converted them into probabilities of taking remediation, by setting all predictors other than the treatment variable at their mean values. This allows us to report the probability that a student at a two-year college would take remedial coursework, compared to the probability that an identical student at a four-year college would take remedial courses, where this hypothetical student is average on all academic background and sociodemographic variables.

The first column in Table 1 labeled "Bivariate" reports the raw effect, with no controls. We see that 58% of NELS:88 students at two-year colleges undertook remedial coursework, compared to 26% of students entering four-year colleges. That difference is statistically highly significant.

The second column in Table 1 reports a logistic regression model in which level of entry to a two- or four-year college predicts whether a student took any remedial coursework, after statistical controls for each student's race and family SES, academic preparation, performance and skill during high school, and for the kind of school attended. With such controls, the difference in remediation attributable to entering a community college rather than a four-year college shrinks: 38% of two-year college entrants took remedial courses, compared to 27% for four-year college entrants, still a statistically significant difference.

The third column of Table 1 provides a propensity matched model to reduce selection bias. This model also employs all the controls utilized in the previous logistic regression.

This counterfactual model again shows a highly significant difference in the likelihood of taking remedial coursework during college when comparing matched two-year college entrants and four-year college entrants, who are otherwise equivalent in terms of academic skills, race, and family background. On average, a two-year college entrant has an 11% higher probability of taking remediation than an otherwise equivalent four-year college entrant (.5236 minus .4181).

The logistic approach and the counterfactual or propensity models are consistent with one another, but they go against conventional wisdom that the reason that students in two-year colleges are more likely to enroll in remedial courses is that those students have weaker academic backgrounds. Two-year colleges are considerably more likely to place a student in a remedial course than four-year colleges are, *even for students with equivalent academic skills and background.*

The second panel in Table 1 reports analyses that examine whether private four-year colleges differ from public four-year colleges in remedial coursework. Since most two-year colleges are public institutions, including them in this analysis could conflate the already-documented association between two-year colleges and remediation with the relationship between public colleges and remediation. To avoid this confusion, students who enrolled in two-year colleges are excluded from this one analysis. The first bivariate column indicates that on average 29%

of students in public four-year colleges took remedial courses compared to 19% of students in private four-year colleges, which is statistically highly significant. The logistic regression in the second column of the table adds controls for family background and high school skills and performance. Even after those controls, a statistically significant difference remains: On average, a student faces a 7% higher probability of taking remediation in a public four-year college than in a private one (.1965 compared to .1273). In the third column, the propensity model minimizes selection effects but continues to show a significant difference: A student in a public four-year college has a 6% higher probability of taking remedial coursework than one in a private four-year college who has an identical high school preparation, test scores, and family background.

The third panel in Table 1 examines the effect of race on a student's probability of taking remediation in college. The bivariate column indicates that on average 61% of non-Hispanic Black students took some remediation, compared to 35% of non-Hispanic White students. (Hispanic and other ethnic groups are excluded from this particular analysis.) The sociologically important question is whether this huge difference disappears after we take into account detailed information on student preparation and achievement in high school, as well as family SES and type of high school and college attended. We find that the racial difference does not disappear, although it shrinks: The logistic regression indicates a statistically significant difference between otherwise equivalent White and Black students, a 16% difference in the probability of undertaking remedial coursework. The propensity matched model in the third column estimates a statistically significant difference of 11% between otherwise identical Black and White students on the probability of enrolling in remedial courses.

Evidently, African American students are significantly more likely to enroll in college remedial courses than are White students with the same academic skills and preparation and social background. Unfortunately, we cannot tell from the NELS:88 data to what extent these African American students are *required* to take remedial coursework, or are *advised* to take such courses, or whether they themselves *choose* to take these courses.

In the bottom panel of Table 1, we examine whether socioeconomic status itself, independent of race and other factors, is associated with taking remedial coursework. In both the logistic regression model and the propensity score model, both of which control for students' academic background and other covariates, there ceases to be a significant SES effect. Evidently, SES is not a significant determinant of taking remedial coursework, independent of high school academic background.

To summarize, *after taking account of family background and academic skills and performance in high school*, we find three separate and independent effects: Students who enter two-year colleges are more likely than equivalent students in four-year colleges to enroll in remedial courses; students who enroll in public colleges are more likely than academically equivalent students in private colleges to take remedial coursework; and African American students are significantly more likely than otherwise similar non-Hispanic White students to enroll in remedial courses.

What Are the Effects of Taking Remedial Courses on Graduation Rates and Time to Degree?

Some critics of college remediation have suggested that remediation has deleterious effects on student progress, while supporters suggest that it helps students. We examined five distinct outcomes: (a) completing 10 or fewer credits; (b) an interrupted education, where a student leaves college for at least one year before completing a degree; (c) whether a student completed any degree (among two-year college entrants only); (d) whether a student completed a bachelor's degree (among four-year college entrants only); (e) time to degree (for all bachelor's degree recipients).

In Table 2, we look at the effect of taking *any remediation* (i.e., one or more remedial courses) on these outcomes. In a later section, we will determine whether students with larger amounts of developmental/remedial coursework follow the same pattern.

The first panel in Table 2 predicts whether a student completed 10 or fewer credits by year 2000; they either dropped out or they made very little progress in college. (Overall, about 9% of NELS:88 students were in this situation.) The first column in Table 2 reports that 11% of remedial students make little progress, compared to about 7% of students who do not enroll in remediation. At first impression, this statistically significant effect suggests that remedial coursework might drastically curtail progress towards the degree; however, there are no controls in this bivariate model. In the second column, in a logistical regression model that includes controls for student academic background in high school, plus sociodemographic controls, *the effect of remediation reverses*: Fewer students with remedial coursework earned 10 or fewer credits, compared to academically and socially similar students with no remedial coursework. This effect is statistically significant but small in magnitude (under 2%). In the third column, a propensity matched analysis also indicates that after one controls for academic preparation, a student's family background, and other covariates, taking one or more remedial courses is significantly associated with a *lower* probability of earning few credits, about a 6% lower probability.

The second panel in Table 2 describes a phenomenon that is especially common among students from less affluent families: leaving college for a substantial time before returning and completing a degree. Although there is a bivariate association between remediation and an interrupted college education, this disappears in both multivariate

Table 2. Effect of Enrolling in One or More Remedial Courses on Student Progress through Higher Education

	Bivariate	Logistic Regression	Propensity Matched
Outcome: Student earned 10 or fewer credits			
Logistic Coefficient	0.456***	−0.634***	−0.593***
Predicted probabilities for:			
Remedial students	0.1120	0.0183	0.0838
Nonremedial students	0.0740	0.0339	0.1420
	N = 6879	N = 6879	N = 3292
Outcome: Student left college for at least one year before receiving first degree			
Logistic Coefficient	0.666***	−0.101	−0.096
Predicted probabilities for:			
Remedial students	0.4248	0.2535	0.3948
Nonremedial students	0.2751	0.2732	0.4179
	N = 6879	N = 6879	N = 3292
Outcome: Student earned a college degree (two-year college entrants only)			
Logistic Coefficient	−0.328***	0.105	0.179
Predicted probabilities for:			
Remedial students	0.2842	0.2882	0.3404
Nonremedial students	0.3553	0.2672	0.3105
	N = 2661	N = 2661	N = 1670
Outcome: Student earned a college degree (four-year college entrants only)			
Logistic Coefficient	−1.159***	−0.316***	−0.288***
Predicted probabilities for:			
Remedial students	0.5211	0.7367	0.5685
Nonremedial students	0.7761	0.7933	0.6373
	N = 4173	N = 4173	N = 1623
Outcome: Years to Bachelor's degree			
OLS Coefficient	0.633***	0.150***	0.211***
Predicted time to degree for:			
Remedial students	5.070	5.100	4.970
Nonremedial students	4.437	4.950	4.759
	N = 3413	N = 3413	N = 1226

Source: NELS:88
* $p < 0.05$ ** $p. < 0.01$ *** $p. < 0.001$

models that control for academic and family background. After controls, there is no statistically significant difference between students who took and did not take remedial courses, in terms of taking time out from college.

The third panel in Table 2 looks solely at entrants to two-year colleges and examines whether taking remedial education affects their chances of completing a degree (an associate degree or higher, since some students transfer to bachelor's programs rather than completing an associate's degree). The bivariate analysis indicates that on average, students who took remediation at a two-year college had significantly lower graduation rates than students at the same kind of institution who did not take remedial coursework. However, after we add controls for family background and academic performance in high school, this effect is reduced to nonsignificance, in both logistic and propensity models. We interpret this as meaning that taking one or more remedial courses in a two-year college does not, in itself, lower a student's chances of graduation. Causal factors that do reduce one's chances of graduating include low family SES, poor high school preparation, and being Black, but not college remediation *per se*.

The fourth panel of Table 2 looks solely at entrants to four-year colleges and examines whether taking remediation affects the probability of graduation with a bachelor's degree. Here the picture is different. In the models that control for high school preparation and family background, including selection effects, taking remedial courses is associated with a significantly lower likelihood of degree completion. In the logistic regression, remedial students have a 6% lower probability of graduating, and in the propensity model, remedial students have a 7% lower probability of completing a degree. Unlike the situation for two-year college entrants, among students in four-year colleges there *is* a statistically significant negative effect of taking remedial coursework on graduation.

The last panel in Table 2 assesses the effects of taking any remedial coursework on time to degree, for the subpopulation of NELS:88 students who completed a bachelor's degree within 8.5 years of leaving high school. Here we find that there is a statistically significant delay associated with taking remedial coursework, after we controlled for other characteristics. However, the magnitude of this effect is quite modest: On average, students with remediation took around 0.2 years longer to graduate, which is between 2 and 3 months extra.

Taken as a whole, these models suggest that taking some remedial or developmental coursework has no negative effects on two-year college entrants' likelihood of gaining a degree but does lower the average chances that a four-year college entrant will graduate by about 6% to 7%, after controlling for academic preparation and high school skills and family background. Nevertheless, in the NELS:88 population, over half of four-year college students who took remedial courses did graduate from college within about 8 years of leaving high school. Thus, taking remediation in a four-year college modestly lowers one's odds of graduating but does not prevent most students completing a bachelor's degree. Taking remedial coursework also slightly increases time to a bachelor's degree. One should also note that so far there is no evidence in any of the multivariate models that remediation on average improves students' chances of graduation in either two- or four-year institutions. However, we shall return to this issue below.

What Are the Effects of Taking MANY Remedial Courses on Graduation Rates and Time to Degree?

We noted earlier that taking many remedial courses is atypical. However, several critics of remediation focus on this group, arguing that they especially are harmed by remediation. We therefore examined the effect of enrolling in *three or more* remedial courses on the same range of outcomes. The results of these analyses are presented in Table 3.

In the top panel, one sees that taking many remedial courses has an unclear relationship to earning 10 or fewer credits. Only in the logistic regression model was there a statistically significant effect: a slightly *lower* likelihood of earning few credits. In the propensity model, this effect was not statistically significant.

The multivariate models in the second panel in Table 3 suggest that there was no significant influence of taking multiple remedial courses on leaving college for a year prior to graduation. Nor was there a discernable effect of taking multiple remedial courses on the likelihood of graduating for two-year college entrants, as the third panel shows. Therefore, for two-year college entrants, even students who take three or more remedial courses are not disadvantaged relative to academically equivalent students who took less or no remediation.

Research by Deil-Amen and Rosenbaum (2002) has given the impression that taking multiple remedial courses is itself a serious barrier to graduation from two-year college. When we controlled for students' academic preparation and abilities leaving high school for a two-year college, we found that taking multiple remedial coursework in a two-year college does not in itself disadvantage these students. Deil-Amen and Rosenbaum did not distinguish between the effects of having a weak high school academic preparation and the effects of taking multiple remedial courses in college. Our analyses suggest that the problem is the former, not the latter. Taking several remedial courses (characterized as being "bogged down" in remedial coursework) does not reduce chances of graduation.

By contrast, for entrants to four-year colleges, the analyses reported in Table 3 suggest that there was a statistically significant disadvantage for students who took three or more remedial courses: Their graduation rates were between 12% and 15% lower than those of students with comparable skills and backgrounds who took fewer or no remedial courses. However, while taking many remedial courses clearly lowers graduation chances for students in bachelor's degree programs, *about one in three students who took many remedial courses nevertheless completed their degree within eight years or so*, overcoming disadvantages in high school preparation and in social background.

Table 3. Effect of Enrolling in Three or More Remedial Courses on Student Progress through Higher Education

	Bivariate	Logistic Regression	Propensity Matched
Outcome: Student earned 10 or fewer credits			
Logistic Coefficient	0.179	–0.933***	–0.908
Predicted probabilities for:			
Multiple remedial students	0.1025	0.0119	0.0968
Other students	0.0871	0.0298	0.2099
	N = 6979	N = 6979	N = 1580
Outcome: Student left college for at least one year before receiving first degree			
Logistic Coefficient	0.784***	–0.024	–0.151
Predicted probabilities for:			
Multiple remedial students	0.4943	0.2617	0.4752
Other students	0.3085	0.2664	0.5130
	N = 6979	N = 6979	N = 1580
Outcome: Student earned a college degree (two-year college entrants only)			
Logistic Coefficient	–0.351**	0.006	0.212
Predicted probabilities for:			
Multiple remedial students	0.2586	0.2802	0.2348
Other students	0.3312	0.2790	0.2751
	N = 2706	N = 2706	N = 1092
Outcome: Student earned a college degree (four-year college entrants only)			
Logistic Coefficient	–1.721***	–0.594***	–0.616***
Predicted probabilities for:			
Multiple remedial students	0.3357	0.6705	0.3358
Other students	0.7385	0.7855	0.4834
	N = 4173	N = 4173	N = 488
Outcome: Years to Bachelor's degree			
OLS Coefficient	0.889***	0.164**	0.334***
Predicted time to degree for:			
Multiple remedial students	5.422	5.151	5.418
Other students	4.533	4.987	5.084
	N = 3413	N = 3413	N = 316

Source: NELS:88
* p < 0.05   ** p. < 0.01   *** p. < 0.001

Among students who obtained a bachelor's degree, we also observed that remediation increased time to degree. For students who took three or more remedial courses in a four-year college, time to degree increased on average between .164 and .334 years, depending on the model. This is a statistically significant but substantively modest delay. In sum, unlike the case for two-year colleges, students in four-year colleges who take many remedial courses are at a disadvantage in earning a degree, over and above any disadvantage stemming from their high school skills and background.

Are Some Types of Remedial Coursework More Consequential Than Others Are?

Adelman (1999) argued that, on average, students who take remedial reading courses are less likely to graduate, whereas those taking remedial mathematics had a better chance of graduation. His analyses were based on simple (uncontrolled) percentages, however, and did not control for students' academic background. One might interpret them as saying that the kinds of students who need remediation in reading tend to come into college with the weakest academic skills and therefore have the lowest rates of graduation. We will ask a quite different question: *after controlling for student academic skills prior to college*, does remedial coursework itself improve or worsen a student's chance of graduation? To pose the question this way, we must separate a student's academic background from whether the student took remedial courses in college. Where we follow Adelman is his insight that it is important to examine whether remediation in math, reading, and writing differ in their consequences.

Table 4 looks individually at the effects of remedial coursework in reading, math, and writing, solely for entrants to four-year colleges. The outcome of interest is whether a student graduates with a degree within 8.5 years of leaving high school. The logistic models examine the effect of taking a particular type of remedial coursework in college, after controlling for a student's family background and high school preparation and skills. In the top panel, we observe a significant *negative effect* on graduation of taking one or more remedial *reading* courses, after controlling for a student's academic and social background. On average, students who took remedial coursework in reading at a four-year college had between a 7% (logistic model) and 11% (propensity model) lower probability of completing a degree than otherwise identical students who did not enroll in remedial reading. This supports Adelman's thesis insofar as reading remediation creates a disadvantage in terms of graduation. However, our analyses also show that 40% of four-year entrants who took remediation in reading nevertheless graduated with a degree. That does not fit Adelman's belief that, "when reading is the core of the problem, the odds of success in college environments are so low that other approaches are called for" (1998, p. 11).

The findings for remedial mathematics coursework were less clear. In the logistic model in Table 4, students who took two or more remedial math classes had on average a 5% lower probability of graduation than students with one or no remedial courses in math had. The pro-

Table 4. Effects of Different Types of Remediation on Senior-College Student Graduation Rates

	Bivariate	Logistic Regression	Propensity Matched
Treatment: Any reading remediation			
Logistic Coefficient	−1.374***	−0.355**	−0.446**
Predicted probabilities for:			
Remedial students	0.4037	0.7164	0.4087
Nonremedial students	0.7279	0.7826	0.5190
	N = 4173	N = 4173	N = 429
Treatment: Two or more math remedial courses			
Logistic Coefficient	−1.416***	−0.260*	−0.464
Predicted probabilities for:			
Remedial students	0.3965	0.7351	0.3343
Nonremedial students	0.7301	0.7825	0.4439
	N = 4173	N = 4173	N = 488
Treatment: Passed all writing remediation etc.			
Logistic Coefficient	−0.920***	−0.039	−0.109
Predicted probabilities for:			
Remedial students	0.5225	0.7740	0.5236
Nonremedial students	0.7330	0.7807	0.5508
	N = 4173	N = 4173	N = 870

Source: NELS:88
* p < 0.05   ** p. < 0.01   *** p. < 0.001

pensity model showed an effect in the same direction, but it was not statistically significant. A cautious interpretation would be that taking remedial coursework in mathematics might have no effect on graduation or possibly a weak negative effect on graduation.

The bottom panel in Table 4 reports that taking remedial courses in writing had no significant effect on graduation, for four-year college students, after controlling for academic background. Both multivariate models are consistent on this.

Overall, then, among entrants to four-year colleges, remediation in reading had a clear negative effect on graduation prospects, remedial mathematics had no effect or possibly a weak negative effect, and remedial writing had no significant impact on graduation.

Interestingly, the pattern for remediation in two-year colleges was quite different. Those results are reported in Table 5. In the top panel, we find that entrants to two-year colleges who took reading remediation were about 11% *more likely* to earn a degree (associate's or bachelor's) with 8 years of high school than academically equivalent students who did not take reading remediation, according to the propensity

Table 5. Effects of Different Types of Remediation on Two-Year College Student Graduation Rates

	Bivariate	Logistic Regression	Propensity Matched
Treatment: Any reading remediation			
Logistic Coefficient	0.040	0.147	0.529*
Predicted probabilities for:			
Remedial students	0.3213	0.3154	0.3348
Nonremedial students	0.3128	0.2751	0.2287
	N = 2706	N = 2706	N = 690
Treatment: Two or more math remedial courses			
Logistic Coefficient	−0.591***	−0.177*	−0.157*
Predicted probabilities for:			
Remedial students	0.2191	0.2514	0.2378
Nonremedial students	0.3326	0.2861	0.2674
	N = 2706	N = 2706	N = 1092
Treatment: Passed all writing remediation etc.			
Logistic Coefficient	0.023	0.278**	0.368**
Predicted probabilities for:			
Remedial students	0.3175	0.3213	0.3193
Nonremedial students	0.3126	0.2640	0.2449
	N = 2706	N = 2706	N = 1220

Source: NELS:88
* p < 0.05   ** p. < 0.01   *** p. < 0.001

model. There was a similar trend in the logistic model, but it did not attain statistical significance. This is the first evidence, albeit weak, that remedial coursework might have a positive impact on students' chances of graduating from college.

In the second panel of Table 5, we note findings for mathematics remediation in two-year colleges. In both the logistic regression analysis and the propensity matched model, we observe a small but statistically significant *negative effect* of taking two or more remedial math courses on graduation rates. Students who take two or more remedial mathematics courses in a two-year college have about a 3% lower likelihood of graduating with a degree, net of high school preparation.

In the bottom panel of Table 5, we see that students who took writing remediation in a two-year college were *more likely* to graduate with a degree (either associate's or bachelor's) than students of equivalent high school skills and social background who did not take remedial writing. Both multivariate models are statistically significant and show the same effect. The difference—a positive effect of remedial or developmental coursework—was 6% in the logistic model and 7% in the propensity model.

Overall, then, Table 5 suggests that for two-year college entrants, after one has controlled for high school preparation and academic skills prior to entering college, taking remedial coursework in writing and perhaps also in reading improves the chances that a student will graduate with a degree. However, remedial coursework in mathematics is associated with slightly lower graduation rates.

The Effect of Successful Completion of Remedial Coursework

In our analyses so far, we have examined whether students who enrolled in remedial coursework were more or less likely to complete a degree. However, substantial numbers of students withdraw from remedial courses, and others do not attend class since there is often no penalty for doing so in non-credit courses. Some scholars argue that in order to assess whether remedial courses improve student skills and enhance chances of graduation, one ought to focus on those students who complete remedial coursework rather than on all who enroll (cf. Bettinger & Long, 2004; Lavin, Alba, & Silberstein, 1981). Most students pass *all* the remedial courses they enroll in writing (68%) and in reading (71%). However, only 30% pass all their remedial math courses: Apparently, the majority of those taking remedial math need more than one attempt before passing.

For each subject area, we decided to contrast those students who successfully completed all their remedial courses in that area with students who did not ever enroll in remedial coursework in that subject, controlling for skills and coursework intensity during high school and for sociodemographic background. In this comparison, we excluded students who took remedial coursework in a given area but either failed a course or withdrew. This provides a different perspective on whether remedial coursework helps: It asks whether students who successfully completed remedial work in an area (reading, writing, or mathematics) had better or worse outcomes than equivalent students who did not undertake remedial coursework at all.

Table 6 reports on these multivariate models, all of which predict graduating with a degree. For remedial courses in reading, we found that two-year college students who passed remedial reading were *more likely to graduate* than were academically and otherwise equivalent students who did *not* take remedial reading. The positive effect was a 11% higher graduation rate in the conventional logistic model, and 8% in the propensity matched model.

This positive influence of remediation was also evident for remedial writing in two-year colleges. Students who passed remedial writing courses were 13% more likely to graduate in both models. There was also an apparent benefit to taking remedial mathematics in the

Table 6. Graduation Rates and Remedial Success: Graduate Rates for Students Who Passed All Remediation, Compared to Those Who Did Not Take Remediation

	Bivariate	Logistic Regression	Propensity Matched
Two-Year College Entrants Only			
Treatment: Passed all reading remediation			
Logistic Coefficient	0.490**	0.477***	0.415**
Predicted graduation rates for:			
Successful remedial students	0.4261	0.3884	0.3388
Nonremedial students	0.3125	0.2827	0.2528
	N = 2508	N = 2508	N = 464
Treatment: Passed all math remediation			
Logistic Coefficient	–0.157	0.490***	–0.030
Predicted probabilities for:			
Remedial students	0.3297	0.3973	0.3404
Nonremedial students	0.3651	0.2876	0.3472
	N = 2009	N = 2009	N = 1160
Treatment: Passed all writing remediation, etc.			
Logistic Coefficient	0.473***	0.591***	0.600***
Predicted probabilities for:			
Remedial students	0.4228	0.4140	0.3908
Nonremedial students	0.3134	0.2812	0.2605
	N = 2407	N = 2407	N = 770
Four-Year College Entrants			
Treatment: Passed all reading remediation			
Logistic Coefficient	–1.241***	–0.337	–0.271
Predicted graduation rates for:			
Successful remedial students	0.4360	0.7236	0.5551
Nonremedial students	0.7278	0.7857	0.4877
	N = 4070	N = 4070	N = 328
Treatment: Passed all math remediation			
Logistic Coefficient	–0.864***	–0.089	–0.066
Predicted probabilities for:			
Remedial students	0.5723	0.7938	0.6066
Nonremedial students	0.7604	0.8079	0.6222
	N = 3833	N = 3833	N = 652
Treatment: Passed all writing remediation, etc.			
Logistic Coefficient	–0.664***	0.270	0.038
Predicted probabilities for:			
Remedial students	0.7327	0.8284	0.5840
Nonremedial students	0.5853	0.7866	0.5931
	N = 4013	N = 4013	N = 582

Source: NELS:88
* p < 0.05   ** p. < 0.01   *** p. < 0.001

conventional logistic regression model (11%), but that effect was not apparent in the propensity matched model.

Overall, however, there is evidence among two-year college entrants that students who passed remedial courses had better educational outcomes than did similar students who never took remedial courses. This positive picture of remedial coursework, however, did not carry over to four-year colleges (the bottom of Table 6). Instead, we observe that those students in four-year colleges who completed remedial reading courses graduated at about the same ratio as similar students who did not take remedial reading (a 7% difference). For remedial writing, the analyses were mixed, with the conventional model indicating a 4% disadvantage, while the propensity model indicated no significant difference between those who passed remedial writing and those who did not take it. Finally, there appeared to be no significant difference between students who completed remedial math and students who never took remediation in mathematics.

In sum, there was evidence that students who successfully completed remedial coursework in two-year colleges gained from that coursework. There was no such positive evidence about remediation in four-year colleges.

Conclusion and Discussion

Our analyses show that remedial coursework was widespread among undergraduates in the high school class of 1992, but did not dominate their college years. Most took only one or two such courses, and most passed those courses successfully, usually in the first year of college.

The common-sense impression that remedial coursework is taken by students with poor high school preparation or very weak academic skills is inaccurate. Our analyses show that many college students with limited academic skills do not take remedial coursework, while substantial numbers of students with strong high school backgrounds nevertheless take remedial courses. Nor is remedial coursework the preserve of the economically disadvantaged: Large proportions of students who graduated from suburban and rural high schools take remedial coursework in college, as do many students from high SES families. These empirical findings contrast with public debates that portray remediation as a preserve of a small group of academic incompetents who have no hope of success in higher education.

Critics have accused public colleges and universities of abandoning their commitment to academic standards, of granting diplomas to undeserving students. Implicit is the claim these colleges have done so to accommodate academically unprepared minority students. The NELS:88 data show that public colleges are more likely to require remedial coursework than private institutions, for equivalently skilled students. In this sense, public institutions appear to have created higher hurdles than their private sector equivalents have created. After controlling for high school preparation and academic skills, we found that a student is also less likely to graduate from a public than from a private university. In addition, Black students are more likely to take remediation than similarly prepared White students are. This is the opposite of the "soft bigotry of low expectations" that critics have claimed operates in public education.

Critics of developmental education suggest that students who need remediation will not be able to graduate. The NELS:88 shows that 28% of remedial students in two-year colleges graduate within 8.5 years (compared to 43% of nonremedial students) and that 52% of remedial students in four-year colleges finish bachelor's degrees (compared to 78% of students without remedial coursework). Looked at another way, 50% of African American bachelor program graduates and 34% of Hispanic bachelor program graduates in the NELS:88 survey graduated after taking remedial coursework. If those students were deemed unsuited for college and denied entry to four-year institutions, a large proportion of the minority graduates in the high school class of 1992 would never have received degrees. (These graduation numbers would be considerably larger if the NELS survey followed students beyond 8.5 years from high school. From our analyses of the NLSY, we find that about a quarter of students who ultimately get a bachelor's degree take longer than that to graduate. So graduation rates measured 8.5 years after high school provide an overly pessimistic picture of the prospects of weaker students.)

Our analyses were able to distinguish the effects of a poor high school academic preparation from the effects of taking remedial coursework in college, and we found that most of the gap in graduation rates has little to do with taking remedial classes in college. Instead, that gap reflects preexisting skill differences carried over from high school. In two-year colleges, we found that taking remedial classes was *not* associated at all with lower chances of academic success, even for students who took three or more remedial courses. Contra Deil-Amen and Rosenbaum's (2002) thesis, in multivariate analyses two-year college students who took remedial courses were somewhat less likely to drop out in the short run, and were no less likely to graduate than were nonremedial students with similar academic backgrounds. In addition, two-year college students who successfully passed remedial courses were more likely to graduate than equivalent students who never took remediation were, suggesting that developmental courses did help those students who completed them. These apparent benefits from taking remediation should not obscure the fact that overall graduation rates in two-year colleges are quite low. Nor should we overlook our finding that taking remediation caused a modest delay in time to degree for two-year college students.

The situation was different among entrants to four-year colleges. At four-year institutions, taking some remedial courses did modestly lower student chances of graduation, even after we took prior academic preparation and skills into account. Student chances of graduation were reduced between 6% and 7%. This should be a matter of concern, but this is not the same as saying that students in four-year colleges who take remediation are unable to graduate. On the contrary, in four-year colleges, the graduation rate for students who took remedial coursework was about two thirds of the graduation rate of students who took no remediation. As was the case for two-year college students, these lower graduation rates faced by students in four-year colleges predominantly reflected skill problems students brought from high school, rather than a negative consequence of taking remedial courses. Nevertheless, taking remedial coursework in reading at a four-year college had a clear negative effect on graduation, even after we controlled for academic skills and background. This did not occur for remedial writing courses. The effect of remedial math courses was ambiguous.

The majority of colleges in the United States are unselective: They admit almost every high school graduate who applies and can pay tuition. Many schools combine open access with requirements that weaker students take remedial or college prep courses in academic areas in which they have problems. Thus, remedial education acts as a gatekeeper and a quality control in higher education, though this function is rarely acknowledged. Students who can successfully pass these courses continue into regular college-level courses. Students who can't make it through remediation either drop out or are academically terminated. Ironically, when colleges require that their students demonstrate proficiency in basic skills by passing remedial courses, they are criticized for wasting the time of the students who fail to overcome these hurdles. At the same time, the provision of remedial courses is perceived by the public as indicating a lack of standards rather than as a mechanism for setting a basic skills standard.

Whether it is desirable for society to offer educational opportunity to students who have a one-in-four chance of graduating from a two-year college, or to students who have a 50% likelihood of graduating from a four-year college, is a complex question. Those students who do earn the degree against the odds enjoy considerably higher incomes. Even those who enter college but don't complete a degree benefit economically, compared to high school graduates. How does one balance the clear benefits of admissions policies for those who succeed against the costs of those who fail? This controversy is also about public finances: How is taxpayers' money best used? Not least, the question touches on issues of inequality and social justice: If children of poor and minority families disproportionately leave high school with poor academic skills, should social policy encourage colleges to redress those skill problems, or should failure at the high school level be irreversible? Currently, college remediation functions partly as a second-chance policy and partly as a form of institutional quality control.

Appendix A

Descriptive Statistics of Variables Used in the Analysis

	NELS Source		Mean	Standard Deviation	Range	Number of Cases
Remediation variables						
R took any remediation	REMCRSE		0.403	0.491	0–1	6879
R took three or more remedial courses	REMCRSE		0.145	0.352	0–1	6879
R took any remedial reading courses	REMREAD		0.092	0.290	0–1	6879
R took two or more remedial math courses	REMMATH		0.119	0.324	0–1	6879
R took any remedial writing or comprehensive language courses	REMFLAG, CRSECODE		0.179	0.383	0–1	6879
R passed all reading remediation	REMFLAG, PASSFLAG		0.067	0.250	0–1	6690
R passed all math remediation	REMFLAG, PASSFLAG		0.193	0.395	0–1	5899
R passed all writing remediation	REMFLAG, PASSFLAG		0.117	0.321	0–1	6485
Outcome variables						
R earned 10 or fewer credits	TCREDB	All	0.089	0.485	0–1	6879
		Remedial	0.112	0.315	0–1	2275
R left college for at least one year before receiving first degree	CONTIN	All	0.335	0.472	0–1	6879
		Remedial	0.425	0.494	0–1	2275
R earned a college degree (community college entrants only)	CONSDEG, REFSELCT	All	0.314	0.464	0–1	3033
		Remedial	0.284	0.451	0–1	1766
R earned a college degree (senior college entrants only)	CONSDEG, REFSELCT	All	0.709	0.454	0–1	3846
		Remedial	0.521	0.500	0–1	1008
Years to bachelor's degree	BACHTME	All	4.581	1.078	2.58–9.42	3059
		Remedial	5.070	1.122	2.66–9.42	696

Background covariates						
White male (dummy)	SEX, RACE	All	0.370	0.483	0–1	6879
		Remedial	0.334	0.472	0–1	2275
Black male (dummy)	SEX, RACE	All	0.041	0.198	0–1	6879
		Remedial	0.075	0.263	0–1	2275
Black female (dummy)	SEX, RACE	All	0.055	0.228	0–1	6879
		Remedial	0.071	0.257	0–1	2275
Hispanic male (dummy)	SEX, RACE	All	0.048	0.213	0–1	6879
		Remedial	0.071	0.256	0–1	2275
Hispanic female (dummy)	SEX, RACE	All	0.048	0.215	0–1	6879
		Remedial	0.075	0.264	0–1	2275
Asian male (dummy)	SEX, RACE	All	0.021	0.141	0–1	6879
		Remedial	0.016	0.125	0–1	2275
Asian female (dummy)	SEX, RACE	All	0.021	0.145	0–1	6879
		Remedial	0.017	0.127	0–1	2275
Other male (dummy)	SEX, RACE	All	0.007	0.081	0–1	6879
		Remedial	0.012	0.107	0–1	2275
Other female (dummy)	SEX, RACE	All	0.008	0.086	0–1	6879
		Remedial	0.013	0.113	0–1	2275
12th grade test score (percentile)	SRTSTPCT	All	59.465	25.972	0–100	6879
		Remedial	44.732	22.623	0–100	2275
8th grade behavior problems scale	BYS55a–BYS55f	All	0.206	0.327	0–2	6879
		Remedial	0.270	0.374	0–2	2275
8th grade standardized test composite	BY2XCOMP	All	53.819	9.619	31–76	6879
		Remedial	48.469	7.785	31–76	2275
High school class rank percentile	CLSSRANK	All	0.591	0.266	0–1	6879
		Remedial	0.478	0.245	0–1	2275
Percent minority students in school (8th grade)	G8MINOR	All	2.718	2.070	0–7	6879
		Remedial	3.212	2.220	0–7	2275

Appendix A (continued)

	NELS Source		Mean	Standard Deviation	Range	Number of Cases
Percent free or reduced lunch students in school (8th grade)	G8LUNCH	All	2.906	2.014	0–7	6879
		Remedial	3.327	2.098	0–7	2275
Parents' highest education level	BYPARED	All	3.344	1.232	1–6	6879
		Remedial	3.038	1.184	1–6	2275
Yearly family income	BYFAMINC	All	10.298	2.217	1–16	6879
		Remedial	9.819	2.338	1–16	2275
Completed "New Basics" curriculum (dummy)	F2RNWB3A	All	0.393	0.488	0–1	6879
		Remedial	0.252	0.434	0–1	2275
Completed pre-calculus course (dummy)	HIGHMATH	All	0.251	0.433	0–1	6879
		Remedial	0.063	0.243	0–1	2275
High school academic intensity top quartile	ACCURHSQ	All	0.251	0.434	0–1	6879
		Remedial	0.094	0.292	0–1	2275
High school academic intensity 2nd quartile	ACCURHSQ	All	0.256	0.437	0–1	6879
		Remedial	0.232	0.422	0–1	2275
High school academic intensity 3rd quartile	ACCURHSQ	All	0.202	0.402	0–1	6879
		Remedial	0.275	0.446	0–1	2275
Urban high school (dummy)	PHSURBAN	All	0.281	0.449	0–1	6879
		Remedial	0.303	0.461	0–1	2275
Suburban high school (dummy)	PHSURBAN	All	0.431	0.495	0–1	6879
		Remedial	0.405	0.491	0–1	2275
Public high school (dummy)	HSTYPE	All	0.890	0.313	0–1	6879
		Remedial	0.918	0.274	0–1	2275
Came to class unprepared	BYS78A-BYS78C	All	0.524	0.871	0–3	6879
		Remedial	0.665	0.980	0–3	2275

Description	Variable	Group	Mean	SD	Range	N
Bored in class	BYS69A, BYS70A, BYS71A, BYS72A, BYS73	All	2.220	0.550	1–4	6879
		Remedial	2.236	0.551	1–4	2275
Retained in grade (before 8th grade)	BYS74	All	0.097	0.294	0–1	6879
		Remedial	0.143	0.347	0–1	2275
Time spent on homework	BYHOMEWK	All	4.220	1.477	1–8	6879
		Remedial	4.019	1.411	1–8	2275
Grades composite (8th grade)	BYGRADS	All	3.105	0.679	0.5–4	6879
		Remedial	2.834	0.649	0.5–4	2275
College degree plans (dummy, 8th grade)	BYPSEPLN	All	0.783	0.412	0–1	6879
		Remedial	0.701	0.458	0–1	2275
Parents educational plans (8th grade)	BYS48A–BYS48B	All	4.917	1.317	0–6	6879
		Remedial	4.741	1.421	0–6	2275
Age first enrolled in college	REFDATE	All	18.923	1.386	14–27	6879
		Remedial	19.046	1.431	14–27	2275
Locus of control (standardized, 8th grade)	BYLOCUS2	All	0.118	0.579	-2.3–1.3	6879
		Remedial	-0.003	0.590	-2.3–1.3	2275
Self-concept (standardized, 8th grade)	BYCNCPT2	All	0.067	0.635	-2.9–1.4	6879
		Remedial	0.015	0.617	-2.9–1.4	2275
First PSE is two-year	REFSELCT	All	0.441	0.497	0–1	6879
		Remedial	0.637	0.481	0–1	2275
First PSE is selective four-year	REFSELCT	All	0.142	0.349	0–1	6879
		Remedial	0.041	0.198	0–1	2275
First PSE is public	LEVLCONT	All	0.756	0.430	0–1	6879
		Remedial	0.859	0.348	0–1	2275
First PSE is for-profit	LEVLCONT	All	0.053	0.224	0–1	6879
		Remedial	0.046	0.210	0–1	2275

Appendix B

Summary of Standard Biases, Comparing Unmatched and Matched Samples

The columns indicate how much the treatment and control groups differ on predictors. E.g., in the unmatched sample, the treatment and control groups differed by more than 0.5 of an s.d. on 12 predictor variables, and between .25 and .5 s.d. on 11 predictors. In the matched sample, biases of this magnitude disappeared.

1. Predictors of remedial course assignment (Tables 2–3)

	Treatment: Level of Entry		Treatment: Public vs. Private		Treatment: Race (Black v. White)		Treatment: Family SES	
	Unmatched sample	Matched sample	Unmatched sample	Matched sample	Unmatched sample	Matched sample	Unmatched sample	Matched sample
Standard Bias of Predictors:								
>0.50	12	—	1	—	7	—	9	—
0.25–0.50	11	—	12	—	8	—	8	—
0.15–0.25	4	—	9	—	7	2	11	1
0.10–0.15	4	2	4	2	4	3	3	1
0.05–0.10	2	12	5	9	2	7	5	8
<0.05	5	24	9	29	2	18	1	27
Standard bias of propensity score	-1.398	-0.001	-0.934	-0.001	-1.831	0.000	-2.566	-0.001

2. Effects of remediation (Tables 4–5)

	Treatment: 1+ remedial courses		Treatment: 3+ remedial courses		Treatment: Reading remediation		Treatment: Math remediation		Treatment: Writing Remediation	
	Unmatched sample	Matched sample	Unmatched sample	Matched sample	Unmatched sample	Matched sample	Unmatched sample	Matched sample	Unmatched sample	Matched sample
Standard bias of predictors:										
>0.50	13	—	16	—	16	—	14	—	7	—
0.25–0.50	12	—	13	—	11	—	15	—	14	—
0.15–0.25	10	—	6	—	7	—	6	—	8	—
0.10–0.15	—	—	—	6	1	7	1	5	1	8
0.05–0.10	4	17	2	14	4	12	4	14	2	10
<0.05	3	25	5	22	4	24	3	23	6	20
Standard bias of propensity score	−1.393	−0.001	−1.375	−0.000	−1.190	−0.000	−1.281	−0.000	−1.103	−0.000

3. Effects of successful remediation (Table 6)

	Treatment: Passed reading remediation		Treatment: Passed math remediation		Treatment: Passed writing remediation	
	Unmatched sample	Matched sample	Unmatched sample	Matched sample	Unmatched sample	Matched sample
Standard bias of predictors:						
>0.50	7	—	8	—	6	—
0.25–0.50	12	—	11	—	12	—
0.15–0.25	8	—	9	—	7	—
0.10–0.15	4	1	2	1	3	3
0.05–0.10	3	15	7	9	5	9
<0.05	4	22	1	28	5	26
Standard bias of propensity score	1.002	0.001	0.709	0.000	0.836	0.000

References

Adelman, C. (1998). The kiss of death? An alternative view of college remediation. *National CrossTalk*, *8*(3), 11.

Adelman, C. (1999). *Answers in the toolbox: Academic intensity, attendance patterns, and bachelor's degree attainment.* Washington, DC: Office of Educational Research and Improvement, U.S. Department of Education. Retrieved from http://www.ed.gov/pubs/Toolbox/toolbox.html

Adelman, C. (2004). *Principal indicators of student academic histories in postsecondary education, 1972–2000.* Washington, DC: U.S. Department of Education, Institute of Education Sciences.

Bennett, W. (1994). *The devaluing of America.* New York: Touchstone.

Bettinger, E., & Long, B. T. (2004). *Shape up or ship out: The effects of remediation on students at four-year colleges* (Working Paper No. 10369). Cambridge, MA: National Bureau of Economic Research. Retrieved from the National Bureau of Economic Research Web site: www.nber.org/papers/w10369

Breneman, D., & Haarlow, W. (1998). *Remediation in higher education.* Washington, DC: Thomas B. Fordham Foundation.

Deil-Amen, R. & Rosenbaum, J. (2002). The unintended consequences of stigma-free remediation. *Sociology of Education*, *75*, 249–268.

DiPrete, T., & Engelhardt, H. (2000). *Estimating causal effects with matching methods in the presence and absence of bias cancellation.* Paper presented at the 2000 annual meeting of the American Sociological Association. Retrieved from http://www.wjh.harvard.edu/~winship/cfa_papers/RESJune12.pdf

Grubb, W. N. (2001). *From black box to Pandora's Box: Evaluating remedial/developmental education* (CRCC Brief No. 11). New York: Community College Research Center, Teachers College, Columbia University.

Harding, D. J. (2002). Counterfactual models of neighborhood effects: The effect of neighborhood poverty on high school dropout and teenage pregnancy. *American Journal of Sociology*, *109*, 676–719.

Harwood, R. (1997, August 25). Flunking the grade and nobody notices. *The Washington Post*, p. A19.

Heckman, J. J., & Hotz, V. J. (1989). Choosing among alternative nonexperimental methods for estimating the impact of social programs: The case of manpower training. *Journal of the American Statistical Association*, *84*, 862–875.

Heckman, J. J., Ichimura, H., Smith, J., & Todd, P. (1998). Characterizing selection bias using experimental data. *Econometrica*, *66*, 1017–1098.

Ignash, J. (1997). Who should provide postsecondary remedial/developmental education? *New Directions in Community Colleges*, *25*, 5–20.

King, G., Honaker, J., Joseph, A., & Scheve, K. (2001). Listwise deletion is evil: What to do about missing data in political science. *American Political Science Review*, *95*, 49–69.

Kozeracki, C. (2002). ERIC review: Issues in developmental education. *Community College Review*, *29*, 83–100.

Lavin, D., Alba, R., & Silberstein, R. (1981). *Right versus privilege: The open admissions experiment at the City University of New York.* New York: Free Press.

Lavin, D., & Weininger, E. (1998). *Proposed new admissions criteria at the City University of New York: Ethnic and enrollment consequences.* Unpublished manuscript, City University of New York Graduate Center, Sociology Program.

Lieberson, S. (1985). *Making it count: The improvement of social research and theory.* Berkeley: University of California Press.

MacDonald, H. (1997). Substandard. *The City Journal, 7*(3). Retrieved from the *City Journal* Web site: http://www.city-journal.org

MacDonald, H. (1998). CUNY could be great again. *The City Journal, 8*(1). Retrieved from the *City Journal* Web site: http://www.city-journal.org

MacDonald, H. (1999). Room for excellence? *The City Journal, 9*(4). Retrieved from the *City Journal* Web site: http://www.city-journal.org

Marcus, J. (2000). Revamping remedial education. *National CrossTalk, 8,* 1.

McCabe, R. (2000). *No one to waste: A report to public decision-makers and community college leaders.* Washington, DC: American Association of Community Colleges, Community College Press.

Merisotis, J., & Phipps, R. (1998). *College remediation: What it is, what it costs, what's at stake?* Washington, DC: Institute for Higher Education Policy.

Payne, E., & Lyman, B. (1996). *Issues affecting the definition of developmental education.* Retrieved from the National Association of Developmental Education Web site: http://www.nade.net/documents/Mono96/mono96.2.pdf

Rosenbaum, J. (2001). *Beyond college for all.* New York: Russell Sage.

Rosenbaum, P. R., & Rubin, D. (1983). The central role of the propensity score in observational studies for causal effects. *Biometrika, 70,* 41–55.

Rosenbaum, P. R., & Rubin, D. (1985). Constructing a control group using multivariate matched sampling methods that incorporate the propensity score. *The American Statistician, 39,* 33–38.

Roueche, J., & Roueche, S. (1999). *High stakes, high performance: Making remedial education work.* Washington, DC: Community College Press.

Soliday, M. (2002). *The politics of remediation.* Pittsburgh, PA: University of Pittsburgh Press.

Traub, J. (1995). *City on a hill: Testing the American dream at City College.* New York: Perseus.

Trombley, W. (1998). Remedial education under attack. *National CrossTalk, 6*(3), 1.

Winship, C., & Morgan, S. L. (1999). The estimation of causal effects from observational data. *Annual Review of Sociology, 25,* 659–707.

Woodham, F. (1998, December 1). Report says remedial classes are cost effective. *Chronicle of Higher Education,* A54.

Unlocking the Gate: What We Know about Improving Developmental Education

Elizabeth Zachry Rutschow and Emily Schneider

This report from MDRC provides an extensive review of the research on "best practices" in developmental education. It also identifies the most promising practices resulting from the past several years of study by MDRC, the Community College Research Center, the National Center for Postsecondary Research, and the Achieving the Dream initiative. Rutschow and Schneider also argue that improving the pedagogy applied to teaching developmental courses should be a key factor in reform efforts.

Interventions for Avoiding Developmental Education

The goal of developmental education is simple: prepare students to engage in college-level work so that they can earn a credential in their field of choice and leave school qualified for a greater range of jobs and salaries. With this goal in mind, two- and four-year institutions have established a system for preparing academically underprepared students for college-level work by devising a sequence of semester-long courses aimed at improving their skills. Generally focused on improving students' reading, writing, and math abilities, most community colleges offer sequences of two to four levels of preparatory work in each of these subject areas.[1] Students are placed into these classes based on their scores on a common placement test, which is designed to assess whether they have the skills to enter directly into college-level courses.[2] Students must work upward from the level to which they are assigned, toward entry into college-level, credit-bearing courses. Additionally, they may be barred from college-level courses in their field of interest until their developmental prerequisites are completed.

While providing a noble opportunity for further preparation, the lengthy sequence of developmental education courses offered at most community colleges has also been criticized for creating an often-insurmountable barrier to students' progress through college. Recent large-scale studies have shown that a majority of students never enroll in or complete the recommended sequence of developmental education courses to which they are referred.[3] This is particularly true of students with multiple developmental needs, as numerous studies have revealed that the number of developmental courses that a student places into is negatively associated with the student's likelihood of completing developmental education courses.[4] Finally, there is mixed evidence on whether developmental education is beneficial for students who are placed into these courses. Some studies have revealed positive outcomes for students who are assigned to developmental education[5] or who complete the developmental education sequence.[6] However, other studies demonstrate that—at least for students at the highest levels of academic preparation—participation in developmental education has little or no effect on subsequent academic performance.[7]

Given these challenges, a number of colleges have begun to focus on helping students better prepare for college-level work before they enter postsecondary education. Usually in collaboration with local high school districts, colleges have sought to identify students who are academically underprepared for college work and to provide them with extra instruction or supports to avoid placement into developmental education courses. The key goal of these programs is to improve students' skills *before* they enter college, thereby allowing them to bypass developmental education and enroll directly in college-level, credit-bearing courses. These programs may be provided by the high school itself and may take place while students are still enrolled in their junior or senior year. Other programs are offered by colleges and provide students with the opportunity to build their skills during the semester or summer before their entry into college. Often, high schools and colleges offer several of these types of programs, thereby providing a number of entry points for additional preparation.

Models for Avoiding Developmental Education

A number of common strategies exist for helping students avoid developmental education. *Dual enrollment programs*, which allow high school students to take college courses while still enrolled in high school, are relatively well-established strategies across U.S. community colleges and have recently been expanded beyond their traditional focus on high-achieving students to include students who have more basic skills needs. Another intervention focused on secondary institutions provides *early assessments* to high school enrollees. In these programs, high school students take the local college placement exam during their junior or senior year, and those who are deemed underprepared for college-level work are encouraged to follow a course of instruction to improve their college readiness before graduating from high school. Colleges have also developed similar types of early assessment programs for recent high school graduates; these programs are then used to recommend entering students to summer bridge programs. *Summer bridge programs* provide the final opportunity for entering students who have tested into developmental education courses to learn or relearn essential knowledge just before their college coursework begins. More information about each of these interventions and the related research is provided below.

Dual Enrollment Programs

As noted above, dual enrollment programs allow students to enroll in college courses and earn college credits while they are still enrolled in high school. Similar to Advanced Placement and International Baccalaureate programs, dual enrollment programs exist in most states and school districts across the country, though the policies around minimum academic requirements, tuition, and course options vary greatly.[8] National data show that nearly every community college in the United States (along with three-quarters of public four-year colleges) offer opportunities for high school students to take courses for college credit within a dual enrollment program and that about 4 percent of high school students take advantage of these programs.[9]

EXAMPLES OF DUAL ENROLLMENT PROGRAMS

While dual enrollment programs have long been a popular option for high-achieving students, they have only recently begun to target less academically prepared students. Although still limited,[10] several models have been developed that create more structured opportunities for at-risk students, at no cost, to attempt courses that require the academic rigor and thinking expected in college-level courses.[11] These programs include both high school and college-level courses, with a focus on college preparatory coursework for students who are academically underprepared in a particular subject. In addition, these programs aim to familiarize students with the college environment and, by doing so, to make the pursuit of a postsecondary degree an imaginable prospect.[12]

Two large-scale interventions—College Now and the Middle/Early College High School movement—provide good examples of well-established dual enrollment programs aimed at academically disadvantaged students. Though begun at Kingsborough Community College in Brooklyn, New York, College Now programs are offered at a number of institutions through[out] the country.[13] Generally, College Now courses are offered at the college campus and are taught by traditional college faculty, or they are delivered at the high school by specially trained high school faculty. Students often take a placement test or other standardized exam to become eligible for the program, and those who score below a minimum threshold are eligible to take developmental-level education courses while still in high school.[14] College Now thus also serves the important purpose of informing students about their readiness for college classes, while giving them an opportunity to improve their skills before enrolling in college.

The Middle/Early College High School movement is an all-encompassing version of dual enrollment. Such programs integrate high school enrollment with the first two years of college, so that students have the opportunity to accumulate credit toward an associate's degree, along with earning their high school diploma. Originally, schools that had these programs were designated "Middle College High Schools" and were located on college campuses. However, with a recent investment from the Bill and Melinda Gates Foundation, the model has expanded and been revamped as stand-alone small high schools, now termed "Early College High Schools."[15] Like students in College Now programs, these students can take a mix of high school and college-level courses, based on their level of preparation and interest.[16] On graduation, they can potentially earn both a high school diploma and an associate's degree.

RESEARCH EVIDENCE SUPPORTING DUAL ENROLLMENT PROGRAMS

Research on dual enrollment programs for academically needy students is relatively limited and is based primarily on studies of College Now programs at colleges in the City University of New York (CUNY) system, where the program was established, and on a developing national study of Early College High Schools.[17] Additionally, most of the available studies tend to focus on the implementation of these interventions or undertake statistical analyses that do not employ rigorous methods, making it difficult to ascertain their true effects on student achievement. While some studies use comparison groups, most of them make simple comparisons that do not take into account such factors as preexisting differences in students' achievement levels.

Evidence about College Now's effectiveness is promising but partial, and none of the available studies specifically examine outcomes for academically underprepared students. (See Table 1.) However, early data showed that the college grade point averages (GPAs) of College Now students were comparable to those of a national sample of freshmen.[18] More recently, comparison studies of CUNY's College Now program found that it had small but statistically significant benefits for students who matriculated at a CUNY college, compared with a group of CUNY freshmen who did not enroll in College Now. Both studies found that College Now students earned more credits and were more likely to persist than students in the comparison group; one study also found a decrease in the likelihood of remediation, and the other found that, among students who were pursuing a bachelor's degree, College Now students also had slightly higher GPAs.[19] Similarly, a large-scale analysis of several College Now programs at vocational high schools and several CUNY campuses found that College Now students were more likely to pursue a bachelor's degree, to earn a higher first-semester GPA, and to earn more college credits after seven semesters of postsecondary enrollment.[20]

Evidence on Middle/Early College High Schools is limited and non-experimental, though more rigorous analyses may be available in the future as a result of an evaluation of Gates Early College High Schools being conducted by the American Institutes for Research (AIR) and SRI International.[21] Early trend data on Middle College High Schools revealed less positive results for academically disadvantaged students, as these students tended to receive worse grades in college than a national sample of freshmen.[22] However, more recent nonexperimental studies have shown more positive results, with one sample of Early College High School students successfully making progress on postsecondary education goals, earning an average of 27 college credits by the end of high school and passing 90 percent of college courses after matriculation.[23] National analyses have further confirmed these positive trends, with 75 percent of 2007 Early College High School graduates earning some college credit and 10 percent on top of those earning enough credits for an associate's degree. Additionally, over 60 percent were accepted to four-year colleges.[24] However, as noted above, these findings should be approached with caution, as they do not account for preexisting differences in students' characteristics and academic achievement, and the only comparison employed is with national trend rates for an observably similar population.

Table 1. Summary of Research on Avoidance Programs

Program	Dual Enrollment		Early Assessment		Summer Bridge Programs
	Middle/Early College High School	College Now	California EAP	El Paso Readiness Initiative	
Rigorous Research					
Findings			Positive outcomes: Students less likely to need math or English remediation		
Studies			Howell, Kurlaender, and Grodsky (2010)		
Promising Trends					
Findings	Mixed outcomes: Substantial progress toward AA in high school; high pass rates in college courses; in one study, lower grades in college level courses	Positive outcomes: In college, more likely to persist, earn more credits; GPAs comparable or higher		Positive outcomes: Increase in students placing into college-level courses and highest level of developmental education; reduction in placement into two lowest levels	Mixed outcomes: Higher levels of persistence and course pass rates; some studies find improvement in skill levels and college readiness
Studies	Greenberg (1988); Kim and Barnett (2008); Jobs for the Future (2009)	Greenberg (1988); Karp et al. (2008); Michalowski (2007); Kleiman (2001)		Kerrigan and Slater (2010)	Garcia (1991); Santa Rita and Bacote (1991); Fitts (1989); Texas Higher Education Coordinating Board (2009); Zuniga (2008); Miller (1990); Ackermann (1990)

Early Assessment Programs

One way to ensure that high school students are college ready is to test their skills with the same assessment instruments that are used to place them in developmental courses when they enroll in college. In this way, students who are academically underprepared for college courses can be identified early and given extra time or tools to strengthen their skills before they arrive at college. As noted above, early assessment programs are generally developed collaboratively by colleges and high school districts.

EXAMPLES OF EARLY ASSESSMENT PROGRAMS

While early assessment programs are a relatively new intervention, two promising, large-scale examples can be seen in the State of California's Early Assessment Program and in El Paso Community College's College Readiness Initiative in El Paso, Texas.

California's Early Assessment Program (EAP) is designed to inform high school juniors, along with their educators and family members, whether the California State University (CSU) system would consider them academically prepared to take college-level courses in English and math. Designed jointly by CSU and the state's Department of Education, the EAP adds optional questions to a mandatory statewide test for eleventh-graders to assess their college readiness, and it provides them with concrete steps to follow if they are deemed academically underprepared. While students who score above a certain threshold on these questions are exempted from the CSU placement exam and remedial coursework, students who score below the threshold can follow several pathways during their senior year to improve their skills, with the goal of being ready for college-level work when they matriculate at a CSU campus. These pathways include taking additional math, reading, or writing courses during their senior year or enrolling in an online math learning program designed by CSU. Ideally, these options will allow students to make an informed decision about enrolling in college and, potentially, will make it possible for them to avoid taking developmental education courses.[25]

A similar program on a smaller scale has been developed at El Paso Community College. The college has implemented an early assessment program—the College Readiness Initiative—in partnership with the University of Texas at El Paso and the local school districts. The College Readiness Initiative is predicated on a common concern about the validity of assessment test results: namely, the belief that some students do poorly on assessment tests when they enroll in college simply because they are unprepared to take the test, not because they are unprepared for college-level coursework itself. To address this, the community college and the university worked with local high schools to develop a protocol for graduating seniors to prepare for this exam. The protocol encourages students to (1) complete a joint application to both institutions; (2) attend an orientation about the college's placement test (ACCUPLACER), which includes an introduction to the high-stakes nature of the test and review materials for the exam; (3) take the placement exam; and (4) meet with a counselor at the high school to review test scores and make decisions about the best way to move forward, given their level of academic preparation. Students qualifying for developmental courses can complete a refresher course in the subject(s) of their weakness or can enroll in a five-week summer bridge course with intensive work in reading, writing, and math. These students can then retake the ACCUPLACER for a final placement score, with the hope that they will be assessed into college-level courses or a more advanced developmental education course.[26]

RESEARCH EVIDENCE SUPPORTING EARLY ASSESSMENT PROGRAMS

Both California's Early Assessment Program and El Paso's College Readiness Initiative have seen positive improvements in students' achievement, with a more rigorous analysis of California's EAP program demonstrating key reductions in the number of students placed into developmental education. (See Table 1.) In a quasi-experimental analysis of the placement patterns at CSU's Sacramento State, students who participated in the EAP were less likely than similar students who did not participate to need developmental English and developmental math (reductions of 6.1 and 4.1 percentage points, respectively).[27] While this study was unable to control for students' motivation levels, it did account for a number of other factors, including differences in students' characteristics and in their high schools.

El Paso Community College undertook a less rigorous, internal evaluation of its College Readiness Initiative and found promising trends in students' placement into developmental education. Over the course of three years, the findings revealed an increase in the number of students placing into college-level courses (ranging from an increase of 2 percentage points in math to 15 percentage points in writing) and who placed into the highest level of developmental education. (Most notably, the proportion of students placing into the highest level of developmental math increased by 13 percent.) These increases were paired with a reduction of 5 to 9 percentage points in the proportions of students placing into the two lowest levels of developmental courses in all subjects.[28] While these trends cannot be causally linked to El Paso's program, they demonstrate that this type of program may be a promising method for reducing placements in developmental education courses.

Summer Bridge Programs

Summer bridge programs can provide a last-minute opportunity for students who qualify for developmental education courses to develop their skills before entry into college. These programs have been popular for a number of years at four-year institutions and have recently become more widely implemented at community colleges.[29] While not providing the residential component that is often associated with four-year colleges' programs, community college summer bridge programs also seek to foster a quick boost in students' skills in a relatively short time frame.

EXAMPLES OF SUMMER BRIDGE PROGRAMS

Though they can take many forms, summer bridge programs generally require students to attend on-campus classes for several weeks during the summer before the fall semester begins. Courses take place during a compressed time period—usually three to five weeks—for students who have taken placement exams and tested into developmental education. Courses may focus on only one academic subject at a time or may touch on all developmental course areas and may range from a quick review of course concepts to more formal classes. Some summer bridge programs also incorporate a college-skills seminar that seeks to introduce students to college life and responsibilities. The goals of these programs vary from efforts to improve students' placement test scores to helping students complete one or more developmental courses before entry into college. Often summer bridge programs are offered free of charge to students as a quick, economical way to improve their academic skills.[30]

RESEARCH EVIDENCE SUPPORTING SUMMER BRIDGE PROGRAMS

Only nonexperimental research is currently available on summer bridge programs, and this research is sparse, though showing somewhat promising results on students' achievement. (See Table 1.) While summer programs at four-year institutions have shown some positive outcomes,[31] research in community colleges has been more limited and has tended to focus on the implementation of programs rather than providing rigorous analyses of student outcomes. Older, simple comparison studies of summer bridge programs in New York and New Jersey showed mixed results; some studies revealed higher levels of persistence and subsequent course pass rates, while another found little change in students' skill levels or GPAs.[32] More recently, internal analyses of student trends from several colleges conducting summer bridge programs in Texas have demonstrated promise, with descriptive statistics showing some improvements in students' study skills and in their readiness for college math and reading.[33]

Building on these positive trends, a more rigorous analysis of summer bridge programs at eight Texas colleges is currently being conducted by the National Center for Postsecondary Research (NCPR).[34] The evaluation uses a random assignment research design to compare the effects of four-week to six-week summer bridge programs on students' college enrollment, need for developmental education, GPAs, persistence, and credit accumulation. This research will help provide more definitive evidence with which to evaluate the effects of bridge programs on students' ability to avoid developmental education.

Summary of Avoidance Models

As can be seen above, very limited evidence is available supporting recent efforts to improve students' chances of avoiding remediation and placing directly into college-level credit-bearing courses. Rigorous evidence is currently limited to an evaluation of California's efforts to provide early assessment to high school students, which has shown positive results in decreasing the number of students placing into developmental education. While many studies have found promising trends related to dual enrollment and summer bridge programs, additional research is clearly needed to confirm what effects these programs have on reducing community college students' need for remediation. Given the promising trends noted with dual enrollment programs and early placement testing, these strategies appear to be the most promising for more rigorous analysis. Key to this research will be a clear demarcation of students' differing levels of need as well as documentation of how programs with differing structures and intensity affect placement into developmental and college-level courses. As the number of academically underprepared students leaving high school continues to rise, such studies will provide critical information about how to better prepare students for full entry into college-level courses and programs.

Accelerating Students' Progress through Developmental Education

One of the key criticisms of developmental education is the lengthy amount of time that many students spend in remedial courses before reaching college-level work. As noted, most community colleges provide multiple levels for each developmental education subject and require students to successfully complete each level before progressing to the next. Given that virtually all these courses are taught as semester-long classes, students who place at the lowest levels in a particular subject take multiple semesters—even years—to complete the course sequence in math, reading, or writing, in order to enroll in college-level courses. To make matters worse, most students do not receive standard college credits for the developmental education courses that they take, nor are these courses transferrable to four-year institutions. Yet students are required to pay for these courses, often using significant chunks of their limited financial aid packages to subsidize the costs.[35]

Recent research has pointed out the difficulties that can be engendered by this long course sequence. For instance, in an analysis of data from Achieving the Dream: Community Colleges Count—a large national initiative now encompassing over 10 percent of community colleges—less than 30 percent of students who place into the lowest levels of developmental math and reading ever complete their developmental education coursework. Often, these students fail to enroll in the first developmental education course to which they were referred, or they do not reenroll in the subsequent level after successfully completing the first recommended course. Additionally, around 10 percent of students who are directed to the lowest level of developmental math successfully complete a college-level math course, while fewer than 30 percent who are directed to the highest level completed these courses.[36] Such findings reveal the enormous hurdles facing students who place into developmental education courses, particularly those with multiple remedial needs.

As a result, greater attention has been placed recently on helping students progress more quickly through the lengthy developmental education sequence. Most frequently, such programs have focused on modifying the timing of these courses, with an effort to condense the amount of time needed to complete a particular level. These reframed courses are generally designed to serve students with variable levels of need, creating alternative options for the pace of instruction, depending on students' skill levels in a particular area. For instance, some colleges offer compressed courses in which students may brush up on their skills, in preparation for direct entry into a college-level course. Other courses offer self-paced instruction, which allows individual students to determine the amount of time to spend on particular tasks or skills. In considering which option to recommend, colleges often refer to students' placement test scores; higher-scoring students are placed into faster-paced review courses, while lower-scoring students are referred to slower-paced instructional models.

Models for Accelerating Students' Progress through Developmental Education

Several models exist for accelerating students' progress through developmental education. With a focus on providing instruction in a shorter time frame, some colleges have developed *fast-track courses* that compress the developmental education curriculum into several weeks or a half semester, allowing students to pass through multiple levels in a single semester. Alternately, other models focus on offering *self-paced instruction through modularized courses.* This approach creates multiple mini-courses that focus on particular skill sets rather than offering the whole curriculum in one continuous course; it allows students to strengthen particular weaknesses that they may have in a subject area while bypassing instruction in their areas of strength. A third model relies on the assumption that students who are deemed developmental-level are capable of the work in college-level courses, given extra assistance or a different curricular approach. This approach of *mainstreaming students directly into college-level courses* offers supplemental supports, such as tutoring or study skills courses, for the group of students who have greater academic needs. Each of these acceleration models and its accompanying research evidence is discussed below, and Table 2 summarizes the research on these strategies.

Fast-Track Courses

As noted above, fast-track courses offer classes in a compressed time frame, usually over several weeks during the summer or in half a semester during the regular school year. Generally, two levels of a particular developmental education subject are offered together and run back to back within the same semester, allowing students to complete both courses within one semester.

Table 2. Summary of Research on Acceleration Strategies

Program	Fast-Track Courses	Modularized Courses	Mainstreaming into College-Level Courses
Rigorous Research			
Findings			Positive outcomes: Higher rates of attempting and completing college-level English and subsequent courses
Studies			(Jenkins et al. (2010)
Promising Trends			
Findings	Positive outcomes: Increased progress through developmental education; increased course pass rates, grades, and rates of persistence	Positive outcomes: Higher pass rate in college-level courses; faster progress through developmental course sequence	Positive outcomes: Higher levels of persistence; comparable or higher pass rates in college-level course
Studies	Brown and Ternes (2009); Zachry (2008); Adams (2003); Brancard, Baker, and Jensen (2006); Bragg (2009)	Bassett (2009); Bragg and Barnett (2009); Epper and Baker (2009)	Goen-Salter (2008); Adams, Gearhart, Miller, and Roberts (p. 303 in this book); Jenkins (2009)

EXAMPLES OF FAST-TRACK COURSES

At Mountain Empire Community College in Big Stone Gap, Virginia, Fast-Track Math provides two levels of developmental math as half-semester courses designed to articulate with each other, with a focus on review and fast-paced instruction. This allows students to complete two developmental course levels in one semester.[37] Similarly, at University of Maryland College Park, students take an accelerated version of the developmental course in the first five weeks of the semester, and then they retake the placement exam. Those whose scores have increased to college-level spend the remainder of the semester in a compressed, intensive version of the college-level course.[38]

Fast-track courses are often designed for developmental education students who are better prepared, and many schools—including these two examples—implement a screening process to ensure that this criterion is met. While most colleges restrict entry to accelerated courses and allow only those students with higher assessment scores to enroll, such practices are not always a requirement. For instance, Community College of Denver's FastStart program mandates that students meet with a counselor to ensure that they understand the course structure and speed, but the college does not have a placement score requirement for entry into these courses.[39]

In addition to compressed instruction, fast-track courses may modify their traditional requirements or pedagogy to better suit the revised structure. For instance, these courses may mandate attendance at every class or may require the cohort to enroll in a student success course, which provides study skills training that is designed to support learning in the developmental-level courses.[40] Additionally, fast-track courses often use computer-aided instruction to facilitate self-paced learning. For example, Community College of Denver's FastStart program utilizes computer tutorials in instruction, allowing faculty to monitor individual students' mastery of particular subjects.[41]

RESEARCH EVIDENCE SUPPORTING FAST-TRACK COURSES

Like most developmental education interventions, little rigorous research exists documenting the success of fast-track courses. However, the simple comparisons used in all available studies demonstrate promising trends. For example, fast-track courses at two Ivy Tech Community College campuses in Evansville and Fort Wayne, Indiana, showed increases in students' course pass rates and fewer withdrawals from accelerated courses when compared with courses offered in the traditional semester-long format.[42] Similarly, in internal evaluations employing simple comparisons between program and nonprogram students, Mountain Empire Community College found that Fast-Track Math students passed the math course and persisted at higher rates.[43]

Exploratory evaluations at University of Maryland College Park found that nearly all the accelerated students moved on to the college-level course, in which they performed at comparable levels to students who went directly into the course. The accelerated program structure also allowed students to pass out of developmental requirements more quickly than students taking the traditional developmental-level class.[44] Likewise, in two nonexperimental evaluations of Community College of Denver's FastStart math program, students were more likely to pass developmental education math classes, gain more developmental education credits, pass college-level math courses, and stay enrolled in the college than students taking the semester-long courses.[45] While these evaluations of FastStart used comparison groups, neither used more rigorous statistical methods to control for preexisting differences between the two groups of students, thereby limiting the reliability of this evidence. Building on these promising results, however, the Community College Research Center (CCRC) will be conducting a quasi-experimental analysis of this program's success as part of its efforts to test a number of promising interventions in developmental education.

Modularized Courses

Another model for accelerating students' progress through developmental education courses is to divide a traditional semester-long course into discrete learning units, or modules, that are designed to improve a particular competency or skill. This approach has become increasingly popular in the last decade, particularly in restructuring developmental math courses.

EXAMPLES OF MODULARIZED COURSES

A number of colleges participating in high-profile developmental education reform movements—such as Achieving the Dream's Developmental Education Initiative and the Charles Stewart Mott Foundation's Breaking Through—have used modularized courses as a way to increase students' progress.[46] While modularized courses can be implemented a number of ways, they generally allow students to prove mastery of particular skills by taking a series of short, focused assessments. After students demonstrate competency, they can move on to more advanced modules.

While some modularized courses are instructor-led, others implement a self-paced format, allowing students to complete particular segments of courses at their own pace. In self-paced modularization programs, such tutorial software packages as MyMathLab, Plato, ALEKS, and Math Zone are often used to supplement in-class instruction or as the primary vehicle tor teaching students new skills. These packages begin by identifying students' skill deficits and then allow them to work independently on building these skills through increasingly challenging content, built around frequent assessments of students' developing abilities.[47]

Math My Way at Foothill Community College in Los Altos Hills, California, and the SMART math program at Jackson State Community College in Tennessee provide two useful examples of modularized math courses. In both programs, the traditional math curriculum has been broken down into a series of modules, with frequent assessments by which students demonstrate their mastery of key concepts. Math My Way splits math students into groups by skill level; each group meets with an instructor for two hours a day, five days a week, to learn and master key concepts through self-paced drills and games (both computer- and paper-based).[48] Jackson State's SMART program is delivered through twelve online instructional modules with supplemental assistance from instructors in a math lab center, where students were required to work at least three hours each week. Students can pass quickly through modules by demonstrating competency in an online pretest at each level; if their skills fall below an 80 percent mastery level, they are required to complete a series of lessons and homework assignments and then pass a proctored posttest. Students can complete the modules at their own pace, and it is possible to complete all three levels of the developmental math sequence in a single semester.[49]

RESEARCH EVIDENCE SUPPORTING MODULARIZED COURSES

Evaluations of these modularized courses reveal promising trends in students' achievement, though the evidence is limited to simple comparisons between program and nonprogram students and, therefore, lacks the rigor needed to make causal inferences about these programs' effectiveness. The evaluations show some promising gains in students' pass rates of both developmental and college-level courses as well as gains in students' GPAs and their persistence into subsequent semesters.[50] For instance, internal evaluations of Foothill's Math My Way program show that students who participated in it had a 20 percent higher pass rate in college-level math than nonparticipants, while Jackson State noted a 20 percentage point increase in students' progress through the developmental sequence, which the college attributed to its new modularized course format.[51]

Mainstreaming into College-Level Courses

Mainstreaming developmental education students into college-level courses is another approach to accelerating their progress that is being explored by a number of community colleges. While different versions of mainstreaming exist, common practices include offering a college-level course with a modified curriculum over a lengthier period of time (usually two semesters) or providing supplemental supports, such as tutoring or additional class periods, for developmental students who are placed into a traditional college-level class. Both approaches rely on the assumption that students who have remedial needs are, with extra assistance, capable of mastering college-level work.

EXAMPLES OF MAINSTREAMING

Yearlong, college-level courses for developmental students have been more popular in four-year colleges, driven by a political interest in minimizing remedial courses at these institutions. Such courses provide the opportunity to earn college credit immediately, and they contextualize skill acquisition with the applications that these competencies have in a college-level course. Additionally, because these courses offer the standard college-level curricula, they align with other college-level courses, effectively bridging the gap that can sometimes occur between the competencies taught in developmental-level courses and those expected in college-level courses. Many courses also emphasize student-centered instructional strategies and rely on a wide range of assessment practices, such as portfolio-based grades. For example, the yearlong Integrated Reading and Writing course at San Francisco State—which replaces semester-long courses in developmental reading, developmental writing, and college composition—reflects a holistic approach to reading and writing, incorporating self-reflective writing and activities to support metacognitive development.[52] Programs at Arizona State University and at City University of New York (CUNY) use similar activities to support active learning and analytic thinking.[53]

At the community college level, mainstreaming has tended to focus on integrating developmental education students into a traditional semester-length, college-level course and on providing additional supports to enhance students' success. For example, in the Accelerated Learning Project (ALP) at Community College of Baltimore County, a limited number of developmental-level students are placed into a college-level English composition course along with students who tested directly into that course. While the standard college-level curriculum is followed, the developmental-level students also enroll in an additional hour-long companion section, in which the same instructor provides extra assistance and guidance.[54] A similar type of immersion program has been run in Aptos, California, through Cabrillo College's Digital Bridge Academy (now the Academy for College Excellence), whereby developmental English students receive a two-week basic skills foundations course followed by enrollment in six integrated courses, including the college-level English course. The program also features supplemental supports for students, including study groups, counseling, and other services.[55]

RESEARCH EVIDENCE SUPPORTING MAINSTREAMING

The most promising evidence for mainstreaming developmental-level students into college-level courses comes from the Community College

Research Center's quasi-experimental evaluations of the Accelerated Learning Program (ALP) at Community College of Baltimore County. When comparing students with similar skill levels and controlling for preexisting characteristics, it was found that students who participated in ALP completed introductory college-level courses, enrolled in and completed additional college English requirements, and attempted college courses at higher rates than non-ALP students.[56]

Less rigorous studies have also shown promising trends. The year-long college-level courses offered to remedial students at four-year colleges have shown promising increases in students' persistence and course pass rates as well as improved comprehension skills. For instance, an internal evaluation of San Francisco State's Integrated Reading and Writing program revealed increases in retention rates, English course pass rates, and the levels of reading comprehension and critical skills thinking for those who participated in the program. Additionally, these students were found to have similar achievement levels in other college-level courses as students who had no remedial needs.[57] Similarly, nonexperimental internal evaluations of ALP found that students participating in the program passed college-level English course at just over 1.5 times the rate of students with similar academic needs who took the college's traditional developmental education sequence.[58] Finally, an evaluation of the Digital Bridge Academy demonstrated that participating students passed college-level English and persisted at higher rates than a comparison group.[59] While these trends cannot be used to establish a causal link between these programs and students' improved achievement, they do reveal that such mainstreaming programs may have an important influence on students' outcomes and should be tested more rigorously to see whether these promising trends hold.

Summary of Acceleration Models

Acceleration strategies—fast-track courses, modularized courses, and mainstreaming—are ripe for more rigorous evaluation. These approaches show trends of relatively strong increases in students' achievement, but only mainstreaming has been tested with a relatively rigorous research design. (See Table 2.) Because students who participate in acceleration programs may have differences in motivation or prior academic achievement, further research is needed to establish a causal link between such programs and any increases observed in student success rates and advancement into college-level work. As these practices are replicated and evaluated more thoroughly, close attention should be paid to the policy environment; resistance to modifying developmental courses in this way has been seen at both the practitioner and the state level, but flexible policies on course credits and prerequisites can also be central to easing implementation.[60] The potential role of technology should also be considered closely by practitioners and researchers, as self-paced instruction seems to enable acceleration programs.[61]

Contextualized Instruction

Throughout the literature on best practices in developmental education, there is a strong conviction that developmental-level skills and knowledge are best learned when applied to content that is relevant to students outside their developmental course curriculum.[62] In many ways, this is a commonsense recommendation, designed to head off the classic question "Why do I have to learn this?"—which can be applied equally to lessons on arithmetic, grammar, or basic essay structures. Importantly, the recommendation is grounded in educational psychology and theories of learning. Research on knowledge transfer has shown that students are better able to apply skills to new situations when they understand the underlying principles and procedures as well as the facts.[63] Additionally, active learning theory suggests that learning is deepest when students personally engage with and interpret material, generating meaning based on their own experiences and knowledge.[64]

Building on these theories, some practitioners have focused on developing instructional models that provide more contextualized learning experiences for students. Generally, *contextualized instructional models* focus on teaching basic skills in reading, writing, and math in conjunction with other course content, giving special attention to students' own personal experiences or learning goals.[65] Contextualized instruction for remedial students may be used to reach two different goals. First, basic skills instruction may rely on a particular course subject, such as nursing or computer technology, to ground students' development of reading, writing, or math skills. In these cases, improvement of students' basic skills, rather than knowledge of content from the field, remains the primary objective. Alternately, contextualized instruction may focus more concretely on developing students' knowledge of an academic discipline or vocational field, with instruction in basic skills as a secondary objective toward better understanding this course content.[66]

Contextualized instructional models are thought to be particularly promising for helping academically underprepared students engage more quickly with their academic or vocational field of interest.[67] Unlike traditional developmental reading, writing, and math courses—which are offered as individualized courses disconnected from other course subjects—contextualized approaches offer more integrated learning environments for developing students' basic skills. By connecting with students' professional interests and providing real-world contexts for the application of basic skills, contextualized learning programs are expected to help developmental students attain skills more quickly.

Models for Contextualized Learning with Developmental Education Students

While contextualized learning has been used in a number of disciplines to promote deeper learning experiences, contextualized approaches for developmental education students have tended to focus on improving basic skills within the context of particular academic or vocational disciplines. In vocational programs, contextualized learning offers students the opportunity to gain professional or technical skills while still enrolled in their precollegiate programs. Contextualized learning may also be used in particular academic subjects to promote students' integration of course concepts with reading, writing, or math skills. Finally, *learning communities*, in which developmental courses are linked with other college-level courses, can provide integrated environments for students to engage with both academic course content and basic skills learning. Each of these contextualized instruction models and its accompanying research evidence is discussed below, and Table 3 summarizes the research on these strategies.

Contextualized Learning in Vocational Programs

A practice gaining much attention in the community college world is contextualized learning opportunities for basic skills students who are interested in vocational or technical fields, such as allied health or early childhood education.[68] These programs may be geared either toward adult basic education students who have yet to earn a high school credential or toward developmental education students who are entering community college. In both cases, students have not yet developed the reading, writing, or math skills needed to earn the credential of interest, and they need additional preparation in these areas to master the course content. Therefore, occupational programs in these colleges have looked to develop integrated vocational and professional training along with substantial basic skills preparation. Many also provide opportunities for direct enrollment in degree or certificate programs, thus accelerating students' completion of these credentials.[69]

EXAMPLES OF CONTEXTUALIZED LEARNING IN VOCATIONAL PROGRAMS

One of the most promising contextualized learning models to date is Washington State's Integrated Basic Education and Skills Training (I-BEST) program, in which English as a Second Language (ESL) and adult basic education instructors work together with career-technical faculty to jointly design and teach occupational courses. In the I-BEST program, basic English instruction is tailored to the language and communication skills needed for students' chosen occupation and are taught in the context of students' workforce training classes. Such comprehensive supports as tutoring, advising, and mentoring are often key program components for assisting students. The primary goal of

Table 3. Summary of Research on Contextualized Instruction Strategies

| Program | Vocational Programs | | Learning Communities |
	I-BEST	Breaking Through	
Rigorous Research			
Findings	Positive outcomes: Increased progress into credit-bearing courses; higher persistence rates; earned more credits that counted toward a credential; higher rate of earning occupational certificates; learning gains on basic skills tests		Modestly positive outcomes: Impacts on student engagement, credits earned, and progression through developmental course sequence; positive effects diminish over time
Studies	Jenkins, Zeidenberg, and Kienzl (p. 294 in this book)		Scrivener et al. (2008); Weiss, Visher, and Wathington (2010); Weissman et al. (2011); Visher, Schneider, Wathington, and Collado (2010)
Promising Trends			
Findings	Positive outcomes: Increases in college credits earned; improvements in access and completion of workforce training; some gains in English language skills	Positive outcomes: Increased rates of college readiness; improvements in progress toward completing occupational certificates	Positive outcomes: Increased student engagement and persistence
Studies	Washington State Board for Community and Technical Colleges (2005)	Bragg and Barnett (2009)	Engstrom and Tinto (2008); Tinto (1997); Zhao and Kuh (2004)

I-BEST is to ensure that students receive at least one year of college training that culminates in the award of a certificate or degree.[70]

Another promising program that emphasizes contextualized learning models is the Charles Stewart Mott Foundation's Breaking Through initiative. Its pilot programs have been tested in a number of community colleges throughout the country, with many focusing on contextualized learning as a key gateway to college success. For instance, Central New Mexico Community College in Albuquerque has implemented the Construction Apprenticeship program, which offers for-credit contextualized courses in math and reading while integrating these skills into other college-level courses, such as carpentry. Similarly, Cuyahoga Community College in Cleveland, Ohio, has created a pre-state-tested Nursing Assistant program that allows individuals who have skills below the eighth-grade level to improve their academic abilities while learning about core concepts in health care and nursing.[71] While many of these programs focus on students in adult basic education programs, several also target developmental education students who have already received a high school credential.

RESEARCH EVIDENCE SUPPORTING CONTEXTUALIZED LEARNING IN VOCATIONAL PROGRAMS

The most promising evidence supporting contextualized learning for students with remedial needs comes from a recent evaluation of Washington State's I-BEST program by the Community College Research Center (CCRC). Building on encouraging results from the state's descriptive analysis, CCRC's evaluation used statewide data to compare I-BEST students with other similarly skilled adult basic education students. Using a multivariate logistic regression analysis and controlling for students' background characteristics, such as socioeconomic status and previous schooling, the analysis found positive effects across the board. Compared with nonparticipating students, those who were in the I-BEST program were significantly more likely to advance into credit-bearing courses, persist in college, earn credits that counted toward a credential, earn an occupational certificate, and make learning gains on basic skills tests. I-BEST students often showed large gains on many of these measures.[72]

Promising evidence also exists documenting the success of several Breaking Through programs. Internal evaluations at some of the participating colleges have shown positive outcomes overall for students who are in the programs, such as increased rates of college readiness and progress toward completing occupational certificates.[73] The findings from this research should be approached with caution, however, as the statistical analyses employed either do not use a comparison group or fail to control for such factors as earlier differences in achievement levels between students who are in the program and those who are not.

Learning Communities

Learning communities are another popular strategy employed by many community colleges to provide contextualized learning experiences for developmental-level students. While variations of this strategy are wide-ranging, the general principle behind learning communities is that students enroll in two or more courses together as a cohort. In the more developed versions of these programs, instructors of these linked courses collaborate to create an integrated curriculum that supports the development of multiple aspects of students' learning. As such, the linked courses generally employ overlapping syllabi and have joint assignments and projects. Additionally, because students proceed through the courses with the same cohort of classmates, learning communities are expected to promote social cohesion and the integration of students within the college campus.[74]

EXAMPLES OF LEARNING COMMUNITIES FOR DEVELOPMENTAL EDUCATION STUDENTS

While learning communities are used with a number of different programs and courses at community colleges, those that involve academically underprepared students often link a developmental education course with a for-credit college-level course. At Queensborough Community College in Queens, New York, developmental math is linked with a variety of college-level courses, such as English, sociology, and business.[75] Another popular strategy is to include a *student success course*, which generally emphasizes the development of study skills and college-going expectations, in order to provide additional advising and supports to students who are adapting to college life. Learning communities at Kingsborough Community College in Brooklyn, New York, use this program model, linking a developmental English course, a content-area college-level course, and a one-credit student success course. Kingsborough's program also includes additional supports, such as enhanced counseling and a voucher to purchase textbooks.

Although most learning communities do not engender the type of workforce or experiential skills that are addressed in other contextualized learning settings, such as vocational programs, the deliberate links that are made between the courses can give students the opportunity to practice in their college-level classes the skills that they are learning in their developmental courses. For instance, linking a developmental reading course with an introductory psychology course allows students the opportunity to use the psychology textbook as a resource for their reading development. Similarly, linking developmental math with an entry-level biology course allows students to apply their developing math knowledge to science problems. Additionally, learning communities that include college-level courses afford developmental students the opportunity to gain credits toward credentials while they are still working to improve their basic skills. Finally, learning communities' general promotion of active learning and student engagement is expected to enhance knowledge acquisition and encourage greater levels of commitment to the institution.[76]

RESEARCH EVIDENCE SUPPORTING LEARNING COMMUNITIES
FOR DEVELOPMENTAL EDUCATION STUDENTS

Learning communities are one of the few strategies for which more rigorous evidence is available. In general, the findings related to learning communities have been positive, though modest, with some studies showing more mixed results. Quasi-experimental studies on the effects of learning communities for both college-level and developmental students at over a dozen institutions have found a significant relationship between students' participation in a learning community and their level of engagement with their classes, fellow students, and faculty. Additionally, students participating in learning communities were found to persist to the following year at significantly higher rates than comparison groups who did not participate, even when controlling for differences in students' background characteristics.[77]

More recent experimental studies testing developmental-level learning communities reinforce many of these positive findings, though showing more modest impacts on students' achievement and persistence in school. For instance, as noted above, Kingsborough developed a relatively comprehensive learning community model for developmental-level English students. This program resulted in improvements in educational outcomes, including the number of credits earned during the semester that students were enrolled in learning communities and students' progression through developmental education. Additionally, students in the learning communities were significantly more likely to pass the standardized CUNY English assessment exams by the end of the second semester after the program, thereby qualifying them to pass out of developmental English and enroll in the college's for-credit introductory English course.[78] Even so, the program had few long-term effects on students' achievement or persistence.

Currently, the National Center for Postsecondary Research (NCPR) is building on this work to conduct experimental evaluations of six different models of learning communities, five of which are geared toward developmental students. Qualitative analyses of learning communities in these colleges have shown that program participation clearly influences students affectively, leading to high levels of engagement and a strong sense of belonging.[79] Emerging results about academic outcomes are mixed. At Hillsborough Community College in Tampa Bay, Florida, learning communities linked a developmental reading course with a student success course but did not integrate course curricula or offer comprehensive supports at the level achieved by Kingsborough's program. The Hillsborough program did not have a meaningful impact on students' academic success within the full sample, but there were some modest positive impacts on educational outcomes among the last group of students, who joined the sample after the program increased its faculty collaboration and curricular integration.[80] However, learning communities for developmental math students at Queensborough Community College and at Houston Community College led to more positive results. Students attempted and passed the math course in the learning communities at significantly higher rates than students in comparison groups. After the program, learning communities students at both schools also progressed along the developmental course sequence more rapidly.[81]

Taken together, these findings suggest that more mature versions of learning communities—those that integrate training for faculty, institutional supports, and strong leadership—may have a greater effect on students' achievement. However, even the effects of these programs have been relatively modest and tended to diminish over time, suggesting that learning communities will not dramatically increase students' success in and progress through developmental education.

Summary of Contextualized Learning Models

Based on the available evidence, developmental education models that offer contextualized learning opportunities hold great promise for helping students build basic skills and advance into college-level courses and beyond. (See Table 3.) Vocational and occupational contextualized learning—at least, as implemented in Washington State's I-BEST program—appears to offer the most encouraging results, as such programs quickly move basic skills students into college-level courses and help them graduate in a compressed amount of time with a certificate or degree. It should be noted, however, that many of the vocational contextualized learning programs worked with adult basic education and ESL students, rather than with those entering college and placing into developmental education programs. Yet, given the promising findings from I-BEST and Breaking Through, developmental education programs should consider how links with occupational courses might further improve students' outcomes. Similarly, more rigorous research should be conducted to validate the promising results of programs based on this model.

Learning communities also provide some heartening news about the potential of contextualized learning for improving student outcomes, although the effects of these programs on long-term outcomes are much more limited. While strong learning community models show some positive effects while students are participating in the programs, less well-developed programs showed fewer effects. Additionally, evidence of academic improvement tended to diminish over time, after the learning communities program ended. This evidence and the strong research models used to document these effects reveal that learning communities may be a less effective method for dramatically changing the overall success of developmental education students. Given this, researchers, policymakers, and practitioners should look toward other methods, which may hold more promise for improving these students' achievement.

Supplemental Supports to Advance Students' Achievement

Most community colleges offer a wide array of services for students in order to support their persistence and advancement in college. The services range from academic counseling for students who are entering college to specialized programs for students with particular interests or backgrounds. Most colleges also offer academic supports—such as individualized tutoring, labs for math or English, and computer tutorials—which are designed to supplement classroom instruction. As such, student support services seek to facilitate academic achievement and remove the barriers that students may experience when seeking a postsecondary credential.

While many developmental education students may take advantage of such services, questions have been raised about whether these more general supports meet the challenges that academically underprepared students may face. Numerous studies have noted that students who place into developmental education arrive at school with more handicaps than the general population of students and are more likely to come from disadvantaged backgrounds that offer little exposure to college expectations.[82] For such reasons, a number of colleges have looked to developing more extensive support services for students who have remedial needs, in an effort to better support their progress in college.

Models for Supplemental Supports with Developmental Education Students

As noted, many studies of the best practices in developmental education encourage integrating multiple student supports into a comprehensive model to foster academic achievement.[83] These services primarily include advising (both academic and career-focused) and academic assistance, such as tutoring or the creation of learning centers, but they can also include workshops or courses designed to teach study strategies and provide opportunities for students to access learning-assistance technology.[84] Generally, recommendations for comprehensive student support services tend to state that the academic instruction and student support service divisions should work collaboratively—on both an institutional and an individual level—to ensure that students are aware of support services and are accessing the ones that best meet their needs.[85]

Unfortunately, limited evidence is available to advance the recommendations for more comprehensive support services. However, several promising models that focus on select support services have shown some encouraging results. First, a number of colleges have looked to implementing *more intensive tutoring services* for developmental education students, particularly through *supplemental instruction programs*, which link tutoring directly with a particular course. Additionally, *intensive advising models*, whereby students meet regularly with a staff or faculty adviser to discuss their course plans and college experiences, have also proved popular among a number of schools as a way to advance students' achievement. Finally, *student success courses*, which provide students with an introduction to college life and study skills training, are another key intervention that colleges are using to improve developmental education students' achievement. Table 4 summarizes the available research on student support services.

Tutoring and Supplemental Instruction

Tutoring is a popular support that has been implemented by a number of colleges as a means to advance developmental education students' achievement.[86] Like many other student support practices, tutoring can take diverse forms. Tutoring can be offered by faculty, staff, or student peers or through computer-assisted instruction with tutorial software packages. Students may receive individualized assistance or may work in small groups with a tutor outside the classroom. On college campuses, tutors may be housed in a stand-alone center or in learning assistance centers, which provide a number of other supports for students' learning.[87] Finally, tutoring can be either more generalized and cover a number of academic subjects or more specialized and focus on a specific curriculum or content area.

One of the more focused models of tutoring that has recently become popular among developmental educators is supplemental instruction. Unlike the more generalized tutoring practices that are independent of students' courses, supplemental instruction is a structured tutoring model that is directly connected to a particular course. Generally, a trained tutor (the "SI leader") or the instructor conducts an additional course section that provides structured assistance to students about the course material or assignments. If someone other than the instructor is the SI leader, that person generally attends the core curriculum class to become familiar with the course material and the instructor's approach. SI leaders may be peer tutors who have already achieved success in the course or may be faculty or staff members who are well versed in the course content. Sessions are often led using active or collaborative learning techniques, which encourage students to more fully interact with the course material. The SI leaders work closely with the instructor leading the course, and they often receive guidance on the content of their sessions.[88]

AN EXAMPLE OF SUPPLEMENTAL INSTRUCTION FOR DEVELOPMENTAL STUDENTS

Supplemental instruction is used widely across the country in a variety of developmental and entry-level courses, all of which have historically high failure rates. One example of structured supplemental instruction

Table 4. Summary of Research on Student Support Services

	Tutoring	Supplemental Instruction	Enhanced Advising	Student Success Courses
Examples	Peer tutoring, tutoring with trained staff person, tutoring labs	Course-based small-group tutoring with trained tutor	Mandatory advising, early alert, "light touch" advising	Orientation course, study skills course, curricula such as On Course
Rigorous Research				
Findings	Positive outcomes: Visits to learning assistance center, paired with a student success course, has positive effects on credits earned, course pass rates, and GPA		Positive outcomes: Intensive advising (plus small stipend) increases persistence and support service access; "light touch" mentoring program decreases course withdrawals and increases credits earned; contact at any intensity level increases success in college-level math and transfer	Positive outcomes: Increased credits earned, course pass rates, GPAs, receipt of credentials, persistence, and transfer to four-year colleges
Studies	Scrivener, Sommo, and Collado (2009)		Scrivener and Weiss (2009); Visher, Butcher, and Cerna (2010); Bahr (2008)	Zeidenberg, Jenkins, and Calcagno (2007); Scrivener, Sommo, and Collado (2009)
Promising Trends				
Findings	Mixed outcomes: Learning centers associated with student achievement; small-group tutors, trained tutors, tutoring related to specific assignments, and personalized systems of instruction seem more helpful than other kinds of tutoring, which show little effect	Positive outcomes: Associated with higher grades and lower withdrawal rates; higher persistence and graduation rates; some studies find more promise for at-risk students	Mixed outcomes: Varied effects for early alert systems, dependent on students' use of recommended services; general and minority-specific advising positively associated with progression through developmental education, grades, and college-level course completion	Positive outcomes: Associated with increased academic outcomes
Studies	Perin (p. 93 in this book); Roueche, Ely, and Roueche (2001); Boylan, Bliss, and Bonham (1997); Maxwell (1990); Topping (1996); Hock, Deshler, and Schumaker (1999)	Arendale (1997); Ramirez (1997); Ogden, Thompson, Russell, and Simons (2003); Zachry (2008); Hodges and White (2001); Bowles, McCoy, and Bates (2008)	Taylor (1996); Boylan, Bliss, and Bonham (1997); Rudmann (1992); Lewallen (1993); Pfleging (2002); Cartnal and Hagen (1999)	Weinstein et al. (1997); Boylan (2002)

is being offered by Mountain Empire Community College in Big Stone Gap, Virginia. Its program, called "Peer-Led Team Learning," provides an extra section of the college's developmental algebra course and meets weekly during an open block of time just before the class begins. The supplemental instruction section is led by a peer tutor, who successfully completed the course in an earlier semester and received training to lead the supplemental section. The peer tutor is also required to regularly attend the developmental algebra course and to work closely with the instructor, who reviews and may modify the tutor's lessons. Like many supplemental instruction programs, Peer-Led Team Learning also emphasizes active learning, with most lessons providing engaging exercises for students to interact with the course content.[89]

RESEARCH EVIDENCE SUPPORTING TUTORING AND SUPPLEMENTAL INSTRUCTION FOR DEVELOPMENTAL EDUCATION STUDENTS

Little rigorous evidence exists documenting the success of either generalized tutoring or supplemental instruction programs for developmental education students. Several challenges also limit the reliability of research demonstrating promising trends. First, student self-selection bias is particularly apparent with tutoring programs, as most studies have not accounted for the motivation of students who seek out tutoring services, which may be correlated with other characteristics that help these students succeed.[90] Additionally, some research has indicated that students who use tutoring and learning assistance centers tend to be older and to have attended college for a longer period of time, making it difficult to generalize conclusions to a larger student population.[91] It can also be challenging to isolate the effects of tutoring from other forms of academic assistance—such as advising or revised pedagogical strategies—as developmental education students often receive multiple services.[92] Finally, few studies focus specifically on developmental education students, making it difficult to disentangle the effects for these students from the effects for the general student population.

Overall, the available data on a variety of tutoring programs have shown mixed results. Some promising trends have been noted for students who utilize learning assistance centers.[93] For instance, one experimental study of a program in which probationary students were required to go to a learning assistance center showed some positive effects on such academic outcomes as credits earned, course pass rates, and grade point averages (GPAs). However, the mandatory visits to the center were offered in conjunction with a required student success course, making it difficult to disentangle which service had the greater effect on students' achievement.[94] Other, nonexperimental studies have found little evidence of improved achievement from tutoring, except when certain types of tutoring were implemented. Those programs with the most promising evidence include small-group tutoring led by a peer, programs designed to help students with specific assignments, and more personalized systems of instruction whereby students go through programmed learning material and a tutor is available for assistance.[95] For a tutoring program to have benefits for students, research on best practices indicates that tutors must receive standardized training.[96]

While supplemental instruction is popular within developmental education, little research is available documenting the results of these programs in community college settings. Nonexperimental internal evaluations of Mountain Empire's Peer-Led Team Learning program revealed promising increases in students' course pass rates, persistence, and GPAs; however, the evaluation had relatively few students and employed only simple comparisons with students who were not enrolled in the program, thereby limiting any causal statements about the program's effects.[97] Other nonexperimental studies conducted in four-year universities have shown positive effects for students who received supplemental instruction in historically difficult entry-level courses.[98] For instance, when using large data sets to compare students who received supplemental instruction and those who did not, the intervention was found to have resulted in higher grades, lower course withdrawal rates, higher GPAs, and higher rates of persistence and graduation.[99] Some studies have also noted positive effects of supplemental instruction with at-risk students, when compared with more traditional students.[100] However, it is important to note that these studies did not effectively control for differences in students' motivation and were, at times, limited by the types of comparisons made between the research groups.

Advising

Developmental educators have also looked toward more intensive advising models to improve remedial students' success. At a minimum, advising in community colleges entails a staff or faculty member's helping students navigate their choice of classes or majors, although advisers in some schools also offer assistance in helping students access campus services or develop career goals or plans. Advising in community college settings tends to be somewhat limited, as advisers often have large caseloads of students—sometimes more than a thousand a semester—making it difficult to give students more personalized attention. High caseloads combined with the fact that at-risk students are far less likely to be proactive and seek out advising opportunities mean that developmental-level students tend to receive quite limited advising.[101]

In order to reverse this trend, some schools have looked to create more intensive advising experiences for students who have remedial needs. One of the most commonly recommended approaches is the reduction of advisers' caseloads, allowing them to meet more frequently with students and provide more personal attention, which can be coupled with mandatory advising for students.[102] A more intensive version of this model has advisers serve as mentors to students, meeting regularly with them to monitor progress and inform them of college services that may assist them with their challenges. Other strategies have focused on implementing early-alert systems, in which faculty and student services staff collaborate to communicate with students who are at risk of failure. Such a system may also include meetings with an adviser to establish a corrective plan of action.[103]

EXAMPLES OF ENHANCED ADVISING FOR DEVELOPMENTAL STUDENTS

Two examples of alternate advising models are found in Ohio and Texas. Lorain County Community College in Elyria, Ohio, and Owens Community College in Toledo offer an enhanced advising program, and South Texas College, in McAllen, has the Beacon Mentoring program, which takes a "light touch" approach to advising.

In the enhanced advising program at Lorain County and Owens, low-income students—who were not all developmental-level—were assigned to a team of counselors with whom they were expected to meet at least twice per semester for two semesters, to discuss academic progress and resolve any issues that might affect their schooling. The caseloads of these counselors were reduced in order to facilitate more frequent, personalized contacts with students.[104]

South Texas took a different approach in its Beacon Mentoring program, choosing to assign faculty or staff mentors to advise students in developmental and introductory math courses. These college employees made several short presentations within students' math classes to describe available resources on campus, and they worked with faculty to identify struggling students and offer them help early on. Some mentors also had more regular contact with their students through personalized meetings or e-mail.[105]

RESEARCH EVIDENCE SUPPORTING ENHANCED ADVISING

A number of rigorous and nonrigorous studies of a variety of advising approaches have been conducted, and they tend to show fairly positive results on developmental education students' achievement. Less rigorous, large-scale studies have noted some positive trends from specialized advising services for developmental education students.[106] Similarly, nonexperimental studies of advising models for minority developmental education students were found to positively influence students' progression through developmental coursework, their grades, and their rates of college-level course completion.[107] Furthermore, some research on early-alert advising models using simple comparisons between program and nonprogram students revealed positive trends in achievement. However, the benefits associated with early-alert programs appeared only when students followed advisers' recommendations for corrective actions, such as attending tutoring. Most early-alert programs did not show meaningful improvements in students' academic achievement.[108]

Rigorous research on various advising models has shown fairly positive results. A large-scale longitudinal control analysis of first-year community college freshmen found that participation in advising at any level of intensity is beneficial for developmental-level students' chances of success in college-level math and for their transfer to a four-year institution, and stronger effects were found for students with the weakest skills.[109] Experimental study results from the Lorain County and Owens enhanced advising models paired with a small stipend reveal some positive outcomes; students who received more personalized attention from their advisers accessed advising services more often and had higher retention rates for the first two semesters following the program. However, the program did not have a positive impact on other academic outcomes, such as course pass rates, credit accumulation, or GPAs.[110]

A random assignment study of the South Texas Beacon Mentoring program provides more encouraging evidence about an advising service with relatively low intensity. While the program did not make a significant difference in the academic outcomes of the overall sample, students in developmental math classes who were visited by a Beacon Mentor withdrew from the course at lower rates and earned more credits at the end of the semester. The program also had some modest positive effects for students who attended part time, as they were found to be less likely to withdraw from and more likely to pass the math class, to earn more credits, and, in the developmental math classes, to score higher on the final exam. However, the effects of the program were relatively modest and did not affect other academic outcomes for these students, such as course pass rates, GPAs, or postprogram persistence.[111]

Student Success Courses

Student success courses have become one of the most popular support interventions among community colleges seeking to improve developmental-level students' achievement. Sometimes referred to as "study skills," "student development," or "new student orientation" courses, student success classes are generally offered as a stand-alone, credit-bearing course for developmental education students or newly entering students at the college. Usually one semester long, student success courses are used to introduce new students to college life, help them learn about the college's services, and give them tools to approach the decisions and responsibilities that they will face as college students. Several recent studies have associated these courses with promising increases in students' academic achievement and persistence in college, leading a number of states and schools to mandate them for newly entering students.[112]

EXAMPLES OF STUDENT SUCCESS COURSES

Student success courses have been linked to developmental math and reading in learning communities at Hillsborough Community College (Tampa Bay, Florida), Houston Community College, and Kingsborough Community College (Brooklyn, New York), providing extra support to students' academic and social integration into college life.[113] Student success courses may also be targeted specifically to at-risk or developmental students; Chaffey College (Rancho Cucamonga, California) uses its student success courses for students who are on probation, and Guilford Technical Community College (Jamestown, North Carolina) targets the courses to students needing one or more developmental education class.[114]

Student success courses may be offered as less intensive, one-credit classes (as was the case at Kingsborough) or as more structured, three-credit classes that provide more opportunities for student interaction (as in Guilford Tech's model). Regardless of the intensity of these programs, however, each of these models shares a focus on developing students' study skills and their knowledge of and expectations for college life.

RESEARCH EVIDENCE SUPPORTING STUDENT SUCCESS COURSES

Student success courses have long been promoted in the research on "best practices" as an important way to help developmental education students acquire better learning strategies, and some practitioner research has shown positive trends in student outcomes.[115] Recently, more rigorous research has confirmed these promising trends. For instance, the Community College Research Center's quasi-experimental analysis of students who enrolled in student success courses in Florida revealed positive effects on students' persistence, degree earning, and transfers, particularly for developmental-level students.[116]

Experimental studies utilizing random assignment methodology have also shown promising effects. For instance, the experimental results of Kingsborough's learning communities model, which incorporated a one-credit student success course, found positive impacts on the number of credits that students earned and on students' progression through developmental education.[117] Similarly, an analysis of Chaffey College's mandatory success course for probationary students—a particularly challenging population—found that students who enrolled in the success course earned more credits, passed more classes, and had higher GPAs than those who did not receive the course. The program also had large, positive effects on getting these students back into good academic standing; at the end of the two-semester follow-up period, there was nearly a 15 percentage point difference between students who received the course and the control group.[118] However, because the success courses at both of these schools were linked to other support services, these results should be approached with caution, as it is difficult to know whether the findings are related to the success courses or to other services offered.

Summary of Student Support Models

Intensive advising, supplemental instruction, and student success courses have each shown some promising effects for increasing developmental-level students' achievement, though their effects appear to be limited. (See Table 4.) For instance, rigorous research on intensive advising and student success courses has documented some positive increases in the number of credits that developmental education students earned; in some cases, these supports have advanced students' progression through developmental education and their success in college-level work. Additionally, there is some suggestive evidence revealing that certain types of tutoring programs and supplemental instruction may produce positive gains in students' success in their courses and persistence in college.

While these findings are promising, none of the student support services described in this [section] have had dramatic effects on helping developmental education students advance more quickly to and through college-level courses. For example, none of the supports studied here provided striking changes in students' course pass rates, GPAs, or credits earned. Additionally, several of the positive findings that were noted during the time when these services were being offered diminished after the programs ended. These findings suggest that while student support services may produce modest gains in achievement, they are unlikely to have more dramatic effects on progress into college-level work and receipt of a credential. While more heartening information may come from the follow-up experimental studies on Chaffey College's student success course and Kingsborough's learning communities, the current evidence implies that reforming student support strategies may be a step in the right direction but is not sufficient, in isolation, to bring remarkable gains in developmental education students' achievement.

Conclusion

The charge of developmental education is clear: to build up the skills of academically underprepared students so that they may be successful in college-level work and progress quickly to a credential that will advance their position in the marketplace. Unfortunately, as the system currently stands, this goal is rarely met. While around 60 percent of community college students begin their college career in developmental courses, less than half of them will make it through these courses successfully.[119] Even more disturbing, from 60 percent to 70 percent of students who take a remedial course never earn a postsecondary degree or credential.[120]

Given these troubling achievement levels, many educators, policy-makers, and foundations are reconsidering the most effective strategies for supporting developmental-level students. As noted in this report, a number of these strategies have exhibited promising trends in increasing the number of students who are ready for college-level work, and some strategies even appear to improve students' receipt of credentials. Generally, the strategies that hold the most promise focus on improving students' skills within a compressed time frame and on linking remediation to relevant college-level work. These include programs that mainstream developmental students into college-level courses with additional supports, programs that provide modularized or compressed courses to allow remedial students to more quickly complete the developmental course sequence, and programs that offer contextualized remedial education within occupational and vocational programs. These strategies tend to modify pedagogical approaches to fit within the programs' nontraditional structures, and they provide clear opportunities for students to remain on a pathway to reaching their college goals rather than becoming mired in multiple semesters or years of remedial work.

While these encouraging findings are a welcome relief for those hoping to advance remedial students' success in college, the relatively modest effects of these programs also need to be taken in context of the larger challenges facing developmental education students. Most of the promising programs cited in this report were conservative efforts to tweak the existing curriculum, and they improved students' academic achievement by only a few percentage points—a small change relative to the large numbers of students failing developmental education courses. Additionally, virtually all these programs are still in the pilot stages and have affected relatively few students, which makes it difficult to ascertain how they might impact the achievement of larger groups of students. Finally, and most importantly, rigorous research demonstrating a clear causal link between these programs and improved student achievement is limited, making it challenging to say with certainty how well these strategies have actually increased students' success.

Given these issues, a number of researchers, policymakers, and foundations have begun to suggest that developmental education in its current form is broken and are calling for a more radical reenvisioning of these programs. Noting that more conventional efforts to improve students' achievement have produced only modest results, some individuals have sought to restructure the core curricula of developmental education programs through innovative models to help students build skills for their education and the workforce. While still new and untested, these ideas offer a fresh perspective for advancing academically underprepared students' success, and they may hold promise for greater improvements in these students' achievement.

Finally, while educators are creating increasingly more novel ways to improve developmental education students' success, the institutional and organizational structures supporting developmental education also present clear challenges for any reform effort. For instance, most developmental education programs are structured around entrance exams, which assess students' skills on entering college and are used to place students into the appropriate developmental education or college-level courses. Given that assessment tests are part of the admissions process at most community colleges, any innovative approach must consider whether and how these tests will be used. Similarly, most community colleges rely heavily on adjunct, or part-time, faculty to teach developmental courses, meaning that large proportions of students are taught by instructors who are less connected to the campus community. Therefore, any reform effort that seeks to reach large groups of developmental education students must find ways to integrate these faculty into the effort—a goal that has proved difficult for many community colleges in the past

Given these challenges, this concluding [section] outlines several promising paradigms for improving developmental education students' success while also detailing key factors to consider in efforts to reform developmental education. First, the [section] delineates a plan for increasing the availability of reliable evidence about the programs and strategies for developmental education students. It then develops an agenda for future innovation in developmental education, focusing both on the reform efforts for which reliable evidence exists as well as on new, more sweeping changes in developmental education curricula. Finally, the [section] discusses several mediating factors that affect the delivery of developmental education, which—with improvement—have the potential to enhance both traditional and innovative practices.

Improving the Quality of Evidence

Currently, there is a dearth of reliable evidence for many of the avoidance, acceleration, contextualization, and support strategies discussed in this report. Only a few experimental and quasi-experimental studies exist that attempt to control for such factors as preexisting differences among students or their motivation levels. While a number of descriptive and correlational analyses exist, these studies rarely provide clear definitions of a program's implementation or characteristics, which limits the conclusions that can be drawn from their results and can also create challenges for replicating the program at other institutions.

Researchers and policymakers should prioritize expanding the field's knowledge about the causal link between new programs and students' achievement. Research designs should be as rigorous as possible, given the intervention and its context; if an experimental study is not feasible, another analytic strategy that minimizes the differences between comparison groups should be used. Such investigations might begin with quasi-experimental analyses, using clearly identified student-level data, which investigate the associations between a new program intervention and students' achievement. Whenever possible, analyses should note and control for such characteristics as preexisting differences in students' achievement levels and differing policies across institutions or states that might affect how students are placed or advanced through developmental education. Similarly, when available, analyses should provide detailed information about programs' implementation and components, to allow for a better understanding of how program structure might be related to outcomes.

While quasi-experimental research is a useful first step in such investigations, more rigorous experimental analyses should also be pursued, when feasible. Experimental analyses, utilizing random assignment methodology, would allow for a causal link to be established between new interventions and any resulting changes in students' achievement. Such experiments would also control for factors like students' motivation level—a challenge that cannot be easily overcome through quasi-experimental research. Again, careful attention should be paid within this research to the structure, programming, and implementation of new strategies, in order to facilitate an understanding of what specific programmatic components may be linked with any improvements in students' achievement.

In considering a research agenda, researchers and policymakers should look to analyze the programs that appear to hold the most promise for rapidly increasing students' progress through developmental education, success in credit-bearing courses, and ultimate completion of a degree. Researchers should actively pursue more innovative programmatic strategies for accomplishing these goals; while tweaks to current developmental education practices may produce some modest results, the available research clearly demonstrates that such small changes are unlikely to produce dramatic improvements in students' achievement. Given that current programs succeed in promoting fewer than half of their students into college-level courses, more drastic changes are undoubtedly needed.

Promising Strategies for Improving Developmental Students' Success

INTERVENTIONS WITH RELIABLE EVIDENCE

As noted above, few developmental education reform efforts have been evaluated rigorously, thereby limiting the number of programs that can be causally linked to improved student achievement. Moreover, experimental evaluations of student support interventions and learning communities reveal that these strategies may have only modest effects on students' achievement.[121] For instance, the most promising of these studies—a random assignment evaluation of Chaffey College's student success course linked with mandatory tutoring—did have large, positive effects on getting probationary students back into good academic standing. However, it only minimally increased these students' grade point averages (GPAs): 7 percent more program students earned a GPA of 2.0 or higher; minor increases in credit earning were primarily a result of enrollment in the success course itself.[122] Similarly, an evaluation of Kingsborough's learning communities concluded that the program drove minor increases in developmental credits earned (by almost one credit) and in the proportion of students who attempted and passed skills tests that would allow them to move on to college-level English (a 6 percentage point increase) but that the program had few long-term effects.[123] Finally, evaluations of advising and mentoring programs at South Texas College, Lorain County Community College, and Owens Community College revealed no sustained increases in the achievement of the overall population of students and increased the number of credits earned by less than a full credit.[124]

Interestingly, earlier quasi-experimental research on some of these programs—learning communities and student success courses—showed more promising results.[125] The differing findings further underscore the need for more rigorous analyses of developmental education reforms, as they suggest that other characteristics, such as students' motivation and self-selection into these programs, may have accounted for the more positive results seen in the quasi-experimental studies. However, the positive experimental findings on learning communities and student support reforms, though at times modest, suggest that these relatively conservative reforms may help improve students' progress through developmental education. As such, colleges may wish to pursue such strategies while also looking for more innovative interventions that may have a larger impact on students' achievement.

Though more rigorous, experimental analysis is needed, quasi-experimental research on other approaches—such as several acceleration and avoidance strategies and contextualized instructional models—have shown great promise for increasing developmental education students' overall achievement, including their progress through developmental education and success in credit-bearing courses. The most promising of these models have focused on integrating developmental education students more quickly into mainstream college programs and providing clear opportunities for them to link their skill development with their field of interest. In particular, quasi-experimental research on Washington State's I-BEST program, which integrates basic skills instruction with vocational and professional training, has revealed substantial improvements in students' progress into credit-bearing courses, credits earned, and attainment of certificates. When controlling for differences in students' background characteristics, researchers found that students in the I-BEST programs earned an average of 14 more college credits than non-I-BEST students and had a higher probability of persisting into the second year (17 percentage points) and of earning an occupational certificate (40 percentage points).[126] Furthermore, the short tracking period of this study (two years) reveals that substantial improvements in achievement among basic skills students may be possible within a relatively short period of time.

While the correlation between participation in I-BEST and better educational outcomes is striking, it is important to note that further research is needed to determine whether a causal link exists between this program and students' increased achievement. I-BEST students' improved success may have resulted from factors unrelated to this program, such as the way students were selected into the program or their relatively higher motivation levels when compared with students not participating in the program. Additionally, though I-BEST was able to increase the rate at which students received certificates, it did not affect students' receipt of an associate's degree. However, these findings do represent one of the most notable improvements in student achievement among the interventions analyzed in this report, demonstrating this program's potential for further replication and study.

Models that help students avoid developmental education before entering college as well as strategies to mainstream students into college-level courses have also demonstrated promise for improving students' achievement. As noted, two quasi-experimental studies of avoidance and mainstreaming revealed modest improvements in developmental education students' success, when controlling for preexisting differences between participating and nonparticipating students. First, a study of California's Early Assessment Program, which gave college placement exams to eleventh-graders and allowed students with lower level skills to build on their abilities while still in high school, was associated with reductions in the number of students needing developmental math (4 percentage points) and English (6 percentage points).[127] Second, Community College of Baltimore County's Accelerated Learning Program (ALP), which mainstreamed developmental English students into college-level English classes, was correlated with substantial improvements in students' pass rates in college-level English. When controlling for student characteristics, there was a 33 percentage point difference between the pass rates of ALP students (71 percent) and non-ALP students (38 percent) in the introductory college-level English course within a year of taking the course. The program was also associated with improvements in the number of college-level courses that ALP students attempted and in the percentage of ALP students who passed the next level of college English.[128]

As with evaluations of Washington State's I-BEST program, these results should be approached with caution, as the improvements cannot be causally linked to these programs, and other, nonintervention-related factors, such as student motivation, may explain some of the positive results noted in these reports. However, the fact that participation in these programs was associated with substantial increases in students' progress into credit-bearing courses, even when controlling for a number of student characteristics, suggests that these programs have important potential for helping decrease the lengthy amount of time that students spend in developmental courses while increasing their progress toward earning a degree or certificate.

When looking to expand or replicate these program models, practitioners and policymakers should pay careful attention to how students with lower-level skills or multiple developmental needs can be better assisted, as these students are the ones most at risk of failure. Washington State's I-BEST model, which worked with students who had skills below the eighth-grade level, provides a useful example of how students with low skill levels may be able to more quickly achieve credentials and degrees that will advance their status in the marketplace. Similarly, California's Early Assessment Program provides increased opportunities for students to understand their academic limitations and advance their basic skills before enrolling in college, which may be particularly beneficial to students who have multiple needs. Developmental education programs should take such findings to heart and consider how variations of these programs might improve the opportunities for their own struggling students.

UNTESTED INNOVATIONS IN DEVELOPMENTAL EDUCATION PRACTICE

While most developmental education reforms have focused on modest tweaks to programs' curricula and practices, a few recent innovations have focused on changing the foundations of these programs in an effort to more quickly advance students into credit-bearing courses and the attainment of postsecondary credentials. For instance, some reformers have sought out technological approaches to instruction as a way to provide more individualized instruction to students. Additionally, policymakers and national leaders have recently made efforts to better align secondary and postsecondary curricula and mandate further preparation in high school in order to increase students' success in college. Finally, other programs have sought to redefine the curricula and practices in both developmental and college-level courses to focus on the key skills that students will need in their careers and to more quickly advance them through introductory college-level courses. While relatively untested, these recent innovations hold clear promise for advancing developmental education students' success and should be a critical part of the research agenda moving forward.

Technology-Aided Approaches to Instruction.   Computer-aided instruction poses a number of new avenues for developmental education instruction. Many colleges have integrated technology into developmental courses that have traditional content and curriculum. Computer programs like MyMathLab, Plato, ALEKS, and Math Zone are used to supplement classroom instruction by means of learning assistance centers or individualized tutoring sessions.[129] Similarly, many colleges are using technology to provide online courses, where all learning takes place remotely, via software.[130] More recently, practitioners have used technology to structure accelerated or modularized courses, which aim to help students progress more quickly through developmental education. In these reforms, software tutorial packages are used to help students focus on particular areas of weakness while allowing them to advance more quickly through other areas of strength. Technological packages have an additional advantage in that they are generally adaptive to diverse circumstances or can be preset to create an individualized program of instruction for each student.[131]

While some efforts have been made to evaluate the use of technology in the classroom, little rigorous research exists documenting the effectiveness of these practices in improving developmental education students' outcomes. Given the utility that technology holds for creating more individualized methods of instruction, researchers, policymakers, and practitioners should seek to better understand how such systems may be used to help students more quickly build their skills. It should also be noted, however, that some nonexperimental studies suggest that technology-aided instruction may have its drawbacks; several simple analyses have revealed that instruction provided wholly through computers may increase the rates of course withdrawal and failure.[132] However, students who remain in computerized courses often perform at similar or higher levels than students who take traditional courses, implying that appropriate assessment and advising might be a step toward ensuring that the students who will benefit from these courses are the ones who actually take them. Moreover, exploratory research into the use of technology in accelerated and modularized courses suggests that these instruments may be most efficacious in supporting innovative course structures, in which they seem to hold more promise for improving students' mastery of course content, course completion, and progress into college-level courses.[133]

Improving the Alignment Between Secondary and Postsecondary Education. As suggested by several of the programmatic interventions discussed in this report, critical challenges remain with regard to aligning the standards and curricula of secondary education with those of postsecondary education. While studies have noted that taking a college preparatory curriculum through the final years of high school may reduce the chances of students needing remediation, others have noted that a substantial proportion of these students still place into developmental coursework when entering college.[134] Similarly, other research has noted a divide between the skills taught in developmental education courses and those required in college-level courses in the same subject.[135]

Given these challenges, a number of states and organizations have begun to focus on eliminating the gap between high school, developmental, and college-level courses. For instance, organizations such as Achieve, Inc., and the American Youth Policy Forum have driven a push for states to require college- and career-ready curricula in high schools; these organizations are also working actively to disseminate best practices in states across the country.[136] Building on these efforts, the National Governors Association and the Council of Chief State School Officers recently announced the Common Core State Standards Initiative, which sets out "clear and consistent goals for learning that will prepare America's children for success in college and work."[137] Such efforts have the potential to take developmental education avoidance strategies—such as early placement testing and precollege preparation—to a national scale by integrating college expectations and standards into the secondary school curricula. Similarly, they could help reduce the number of students placing into developmental education as students are better able to develop the skills needed for college-level work while still in high school.

Better alignment of secondary, developmental, and college-level curricula is perhaps one of the most important frontiers for improving students' avoidance of developmental education and their progress through college. As demonstrated by the avoidance strategies discussed [earlier], helping high school students develop a clear perspective on how their skills and abilities match expectations for college students and allowing them additional preparation time before entering college has real promise for helping students reach college-level coursework quickly. Given the important influence that such alignment can have on developmental education students' success, researchers and policymakers should prioritize research in this area and seek to better understand how these policy efforts are changing students' educational experiences and achievement.

Transforming Developmental and College-Level Curricula and Practice. While a number of efforts are being made to better align secondary and college curricula, even more innovative efforts are taking place within colleges in an attempt to better align developmental and college-level practices and to advance remedial students' progress to college-level work. One of the most transformative of these movements is the Statistics Pathway (also known as Statway), a collaborative project being launched by the Carnegie Foundation for the Advancement of Teaching and the Charles A. Dana Center at the University of Texas at Austin. Arguing that statistical reasoning and data analysis are key requirements for many of today's growing occupations, Statway seeks to realign colleges' math curricula to focus on statistics rather than the algebra and calculus content currently required.[138] This transformed math curricula offered to entering college students in nontechnical fields, and it seeks to advance students who lack basic math skills through an introductory college-level statistics curricula in one year. Thus, the initiative seeks to better prepare students for the needs of the workforce while also helping basic skills students move more quickly through their math courses—a critical consideration, given that developmental math tends to present the highest hurdle to developmental education students.[139]

Such efforts to dramatically transform both developmental and college-level math curricula and to move students more quickly through basic skills work represent a distinct departure from past developmental education reforms, which have focused primarily on tweaking particular aspects of instruction and less on changes in course content. Programs such as Statway provide a unique answer to researchers' recent calls for more drastic changes in developmental education and provide a promising venue for exploring how more dramatic reforms may affect students' outcomes. Given the limited impact that previous reforms have had on students' achievement, researchers and policymakers should prioritize investigations into these more innovative designs and should pay close attention to how these efforts affect students' progress through developmental education and into college-level courses.

Acceleration Models. As discussed, a number of colleges are now experimenting with ways to accelerate students' progress through developmental education. While little rigorous research exists documenting the success of these programs, a number of internal and descriptive evaluations have shown that these programs hold great promise for increasing students' success. As noted above, Community College of Baltimore County's practice of mainstreaming developmental education students into college-level courses has helped students gain quicker access to and success in college-level courses. However, other approaches— such as modularizing developmental education courses into mini-classes focused on discrete skills or creating compressed courses by which students can quickly cover course material—have also shown promise for helping students move more quickly into credit-bearing courses. While limited evidence exists about these programs, practitioners and researchers should explore accelerated courses as an important avenue for moving students more quickly through remedial coursework and into college-level courses.

Additional Considerations for Future Research and Practice

While a number of promising innovations in developmental education are under development, most of these reform efforts will also need to consider how to tackle several institutional issues that are at the core of developmental education programming and practice. For instance, most developmental education programs rely on entrance exams or placement tests to funnel students into the appropriate course levels. The tests thus play a large role in determining the length of students' tenure in developmental education—an issue that most practitioners will need to face when developing new reforms. Educators should also consider which faculty members will be implementing classroom innovations and how these individuals will be trained in newly developed methodologies. The following sections outline some of the challenges that these issues pose for developmental education reform and make some recommendations about how practitioners, researchers, and policymakers might approach these difficulties.

PLACEMENT ASSESSMENTS

On entering community college, most students are required to take an entrance exam, which assesses their current math, reading, and writing skills and is used to place them into the appropriate developmental or college-level courses. While the tests are designed to aid colleges' placement practices and were encouraged within earlier developmental education research, much debate exists as to the validity of these assessments and their benefits for students. First, colleges across the country have established different cutoff scores for placement into developmental education, creating questions about how well these tests demarcate a true deficit in students' skills.[140] Additionally, recent research reports, employing sophisticated statistical methods, have shown that students with skill levels denoted by some colleges as developmental performed successfully in college-level courses.[141] Finally, these assessments are not diagnostic and provide little information about how instruction could improve students' skills, making their validity for classroom assignment questionable.[142]

Given the important role that assessment and placement play in defining students' college careers, researchers and policymakers should place a high priority on developing more nuanced placement methods and on understanding how they affect students' progress through college. Much as four-year colleges use a compendium of resources to assess students' skills, community colleges should seek to diversify their methods. In particular, assessments that are more diagnostic—which delineate particular skill weaknesses and strengths—would help practitioners better understand the level of students' deficiencies (or lack thereof) while also providing clearer guides for classroom practice and instruction. Such tests would be particularly useful for certain classroom reforms, such as fast-track or modularized courses, as they would help to place students into the appropriate class format.

While some developers of the current placement tests have began to provide more diagnostic tools to accompany their tests,[143] other, more comprehensive assessments should be identified and researched in order to see whether more valid measures can be used for placing students into different levels of developmental education. Effective measures used in secondary schools for diagnosing reading, writing, and math deficiencies would be one place to begin, as these assessments have already been validated for classroom use. Other assessments, such as those designed to measure students' affective characteristics, could also be an option, as these tests might be useful in considering other supports that might help improve students' success, such as more intensive advising or mentoring.[144]

ADJUNCT FACULTY

Studies have clearly demonstrated that a large majority of developmental education classes are taught by adjunct, or part-time, faculty. While consistent estimates are difficult to find, national surveys have found that up to three-quarters of developmental courses in community colleges are taught by adjuncts.[145] While adjunct faculty make invaluable contributions to the nation's higher education system, they can also suffer several major disadvantages as a result of their employment status. For instance, adjunct faculty are generally paid only for their time teaching in the classroom, which can limit their involvement in other activities at the college, such as departmental decision-making and piloting new programmatic strategies. Additionally, adjuncts tend to work multiple jobs, which usually makes them less accessible to students or other faculty. Finally, adjunct faculty are rarely paid for professional development, thus restricting their chances of being trained to fully implement programs seeking to transform developmental education practice.[146]

Given that adjunct faculty have the greatest access to developmental education students, educators and policymakers need to pay close attention to integrating them into interventions, particularly when considering how to scale new strategies to reach larger populations of students. While a number of community college initiatives and developmental educators recommend such integration, few structures currently exist in the community college environment to make such practices a reality, and so very few adjuncts become deeply involved in colleges' work.[147] Indeed, numerous colleges have cited budget limitations as the key reason why adjunct faculty are employed at such high numbers, thus revealing the substantial challenges that colleges face in providing additional support to these faculty.[148]

These issues suggest that more fundamental changes in community college programming and practices may be needed in order to bring larger proportions of adjunct faculty into colleges' implementation of new reforms. For instance, higher-level policies, allowing for additional resources to be funneled to the preparation of adjunct faculty, might help colleges overcome some of the limitations that they face in readying personnel to lead new instructional interventions. Similarly, finding ways to standardize practices across full-time and adjunct faculty will require deeper investment in a college's ongoing professional development activities (which is itself an important field for future research, as discussed below).

CLASSROOM INSTRUCTIONAL PRACTICE

Several studies have demonstrated that the level of quality and effectiveness of instruction are among the most important factors influencing developmental students' academic performance and that classroom experiences are an important predictor of commitment to the institution for students at all levels.[149] Researchers, however, have given only cursory treatment to instructors' pedagogy and practice within the classroom, and currently no rigorous studies have attempted to document how different instructional practices affect student outcomes.[150] Theoretical and best-practices research have hypothesized that certain pedagogical techniques—such as active, or "constructivist," learning, in which students play a critical role in facilitating and evaluating their own learning—provide promising methods for classroom instruction.[151] However, although some researchers have attempted to document the variation in developmental education instruction and have found correlational evidence that active learning is beneficial to developmental-level students, currently no standardized techniques exist for assessing the effectiveness of various pedagogical practices.[152]

Given the important role that pedagogy and instruction play in student learning, practitioners, policymakers, and researchers should pay close attention to the variations in instruction and should develop more standardized measures for assessing the effectiveness of different practices. In order to undertake this work, these individuals might identify particular instructors who have high levels of success and then determine what practices make their instruction effective. Similarly, researchers might look to develop a standardized classroom observation instrument, which would allow for a more consistent method of assessing instruction across different classrooms and schools. Finally, rigorous evaluations of new reforms and innovations should be accompanied by more intensive observations of actual classroom instruction. This would allow researchers to evaluate the continuity of implementation across classrooms, and it would help policymakers and practitioners to better understand what practices and pedagogies facilitate student achievement.

PROFESSIONAL DEVELOPMENT

Professional development is also a critical consideration in developmental education practice and reform. As might be expected, classroom instructors and other support staff play a key role in implementing reforms to improve students' success and, as such, may require substantial training to learn the methodology behind the new practices. Professional development is particularly important for developmental education instructors, as these individuals tend to have limited previous training for teaching basic skills students.[153] Unfortunately, studies have found that most community colleges provide only episodic staff development activities, which tend to take the form of one-day workshops or seminars led by outside experts, or else informal and isolated conversations among colleagues or departmental meetings that focus on logistics or content knowledge rather than pedagogy.[154] Sadly, studies have revealed that such isolated professional development does little to change individuals' everyday practice, as they become subsumed in normal routines and have little support for integrating new learning into their practice.[155] Moreover, little research has been done within community colleges to determine whether and how a particular professional development activity may have influenced faculty practice or student outcomes.[156]

While research in middle and high schools has shown that professional development reforms alone do not necessarily lead to improved student achievement,[157] a more systematic approach to professional development activities can be a vital tool in colleges' efforts to implement large-scale reforms aimed at increasing developmental education students' success. As such, policymakers and reformers should place a high priority on developing more integrated approaches to professional development that are designed to provide ongoing support to faculty and staff implementing new reforms and to assist them in bringing this new learning into their actual classroom practice. Promising methods have been developed at a few colleges, including the efforts of several California community colleges to create Faculty Inquiry Groups, which provide opportunities for regular collaboration and reflection on specific goals for student success.[158] Patrick Henry Community College in Martinsville, Virginia, has developed a training center—the Southern Center on Active Learning Excellence—to support the institutionalization of pedagogical practices that encourage active and collaborative learning. This center provides a number of ongoing opportunities for faculty and staff training, including free courses to learn different pedagogical approaches, coaching and mentoring in implementing these practices, examples of classroom lessons, surveys for students, and training institutes for other colleges to learn about collaborative learning.[159] Innovations like these represent promising steps toward a more integrated approach for faculty and staff training, which, in turn, may create a more systematic approach to implementation of reforms while supporting their wide-scale adoption.

Similarly, given the dearth of rigorous research on the effects of professional development in community colleges, researchers should seek to develop new inquiries into this field. One useful approach would be to create a more holistic research process for observing program implementation, which would provide on-the-ground time to assess instructors' training and the consistency with which they implement new methodologies within their actual practice. As with research into instructional practices, developing more standardized techniques for evaluating the effectiveness of colleges' training practices would allow for more concrete comparisons across different institutions. These instruments might seek to document such factors as the depth and intensity of colleges' training programs, their institution of research-based principles and practices, the ongoing supports provided for classroom implementation, and the actual integration of the new knowledge and methods into classroom instruction.

Conclusion

Developmental education remains a field ripe for further research and innovation. With multiple studies revealing alarmingly low success rates for developmental students, these programs can no longer afford to focus on the status quo. Research to date clearly demonstrates that minor modifications in developmental education programs are insufficient for producing dramatic improvements in student achievement. Given this, educators, policymakers, and researchers should continue to question the traditional developmental course sequence and should turn to more innovative efforts aimed at transforming the educational experience of academically underprepared students. Creating ever more novel ways to improve students' achievement and providing rigorous, reliable evidence for the successes of these new innovations are two actionable steps that educators, policymakers, and researchers can take to allow academically disadvantaged students the opportunity to achieve the college and career dreams that they are so avidly pursuing.

Appendix A

List of Journals Reviewed

The journals listed below were searched by keywords that include "basic skills," "community college," "developmental education," and "remedial education."

American Educational Research Journal
Community College Journal of Research and Practice
Education and Information Technologies
Education Technology Research and Development
Educational Assessment, Evaluation and Accountability
Educational Evaluation and Policy Analysis
Educational Research for Policy and Practice
Educational Studies in Mathematics
*Higher Education: The International Journal of Higher Education
and Educational Planning*
Industry and Higher Education
Innovative Education
Journal of College Student Development

Journal of Developmental Education
Journal of Higher Education
New Directions for Community Colleges
New Directions for Higher Education
New Directions for Teaching and Learning
New Directions in Adult and Continuing Education
New England Journal of Higher Education
Opportunity Matters
Research in Developmental Education
Research in Higher Education
Review of Higher Education
Review of Research in Education

Notes

1. Bailey, Jeong, and Cho (p. 125 in this book); Parsad and Lewis (2003).
2. Common placement tests include the ACCUPLACER (developed by the College Board) and COMPASS (developed by ACT, Inc.). However, each college (or district) chooses which test(s) to accept and where to set the cutoff scores for college-level coursework.
3. Bailey, Jeong, and Cho (p. 125 in this book); Jenkins, Jaggars, and Roksa (2009).
4. Bahr (2010); Bailey, Jeong, and Cho (p. 125 in this book); Jenkins, Jaggars, and Roksa (2009).
5. Bettinger and Long (2009); Lesik (2006).
6. Bahr (2010); Attewell, Lavin, Domina, and Levey (p. 153 in this book).
7. Calcagno and Long (2008); Martorell and McFarlin (2007).
8. Bailey, Hughes, and Karp (2003).
9. Kleiner and Lewis (2005).
10. In the 2002–2003 school year, 110 institutions offered dual enrollment programs specifically targeting at-risk students; these programs served about 6,400 students (Kleiner and Lewis, 2005).
11. American Institutes for Research and SRI International (2007); Jobs for the Future (2009); Karp et al. (2008).
12. American Institutes for Research and SRI International (2007); Kleiman (2001). See also the Web sites for College Now in New York (http://collegenow.cuny.edu) and the Early College High School Initiative (www.earlycolleges.org).
13. Kleiman (2001). Examples of other colleges with College Now programs include Lane Community College in Eugene, OR (http://www.lanecc.edu/hsconnections/collegenow/index.html); Linn-Benton Community College in Albany, OR (http://www.linnbenton.edu/go/collegenow); Mt. Hood Community College in Gresham, OR (http://www.mhcc.edu/CollegeNow/); and Allan Hancock College in Santa Maria, CA (http://www.hancockcollege.edu/Default.asp?Page=740).
14. Kleiman (2001).
15. Golann and Hughes (2008).
16. Kim and Barnett (2008).

17. Michalowski (2007); American Institutes for Research and SRI International (2007); Karp et al. (2008).
18. Greenberg (1988).
19. Michalowski (2007); Kleiman (2001).
20. Karp et al. (2008). Like the previously cited studies, this study employed some controls for background characteristics but did not use a quasi-experimental design; therefore, these results are categorized as promising trends.
21. Much of this work to date has been about the implementation of the programs and students' experiences in the programs. For example, see American Institutes for Research and SRI International (2007) and other reports in this series.
22. Greenberg (1988).
23. Kim and Barnett (2008).
24. Jobs for the Future (2009).
25. Howell, Kurlaender, and Grodsky (2010).
26. Kerrigan and Slater (2010).
27. Howell, Kurlaender, and Grodsky (2010).
28. Kerrigan and Slater (2010).
29. Ackermann (1990); Fitts (1989); Garcia (1991); Miller (1990); Santa Rita and Bacote (1991); Barnett (2009).
30. Barnett (2009).
31. Garcia (1991); Ackermann (1990).
32. Santa Rita and Bacote (1991); Miller (1990); Fitts (1989).
33. Texas Higher Education Coordinating Board (2009); Zuniga (2008).
34. Barnett (2009).
35. Melguizo, Hagedorn, and Cypers (2008).
36. Bailey, Jeong, and Cho (p. 125 in this book).
37. Zachry (2008).
38. Adams (2003).
39. Bragg (2009).
40. Zachry (2008); Bragg (2009).
41. Epper and Baker (2009).
42. Brown and Ternes (2009), as cited in Edgecombe (p. 256 in this book).
43. Zachry (2008).
44. Adams (2003).
45. Brancard, Baker, and Jensen (2006); Bragg (2009).
46. See the Web sites of these initiatives for a list of project participants and the developmental education strategies that they use: Developmental Education Initiative (http://www.deionline.org/); Breaking Through (http://www.breakingthroughcc.org).
47. Epper and Baker (2009).
48. Epper and Baker (2009).
49. Bassett (2009).
50. Bassett (2009); Bragg and Barnett (2009); Epper and Baker (2009).
51. Epper and Baker (2009); Bassett (2009). These positive results were also enabled by the flexible math requirements put in place by Jackson State as part of its redesign. Administrators used the modules to redefine the math competencies necessary for each program of study, which reduced the requirements for all but seven majors.

52. Goen-Salter (2008).
53. Glau (2007); Gleason (2000). The CUNY program ended as a result of the institutional decision to relegate all developmental-level students to the system's community colleges, rather than providing remediation at the four-year colleges as well.
54. Adams, Gearhart, Miller, and Roberts (p. 303 in this book).
55. Jenkins (2009). The Digital Bridge Academy has since been restructured to replace the college-level English course with a reading lab and a literacy skills course, and so its current incarnation should not be considered a mainstreaming strategy. The restructuring decision was made in response to state policies about prerequisites for developmental-level students.
56. Jenkins et al. (2010).
57. Goen-Salter (2008).
58. Adams, Gearhart, Miller, and Roberts (p. 303 in this book).
59. Jenkins (2009).
60. Moltz (2010); Jenkins (2009); Gleason (2000); Bassett (2009).
61. Epper and Baker (2009).
62. Center for Student Success (2007); Grubb and Associates (1999); McCabe and Day (1998); American Mathematical Association of Two-Year Colleges (AMATYC) (2006); Simpson, Stahl, and Francis (2004).
63. Gillespie (2002); Berns and Erickson (2001).
64. Center for Student Success (2007); Grubb and Associates (1999); De Corte (2007); Dirkx and Prenger (1997).
65. Baker, Hope, and Karandjeff (2009).
66. Perin (p. 93 in this book).
67. Grubb and Kraskouskas (1992); Berns and Erickson (2001); Perin (2001); Badway and Grubb (1997).
68. Baker, Hope, and Karandjeff (2009); Berns and Erickson (2001); Jobs for the Future (2010).
69. Jobs for the Future (2010); Washington State Board for Community and Technical Colleges (2005).
70. Washington Stale Board for Community and Technical Colleges (2005).
71. Bragg and Barnett (2009).
72. Jenkins, Zeidenberg, and Kienzl (p. 294 in this book).
73. Bragg and Barnett (2009).
74. Tinto (1975, 1987); Visher, Schneider, Wathington, and Collado (2010).
75. Weissman et al. (2011).
76. Tinto (1997); Visher, Schneider, Wathington, and Collado (2010).
77. Engstrom and Tinto (2008); Tinto (1997); Zhao and Kuh (2004).
78. Scrivener et al. (2008).
79. Visher, Schneider, Wathington, and Collado (2010).
80. Weiss, Visher, and Wathington (2010).
81. Weissman et al. (2011).
82. Adelman (2004); Attewell, Lavin, Domina, and Levey (p. 153 in this book); Hagedorn et al. (1999); Goldrick-Rab (2007).
83. Boylan (2002); McCabe and Day (1998); Center for Student Success (2007); Sperling (2009).
84. American Mathematical Association of Two-Year Colleges (AMATYC) (2006); Boylan (2002).
85. Center for Student Success (2007); Weissman et al. (2009).
86. Brock et al. (2007).

87. American Mathematical Association of Two-Year Colleges (AMATYC) (2006); Perin (p. 93 in this book); Maxwell (1990).
88. Arendale (1997).
89. Zachry (2008).
90. Xu, Hartman, Uribe, and Mencke (2001).
91. Bannier (2007).
92. Xu, Hartman, Uribe, and Mencke (2001).
93. Perin (p. 93 in this book); Roueche, Ely, and Roueche (2001).
94. Scrivener, Sommo, and Collado (2009).
95. Maxwell (1990); Topping (1996); Hock, Deshler, and Schumaker (1999).
96. Boylan, Bliss, and Bonham (1997).
97. Zachry (2008).
98. Maxwell (1990); Hock, Deshler, and Schumaker (1999).
99. Arendale (1997); Bowles, McCoy, and Bates (2008); Hodges and White (2001); Ogden, Thompson, Russell, and Simons (2003); Ramirez (1997).
100. Ogden, Thompson, Russell, and Simons (2003); Ramirez (1997).
101. Grubb (2001).
102. Sperling (2009).
103. Pfleging (2002).
104. Scrivener and Weiss (2009).
105. Visher, Butcher, and Cerna (2010).
106. Boylan, Bliss, and Bonham (1997); Light (2001).
107. Taylor (1996); the program (*Puente*, in California) also has a coursework component whereby students take English courses especially designed for Latino students.
108. Lewallen (1993); Pfleging (2002); Cartnal and Hagen (1999); Rudmann (1992).
109. Bahr (2008).
110. Scrivener and Weiss (2009).
111. Visher, Butcher, and Cerna (2010). Similarly positive effects were noted in a random assignment study of "light touch" mentoring for a more general college population (Bettinger and Baker, 2010).
112. Scrivener, Sommo, and Collado (2009); Zeidenberg, Jenkins, and Calcagno (2007); Derby and Smith (2004).
113. Weiss, Visher, and Wathington (2010); Scrivener et al. (2008); Weissman et al. (2011).
114. Scrivener, Sommo, and Collado (2009); Zachry and Orr (2009).
115. Boylan (2002); Weinstein et al. (1997).
116. Zeidenberg, Jenkins, and Calcagno (2007).
117. Scrivener et al. (2008).
118. Scrivener, Sommo, and Collado (2009). MDRC is conducting an additional random assignment study of Guilford Tech's student success course for developmental education students; results are due by the end of 2011.
119. Adelman (2004); Attewell, Lavin, Domina, and Levey (p. 153 in this book); Bailey, Jeong, and Cho (p. 125 in this book).
120. Adelman (2004).
121. While programs at most of these colleges targeted both developmental and college-level students, the sample population in each of these studies included a large proportion of developmental education students.
122. Scrivener, Sommo, and Collado (2009).
123. Scrivener et al. (2008).

124. Scrivener and Weiss (2009); Visher, Butcher, and Cerna (2010).
125. Engstrom and Tinto (2008); Tinto (1997); Zhao and Kuh (2004); Zeidenberg, Jenkins, and Calcagno (2007).
126. Jenkins, Zeidenberg, and Kienzl (p. 294 in this book).
127. Howell, Kurlaender, and Grodsky (2010).
128. Jenkins, Speroni, Belfield, Jaggars, and Edgecombe (2010).
129. Epper and Baker (2009).
130. Carpenter, Brown, and Hickman (2004); Zavarella and Ignash (2009); Creery (2001); McClenden and McArdle (2002); Weems (2002); Blackner (2000).
131. Epper and Baker (2009).
132. Boylan (2002); Jaggars and Bailey (2010); Zavarella and Ignash (2009).
133. Epper and Baker (2009).
134. Attewell, Lavin, Domina, and Levey (p. 153 in this book); Fine, Duggan, and Braddy (2009); Hoyt and Sorenson (2001).
135. Boylan (2002); Roueche and Roueche (1993).
136. Achieve, Inc. (2010); American Youth Policy Forum (AYPF) (2009).
137. National Governors Association (2010).
138. Bryk and Treisman (2010).
139. Bailey, Jeong, and Cho (p. 125 in this book).
140. Safran and Visher (2010); Attewell, Lavin, Domina, and Levey (p. 153 in this book).
141. Bettinger and Long (2009).
142. Safran and Visher (2010).
143. For instance, the College Board has developed a diagnostic tool for the ACCUPLACER tests, which many community colleges use for assessment and placement (Hughes and Scott-Clayton, 2010).
144. Hughes and Scott-Clayton (2010); Boylan (p. 325 in this book).
145. Boylan, Bonham, Jackson, and Saxon (1994); Gerstein (2009); Shults (2000).
146. Gerstein (2009); Schuetz (2002).
147. Boylan (2002); Zachry (2008); Rutschow et al. (2011); Center for Student Success (2007).
148. Rutschow et al. (2011).
149. Boylan (2002); Strauss and Volkwein (2004); Tinto (1975).
150. Grubb and Associates (1999).
151. Boylan (2002); Grubb and Associates (1999); Simpson, Stahl, and Francis (2004); Center for Student Success (2007). These recommendations do not entirely discount lectures but suggest that students are more likely to succeed if they are exposed to a variety of pedagogical techniques that encourage active rather than passive learning.
152. Grubb and Associates (1999); Schwartz and Jenkins (2007); Braxton, Milem, and Sullivan (2000); Weinstein et al. (1997); Kuh, Pace, and Vesper (1997); DePree (1998); Chaffee (1992).
153. Shults (2000).
154. Grubb and Associates (1999); Murray (2002); Gerstein (2009).
155. Troen and Boles (2003).
156. Chism and Szabo (1997).
157. Some studies, which have focused on the effects of increased professional development on student outcomes, have had disappointing results (Cor-

rin et al., 2008; Garet et al., 2010). However, systematic professional development and training remain key in other K–12 efforts that have seen some success in increasing students' academic and workforce outcomes (Darling-Hammond et al., 2009).

158. Carnegie Foundation for the Advancement of Teaching (2008).

159. Rutschow et al. (2011); Zachry (2008).

References

Achieve, Inc. 2010. *On the Road to Implementation: Achieving the Promise of the Common Core State Standards.* Washington, DC: Achieve, Inc.

Ackermann, S. P. 1990. "The Benefits of Summer Bridge Programs for Underrepresented and Low-Income Students." Paper presented at the Annual Meeting of the American Educational Research Association, Boston, April 16–20.

Adams, William W. 2003. *Developmental Mathematics: A New Approach.* Mathematical Association of America (MAA). Web site: http://www.maa.org/features/112103devmath.html.

Adelman, Clifford. 2004. *Principal Indicators of Student Academic Histories in Postsecondary Education, 1972–2000.* Washington, DC: Institute of Education Sciences, U.S. Department of Education.

American Institutes for Research and SRI International. 2007. *Evaluation of the Early College High School Initiative: Select Topics on Implementation.* Report prepared for the Bill and Melinda Gates Foundation. Washington, DC: American Institutes for Research and SRI International.

American Mathematical Association of Two-Year Colleges (AMATYC). 2006. *Beyond Crossroads: Implementing Mathematics Standards in the First Two Years of College.* Memphis, TN: American Mathematical Association of Two-Year Colleges.

American Youth Policy Forum (AYPF). 2009. "Linking Second and Postsecondary Systems Lessons from Indiana." Issue Brief. Washington, DC: American Youth Policy Forum.

Arendale, David. 1997. "Supplemental Instruction (SI): Review of Research Concerning the Effectiveness of SI from the University of Missouri-Kansas City and Other Institutions from Across the United States." Proceedings of the 17th and 18th Annual Institutes for Learning Assistance Professionals. Tucson: University Learning Center, University of Arizona.

Badway, Norena, and W. Norton Grubb. 1997. *A Sourcebook for Reshaping the Community College: Curriculum Integration and the Multiple Domains of Career Preparation*, Vols. I and II. Berkeley, CA: National Center for Research in Vocational Education.

Bahr, Peter Riley. 2008. "Cooling Out in the Community College: What Is the Effect of Academic Advising on Students' Chances of Success?" *Research in Higher Education* 49: 704–732.

Bahr, Peter Riley. 2010. "Revising the Efficacy of Postsecondary Remediation: The Moderating Effects of Depth/Breadth of Deficiency." *Review of Higher Education* 33, 2: 177–205.

Bailey, Thomas, Katherine L. Hughes, and Melinda Mechur Karp. 2003. "Dual Enrollment Programs: Easing Transitions from High School to College." CCRC Brief No. 17. New York: Community College Research Center, Teachers College, Columbia University.

Baker, Elaine DeLott, Laura Hope, and Kelley Karandjeff. 2009. *Contextualized Teaching and Learning: A Faculty Primer (A Review of Literature and Faculty Practices with Implications for California Community College Practitioners)*. Sacramento: Center for Student Success/RP Group and the Academic Senate for California Community Colleges.

Bannier, Betsy. 2007. "Predicting Mathematics Learning Center Visits: An Examination of Correlating Variables." *Learning Assistance Review* 12, 1: 7–16.

Barnett, Elisabeth. 2009. "Developmental Summer Bridges: Young Texans on the Road to College." Presentation at the Annual Conference of the League for Innovation in the Community College, Reno, NV, March 17.

Bassett, Mary Jane. 2009. *Tennessee Board of Regents: Developmental Studies Redesign Initiative.* "Jackson State Community College, Course Title: Basic Math, Elementary Algebra and Intermediate Algebra." Web site: http://www.thencat.org/States/TN/Abstracts/JSCC%20Algebra_Abstract.htm.

Berns, Robert G., and Patricia M. Erickson. 2001. "Contextual Teaching and Learning: Preparing Students for the New Economy." The Highlight Zone: Research @ Work, No. 5. Columbus, OH: National Center for Career and Technical Education.

Bettinger, Eric, and Rachel Baker. 2011. "The Effects of Student Coaching in College: An Evaluation of a Randomized Experiment in Student Mentoring." Paper presented at the Society for Research on Educational Effectiveness Conference, Washington, DC, March 3–5.

Bettinger, Eric P., and Bridget Terry Long. 2009. "Addressing the Needs of Underprepared Students in Higher Education: Does College Remediation Work?" *Journal of Human Resources* 44, 3: 736–771.

Blackner, D. B. 2000. "Prediction of Community College Students' Success in Developmental Math with Traditional Classroom, Computer-Based On-Campus and Computer-Based at a Distance Instruction Using Locus of Control, Math Anxiety and Learning Style." Doctoral dissertation. Available from ProQuest Dissertations and Theses database: UMI No. 3064379.

Bowles, Tyler J., Adam C. McCoy, and Scott Bates. 2008. "The Effect of Supplemental Instruction on Timely Graduation." *College Student Journal* 42, 3: 853–859.

Boylan, Hunter R. 2002. *What Works: Research-Based Practices in Developmental Education*. Boone, NC: Continuous Quality Improvement Network and the National Center for Developmental Education, Appalachian State University.

Boylan, Hunter R., Leonard B. Bliss, and Barbara S. Bonham. 1997. "Program Components and Their Relationship to Student Performance." *Journal of Developmental Education* 20, 3: 2–8.

Boylan, Hunter R., Barbara S. Bonham, James Jackson, and D. Patrick Saxon. 1994. "Staffing Patterns in Developmental Education Programs: Full-Time/Part-Time, Credentials, and Program Placement." *Research in Developmental Education* 11, 5.

Bragg, Debra D. 2009. *Community College of Denver* Breaking Through *Outcomes Report*. Denver, CO: Community College of Denver.

Bragg, Debra D., and Elisabeth Barnett. 2009. *Lessons Learned from* Breaking Through. *In Brief.* Champaign, IL: Office of Community College Research and Leadership. Web site: http://occrl.ed.uiuc.edu.

Brancard, Ruth, Elaine DeLott Baker, and Laura Jensen. 2006. *Accelerated Developmental Education Project: Research Report (Community College of Denver).* Denver, CO: Community College of Denver.

Braxton, John M., Jeffrey F. Milem, and Anna Shaw Sullivan. 2000. "The Influence of Active Learning on the College Student Departure Process: Toward a Revision of Tinto's Theory." *Journal of Higher Education* 71, 5.

Brock, Thomas, Davis Jenkins, Todd Ellwein, Jennifer Miller, Susan Gooden, Kasey Martin, Casey MacGregor, and Michael Pih. 2007. *Building a Culture of Evidence for Community College Student Success: Early Progress in the Achieving the Dream Initiative.* New York: MDRC.

Brown, R., and R. Ternes. 2009. *Final Report to the Lilly Endowment Grant: Grant for Targeted and Accelerated Remediation.* Unpublished. Indianapolis: Ivy Tech.

Bryk, Anthony, and Uri Treisman. 2010. "Make Math a Gateway, Not a Gatekeeper." *Chronicle of Higher Education* (April 18).

Calcagno, Juan Carlos, and Bridget Terry Long. 2008. *The Impact of Postsecondary Remediation Using a Regression Discontinuity Approach: Addressing Endogenous Sorting and Noncompliance.* NCPR Working Paper. New York: National Center for Postsecondary Research.

Carnegie Foundation for the Advancement of Teaching. 2008. "Strengthening Pre-Collegiate Education in Community Colleges: Project Summary and Recommendations." Stanford, CA: Carnegie Foundation for the Advancement of Teaching.

Carpenter, Trudy G., William L. Brown, and Randall C. Hickman. 2004. "Influences of Online Delivery on Developmental Writing Outcomes." *Journal of Developmental Education* 28, 1: 14–18, 35.

Cartnal, Ryan, and Peter F. Hagen. 1999. *Evaluation of the Early Alert Program, Spring 1999* (Cuesta College, California). ERIC ED 441 541.

Center for Student Success. 2007. *Basic Skills as a Foundation for Student Success in California Community Colleges.* Sacramento: Research and Planning Group for California Community Colleges.

Chaffee, John. 1992. "Critical Thinking Skills: The Cornerstone of Developmental Education." *Journal of Developmental Education* 15, 3: 2–4.

Chism, Nancy Van Note, and Borbala Szabo. 1997. "How Faculty Development Programs Evaluate Their Services." *Journal of Staff, Program, and Organizational Development* 15, 2.

Corrin, William, Marie-Andrée Somers, James J. Kemple, Elizabeth Nelson, and Susan Sepanik with Terry Salinger and Courtney Tanenbaum. 2008. *The Enhanced Reading Opportunities Study: Findings from the Second Year of Implementation.* New York: MDRC.

Creery, Katherine W. 2001. "Comparison of Lecture, Self-Paced, and On-Line Courses." NADE Selected Conference Papers, Vol. 7. Louisville, KY: National Association of Developmental Education.

Darling-Hammond, Linda, Ruth Chung Wei, Alethea Andree, Nikole Richardson, and Stelios Orphanos. 2009. *Professional Learning in the Learning Profession: A Status Report on Teacher Development in the United States and Abroad.* Stanford, CA: National Staff Development Council and the School Redesign Network.

De Corte, Erik. 2007. "Learning from Instruction: The Case of Mathematics." *Learning Inquiry* 1: 19–30.

DePree, J. 1998. "Small-Group Instruction: Impact on Basic Algebra Students." *Journal of Developmental Education* 22, 1: 2–5.

Derby, D. C., and T. Smith. 2004. "An Orientation Course and Community College Retention." *Community College Journal of Research and Practice* 28, 9: 763–773.

Dirkx, John M., and Suzanne M. Prenger. 1997. *A Guide to Planning and Implementing Instruction for Adults: A Theme-Based Approach.* San Francisco: Jossey-Bass.

Engstrom, Cathy McHugh, and Vincent Tinto. 2008. "Learning Better Together: The Impact of Learning Communities on the Persistence of Low-Income Students." *Opportunity Matters* 1.

Epper, Rhonda M., and Elaine DeLott Baker. 2009. *Technology Solutions for Developmental Math: An Overview of Current and Emerging Practices.* Report funded by the William and Flora Hewlett Foundation and the Bill and Melinda Gates Foundation.

Fine, Anne, Mickle Duggan, and Linda Braddy. 2009. "Removing Remediation Requirements: Effectiveness of intervention Programs." *PRIMUS* 19, 5: 433–446.

Fitts, J. D. 1989. "A Comparison of Locus of Control and Achievement Among Remedial Summer Bridge and Nonbridge Students in Community Colleges in New Jersey." Paper presented at the Annual Meeting of the American Educational Research Association, San Francisco, March 27–31.

Garcia, Phillip. 1991. "Summer Bridge: Improving Retention Rates for Underprepared Students." *Journal of the Freshman Year Experience* 3, 2: 91–105.

Garet, Michael S., Andrew J. Wayne, Fran Stancavage, James Taylor, Kirk Walters, Mengli Song, Seth Brown, Steven Hurlburt, Pei Zhu, Susan Sepanik, and Fred Doolittle. 2010. *Middle School Mathematics Professional Development Impact Study: After the First Year of Implementation.* Washington, DC: Institute of Education Sciences, U.S. Department of Education.

Gerstein, Amy. 2009. *Community College Faculty and Developmental Education: An Opportunity for Growth and Investment.* Stanford, CA: Carnegie Foundation for the Advancement of Teaching.

Gillespie, Marilyn K. 2002. *EFF Research Principle: A Contextualized Approach to Curriculum and Instruction.* Washington, DC: National Institute for Literacy.

Glau, Gregory. 2007. "Stretch at 10: A Progress Report on Arizona State University's Stretch Program." *Journal of Basic Writing* 26, 2: 30–48.

Gleason, Barbara. 2000. "Evaluating Writing Programs in Real Time: The Politics of Remediation." *College Composition and Communication* 51, 4: 560–588.

Goen-Salter, Sugie. 2008. "Critiquing the Need to Eliminate Remediation: Lessons from San Francisco State." *Basic Writing* 27, 2: 81–105.

Golann, Joanne Wang, and Katherine L. Hughes. 2008. *Dual Enrollment Policies and Practices: Earning College Credit in California High Schools.* San Francisco: James Irvine Foundation.

Goldrick-Rab, Sara. 2007. "Promoting Academic Momentum at Community Colleges: Challenges and Opportunities." CCRC Working Paper No. 5. New York: Community College Research Center, Teachers College, Columbia University.

Greenberg, Arthur Richard. 1988. "High School Students in College Courses: Three Programs." *New Directions for Community Colleges* 63: 69–84.

Grubb, W. Norton. 2001. *"Getting into the World": Guidance and Counseling in Community Colleges.* New York: Community College Research Center, Teachers College, Columbia University.

Grubb, W. Norton, and Associates. 1999. *Honored but Invisible: An Inside Look at Teaching in Community Colleges.* New York: Routledge.

Grubb, W. Norton, and Eileen Kraskouskas. 1992. *A Time to Every Purpose: Integrating Occupational and Academic Education in Community Colleges and Technical Institutes.* Berkeley, CA: National Center for Research in Vocational Education.

Hagedorn, Linda Serra, M. Vali Siadet, Shereen F. Fogel, Amaury Nora, and Ernest T. Pascarella. 1999. "Success in College Mathematics: Comparisons Between Remedial and Nonremedial First-Year College Students." *Research in Higher Education* 40, 3: 261–284.

Hock, Michael F., Donald D. Deshler, and Jean B. Schumaker. 1999. "Tutoring Programs for Academically Underprepared College Students: A Review of the Literature." *Journal of College Reading and Learning* 29: 101–122.

Hodges, Russ, and William G. White, Jr. 2001. "Encouraging High-Risk Student Participation in Tutoring and Supplemental Instruction." *Journal of Developmental Education* 24, 3: 2–10.

Howell, Jessica S., Michal Kurlaender, and Eric Grodsky. 2010. "Postsecondary Preparation and Remediation: Examing the Effect of the Early Assessment Program at California State University." *Journal of Policy Analysis and Management* 29, 4: 726–748.

Hoyt, Jeff E., and Colleen T. Sorenson. 2001. "High School Preparation, Placement Testing, and College Remediation." *Journal of Developmental Education* 25, 2: 26–34.

Hughes, Katherine, and Judith Scott-Clayton. 2010. "Assessing Developmental Assessment in Community Colleges: A Review of the Literature." CCRC Working Paper No. 19. Presented at the NCPR Developmental Education Conference: What Policies and Practices Work for Students? New York, September 23–24.

Jaggars, Shanna Smith, and Thomas Bailey. 2010. *Effectiveness of Fully Online Courses for College Students: Response to a Department of Education Meta-Analysis.* New York: Community College Research Center, Teachers College, Columbia University.

Jenkins, Davis. 2009. "Educational Outcomes of the Digital Bridge Academy: Findings from a Multivariate Analysis." Presentation at the Conference of the League for Innovation in Community College, Reno, NV, March 16.

Jenkins, Davis, Shanna Smith Jaggars, and Josipa Roksa. 2009. *Promoting Gatekeeper Course Success Among Community College Students Needing Remediation: Findings and Recommendations from a Virginia Study (Summary Report).* New York: Community College Research Center, Teachers College, Columbia University.

Jenkins, Davis, Cecilia Speroni, Clive Belfield, Shanna Smith Jaggars, and Nikki Edgecombe. 2010. "A Model for Accelerating Academic Success of Community College Remedial English Students: Is the Accelerated Learning Program (ALP) Effective and Affordable?" CCRC Working Paper No. 21. New York: Community College Research Center, Teachers College, Columbia University.

Jobs for the Future. 2009. *Early College High School Initiative: A Portrait in Numbers.* Boston: Jobs for the Future.

Jobs for the Future. 2010. *Contextualization Toolkit: A Tool for Helping Low-Skilled Adults Gain Postsecondary Certificates and Degrees.* Boston: Jobs for the Future.

Karp, Melinda Mechur, Juan Carlos Calcagno, Katherine L. Hughes, Dong Wook Jeong, and Thomas Bailey. 2008. "Dual Enrollment Students in Florida and New York City: Postsecondary Outcomes." CCRC Brief No. 37. New York: Community College Research Center, Teachers College, Columbia University.

Kerrigan, Monica Reid, and Doug Slater. 2010. *Collaborating to Create Change: How El Paso Community College Improved the Readiness of Its Incoming Students Through Achieving the Dream.* Report No. 4 in the Achieving the Dream Culture of Evidence Series. New York: Community College Research Center and MDRC.

Kim, Jennifer E., and Elisabeth Barnett. 2008. "2007–08 MCNC Early College High School Students: College Coursework Participation and Performance." New York: National Center for Restructuring Education, Schools, and Teaching, Teachers College, Columbia University.

Kleiman, Neil Scott. 2001. "Building a Highway to Higher Ed: How Collaborative Efforts Are Changing Education in America." New York: Center for an Urban Future. ERIC ED 453 738.

Kleiner, Brian, and Laurie Lewis. 2005. "Dual Enrollment of High School Students at Postsecondary Institutions: 2002–03." NCES 2005-008. Washington, DC: National Center for Education Statistics, Institute of Education Sciences, U.S. Department of Education.

Kuh, George D., C. Robert Pace, and Nick Vesper. 1997. "The Development of Process Indicators to Estimate Student Gains Associated with Good Practices in Undergraduate Education." *Research in Higher Education* 38, 4: 435–454.

Lewallen, Willard Clark. 1993. *Early Alert: A Report on Two Pilot Projects at Antelope Valley College.* ERIC ED 369 452.

Lesik, Sally Andrea. 2006. "Applying the Regression-Discontinuity Design to Infer Causality with Non-Random Assignment." *Review of Higher Education* 30, 1: 1–19.

Light, Richard J. 2001. *Making the Most of College: Students Speak Their Minds.* Cambridge, MA: Harvard University Press.

Martorell, Paco, and Isaac McFarlin. 2007. "Help or Hindrance? The Effects of College Remediation on Academic and Labor Market Outcomes." Unpublished manuscript.

Maxwell, Martha. 1990. "Does Tutoring Help? A Look at the Literature." *Review of Research in Developmental Education* 7, 4: 1–5.

McCabe, Robert H., and Philip R. Day (eds.). 1998. *Developmental Education: A Twenty-First Century Social and Economic Imperative.* Laguna Hills, CA: League for Innovation in the Community College.

McClenden, Marie, and Michele McArdle. 2002. "Comparing Alternative Algebraic Modalities for Remedial Students." Paper presented at the Chair Academy Leadership Conference, Kansas City, MO, February 28–March 2. ERIC ED 464 568.

Melguizo, Tatiana, Linda Serra Hagedorn, and Scott Cypers. 2008. "Remedial/Developmental Education and the Cost of Community College Transfer: A Los Angeles County Sample." *Review of Higher Education* 31, 4: 401–431.

Michalowski, Sam. 2007. *Positive Effects Associated with College Now Participation.* New York: Collaborative Programs Research and Evaluation, City University of New York.

Miller, M. F. 1990. *1990 Pre-Freshman Summer Program: Post-Program Self-Study Report.* ERIC ED 337 213.

Moltz, David. 2010. "Competing Principles." *Inside Higher Education* (June 28).

Murray, John P. 2002. "The Current State of Faculty Development in Two-Year Colleges." *New Directions for Community Colleges*, 18: 89–98.

National Governors Association. 2010. "National Governors Association and State Education Chiefs Launch Common State Academic Standards." Press release. Washington, DC: National Governors Association.

Ogden, Peggy, Dennis Thompson, Art Russell, and Carol Simons. 2003. "Supplemental Instruction: Short- and Long-Term Impact." *Journal of Developmental Education* 26, 3: 2–8.

Parsad, Basmat, and Laurie Lewis. 2003. "Remedial Education at Degree-Granting Postsecondary Institutions in Fall 2000." NCES 2004-010. Washington, DC: National Center for Education Statistics, Institute of Education Sciences, U.S. Department of Education.

Perin, Dolores. 2001. "Academic-Occupational Integration as a Reform Strategy for the Community College: Classroom Perspectives." *Teachers College Record* 103: 303–335.

Perin, Dolores. 2005. "Institutional Decision Making for Increasing Academic Preparedness in Community Colleges." *New Directions for Community Colleges* 129: 27–38.

Pfleging, Elizabeth. 2002. "An Evaluation of the Early Alert Program at Columbia College." Unpublished doctoral dissertation. ERIC ED 478 596.

Ramirez, Gen M. 1997. "Supplemental Instruction: The Long-Term Impact." *Journal of Developmental Education* 21, 1.

Roueche, John, Eileen Ely, and Suanne Roueche. 2001. *In Pursuit of Excellence: The Community College of Denver.* Washington, DC: Community College Press.

Roueche, John, and Suanne Roueche. 1993. *Between a Rock and a Hard Place: The At-Risk Student in the Open Door College.* Washington, DC: Community College Press.

Rudmann, Jerry. 1992. *An Evaluation of Several Early Alert Strategies for Helping First Semester Freshmen at the Community College and a Description of the Newly Developed Early Alert Retention System (EARS) Software.* Irvine, CA: Irvine Valley College.

Rutschow, Elizabeth Zachry, Lashawn Richburg-Hayes, Thomas Brock, Genevieve Orr, Oscar Cerna, Dan Cullinan, Monica Reid Kerrigan, Davis Jenkins, Susan Gooden, and Kasey Martin. 2011. *Turning the Tide: Five Years of Achieving the Dream in Community Colleges.* New York: MDRC.

Safran, Stephanie, and Mary G. Visher. 2010. "Case Studies of Three Community Colleges: The Policy and Practice of Assessing and Placing Students in Developmental Education Courses." NCPR Working Paper. New York: MDRC.

Santa Rita, E., and J. B. Bacote. 1991. "The College Discovery Summer Program: Its Effects on Persistence and Academic Performance." New York: Bronx Community College. ERIC ED 338 290.

Schuetz, Pam. 2002. "Instructional Practices of Part-Time and Full-Time Faculty." *New Directions for Community Colleges*, 118: 39–46.

Schwartz, Wendy, and Davis Jenkins. 2007. *Promising Practices for Community College Developmental Education: A Discussion Resource for the Connecticut Community College System*. New York: Community College Research Center, Teachers College, Columbia University.

Scrivener, Susan, Dan Bloom, Allen LeBlanc, Christina Paxson, Cecilia Elena Rouse, and Colleen Sommo with Jenny Au, Jedediah J. Teres, and Susan Yeh. 2008. *A Good Start: Two-Year Effects of a Freshmen Learning Community Program at Kingsborough Community College*. New York: MDRC.

Scrivener, Susan, Colleen Sommo, and Herbert Collado. 2009. *Getting Back on Track: Effects of a Community College Program for Probationary Students*. New York: MDRC

Scrivener, Susan, and Michael J. Weiss with Jedediah J. Teres. 2009. *More Guidance, Better Results? Three-Year Effects of an Enhanced Student Services Program at Two Community Colleges*. New York: MDRC.

Shults, Christopher. 2000. *Remedial Education: Practices and Policies in Community Colleges*. Washington, DC: American Association of Community Colleges.

Simpson, Michele L., Norman A. Stahl, and Michelle Anderson Francis. 2004. "Reading and Learning Strategies: Recommendations for the 21st Century." *Journal of Developmental Education* 28, 2.

Sperling, Charmian B. 2009. "Massachusetts Community Colleges Developmental Education Best Policy and Practice Audit: Final Report." Boston: Massachusetts Community College Executive Office and Jobs for the Future.

Strauss, Linda C, and J. Fredericks Volkwein. 2004. "Predictors of Student Commitment at Two-Year and Four-Year Institutions." *Journal of Higher Education* 75, 2: 203–227.

Taylor, A. 1996. "The Puente Program: Latino Student Outcomes in English 96 and 1A, 1993–1995." San Francisco: City College of San Francisco, Office of Research, Planning and Grants. Web site: http://www.ccsf.edu/Offices/Research_Planning/planning/puente.htm.

Texas Higher Education Coordinating Board. 2009. *Consolidated Annual Program Evaluation Report: THECB Funded Programs (Fiscal Year 2008)*. Austin: Texas Higher Education Coordinating Board.

Tinto, Vincent. 1975. "Dropout from Higher Education: A Theoretical Synthesis of Recent Research." *Review of Education Research* 45: 89–125.

Tinto, Vincent. 1987. *Leaving College: Rethinking the Causes and Cures of Student Attrition*. Chicago: University of Chicago Press.

Tinto, Vincent. 1997. "Classrooms as Communities: Exploring the Educational Character of Student Persistence." *Journal of Higher Education* 68, 6: 599–623.

Topping, K. J. 1996. "The Effectiveness of Peer Tutoring in Further and Higher Education: A Typology and Review of the Literature." *Higher Education: The International Journal of Higher Education and Educational Planning* 32: 321–345.

Troen, Vivian, and Katherine C. Boles. 2003. *Who's Teaching Your Children? Why the Teacher Crisis Is Worse Than You Think and What Can Be Done About It*. New Haven, CT: Yale University Press.

Visher, Mary G., Kristin F. Butcher, and Oscar S. Cerna with Dan Cullinan and Emily Schneider. 2010. *Guiding Developmental Math Students to Campus Services: An Impact Evaluation of the Beacon Program at South Texas College.* New York: MDRC.

Visher, Mary G., Emily Schneider, Heather Wathington, and Herbert Collado. 2010. *Scaling Up Learning Communities: The Experience of Six Community Colleges.* New York: MDRC.

Washington State Board for Community and Technical Colleges. 2005. *I-BEST: A Program Integrating Adult Basic Education and Workforce Training.* Research Report No. 05-2. Olympia: Washington State Board for Community and Technical Colleges.

Weems, Gail H. 2002. "Comparison of Beginning Algebra Taught Onsite Versus Online." *Journal of Developmental Education* 26, 1: 10–18.

Weinstein, Claire Ellen, Gary Hanson, Lorrie Powdrill, Linda Roska, Doug Dierking, Jenefer Husman, and Erin McCann. 1997. "The Design and Evaluation of a Course in Strategic Learning." Web site: www.nade.net/documents/SCP97/SCP97.20.pdf.

Weiss, Michael J., Mary G. Visher, and Heather Wathington with Jedediah J. Teres and Emily Schneider. 2010. *Learning Communities for Students in Developmental English: An Impact Study at Hillsborough Community College.* New York: MDRC.

Weissman, Evan, Kristin F. Butcher, Emily Schneider, Jedediah Teres, Herbert Collado, and David Greenberg with Rashida Welbeck. 2011. *Learning Communities for Students in Developmental Math: Impact Studies at Queensborough and Houston Community Colleges.* New York: MDRC.

Weissman, Evan, Oscar Cerna, Christian Geckeler, Emily Schneider, Derek V. Price, and Tom J. Smith. 2009. *Promoting Partnerships for Student Success: Lessons from the SSPIRE Initiative.* New York: MDRC.

Xu, Yonghong, Stacey Hartman, Guillermo Uribe, and Reed Mencke. 2001. "The Effects of Peer Tutoring on Undergraduate Students' Final Scores in Mathematics." *Journal of College Reading and Learning* 32, 1: 22–31.

Zachry, Elizabeth M. with Emily Schneider. 2008. *Promising Instructional Reforms in Developmental Education: A Case Study of Three Achieving the Dream Colleges.* New York: MDRC.

Zachry, Elizabeth, and Genevieve Orr. 2009. *Building Student Success from the Ground Up: A Case Study of an Achieving the Dream College.* New York: MDRC.

Zavarella, Carol A., and Jan M. Ignash. 2009. "Instructional Delivery in Developmental Mathematics: Impact on Retention." *Journal of Developmental Education* 32, 3: 2–8.

Zeidenberg, Matthew, Davis Jenkins, and Juan Carlos Calcagno. 2007. "Do Student Success Courses Actually Help Community College Students Succeed?" CCRC Brief No. 36. Community College Research Center, Teachers College, Columbia University.

Zhao, Chun-Mei, and George D. Kuh. 2004. "Adding Value: Learning Communities and Student Engagement." *Research in Higher Education* 45, 2: 115–138.

Zuniga, Robin. 2008. *Developmental Education Summer Bridge Program: Texas Higher Education Coordinating Board, Cross-Site Evaluation Final Report.* Austin: Texas Higher Education Coordinating Board.

Chapter 2 Questions for Further Reflection

1. How well are developmental courses and support services integrated at your institution?

2. What can you do to improve the level of integration between developmental courses and academic support services?

3. Research suggests students who place into a sequence of developmental courses often fail to complete the sequence. What are some of the reasons for this that are not addressed in this chapter?

4. Many of the authors in this chapter discuss policy issues in developmental education. What policies do you think would do the most to improve developmental education on your campus? In your state?

5. What can you and your professional colleagues do to influence policy makers in your state?

6. What academic support services have the most potential for being fully integrated into academic courses?

3

Innovative Practices in Developmental Education

M ost policies affecting higher education are made at the state level. Legislators and state higher education executive offices generally do not consult practitioners in establishing statewide policies; or if they do, the consultation is brief and random. Consequently, state higher education policy frequently flows downhill, and at the bottom of that hill are the professionals who have to implement it, often without having been involved in developing the policy, or without understanding how or why it was made.

Many developmental educators are in this position today. There is a great deal of policy making going on that will affect developmental education at the campus level for many years to come. Much of what happens in the future of developmental education will be driven by emerging policies based on economic, social, and demographic considerations. Some of it may also be driven by sound research on developmental education. One might debate the wisdom of various state policies on developmental education or the widespread applicability of some innovations, but it is hard to disagree with the premises on which they are based. Unfortunately, the failure of policy makers to involve practitioners in policy discussions and subsequent implementation has the potential to erode the effectiveness of even sound policies.

It is important, therefore, for practitioners in the field to understand not only what policies mean but also what drives their development and implementation. Developmental educators should understand that today there are two themes driving many of the policy initiatives in developmental education: completion and acceleration. The college completion agenda is based on well-documented workforce and economic needs. Researchers have determined that there is a direct relationship between the educational attainment and economic development of a region (Aghion, Boustan, Hoxby, & Vandenbussche, 2009; Hanushek, Jamison, Jamison, & Woessmann, 2008; McCabe, 2003). The message is simple and direct—a well-educated workforce contributes to an improved economy.

Obviously, legislators and policy makers are interested in promoting an improved economy. However, various analyses of our college and university completion rates suggest that we are not producing enough college graduates to meet the needs of our economy. Carnevale, Smith, and Strohl (2010), for instance, point out that although our economy's need for college-educated workers is increasing, our level of college degree conferment has remained relatively stable. Carnevale and Rose (2011) project that we will need to graduate 12 million more college and university students than currently in order to meet workforce needs by 2025. According to a recent report from Complete College America (2011), "Given changing demographics, our country will simply not be economically competitive unless more students succeed" (p. 3).

If we are going to increase our college completion rates the most obvious vehicle for producing that increase is the community college. As O'Banion (2012) points out, our community colleges can produce associate degrees in only two years as well as a variety of shorter-term but meaningful work credentials in a year or less. Furthermore, community colleges are able to understand and respond to local labor needs more quickly than just about any other type of institution (Cohen & Brawer, 2008).[1]

Unfortunately, Bailey, Calcagno, Jenkins, Leinbach, and Kienzl (2006) estimate that the six-year community college graduation rate is just over 28 percent.[2] (Given the shortcomings of our reporting systems, it is impossible to determine whether the other 72 percent drop out, transfer to another institution, or complete degrees or certificates at their original institution after six years.) According to a report from Complete College America, about 56 percent of university students graduate within six years (Complete College America, 2012). These circumstances represent the primary reasons why there is so much pressure on postsecondary institutions, particularly community colleges, to improve student completion rates.

It should be noted at the outset that it is unlikely we can increase the number of college graduates by recruiting and graduating more middle-income students. According to Carnevale and Fry (2001), most of the students in this group who want to go to college are already doing so. The National Center for Education Statistics (2008), for instance, reports that students from the top 25 percent of the U.S. national income distribution are almost twice as likely to enter postsecondary education immediately after high school graduation than students from the lowest 25 percent of that distribution. The only way we can increase the number of college graduates is by increasing the number of people from lower income brackets who go to college.

People from lower income brackets, however, often bring weak academic skills to college. Zwick and Green (2007) report that there is a high correlation between family income and SAT scores, with students from the lowest income level attaining the lowest scores. In a study of California community colleges, Howell (2011) found that low-income students are disproportionally represented in remedial courses. Yet placement into remedial courses means that students have to take additional courses and pay extra money to obtain their college degrees. At some institutions, students placing into the lowest levels of the remedial course sequence in three subject areas would have to complete seven or eight courses (or twenty-one to twenty-four hours of credit) before being eligible to take their first college-level credit course. This is a particularly difficult burden for the nation's poor and may contribute to the low completion rates among students taking remedial courses.

According to Bailey and Cho (2010), less than 25 percent of those taking remedial courses complete an associate degree within eight years of enrollment (though, of note, part-time and older students were excluded from this study). Citing data from the Department of Education's National Education Longitudinal Study, Brock (2011) reports that only 28 percent of those taking remedial courses complete an associate degree or other credential within eight and a half years of enrollment in a community college compared to 43 percent of those taking no remedial courses.[3]

A recent report from Complete College America (2011) claims that time is the enemy of college completion. The longer a student takes in working toward a degree, the less likely the student is to attain that degree. This is where the acceleration of developmental education comes into play. Participating in long sequences of remedial courses, having to spend an entire semester in each course, and often having to retake one or more courses in the sequence can make remediation an unacceptably time-consuming and expensive venture. This is particularly true for those students who can least afford to pay the price in time or money that is necessary to participate in remediation. The bottom line here is that unless we can reduce the time students spend in remedial courses, we will never be able to attain the college completion rates necessary to meet future workforce needs.

All this has led and will continue to lead to policy initiatives and innovations designed to reduce the amount of time students spend in remedial courses. In the name of acceleration, state systems are establishing policies and developmental educators are implementing innovations providing summer bridge programs, shortened and accelerated remedial courses, computer-based teaching and tutoring, contextualized learning, and mastery learning.

This chapter addresses some of the most promising among these initiatives and innovations that will, no doubt, influence the direction of developmental education for years to come. The chapter begins with a brief summary by Nikki Edgecombe of developmental education acceleration efforts in community colleges and then describes them in greater detail. Deloris Perin's article discussing the contextualization of developmental education is followed by Davis Jenkins, Matthew Zeidenberg, and Gregory Kienzl's brief summary of Washington State's I-BEST Program, one of the most successful examples of contextualization. Peter Adams, Sarah Gearhart, Robert Miller, and Anne Roberts then describe the Community College of Baltimore County's highly successful Accelerated Learning Program. This is followed by a brief description of various summer bridge programs participating in an ongoing study by Elizabeth A. Barnett, Rachel Hare Bork, Alexander K. Mayer, Joshua Pretlow, Heather D. Wathington, and Madeline Joy Weiss. These programs are designed to help students complete remediation before starting college. Hunter Boylan then discusses a model for more carefully targeting interventions to student characteristics, and Caroline Sheldon and Nathan Durdella follow with a description of the impact of compressed courses on student achievement. Barbara Bonham and Hunter Boylan come next with a summary of recent initiatives that will guide developmental mathematics reform in the future. The final articles in this chapter, by Douglas Holschuh and David Caverly; Melissa Burgess and David Caverly; and David Caverly, Anne Ward, and Michael Caverly; describe available technologies and discuss ways in which developmental educators can use them.

Notes

1. Of course, universities also have an important role to play in producing thoughtful liberal arts and well-trained professional school graduates. Although they cannot generate credentialed workers as quickly as community colleges, universities are still the labor market's primary provider of teachers, technicians, accountants, business managers, social workers, and other high-skilled professionals.

2. According to a report from the National Center for Education Statistics (Horn, 2009), only 10 percent of entering community college students complete an associate degree within three years and only 5 percent complete a vocational or technical certificate in that time period. This figure may be accurate but it fails to take into account the fact that the majority of community college students are enrolled part-time. For them, completing a degree or certificate in three years is unlikely to begin with.

3. The Brock study, however, has some of the same limitations as that of Bailey and Cho. Although reports on college completion rates are subject to a number of limitations, whatever the true numbers may be they are probably insufficient to meet current and future workforce demands.

References

Aghion, P., Boustan, L., Hoxby, C., & Vandenbussche, J. (2009, March). *The causal impact of education on economic growth: Evidence from the U.S.* Boston, MA: Center for Education Policy Research, Harvard University.

Bailey, T., Calcagno, J., Jenkins, D., Leinbach, T., & Kienzl, G. (2006). Is the Student-Right-To-Know all you should know? An analysis of community college graduation rates. *Research in Higher Education, 47*(5), 491–519.

Bailey, T., & Cho, S-W. (2010, September). *Developmental education in community colleges.* Issue brief prepared for the White House Summit on Community Colleges. New York, NY: Community College Research Center, Teachers College, Columbia University.

Brock, T. (2011). Young adults in higher education: Barriers and breakthroughs to success. *Future of Children, 20*(1), 109–132.

Carnevale, A., & Fry, R. (2001). *Economics, demography, and the future of higher education policy.* Princeton, NJ: Educational Testing Service.

Carnevale, A., Smith, N., & Strohl, J. (2010, June). *Help wanted: Projection of jobs and education requirements through 2018.* Washington, DC: Center on Education and the Workforce, Georgetown University.

Carnevale, A., & Rose, S. (2011). *The undereducated American.* Washington, DC: Center on Education and the Workforce, Georgetown University.

Cohen, A., & Brawer, F. (2008). *The American community college.* San Francisco, CA: Jossey-Bass.

Complete College America. (2011, September). *Time is the enemy: The surprising truth behind why today's college students aren't graduating and what needs to change.* Washington, DC: Complete College America.

———. (2012, Spring). *Remediation: Higher education's bridge to nowhere.* Washington, DC: Complete College America.

Hanushek, E., Jamison, D., Jamison, E., & Woessmann, L. (2008). Education and economic growth. *Education Next, 8*(2), 62–70.

Howell, J. S. (2011). What influences students' need for remediation in college: Evidence from California. *Journal of Higher Education, 82*(3), 292–318.

Horn, L. (2009). *On track to complete? A taxonomy of beginning community college students and their outcomes three years after enrolling: 2003–04 through 2006.* Washington, DC: National Center for Education Statistics, Institute for Education Sciences, U.S. Department of Education.

McCabe, R. H. (2003). *Yes we can! A community college guide for developing America's underprepared.* Phoenix, AZ: League for Innovation in the Community College.

National Center for Education Statistics. (2008). *The condition of education 2008.* Washington, DC: U.S. Department of Education.

O'Banion, T. (2012). Pathways to completion: Guidelines to boosting student success. *Community College Journal, 82*(1), 28–35.

Zwick, R., & Green, J. (2007). New perspectives on the correlation of SAT scores, high school grades, and socio-economic factors. *Journal of Educational Measurement, 44*(1), 23–45.

Additional Readings

Lumina Foundation (2010, September). *A stronger nation through higher education.* Indianapolis, IN: Lumina Foundation.

National Center for Education Statistics. (2011, November). *Community college student outcomes: 1994–2009.* Web Tables, NCES 2012-253. Washington, DC: U.S. Department of Education.

Accelerating the Academic Achievement of Students Referred to Developmental Education

Nikki Edgecombe

Edgecombe's article is the most extensive review of the literature currently available on various approaches to accelerating student completion of developmental courses. It discusses each approach, describes what research has to say, and provides recommendations for practice. Edgecombe concludes that while these approaches show promise, none of them has yet been validated by extensive empirical research.

Mounting evidence suggests that the traditional sequence of developmental education courses hinders community college students from entering college-level coursework and ultimately earning a credential. For example, using data from colleges participating in the Achieving the Dream initiative, an analysis by Bailey, Jeong, and Cho (2010) found that only 33% of students referred to developmental math and 46% of students referred to developmental reading completed their recommended course sequence within three years. Among students referred to the lowest levels of developmental education (or "remediation"; I use these terms interchangeably), only 17% of math students and 29% of reading students completed the entire sequence of three or more term-length courses. The traditional sequence of developmental courses undermines academic achievement in part because it has a multitude of exit points. Many students never enroll in the courses to which they are initially referred; others drop out between courses in the sequence. This has led a number of practitioners to experiment with restructuring the developmental sequence.

Acceleration is an increasingly popular strategy for improving the outcomes of students referred to developmental education. Advocates of acceleration argue that a greater portion of students may complete remediation and succeed in college-level courses if colleges either help them complete requirements more quickly or enroll them in higher-level courses while providing effective academic support. This Brief, based on a longer literature review, explores the evidence on the effects of acceleration, describes different acceleration models that are used with developmental education students, and discusses ways of dealing with challenges involved in implementing acceleration strategies.

Acceleration involves the reorganization of instruction and curricula in ways that expedite the completion of coursework or credentials. Many accelerated course formats require as many instructional contact hours as traditional classes, but those hours occur within a truncated time frame. Although this Brief focuses on the application of this approach in developmental education, acceleration is ubiquitous in higher education, and there is an expansive literature describing its various manifestations, including summer school and other courses with non-traditional term lengths. For developmental education, acceleration involves a departure from the traditional multi-course sequence in favor of a more streamlined structure intended to better support students' learning objectives and to accommodate students' complicated lives by reducing the time required to complete academic requirements.

Models of Acceleration

The review summarized here draws on a variety of sources, including articles, books, and dissertations dating back to 1990. In order to be included, studies had to present student outcome data on measures such as course success rates, sequence completion rates, grade point averages, subsequent course performance, or credential completion. While twelve relevant empirical studies were found, most of these did not include control groups, which omits the inferences that can be drawn from their results. A scan of the literature uncovered a variety of acceleration models, which are categorized below. (It is important to note that individual programs may integrate multiple design elements.) Excluded from this categorization are short-term intensive programs designed to improve students' performance on entry assessments so that they may bypass remediation.

Course Restructuring

Many acceleration models restructure courses by reorganizing instructional time or modifying curriculum to reduce the time necessary to fulfill developmental education requirements. Course restructuring accelerates students' completion of the developmental education sequence by eliminating course requirements and incorporating content with stronger linkages to the college curriculum.

COMPRESSED COURSES

Compressed courses allow students to complete multiple sequential courses in one semester. Typically, the content of a single course is compressed into a seven- or eight-week segment, which is followed immediately by the next course in the sequence, also taught in a compressed format. The instructional contact hours are the same as in a traditional 16-week course, so class periods tend to be longer and generally require instructors to modify lesson plans.

Learning outcomes for compressed courses are often comparable to, if not better than, learning outcomes for semester-length courses. Sheldon and Durdella (see p. 339 in this book) compared the success rates of students who took compressed (i.e., 5–9 week) and full-semester (i.e., 15–18 week) courses in developmental English, reading, and math and found higher course completion rates (with a grade of C or higher) among students taking the compressed format. Preliminary (Brancard, Baker, & Jensen, 2006) and subsequent (Bragg, 2009) descriptive studies of the Community College of Denver's FastStart program analyzed longer-term student outcomes. FastStart offers a range of compressed and paired developmental education course options, combining two to four courses in a single semester. Brancard et al. (2006) concluded that FastStart students had higher course completion rates than non-FastStart students. Bragg (2009) found that FastStart students completed more developmental math courses, earned more developmental math credits, and were more likely to pass college-level math courses. Bragg and Barnett (2008) also note that longer instructional blocks allow redundancies across the curricula to be reduced.

PAIRED COURSES

Paired courses link developmental and college-level courses with complementary subject matter, such as an upper-level developmental writing course and a college literature course. This allows students to begin to accrue college credit earlier than they would if they were required to complete developmental education first, eliminates exit points between courses that would otherwise be taken in different semesters, and makes basic skills instruction more relevant through linkages with the college curriculum. Students may also feel more like "real" college students and benefit psychologically from tackling higher-level coursework instead of rehashing high school content.

Paired courses may promote a level of connectedness and peer support that is absent from typical courses. According to Karp (2011), cohorts encourage persistence by helping students feel connected to school, and the relationships that develop in cohorts can provide students with access to information that may help them achieve their academic goals. Cohorts also are associated with stronger social relationships and improved retention in the learning communities literature (see, e.g., Engstrom & Tinto, 2008).

CURRICULAR REDESIGN

Curricular redesign accelerates student progression by decreasing the number of developmental courses students must take. Redundant content is eliminated, and the remaining curriculum is modified to meet the learning objectives of a particular intervention or academic pathway. For example, the curricula of multiple developmental education courses can be consolidated into a single-semester course.

Hern's (2010) comparison of a one-semester course and a two-semester sequence in developmental reading and writing at Chabot College found that a significantly higher percentage of students who took the accelerated course successfully completed their developmental English requirements, compared with students who enrolled in the traditional sequence. Hern also compared the outcomes of students enrolled in Statpath, an experimental course in developmental statistics at Los Medanos College, with the outcomes of students in the traditional developmental math sequence. Among students who were originally referred to the lowest level of developmental math, more than a third of Statpath students went on to complete college statistics, compared with only a small percentage of students who enrolled in the traditional sequence. While these results are promising, the conclusions that can be drawn from them are limited since the analyses are descriptive and do not control for observable student characteristics.

The conversion of developmental content into modules is another curricular redesign strategy. Since students may need to spend more time mastering certain competencies and less on others, modules may accelerate student progress by permitting a customized approach to learning, allowing practitioners to address particular skills. The use of modules also allows for a focus on only those competencies that are necessary for success in specific academic pathways (for example, some programs require more math skills than others). A study by South Texas College (2010) found that self-paced modules in mathematics yielded higher course completion rates than traditional courses, but the reliability of this study's results is limited due to its small sample sizes.

Mainstreaming

Mainstreaming strategies accelerate students' progress by placing students referred to developmental education directly into college-level courses. Colleges may choose to recruit students with higher developmental placement scores for mainstreaming programs, since those students are more similar to their college-ready peers. Mainstreaming may reduce the negative implications surrounding the distinction between developmental and college-ready students (Levin & Hopfenberg, 1991).

MAINSTREAMING WITH SUPPLEMENTAL SUPPORT

Mainstreaming with supplemental support involves placing students with developmental education referrals directly into introductory college-level courses and providing additional instruction through mandatory companion classes, lab sessions, or other learning supports designed to promote success in the college course. During these sessions, students may review concepts presented in the college course in greater depth, address particular skills necessary to complete an assignment, or preview upcoming lessons. Moreover, with college-ready and underprepared students in the same classroom, there are opportunities for students referred to developmental education to be exposed to the work habits of higher-achieving students and to engage with a more challenging and enriching curriculum.

Evidence suggests that mainstreaming improves short- and long-term academic outcomes for underprepared students. The Accelerated

Learning Program (ALP) at the Community College of Baltimore County permits upper-level developmental writing students to enroll directly in English 101 while taking a companion course that provides extra academic support. Jenkins, Speroni, Belfield, Jaggars, and Edgecombe (2010) found that compared with non-ALP students, ALP students complete both the introductory college-level course and the subsequent college English requirement at a higher rate and attempt more college courses.

BASIC SKILLS INTEGRATION

Integrating basic skills instruction into college-level courses is a form of contextualization and a means to accelerate student progress. Integration is designed to address students' academic deficiencies in instructional contexts that are mere relevant than traditional developmental classes (Perin, p. 93 in this book).

Washington State's Integrated Basic Education and Skills Training (I-BEST) program integrates basic skills instruction into college-level occupational courses that are jointly taught by career-technical faculty and basic skills instructors. The I-BEST model embeds basic skills education into a highly relevant context, workforce training, in order to make the learning more meaningful and expedite progress on college-level coursework. Findings by Jenkins, Zeidenberg, and Kienzl (2009) suggest that participation in I-BEST is associated with an increased number of college credits earned, persistence to the subsequent academic year, attainment of a credential, and achievement of point gains on basic skills tests.

Challenges and Recommendations

The trend toward accelerating the academic progress of students referred to developmental education continues to gain momentum based on a limited but promising empirical evidence base. This section explores the challenges community colleges face in implementing acceleration programs and presents recommendations for increasing the availability of higher-quality acceleration models; creating the conditions most likely to support successful adoption, implementation, and scaling; and generating rigorous and actionable data on the efficacy of acceleration.

Assessment and Placement

The sorting function of the assessment and placement process reinforces the sequential structure of developmental education, which may hamper student progress. Most colleges rely on standardized tests to place students at the appropriate levels of instruction, despite well-documented evidence of the limitations of these instruments (Hughes & Scott-Clayton, 2011). Moreover, mandatory placement policies that require students to complete developmental education before pursuing advanced courses may undermine participation in accelerated pathways, particularly those mainstreaming models that attempt to place higher-scoring developmental students directly into college courses.

Research suggests that assessment and placement instruments and policies should be reconceived in order to match students more precisely with academic interventions that meet their needs (Hughes & Scott-Clayton, 2011). Test makers have responded to concerns about the limitations of placement tests by creating diagnostic assessments, but these remain infrequently used due to the additional time and costs required to administer them. Similar obstacles hinder the use of supplemental measures for course placement, such as high school transcripts or student interviews. State policymakers may nonetheless want to reconsider policies related to assessment.

Course Development and Curricular Alignment

Strict system or college guidelines regarding course content and sequencing can undermine attempts to implement acceleration models, particularly those models that rationalize curricula or do not adhere to the traditional developmental education sequence. Courses designed to more closely align with degree program pathways or the college curriculum more generally may include content that varies significantly from the traditional developmental curriculum. While better alignment may improve outcomes (Jenkins, 2011), variability in comparable-level courses among developmental education offerings may generate confusion regarding the best course-taking options for students.

Although they may be constrained by policy, academic administrators, faculty senates, and other course-monitoring bodies within colleges may want to consider reevaluating what students in developmental education are asked to learn and why. In instances where there is no clear connection between required content or desired skill development and the college-level curriculum, practitioners should consider rationalizing content and seeking means to accelerate student progress. Regular audits of courses and degree program requirements are recommended to ensure that students are not being asked to master out-of-date concepts or demonstrate irrelevant skills.

Student Recruitment

It can be challenging to recruit students to participate in accelerated programs. Entry assessment results are often the only data point used to determine the appropriateness of an educational pathway. The effective marketing of accelerated developmental education alternatives—both to students and to those who help them decide which courses to take—is underemphasized. Pre-term information sessions with counselors could help to steer more students to appropriate courses. Communications to students through email, text message, and announcement boards could highlight developmental education alternatives and direct students to counselors and program staff for further information. Moreover, the use of more actionable assessments can provide advisors and students with additional feedback, which may enable them to make better placement decisions (Hughes & Scott-Clayton, 2011).

Faculty Resistance

Faculty members may be resistant to change, which can affect their willingness to participate in accelerated instructional reform. Many may believe that developmental education students need slower-paced instruction or that academic standards are inevitably lowered in compressed courses. The dearth of rigorous research on student outcomes gives acceleration advocates little hard evidence to quell this skepticism.

Faculty resistance may be reduced if faculty feel that they have a role in leading instructional reforms. Institutions can encourage faculty to participate in acceleration efforts by developing faculty inquiry groups to evaluate reforms and using their results to further improve programs.

Financial Sustainability

The imperative for improved student outcomes is coming at a time when community colleges are facing serious budget challenges. Colleges should consider rigorously assessing innovations in order to identify, sustain, and expand funding for those associated with superior student outcomes. Policymakers and practitioners may find cost-effectiveness analyses particularly useful when making resource allocation decisions. The availability of rigorous analysis of the cost per successful student can be used in conjunction with student outcome data to determine whether it is appropriate to scale up or discontinue acceleration models.

Administrative Logistics

Certain acceleration models present logistical challenges by virtue of their programmatic features. For example, compressed courses, which sometimes have class periods lasting as long as four or five hours, may produce significant course and room scheduling problems. Models that mainstream a small number of students into a college course may struggle to find space to conduct the companion course. The use of nontraditional instructional spaces, such as small-group study rooms at libraries and conference rooms, is emerging as a potential solution to the space constraint issue.

The lack of flexibility of student information systems can also pose a challenge. Self-paced modules, for example, can be problematic from a record-keeping perspective if not explicitly apportioned by credit and if students do not complete all of the modules in a 16-week semester. While grades of "Incomplete" or "Re-enroll" can serve as placeholders in the system, they do not allow administrators to accurately assess students' progress. Increasingly, though, vendors are willing to work with state systems and colleges to ensure that their products meet the dynamic needs of end-users.

Actionable Research

While acceleration strategies are gaining in popularity, research evidence on acceleration remains thin and may not represent the diversity of programs in operation. Currently, the most commonly used outcome measures focus on academic progression rather than student learning, and there is little data on the institutional contexts that support the use of acceleration.

A strong evidence base is critical to the legitimacy of acceleration and should reflect relevant research questions and rigorous methods, providing information about the effectiveness of acceleration as well as issues that institutions encounter during implementation. In order to improve the empirical evidence base for acceleration and clearly indicate whether it negatively impacts academic standards, it is recommended that institutions develop department-wide learning outcomes for specific courses measured by common assessments (Jenkins, 2011). The rigorous evaluation of those learning outcomes across course formats can more effectively address questions about student outcomes and academic rigor. Further, a focus on pedagogical improvement is needed to improve understanding of the factors that influence student performance. Researchers should conduct classroom-based fieldwork that catalogs, analyzes, and evaluates instructional practice.

Conclusion

The evidence on acceleration, while limited, is promising, and acceleration is gaining popularity as a means to improve outcomes for students referred to developmental education. Yet colleges often face obstacles to implementation, including rigid assessment and placement policies, curricular misalignment, recruitment challenges, faculty resistance, unsustainable funding, and logistic impediments. After implementation, challenges persist throughout the scaling process, which has financial and human resource implications and can require substantial changes to policy regarding placement, course content, or course sequencing as well as shifts in expectations for students and faculty.

Despite these challenges, the evidence on acceleration and the growing interest in this strategy should encourage practitioners, policymakers, and researchers to think boldly about how to improve the current course delivery system in community colleges. To reach the ambitious credential completion goals set by the Obama administration and the philanthropic community, institutions will need to radically rethink current policy and practice, challenge institutional norms, and be willing to reallocate resources to unconventional interventions that are shown to enhance academic achievement.

References

Bailey, T., Jeong, D. W., & Cho, S.-W. (2010). Referral, enrollment, and completion in developmental education sequences in community colleges. *Economics of Education Review, 29*(2), 255–270.

Bragg, D. D. (2009). *Community College of Denver: Breaking Through outcomes report.* Denver, CO: Community College of Denver.

Bragg, D. D., & Barnett, E. A. (2008). *Final report of the Charles Stewart Mott Breaking Through Initiative.* Unpublished manuscript.

Brancard, R., Baker, E. D., & Jensen, L. (2006). *Accelerated Developmental Education Project research report.* Denver, CO: Community College of Denver.

Engstrom, C. M., & Tinto, V. (2008). Learning better together: The impact of learning communities on the persistence of low-income students. *Opportunity Matters, 1,* 5–21.

Hern, K. (with Snell, M.). (2010). *Exponential attrition and the promise of acceleration in developmental English and math.* Hayward, CA: Chabot College.

Hughes, K. L., & Scott-Clayton, J. (2011). *Assessing developmental assessment in community colleges* (CCRC Working Paper No. 19, Assessment of Evidence Series). New York, NY: Columbia University, Teachers College, Community College Research Center.

Jenkins, D. (2011). *Redesigning community colleges for completion: Lessons from research on high-performance organizations* (CCRC Working Paper No. 24, Assessment of Evidence Series). New York, NY: Columbia University, Teachers College, Community College Research Center.

Jenkins, D., Speroni, C., Belfield, C., Jaggars, S. S., & Edgecombe, N. (2010). *A model for accelerating academic success of community college remedial English students: Is the Accelerated Learning Program (ALP) effective and affordable?* (CCRC Working Paper No. 21). New York, NY: Columbia University, Teachers College, Community College Research Center.

Jenkins, D., Zeidenberg, M., & Kienzl, G. S. (2009). *Educational outcomes of I-BEST, Washington State Community and Technical College System's Integrated Basic Education and Skills Training program: Findings from a multivariate analysis* (CCRC Working Paper No. 16). New York, NY: Columbia University, Teachers College, Community College Research Center.

Karp, M. M. (2011). *Toward a new understanding of non-academic student support: Four mechanisms encouraging positive student outcomes in the community college* (CCRC Working Paper No. 28, Assessment of Evidence Series). New York, NY: Columbia University, Teachers College, Community College Research Center.

Levin, H. M., & Hopfenberg, W. A. (1991). Don't remediate: Accelerate! *Principal Magazine, 70*(2), 11–13.

South Texas College, Office of Institutional Effectiveness and Assessment. (2010). *Accelerating developmental math* (Intervention Assessment Brief, Vol. 1, Issue 3).

Facilitating Student Learning through Contextualization: A Review of Evidence

Dolores Perin

Dolores Perin argues that low-skilled students can progress more quickly through contextualized instruction and presents evidence to support this contention. The article reviews the literature on the most common forms of contextualization and discusses how they are implemented. A very useful list of recommendations for implementing contextualized developmental education concludes this article.

Proficiency in reading, writing, and mathematics is key to academic learning, but courses in these foundational skills[1] are conventionally taught separately from the disciplines to which the skills must be applied. For example, students may be taught writing skills in a developmental English class and then be expected to apply them in a college-level history class. Several problems arise with this structure. First, for reasons still to be determined, learners, even the most proficient, often do not readily transfer newly learned skills to novel settings (Barnett & Ceci, 2002). Second, students may not be motivated to learn the skills taught in developmental education courses because they do not perceive them to be directly connected to their personal educational goals (Cavazos, Johnson, & Sparrow, 2010). Third, weaknesses in academic skills may not be addressed by the disciplinary instructor whose objective is to teach the subject matter, not basic skills (Fisher & Ivy, 2005).

This situation has serious implications for the academic trajectory of the many students who enter community colleges without the ability to read, write, or solve mathematics problems at the college level. However, bringing basic skills and content area instruction closer together may increase proficiency in reading, writing, and mathematics skills as well as the capacity of students to apply those skills in meaningful ways to academic tasks (Baker, Hope, & Karandjeff, 2009; Heller & Greenleaf, 2007; Lee & Spratley, 2010). In particular, developmental educators have suggested that basic skills instruction should use "authentic materials like the textbooks used in college courses such as psychology or biology" (Simpson, Hynd, Nist, & Burrell, 1997, p. 41). Simpson et al. (1997) contrasted such "embedded" instruction with the predominant "generic" approach (p. 42), in which technical aspects of literacy or mathematics are taught apart from content. Embedding developmental education instruction in disciplinary content may be helpful because basic-skill demands differ considerably across disciplines (Goldman & Bisanz, 2002; Stahl & Shanahan, 2004). Furthermore, generic instruction has been criticized as uninteresting and ineffective (Grubb et al., 1999). In contrast, "people learn when they have a need that is meaningful and real" (Goode, 2000, p. 270). For many students, what is real is their career goals, which are furthered by the completion of a specific degree or certificate program. Thus, using authentic materials may result in more active, generalizable learning (Simpson & Nist, 2002). The purpose of this article is to examine evidence for the embedding of basic skills instruction through *contextualization*.

Contextualization has been defined as "a diverse family of instructional strategies designed to more seamlessly link the learning of foundational skills and academic or occupational content by focusing teaching and learning squarely on concrete applications in a specific context that is of interest to the student" (Mazzeo, Rab, & Alssid, 2003, pp. 3–4). As passing the disciplinary courses needed to earn a desired college credential is assumed to be of considerable interest to students, the specific content of these courses can create a context for the learning of reading, writing, and mathematics skills that are authentic and personally meaningful to them (Kalchik & Oertle, 2010). The alignment and integration of developmental and disciplinary courses has been associated with positive student outcomes (Levin, Cox, Cerven, & Haberler, 2010; Weiss, Visher, & Wathington, 2010) and connections between basic skills and disciplinary learning are highlighted in the national literacy standards for career and college readiness (National Governors' Association and Council of Chief State School Officers, 2010).

Identification of Studies

Literature was sought that focused on contextualization as a form of instruction in reading, writing, or mathematics. A keyword search for sources (journal articles, books, and technical reports) dated 1990 to 2010 was conducted using the ERIC, JSTOR, and Education Full Text databases, augmented by searches of the Web of Science Social Science Citation Index, Google Scholar, and bibliographies in identified references as well as by a hand search of the journals relevant to the purpose of the study, including *Community College Review, Community College Journal of Research and Practice*, and *Journal of Developmental Education*. Works were selected if they reported instructional procedures for the contextualization of basic academic skills or measured student outcomes associated with the approach. The contextualization of English as a second language (e.g., Song, 2006) and content area instruction (e.g., Reisman & Wineburg, 2008) was beyond the scope of this review. The initial intention was to confine the search to work in community colleges, but because a shortage of research on contextualization in this setting was immediately apparent, the search also screened in reports on contextualization in adult literacy and K–12 education. The search identified 61 sources, of which 34 were descriptive and 27 were quantitative reports. Later in this article, selected studies with quantitative evidence are discussed. A full bibliography, listing both the descriptive and quantitative work, is available from the author.

Terminology

Numerous terms are used in the literature for contextualization, both of basic skills and other areas, including *contextual teaching and learning* (Baker et al., 2009; Johnson, 2002), *contextualized instruction* (Parr, Edwards, & Leising, 2008; Wisely, 2009), *content area literacy* (McKenna & Robinson, 2009), *embedded instruction* (Simpson et al., 1997), *writing-to-learn* (Klein, 1999; McDermott, 2010), *integrative curriculum* (Dowden, 2007), *situated cognition* (Hattie, Biggs, & Purdie, 1996; Stone, Alfeld, Pearson, Lewis, & Jensen, 2006), *problem-based learning* (Gijbels, Dochy, Van den Bossche, & Segers, 2005), *theme-based instruction* (Dirkx & Prenger, 1997), *anchored instruction* (Bottge, Rueda, Serlin, Hung, & Jung, 2007), *curriculum integration* (Badway & Grubb, 1997), *academic-occupation integration* (Bragg, Reger, & Thomas, 1997; Grubb & Kraskouskas, 1992; Perin, 2001; Prentice, 2001), *work-based learning* (Raelin, 2008), and *functional context education* (Sticht, 2005). Furthermore, contextualization is an important component of learning communities involving developmental education and college English courses (Fallon, Lahar, & Susman, 2009; Tai & Rochford, 2007; Weiss et al., 2010) as well as workplace literacy (Mikulecky & Lloyd, 1997). Regardless of the term used, all of these applications center on the practice of systematically connecting basic skills instruction to a specific content that is meaningful and useful to students.

Extent of Use of Contextualization in Basic Skills Instruction

Estimating the extent of contextualization of basic skills instruction in community colleges is difficult, but the use of contextualization seems rare. A study in one state found the practice to be infrequent and confined mostly to mathematics instruction (Wisely, 2009). A search for contextualization in the form of academic integration at community colleges in several states also found low usage (Perin, 2001). Although learning communities connecting developmental and college-level content courses have been described (Weiss et al., 2010), it is not known whether these efforts last only when external funding is available or whether they are becoming regular practice. If contextualization is rare, it may be because it is expensive; Jenkins, Zeidenberg, and Kienzl (2009) reported that a program integrating adult basic education and college-credit occupational courses in the state of Washington received 75% more funds per student than did traditional basic skills and vocational courses. Other reasons for the low use of contextualization may be a lack of awareness of its existence and benefits, the effort required to modify curriculum, and general resistance to moving toward an interdisciplinary focus. If the research indicates positive outcomes and colleges wish to implement contextualization, these barriers will need to be overcome.

Two Forms of Contextualization of Basic Skills Instruction

An examination of the literature indicates that contextualization is implemented in two distinct forms, *contextualized* and *integrated* instruction. This distinction has not been made explicit in previous literature, but it is an important contrast for instructional design because each form of contextualization involves different teaching staff and instructional emphases. Contextualized instruction is employed by instructors of reading, writing, and mathematics, whereas integrated instruction is the province of discipline-area instructors.[2] To maintain consistency with previous literature, the umbrella term *contextualization* is used here to refer collectively to the two forms of instruction.

Contextualized basic skills instruction involves the teaching of reading, writing, or mathematics skills against a backdrop of specific subject matter such as philosophy (Snyder, 2002), statistical process control (Baker et al., 2009), allied health (Shore, Shore, & Boggs, 2004), business (Weiss et al., 2010), history (De La Paz, 2005), and science. The primary objective is to teach the academic skills rather than the subject matter, although there may be some implicit learning of the content as students are exposed systematically to material in the same discipline as they practice the basic skills over time. Although many developmental reading instructors routinely use passages from content area textbooks, what is different about contextualized instruction is the systematic use of text from a single college-credit subject area.

Whereas the venue for contextualized basic skills instruction is the basic skills classroom, *integrated basic skills instruction* occurs in content area classrooms. Examples have been reported for college courses in business and allied health (Artis, 2008; Badway & Grubb, 1997; Cox, Bobrowski, & Spector, 2004; Perin, 2001) and in K–12 science, social studies, and career and technical education (Barton, Heidema, & Jordan, 2002; Bulgren, Marquis, Lenz, Schumaker, & Deshler, 2009; De La Paz & Felton, 2010; Krajcik & Sutherland, 2010; Massey & Heafner, 2004; McDermott, 2010; Nokes, 2008; Parr et al., 2008; Stone et al., 2006; Tilson, Castek, & Goss, 2010). Integrated instruction may be needed when a content instructor observes that many students are having difficulty with the basic skills needed to learn the material, such as, in one example, when teachers found it necessary to "sneak in" reading comprehension strategies in a college course on symbolic logic (Higbee, Lundell, & Arendale, 2005, p. 328).

While contextualized instruction aims to teach basic skills for the purpose of meaningful application, the goal of integrated instruction is to teach the disciplinary content, not basic skills; however, teaching basic skills is a necessary step toward critical thinking about the content (Pearson, 2010). As instruction must be customized for specific contexts, both approaches can require considerable effort on the part of instructors. However, given the serious difficulties with basic academic skills seen in both secondary and postsecondary classrooms in the United States (Bailey, Jeong, & Cho, 2009; Grigg, Donahue, & Dion, 2007; Salahu-Din, Persky, & Miller, 2008), it is important to find instructional methods that can promote improved outcomes. Theories of the transfer of learning as well as theories of learner motivation suggest that contextualization may serve this purpose.

Theoretical Framework: Underlying Mechanisms

The goal of contextualization is to create conditions for more effective learning, expressed, for example, in better skills, higher grades and rates of retention in courses, and progression to more advanced course work. Whether instruction is contextualized or integrated, the connection of basic skills instruction to applications and life goals is consistent with constructivism, which places students' interests and needs at the center of education (Dewey, 1916/1966; Dowden, 2007).

From a cognitive perspective, contextualization is thought to promote transfer of learning and the retention of information (Boroch et al., 2007; Dirkx & Prenger, 1997; Karweit, 1998; Stone et al., 2006; Weinbaum & Rogers, 1995). Stone et al. (2006) hypothesized that "the creation of explicit connections between situations is critical if students are to transfer their knowledge and skills outside the classroom, whether it is to another context or to an abstract testing situation" (p. 11). However, knowing when and where one should apply a previously learned skill requires metacognitive and self-regulation abilities that low-skilled students may lack (Bailer, 2006; Fox, 2009; Mayer & Wittrock, 1996; Nash-Ditzel, 2010). Linking basic skills instruction directly to authentic content area applications that students will encounter in a disciplinary course may increase the likelihood that skills will be transferred to that particular setting.[3]

Barnett and Ceci (2002) proposed that the extent to which the transfer of skills occurs will vary according to the type of skill being targeted, how transfer is measured, the demands placed on memory of the skill to be transferred, and the distance between learning and transfer. According to this framework, the distance between original learning and eventual transfer can be measured in terms of the similarity of the two domains; the physical, temporal, functional, and social contexts also come into play, as does the modality for expressing transfer. In the present context, modality is the application of a skill, such as verbalizing how a mathematics problem is solved in an accounting class or writing a summary in a history class.

In addition to the cognitive mechanism of transfer of learning, possible benefits of contextualization may be explained by the affective mechanism of intrinsic motivation, where a learner is drawn to engage in a task because it is perceived as interesting, enjoyable, or useful (Baker & Wigfield, 1999; Becker, McElvany, & Kortenbruck, 2010; Ryan & Deci, 2000). Academically underprepared college students may not be drawn to learn basic skills that they should have learned much earlier in their academic history (Cavazos et al., 2010; Dean & Dagostino, 2007; Gardenshire-Crooks, Collado, Martin, & Castro, 2010). Having graduated from high school, they may not realize that their academic skills are not at college standard, and they may resist the need yet again to sit in classrooms that teach basic skills. Levin and Calcagno (2008) summarized students' low motivation to learn from generic basic skills instruction:

> [Skill and drill] pedagogy has many drawbacks, including the fact that many remedial students face serious attitudinal obstacles that prevent them from learning in this way. Often it is the same style that the students were exposed to in high school and that may have contributed to their difficulties in the first place. Beyond that, its abstract and isolated nature may prevent students from seeing the usefulness of what is being taught in real-world situations and from applying the skills that are learned to later academic and vocational coursework. (Levin & Calcagno, 2008, p. 185)

Furthermore, underprepared students may not be motivated to attend class regularly and apply themselves to learning because they dislike appearing incompetent (Dean & Dagostino, 2007) or because of competing job and family responsibilities (Caverly, Nicholson, & Radcliffe, 2004; Kozeracki, 2005). Extrapolating from research on motivation, it is possible that students may be more inclined to try to overcome such obstacles if explicit connections are made in class between basic skills and personally meaningful content applications (Berns & Erickson, 2001; Bond, 2004; Boroch et al., 2007; Guthrie, Anderson, Alao, & Rinehart, 1999; Johnson, 2002; National Council for Workforce Education & Jobs for the Future, 2010; Shore et al., 2004; Sticht, 2005).[4] Similarly, workplace literacy students, who may not generally see the appeal of basic skills instruction, may be more motivated to learn the skills when instruction is connected to job-specific applications (Jenkins et al., 2009; Sticht, Armstrong, Hickey, & Caylor, 1987; Washington State Board for Community and Technical Colleges, 2005).

Evidence on Contextualization

Twenty-seven studies provided evidence on contextualization. Sixteen of the studies were on contextualized instruction, 10 were on integrated instruction, and a further study, by Wisely (2009), reported on both contextualized and integrated instruction. Quantitative studies of contextualized instruction were conducted with college academic programs (six studies), adult basic education (six studies), and K–12 academic education (four studies of each), but no studies involving career and technical education (CTE) students were found for this form of contextualization. Five of the six studies on contextualized instruction in college involved developmental education (Caverly et al., 2004; Perin & Hare, 2010; Shore et al., 2004; Snyder, 2002; Wisely, 2009), and one (Martino, Norris, & Hoffman, 2001) focused on low-achieving students in a college-level content course. Among the six studies involving adult basic education students, five were conducted with workplace literacy programs (Ekkens & Winke, 2009; Lazar, Bean, & Van Horn, 1998; Mikulecky & Lloyd, 1997; Perin, 1997; Sticht, 1995) and one was conducted with a prison sample (Dirkx & Crawford, 1993). Three of four studies of K–12 contextualized instruction focused solely on mathematics (Bottge, 1999; Bottge & Hasselbring, 1993; Brenner et al., 1997), and one dealt with writing instruction (De La Paz, 2005).

Four of the 10 studies on integrated instruction were conducted with CTE programs, two in college (Cox et al., 2004; Jenkins et al., 2009) and two in secondary education (Parr et al., 2008; Stone et al., 2006). The other six studies were in academic programs in elementary (Guthrie et al., 1999; Tilson et al., 2010) and secondary education (Bulgren et al., 2009; De La Paz & Felton, 2010; Greenleaf et al., 2010; Vaughn et al., 2009). No studies of integrated instruction at the college level were identified.

Many of the studies had methodological weaknesses that limited conclusions that could be drawn about the effectiveness of contextualization. A table summarizing the studies and their limitations is available from the author. Twelve studies (six on contextualized and six on integrated instruction) that offer the best evidence for the impact of contextualization on basic skills are summarized in the next section.[5]

Contextualized Instruction

COLLEGE SETTINGS

Perin and Hare (2010) created a curricular supplement to provide developmental education students with weekly practice in selected reading and writing skills to complement their work in the classroom. The practice focused on written summarization, question generation, vocabulary, and persuasive writing skills. Students in 12 developmental reading and English classrooms in two community colleges were randomly assigned to two conditions. Both conditions practiced the same skills but used different text. In one condition called "science," the skills practice was contextualized in passages from biology textbooks. In the other condition called "generic," the students engaged in the same practice but instead of using science text, read passages on a wide assortment of topics taken from developmental education textbooks. A third group was a purposive sample of four classrooms that served as a business-as-usual comparison group. Both the science and generic groups showed statistically significant higher gain on three variables on a researcher-developed written summarization measure (the proportion of main ideas from source text, accuracy of information, and word count) than the comparison group, and the science group showed greater gain than the generic group on two summarization variables (proportion of main ideas and accuracy), with effect sizes of 0.33 to 0.62 *SD* units. However, pre-post gain on a generic standardized test of reading was not associated with participation in the instruction. The findings for the summarization measure suggest that systematic practice contextualized in content-specific text helps students learn to summarize the type of material they need to read to learn in college-credit courses. At the same time, the study is limited by the fact that it involved independent practice rather than direct instruction, and students received only a small amount of feedback, raising the possibility that results were perhaps due at least in part to student-related variables. Also, because randomization occurred within classrooms, there may have been contamination between conditions.

Caverly et al. (2004) investigated the use of a contextualized reading comprehension strategy with first-semester students in developmental reading classrooms in a 4-year college. Instruction was anchored in chapters from textbooks used in core curriculum courses that the students would have to pass to complete their degree. A strategy was taught based on the mnemonic "PLAN" (Predict, Locate, Add, and Note). Students first predicted what would be in the textbook chapters and examined the title, introduction, subtitles, pictures, graphs, summaries, and the use of boldface and italics. From the predictions and examination of the text, the students created a concept map (visual display of the information) and ascertained how they would approach the reading task. Next, they checked items in the concept map that they already knew and marked unfamiliar information with a question mark. They then read the text and expanded the concept map using new information. In the last step of the strategy, students reflected on what they had learned and estimated how well they thought they could now satisfy the task demands they had identified before reading. The students applied the strategy to both well- and poorly written textbook passages. Also, to promote transfer of learning, they were asked to apply it in other classes and were required to summarize this in writing.

Statistically significant differences were found between students ($n = 56$) who took the contextualized reading course and students in a random sample ($n = 72$) who had the same pretest reading levels but did not take developmental education. Measures used in the analysis were scores on a statewide standardized reading test as well as grades in a subsequent college-level history course with high reading demands. This study suggests that the strategy of contextualized instruction promoted achievement in college-credit courses, but the conclusions are tentative because the comparison group did not take developmental education, leaving a question as to what, specifically, was responsible for the improved performance: the developmental education course in general, the instructional strategy, or a combination of the two. Also, students who choose to take developmental education may differ from those who do not on variables (e.g., motivation) that may explain the group difference.

Similar to Caverly et al. (2004), Shore et al. (2004) contextualized basic skills instruction in college course content. Community college developmental mathematics students who were preparing for degrees in various health professions were taught problems based on topics from allied health (respiratory therapy, radiology, occupational therapy, medical laboratory, and physical therapy) and nursing curricula. The problems were developed collaboratively by a group of health and developmental education instructors who observed each other's classes. For example, a problem was developed to teach students to interpret a graph illustrating the relationship between the percentage of normal glomerular filtration, as measured by creatine clearance, and blood urea nitrogen; this information is used to yield a function needed by nurses when analyzing a patient's kidney function. Data were collected for cohorts over a 3-year period.

Compared with a comparison group made up of sections of a traditional developmental mathematics course, students receiving the contextualized instruction in the first 2 years of the study earned better mathematics scores and were more likely to respond on a questionnaire that they found the instruction useful. The proportion of contextualized problems on the mathematics test increased each year over the 3-year project period, increasing to 70% in the third year. The contextualization group participating in the third year did not show an advantage over the comparison group, which was attributed by the researchers to a larger number of seriously underprepared students than in previous years and to the fact that the contextualized problems were harder than the traditional problems. The positive findings for contextualization in the first 2 years of the study are encouraging, but firm conclusions cannot be drawn because it was not stated how classrooms were assigned to conditions or whether the groups had equivalent mathematics scores at the pretest stage. Furthermore, the authors referred to pre- and posttests but neither the specific amount of gain nor the statistics were reported.

ADULT BASIC EDUCATION

Based on a program evaluation, Mikulecky and Lloyd (1997) reported outcomes of contextualized instruction for 180 incumbent workers in six companies who participated in work-related literacy classes. The instruction was provided in five of the companies for 20 to 60 hours and for 200 hours in another—equivalent, as the authors pointed out, to 6 or 7 weeks of high school. Participants' initial reading levels ranged from high elementary school grades to college level. The industries in which the instruction was contextualized included automobile and other manufacturers, a prison, an insurance company, and a hospital. For example, hospital workers and correctional officers were taught writing skills needed to improve the quality of written reports and memoranda, and gasket makers were taught reading skills using company newsletter articles, procedure manuals, and productivity graphs. Some of the participants were taught skills to prepare for promotion tests.

Literacy gains were measured using pre and post self-reports on literacy practices, beliefs, and plans as well as self-reports on strategies used to read a workplace newsletter and on performance on a work-related reading scenario. The researchers created scores from the self-reports, compared the pre and post scores using t tests, and, finally, expressed the amount of gain on a 3-point scale (positive, neutral, and negative gain). Statistically significant gain was found on the reading scenario, reading strategies, literacy beliefs, and plans, and the gains in one company were higher than those for a waiting-list comparison group from the same company. Overall, increases in skill were found for students in classrooms in which more than 70% of instructional time was spent on reading and writing activities and in which students discussed and received feedback on reading and writing processes. Although encouraging, this is tentative because it is based on self-reports, which can be subjective.

SECONDARY EDUCATION

De La Paz (2005) contextualized writing instruction in social studies content in eighth-grade English language arts classrooms. This instruction took place after students had learned an approach to historical reasoning in the social studies class. In the language arts class, the students were taught self-regulation strategies to set and monitor progress toward reading and writing goals and to write persuasive essays on controversies related to westward expansion. The essay-writing instruction was contextualized in textbook passages, primary documents, and secondary sources from the social studies class based on two mnemonics, STOP (Suspend judgment; Take a side; Organize ideas; Plan as you write) and DARE (Develop a topic sentence; Add supporting ideas; Reject an argument for the other side; End with a conclusion). Students engaged in essay-writing practice using the self-regulation and mnemonic strategies until they were able to plan and compose an essay of at least five paragraphs within one class period after reading a set of social studies documents. Compared with a group receiving traditional instruction (no historical reasoning or contextualized writing instruction), the contextualized strategy group showed greater gain on measures of essay length, persuasive quality, the number of arguments included in the essay, and historical accuracy (effect sizes $d = 0.57$ to $d = 1.23$), providing some support for contextualization. Furthermore, the effects were seen for learners over a range of ability levels, from students with learning disabilities to average- and high-achieving learners. However, a post-only design was used, and although group pretest achievement scores did not differ, the comparison group was made up of English language learners, raising the possibility that there may have been unmeasured pretest differences between groups. Furthermore, the experimental condition consisted of both contextualization and strategy instruction, clouding attribution of results.

Brenner et al. (1997) conducted a contextualized mathematics intervention using an everyday life scenario. Seventh and eighth graders in a pre-algebra class were taught problem-solving skills including the manipulation of symbols in equations. Specifically, students learned to produce and represent functions such as $y = mx + b$. The problems were cast in a hypothetical scenario involving the selection of a pizza company as a vendor for the school cafeteria. Lessons included taste tests with data collection on student preferences, a computer malfunction scenario in which students searched for errors in the pizza maker's order forms and invoices, a pizza delivery game in which students had to determine the correct destination, formulas related to advertising the pizza, and tables about profit and loss in the pizza business. Students frequently worked in cooperative groups to discuss and solve the problems. Three teachers taught two sections each, one contextualized and one traditional; the classes were randomly assigned among teachers to treatment and control conditions, and the classrooms for each teacher were randomly assigned to conditions. Several curriculum-based and transfer measures were administered to test students' ability to represent and solve word problems. Participants in the intervention showed greater gain than the control group in the representation of problems, such as depicting the word problems in the form of tables and graphs. Both fluent speakers and English language learners showed this benefit.

The design of the study did not permit a clear attribution of the findings to contextualization. The intervention and control conditions differed not only in the use of contextualized materials but also in whether cooperative learning was used. Furthermore, because the materials were contextualized, the treatment focused more on problem representation than the symbol manipulation that, according to the researchers, is characteristic of traditional mathematics instruction at this level. In fact, the performance of the control group was better on symbol manipulation.

Integrated Instruction

CTE (COLLEGE)

Jenkins et al. (2009) studied student outcomes in the Integrated Basic Education and Skills Training (I-BEST) program, a special initiative that combines CTE and adult basic education in community colleges throughout the state of Washington.[6] Students in this program are enrolled in noncredit adult basic education and simultaneously take a college-credit occupational course that integrates instruction in occupationally related reading, writing, and mathematics. Instruction lasts one college quarter, in accordance with the statewide community college calendar. Although the content and number of hours of instruction varies across sites, there is a stipulation that both an occupational and a basic skills instructor must be present in the classroom for at least half of the total instructional time. (It is not reported how this time is distributed across class sessions.)

Two-year outcomes were compared between a cohort of 900 I-BEST students and two other samples of adult basic education students: one group that did and another group that did not enroll in a traditional, college-level CTE course at the same time as the I-BEST students. The comparisons controlled for age, gender, intent (vocational or academic), enrollment status (full- or part-time) when first enrolled, and educational history. Net of controls, I-BEST students were more likely than the traditional group to take subsequent credit-bearing courses, earn credits toward a certificate or degree, persist to the next college year, and show gain in basic skills. I-BEST students' basic skills improvement was 18% higher than adult basic education students who did not enroll in a traditional occupational course and 9% higher than adult basic education students who took an occupational course. Thus, the major advantage of I-BEST was seen when the comparison group took only adult basic education but not an occupational course. These results provide encouraging evidence for integrated instruction, but conclusions remain tentative as the sample was self-selected, raising the possibility that results could be attributed at least partially to student motivation. As the authors noted, I-BEST correlated with, but did not necessarily cause, the positive outcomes.

CTE (SECONDARY EDUCATION)

Stone et al. (2006) investigated the effects of integrating mathematics instruction into five CTE areas (agriculture, auto technology, business and marketing, health, and information technology) using a "Math-in-CTE" model. The purpose of the instruction was to broaden students' knowledge of mathematics concepts they learned in CTE and have students "recognize how to solve practical problems by using mathematics in their occupational area; recognize math occurring in other contexts; and do so without diminishing the acquisition of technical knowledge in the course" (p. 5). However, it was not explained why technical knowledge might diminish by a broadened approach to mathematics instruction, which assumed prior knowledge of algebra. Initially, highly contextualized mathematics problems were taught, along with more abstract examples. For instance, when students used a T-square during instruction in agricultural mechanics, the teacher presented the Pythagorean theorem by showing the formula $a^2 + b^2 = c^2$. However, ultimately, the goal was that "students would see the math as an essential component of the CTE content, a tool—like a saw, wrench, or thermometer—needed to successfully solve workplace problems" (p. 6).

Teachers in 12 states were recruited on a volunteer basis and randomly assigned to conditions (57 experimental and 74 control). The CTE teachers in the experimental condition collaborated with mathematics teachers to identify mathematics problems embedded in the existing CTE curricula and to create lessons highlighting mathematical operations. The math-enhanced CTE lessons constituted 10% of instructional time over one academic year. The mathematics lessons contained seven-elements: introduce the CTE lesson; assess mathematics skills relating to the CTE lesson; work through a mathematics problem embedded in the CTE lesson; work through related, contextualized examples; work through traditional mathematics examples; have students demonstrate their understanding; and mathematics questions in formal assessment at the end of the CTE unit or course (Stone et al., 2006, p. 12).

Pre- and posttests on two standardized mathematics tests, the TerraNova and Accuplacer, showed significantly greater gain for the experimental group (effect sizes 0.42 and 0.55). When occupational tests used in each participating classroom were administered at posttest, no significant differences were found between the experimental and control groups. The authors interpreted this to mean that the mathematics instruction was not detrimental to a growth of knowledge in the CTE field, but because the mathematics enhancement was presumably in the interest of an increase in occupational knowledge, the findings can also be interpreted to mean that the mathematics enhancement did not advance CTE performance.

ACADEMIC PROGRAMS (K–12)

Building on De La Paz's (2005) eighth-grade study of contextualized instruction described earlier, De La Paz and Felton (2010) investigated the effects of instruction that focused on both historical reasoning and persuasive writing in an eleventh-grade 20th century history course. Whereas in the earlier study, the writing skills were taught by language arts teachers, in the De La Paz and Felton study, history teachers provided this instruction.

Participants were students (n = 79) in experimental classrooms and students (n = 81) in business-as-usual comparison classrooms in two schools. In the experimental (integrated instruction) condition, the history teachers introduced and modeled steps in the writing of persuasive essays on historical topics and then taught the content using the historical reasoning strategy. Then, the students were given guided practice in the writing of two persuasive essays on the history topics using the STOP and DARE mnemonics from De La Paz's 2005 study. Instruction and guided practice focused on writing a topic sentence stating a position on a historical controversy, providing reasons, using evidence to support claims, presenting a counterargument (with evidence), and refuting the opposing point of view, presenting new evidence.

Pre- and posttest persuasive essays were analyzed for length, persuasive quality, and historical accuracy. At posttest, the essays written by the experimental group were longer ($d = 0.66$), approximately one third more likely to include elaborated claims, and three times more likely to include elaborated rebuttals than the essays written by the comparison group (controlling for essay length); in addition, the experimental group's essays cited historical documents in support of claims more often (effect size 1.42 *SD* units). These results support the practice of integrated instruction, although, as with the De La Paz (2005) study, it is not possible to determine whether the positive outcome was attributable to contextualization or the instructional strategies.

A study of integrated instruction was conducted by Vaughn et al. (2009) with low-income seventh-grade social studies students, approximately one third of whom spoke Spanish as a native language and were not proficient speakers of English. Assignment to condition was unusually rigorous; first, students were randomly assigned to classrooms and then classrooms were randomly assigned to an intervention or business-as-usual control condition. The social studies material was identical in both conditions. The intervention involved explicit reading comprehension and vocabulary instruction; the control group did not receive any literacy instruction but only focused on the social studies content. The integrated instruction was delivered for 50 minutes per day, 5 days per week for 9 to 12 weeks. Four new vocabulary words were taught per day. All vocabulary was drawn directly from the social studies text.

To teach vocabulary after giving an overview of a "big idea" relating to the historical topic, the teacher pronounced each vocabulary word, identified a Spanish cognate or translated the word into Spanish, provided a definition in everyday language, showed a visual representation of the word, and put each word into two sentences, one in historical context from the class reading and the other relating to students' everyday life experience. The students then discussed each word in pairs. A 2-to-4-minute video clip on the topic was then shown and discussed. Then a graphic organizer was used to support silent and oral reading comprehension, and students worked in pairs to read the text and answer questions. In the paired reading, one student read while the other followed along, with the first student interrupting to correct the reader as needed. The teacher then led a whole-class discussion of the answers to the questions and, as a writing activity, worked with students to summarize information on the topic using the graphic organizer.

On researcher-developed measures of vocabulary matching and reading comprehension, the experimental group showed greater gain than the control group, with effect sizes of $g = 1.12$ for reading comprehension and $g = 0.53$ for vocabulary. Importantly, the integrated instruction was equally effective with proficient and less proficient speakers of English.

Bulgren et al. (2009) used a short-term "content-enhancement routine" (CER, p. 274) with typically developing and learning disabled (LD) students ($n = 36$) in grades 9 to 12. Students were randomly assigned to CER and control groups, using stratification to ensure equal representation of LD and non-LD students. The CER group learned a strategy for taking notes and learning vocabulary based on a 30-minute film on ozone depletion as the basis of an essay on climate change. The note-taking process was taught using a "question exploration guide," an organizational structure for recording important information in the film. Sections of the guide listed several questions that students had to answer, including "What is the critical question?" "What are the key terms and explanations?" "What are the supporting questions and answers?" and "What is the main idea answer?" Other questions related to experiments that could be conducted as well as to how knowledge about ozone depletion could be applied to individual lives. The control group viewed the film twice and was asked to take notes with no further instruction.

Outcome measures were writing quality and content knowledge exhibited in posttest essays on a topic related to ozone depletion. Writing quality referred to the ideas expressed in the essay as well as organization, voice, word choice, sentence construction, and the use of written English conventions. The content score measured identification of the problem, cause, effect, solution, and the writer's conclusion on the issue. At posttest, the essay quality of the experimental group was 25% better than that of the control group ($d = 1.32$). Superior gains for the treatment group were seen for every writing quality variable except writing conventions. The CER group also showed greater gain than the control group on content knowledge ($d = 0.74$). However, when the scores for the LD and typically developing students were disaggregated, only the typically developing students showed greater gain than the control group ($d = 2.0$). The results of this integrated instruction approach are encouraging, but conclusions are limited by the fact that the activity in the control condition seems considerably less compelling. Other methodological limitations are that instruction was delivered by researchers rather than classroom teachers and the intervention was very short, lasting only two sessions.

Similar to Bulgren et al. (2009), Tilson et al. (2010) taught an experimental science unit that integrated literacy instruction. Whereas the study conducted by Bulgren et al. was a small-scale experiment in secondary education, participants in the study conducted by Tilson et al. were fourth graders in 94 classrooms in 48 elementary schools. Students were randomly assigned to experimental classrooms ($n = 217$ students) or control classrooms ($n = 241$ students). The science unit taught concepts on physical science (light and energy), with 40% of instructional time spent on science, 40% on literacy (reading, writing, speaking, and listening), and 20% on formative assessment.

Several types of science-related writing were embedded in the science instruction, including the recording of data, written responses to informational text, and reports on what students learned in group discussions. Instruction was provided on constructing topic sentences, including supporting evidence, and using scientific vocabulary in precise ways. The teacher modeled the entire writing process at the beginning of the unit. Moreover, the students were taught to use graphic organizers and worked in pairs to plan writing tasks. As an example of the integrated instruction, one of the lessons involved testing various materials to investigate the phenomenon of reflection. Students created a data table and read a text on the topic, after which they wrote explanations on the nature of reflection.

In the control condition, students used the same text and experiential activities but, instead of explicit strategy instruction, they only engaged in reading and writing practice. All students were tested pre and post on writing skills using an experimenter-designed instrument. The quality of students' writing was scored on the accuracy of the science content, the use of evidence, the quality of the introduction and conclusion, the clarity of expression, vocabulary usage, and vocabulary count (defined as how many of 32 science terms targeted during instruction were included in the writing sample). The treatment group showed greater gain from pre to post than the control group on all of the writing measures except vocabulary usage and quality of conclusion ($d = 0.69$ on a composite score of all of the writing dimensions). As with De La Paz (2005) and De La Paz and Felton (2010), a clear attribution cannot be made to contextualization in itself because the treatment was confounded with strategy instruction.

Trends in the Research

The studies identified in this review suggest that contextualization of basic skills instruction, especially when coupled with explicit strategy instruction, is a promising approach for academically underprepared community college students. Conclusions are tentative, however, because of the shortage of rigorous studies with college populations. Research with K–12 samples was included in the review because there was relatively little information on the use of contextualization with students in college or adult education settings, but there does not seem to be any reason why findings from elementary and secondary education cannot be extrapolated to older adolescent and adult learners.

Outcome measures for almost all of the studies focused exclusively on and found gains for specific basic skills outcomes, such as reading, writing, or mathematics scores. All of the outcomes of contextualization for basic skills achievement were positive, although there was minor variation in outcomes for subskills and different measures. It is also of note that most of the studies compared contextualization with a business-as-usual comparison group, indicating that contextualization is more effective than standard, noncontextualized practice. This is a good start in examining the potential of contextualization, but more definitive conclusions can only be made when contextualization is compared with other instruction in addition to conventional approaches so that effects of attention and novelty can be ruled out.

An assumption underlying integrated instruction is that when basic skills instruction is incorporated in disciplinary instruction, ability in both academic skills and content knowledge should increase. However, in five studies of integrated instruction that measured outcomes on knowledge development in a content area (Bulgren et al., 2009; De La Paz & Felton, 2010; Parr et al., 2008; Stone et al., 2006; Tilson et al., 2010), two found no improvement in content knowledge (Parr et al., 2008; Stone et al., 2006). Both of these studies embedded mathematics in occupational courses in high school CTE. As strong claims are made for the advantages of combining literacy with subject-area instruction, these mixed findings are disappointing and warrant further research.

Only two studies, Wisely (2009) and Jenkins et al. (2009), provided data on college advancement. Wisely found that participation in contextualization was associated with completion of developmental education courses and the speed of entry into, as well as the performance and completion of, college-level courses. However, these positive effects were limited to non-White students; no effect of contextualization was found for White students. Jenkins et al. found that adult education students who attended occupational classes that integrated basic skills and content area instruction were more likely than adult education students who either did or did not enroll in a traditional occupational course to take subsequent credit-bearing courses, earn credits toward a college credential, persist to the next college year, and show greater gain in basic skills. Given practitioners' enthusiasm about the value of contextualization (see program descriptions in Baker et al., 2009; Boroch et al., 2007; California Community Colleges, 2008), it is unfortunate that more evidence is not available.

Practical Implications

The presence of large numbers of low-skilled students in colleges, especially community colleges, along with low rates of retention and progress in course work (Bailey et al., 2009) and recent findings that traditionally low graduation rates are not increasing (Radford, Berkner, Wheeless, & Shepherd, 2010) suggest that instruction of academically underprepared college students needs to be reformed. Among the many different innovations under way that attempt to promote the learning of low-skilled college students (Perin & Charron, 2006), contextualization seems to have the strongest theoretical base and perhaps the strongest empirical support. (There is a striking lack of evidence for most instructional approaches used to teach foundational skills in community colleges; see Levin and Calcagno, 2008.) Both forms of contextualization (i.e., contextualized and integrated instruction) are supported by quantitative studies that include control or comparison groups. There are more studies on contextualized than integrated instruction, but both forms of contextualization appear potentially valuable.

Moving toward contextualization in general, and contextualized or integrated instruction in particular, will depend on practical conditions internal to the colleges. Most important among these conditions are instructors' willingness to modify their instruction and colleges' ability to provide incentives and support for this change. Many developmental education instructors are not highly aware of the day-to-day reading and writing requirements that students find so difficult in college-credit disciplinary courses. Furthermore, instructors tend to be strongly committed to the generic, decontextualized instruction in reading, writing, and mathematics that predominates in developmental education (Grubb et al., 1999). However, disciplinary instructors may be equally unwilling to consider contextualization because they feel that basic skills instruction is beyond their range of responsibility or competence. Strong college leaders will need to provide ongoing direction and support for either version of contextualization.

The following recommendations are offered to support the implementation of contextualization in community colleges to promote improved student outcomes.

1. Carefully select the context for basic skills instruction. Indeed, the selection of this context is perhaps the greatest challenge to contextualization. Instructors understandably do not wish to teach academic skills too narrowly. It may be most effective to segment basic skills instruction according to students' career goals so that different developmental education courses are contextualized in content from course work needed for a given degree or certificate. Selection of college-credit courses with high enrollments but low success rates may be a useful direction. Block scheduling of developmental education students to provide appropriate contextualization will be needed. These reforms will initially take much effort but may be more effective than current developmental education practice.

2. Create conditions for interdisciplinary collaboration so that basic skills and content area instructors can familiarize each other with their curricula, assessment approaches, standards, and teaching techniques (Baker et al., 2009; Greenleaf et al., 2010; Kalchik & Oertle, 2010; Perin, 2005; Shore et al., 2004; Stone et al., 2006). It is important that instructors visit each other's classrooms, discuss their educational philosophy and instructional techniques,

jointly analyze the literacy and mathematics demands of content instruction, look for intersects between their instructional topics, and collaborate to align curricula so that students can be taught reading, writing, or mathematics skills that are directly applicable to the subject areas they are learning. Substantial time is required for this effort. Although salary and time constraints are a major challenge, part-time instructors should be integral to this effort because they form a large proportion of the developmental education faculty.

3. Provide ongoing professional development led by experienced trainers, coaches, and mentors to initiate and support contextualization. Professional development leaders should be experts from within the institution rather than outsiders (Kozeracki, 2005). Formal professional development should be conducted with interdisciplinary groups of instructors and should be designed to meet tangible targets for implementing contextualized or integrated courses. Evidence-based professional development methods should be used, such as interdisciplinary inquiry-based approaches that involve coaching and intensive institutes (Greenleaf et al., 2010). Furthermore, professional development should be guided by common cross-discipline agreement on desired learning outcomes for contextualization and the means of achieving them (Baker et al., 2009). Follow-up activities and supportive monitoring should be provided after the conclusion of formal training sessions to maintain instructors' interest and ability to contextualize or integrate basic skills instruction. Greenleaf et al. (2010) noted that "a long history of research in reading has demonstrated that reading comprehension strategies are not often taught in subject-area classes, even when teachers are trained to use these strategies during subject-area teaching" (p. 15). To avoid this situation, follow-up support by respected instructional leaders will be needed.

4. Develop assessment procedures that incorporate both basic skills and content area knowledge to evaluate the effects of contextualization. For example, in the study conducted by Shore et al. (2004), developmental mathematics and allied health instructors collaborated to create allied health mathematics problems. Both De La Paz and Felton (2010) and Perin and Hare (2010) included measures of content accuracy in instruments to measure contextualized writing, and Guthrie et al. (1999) developed fine-grained assessment methods that simultaneously measured reading comprehension strategies and science knowledge. It appears that such measures will need to be locally developed because disciplinary curricula tend to change, and conventional standardized tests do not capture students' progress in contextualized basic skills (Greenleaf et al., 2010), although customized subject-specific basic skills tests can be developed and normed (Lazar et al., 1998).

5. As the basis of contextualization of basic skills instruction in community colleges, select discipline-area courses that are needed for graduation by large numbers of students but have high failure rates. As contextualization is a labor-intensive initiative, it will be necessary to select courses for implementation. Initial attempts should focus on courses that have the highest need, represented by failure rates. Anecdotal evidence suggests that introductory science courses such as anatomy and physiology, required for graduation in popular majors such as allied health, may be a useful place to start because these courses display high failure rates, and studies are available on the contextualization of basic skills in science (Bulgren et al., 2009; Guthrie et al., 1999; McDermott, 2010; Shore et al., 2004).

6. When contextualized courses are established, collect outcome data for examination by instructors and administrators. Instructors who implement contextualization and administrators who support this effort should be made aware of both short- and longer-term outcomes such as the rate of passing basic skills and disciplinary courses, grade point average, semester-to-semester retention, and degree or certificate attainment. Evaluating contextualization in this way will indicate whether the effort is worthwhile and may point to the need for modification of teaching techniques.

Future Research Directions

Many approaches to the instruction of academically underprepared students have been tried, but their level of effectiveness is often unknown (Perin & Charron, 2006). Furthermore, it is not clear that improving instruction is itself high on the community college educational reform agenda. For example, a study of a well-funded reform effort, "Achieving the Dream," reported that only 27% of a set of student achievement–oriented reform strategies implemented by 26 community colleges focused on changes in classroom instruction (Rutschow et al., 2011, Figure 5.2, p. 76). Colleges might be more likely to reform instruction if there were more evidence on which to base such efforts.

The lack of rigorous research suggests that it is currently premature to invest substantial funds in contextualization. However, practitioners have been enthusiastic about it for many years, trends in the available research are positive, and the approach is consistent with theories of learning and motivation. For these reasons, it would be worthwhile to mount a rigorous research and development effort to gather information about the potential efficacy of this approach, specifically with low-skilled adult learners, whether in community college degree and certificate programs or adult basic education programs.

A premise underlying the practice of contextualization of basic skills is that students are more likely to transfer the skills to subject-area learning when the instruction is connected to these subject areas rather than taught abstractly. A topic that has not been addressed in studying the effects of contextualization on transfer of learning is possible interactions between student ability, student motivation, type of skill to be learned, and amount of contextualization. Thus, in either research and development studies or basic research investigations, moderators of the possible effects of contextualization should be identified. Experiments investigating contextualization should include a comparison of performance on alternate approaches as well as business-as-usual comparison groups to ensure that effects of contextualization are not attributable simply to novelty or increased attention.

Anecdotal evidence from practitioners (e.g., Baker et al., 2009; Boroch et al., 2007; Johnson, 2002) suggests that lower-skilled students benefit from contextualization, not because it helps them become flexible learners but only because it increases their mastery of basic skills as well as the likelihood of transfer of basic skills to content courses that is not occurring in traditional, decontextualized learning environments. There is very little research on the relationship between contextualization of basic skills instruction and subsequent course work, and based on the small number of available studies, it is not possible to attribute the gains exclusively to contextualization. Future research paradigms should control for variables such as the nature of the course, teacher expertise, and cognitive and affective characteristics of learners.

The issue of dosage of contextualization should also be studied in light of claims that instruction can be overcontextualized and as such can be counterproductive (e.g., see Bransford, Brown, & Cocking, 2000). Another area that needs attention is the nature of the dependent variable used in studies of contextualization. The studies in this review varied on whether they measured both basic skills and subject-area gain or just the former. Dependent variables in future research on contextualization of basic skills should include both basic skills and content knowledge because the intent is to bring the two areas closer together and increase learning in both.

Conclusion

The contextualization of basic skills in disciplinary content is used in elementary, secondary, adult, and postsecondary education as a way to engage students, deepen content learning, and promote transfer of skill. The approach is well grounded in psychological theories of transfer and motivation. There is support in the literature for two forms of contextualization identified in this review: contextualized instruction, which is taught by developmental education instructors and English language arts teachers, and integrated instruction, which is provided by discipline-area instructors.

There is more descriptive than evaluative literature, but the 27 quantitative studies found in this review, taken together, suggest that contextualization has the potential to promote short-term academic achievement and longer-term college advancement of low-skilled students. However, the studies suggest that considerable effort is needed to implement contextualization because instructors need to learn from each other and collaborate across disciplines, a practice that is not common in college settings. Furthermore, there is very little information on cost or what would be needed to scale up contextualization. However, the available evidence, taken in combination with practitioners' considerable enthusiasm for contextualization, suggests that this approach is a useful step toward improving the outcomes of academically underprepared college students.

Notes

1. The terms *foundational skills*, *basic skills*, and *developmental education* are used interchangeably in this article to refer to preparation in reading, writing, and mathematics that aims to bring underprepared students' skills to the college level. A further point is to recognize that all of these terms imply assumptions about the nature of learning. It is possible to interpret the word *skill* as implying a behaviorist framework, which is at odds with a view of learning as essentially sociocultural. The term *skill* is used here as shorthand for ability to engage in the reading, writing, and mathematics activities that undergird and are necessary for learning from the postsecondary curriculum. Also, the current intent is to be neutral with regard to explanations for the term *low skills*; no negative connotation should be inferred.

2. In rare cases, contextualization of reading, writing, or mathematics has been used in learning communities that link upper-division college courses, such as advanced composition and abnormal psychology (Cargill & Kalikoff, 2007).

3. Cognitive theory on transfer has a long history of unresolved debates (Anderson, Reder, & Simon, 1996; Barnett & Ceci, 2002; Billing, 2007; Bransford et al., 2000; Detterman & Sternberg, 1993; Greeno, 2009; Mikulecky, 1994; Perkins & Salomon, 1989; Smagorinsky & Smith, 1992; Son & Goldstone, 2009). One problem is the lack of a commonly agreed-on definition of transfer (Barnett & Ceci, 2002), but a more pressing question is that of "dosage," that is, how much contextualization is required to facilitate the transfer of learning. More specifically, the debate has focused on creating flexible learners who will apply knowledge and skill to diverse situations. It has been theorized that overcontextualization limits learners' flexibility in applying new knowledge and skill (Bransford et al., 2000). The debate has a slightly different focus from that in the current review, which is narrower in its concern with the learning and application of basic literacy and mathematics skills by low-achieving students. From a pragmatic point of view, although too much contextualization may inhibit flexibility in the application of skills, the simple application of basic skills to a subject area would be an improvement over the current situation in which many low-skilled students do not apply basic skills they have learned in remedial settings once in the content classroom. Furthermore, it appears that transfer is difficult to discern even when explicit instruction in transfer is provided (Hendricks, 2001).

4. The hypothesis here is that level of intrinsic motivation predicts level of future engagement in course work. However, it is noted that intrinsic motivation to read has not been found to be a statistically significant predictor of future reading ability. Rather, level of intrinsic motivation to read loses its independent predictiveness once prior reading ability is accounted for (Becker et al., 2010). The same may be true for intrinsic motivation as a predictor of students' engagement in learning, with the result that motivation may be confounded with prior academic achievement in predicting future course engagement

5. Most of the studies of contextualization in college settings have serious limitations. However, all of the studies of contextualization in college identified in the search for this review are included in the following section because we are most concerned with this particular sector.

6. In the state of Washington, adult basic education serves students based on tested skill levels and, consequently, overlaps with developmental education courses.

References

Anderson, J. R., Reder, L. M., & Simon, H. A. (1996). Situated learning and education. *Educational Researcher, 25*(4), 5–11.

Artis, A. B. (2008). Improving marketing students' reading comprehension with the SQ3R method. *Journal of Marketing Education, 30,* 130–137.

Badway, N., & Grubb, W. N. (1997). *A sourcebook for reshaping the community college: Curriculum integration and the multiple domains of career preparation* (MDS-782, Vols. I–II). Berkeley, CA: National Center for Research in Vocational Education.

Bailer, D. L. (2006). *A multivariate analysis of the relationship between age, self-regulated learning, and academic performance among community college developmental education students* (Unpublished doctoral dissertation). Touro University International, Cypress, CA.

Bailey, T. R., Jeong, D. W., & Cho, S. W. (2009). Referral, enrollment, and completion in developmental education sequences in community colleges. *Economics of Education Review, 29,* 255–270.

Baker, E. D., Hope, L., & Karandjeff, K. (2009). *Contextualized teaching and learning: A faculty primer.* Retrieved from http://www.careerladdersproject.org/docs/CTL.pdf

Baker, L., & Wigfield, A. (1999). Dimensions of children's motivation for reading and their relations to reading activity and reading achievement. *Reading Research Quarterly, 34,* 452–477.

Barnett, S. M., & Ceci, S. J. (2002). When and where do we apply what we learn? A taxonomy for far transfer. *Psychological Bulletin, 128,* 612–637.

Barton, M. L., Heidema, C., & Jordan, D. (2002). Teaching reading in mathematics and science. *Educational Leadership, 60*(3), 24–29.

Becker, M., McElvany, N., & Kortenbruck, M. (2010). Intrinsic and extrinsic reading motivation as predictors of reading literacy: A longitudinal study. *Journal of Educational Psychology, 102,* 773–785.

Berns, R. G., & Erickson, P. M. (2001). Contextual teaching and learning: Preparing students for the new economy. *The highlight zone.* Research @ Work (No. 5). (ERIC Document Reproduction Service No. ED452376)

Billing, D. (2007). Teaching for transfer of core/key skills in higher education: Cognitive skills. *Higher Education, 53*, 483–516.

Bond, L. P. (2004, January). *Using contextual instruction to make abstract learning concrete.* Alexandria, VA: Association for Career and Technical Information. Retrieved from http://www.acteonline.org/content.aspx?id=5822 &terms=Using+Contextual+Instruction+to+Make+Abstract#contextual

Boroch, D., Filipot, J., Hope, L., Johnstone, R., Mery, P., Serban, A., & Gabriner, R. S. (2007). *Basic skills as a foundation for student success in California community colleges.* Sacramento: Center for Student Success, Research and Planning Group, Chancellor's Office, California Community Colleges. Retrieved from http://css.rpgroup.org

Bottge, B. A. (1999). Effects of contextualized math instruction on problem solving of average and below-average achieving students. *Journal of Special Education, 33*, 81–92.

Bottge, B. A., & Hasselbring, T. S. (1993). A comparison of two approaches for teaching complex, authentic mathematics problems to adolescents in remedial math classes. *Exceptional Children, 59*, 556.

Bottge, B. A, Rueda, E., Serlin, R. C., Hung, Y.-H., & Jung, M. K. (2007). Shrinking achievement differences with anchored math problems: Challenges and possibilities. *Journal of Special Education, 41*, 31–49.

Bragg, D. D., Reger, W. I. V., & Thomas, H. S. (1997). *Integration of academic and occupational education in the Illinois Community College System.* Springfield: Illinois Community College Board. (ERIC Document Reproduction Service No. ED418757)

Bransford, J. D., Brown, A. L., & Cocking, R. R. (2000). *How people learn: Brain, mind, experience, and school.* Washington, DC: National Academy Press. Retrieved from http://www.nap.edu/

Brenner, M. E., Mayer, R. E., Moseley, B., Brar, T., Durán, R., Reed, B. S., & Webb, D. (1997). Learning by understanding: The role of multiple representations in learning algebra. *American Educational Research Journal, 34*, 663–689.

Bulgren, J., Marquis, J., Lenz, B. K., Schumaker, J. B., & Deshler, D. D. (2009). Effectiveness of question exploration to enhance students' written expression of content knowledge and comprehension. *Reading & Writing Quarterly, 25*, 271–289.

California Community Colleges. (2008). Teaming up for green technology. *Getting It Done with WPLRC, 6*(5), 1–2. Retrieved from http://www.wplrc.org/ app/doc/WPLRC%20Getting%20It%20Done%20Vol6-5.pdf

Cargill, K., & Kalikoff, B. (2007). Linked psychology and writing courses across the curriculum. *Journal of General Education, 56*, 83–92.

Cavazos, J. J., Johnson, M. B., & Sparrow, G. S. (2010). Overcoming personal and academic challenges: Perspectives from Latina/o college students. *Journal of Hispanic Higher Education, 9*, 304–316.

Caverly, D. C., Nicholson, S. A., & Radcliffe, R. (2004). The effectiveness of strategic reading instruction for college developmental readers. *Journal of College Reading and Learning, 35*, 25–49.

Cox, P. L., Bobrowski, P. E., & Spector, M. (2004). Gateway to business: An innovative approach to integrating writing into the first-year business curriculum. *Journal of Management Education, 28*, 62–87.

De La Paz, S. (2005). Effects of historical reasoning instruction and writing strategy mastery in culturally and academically diverse middle school classrooms. *Journal of Educational Psychology, 97*, 139–156.

De La Paz, S., & Felton, M. K. (2010). Reading and writing from multiple source documents in history: Effects of strategy instruction with low to average high school writers. *Contemporary Educational Psychology, 35,* 174–192.

Dean, R. J., & Dagostino, L. (2007). Motivational factors affecting advanced literacy learning of community college students. *Community College Journal of Research and Practice, 31,* 149–161.

Detterman, D. K., & Sternberg, R. J. (Eds.). (1993). *Transfer on trial: Intelligence, cognition, and instruction.* Norwood, NJ: Ablex.

Dewey, J. (1966). *Democracy and education.* New York, NY: Free Press. (Original work published 1916)

Dirkx, J. M., & Crawford, M. (1993). Teaching reading through teaching science: Development and evaluation of an experimental curriculum for correctional ABE programs. *Journal of Correctional Education, 44,* 172–176.

Dirkx, J. M., & Prenger, S. M. (1997). *A guide for planning and implementing instruction for adults: A theme-based approach.* San Francisco, CA: Jossey-Bass.

Dowden, T. (2007). Relevant, challenging, integrative and exploratory curriculum design: Perspectives from theory and practice for middle level schooling in Australia. *Australian Educational Researcher, 34,* 51–71.

Ekkens, K., & Winke, P. (2009). Evaluating workplace English language programs. *Language Assessment Quarterly, 6,* 265–287.

Fallon, D., Lahar, C. J., & Susman, D. (2009). Taking the high road to transfer: Building bridges between English and psychology. *Teaching English in the Two-Year College, 37*(1), 41–55.

Fisher, D., & Ivy, G. (2005). Literacy and language as learning in content-area classes: A departure from "Every Teacher a Teacher of Reading." *Action in Teacher Education, 27*(2), 3–11.

Fox, E. (2009). The role of reader characteristics in processing and learning from informational text. *Review of Educational Research, 79,* 197–261.

Gardenshire-Crooks, A., Collado, H., Martin, K., & Castro, A. (2010). *Terms of engagement: Men of color discuss their experiences in community college.* New York, NY: Manpower Demonstration Research Corporation. (ERIC Document Reproduction Service No. ED508982)

Gijbels, D., Dochy, F., Van den Bossche, P., & Segers, M. (2005). Effects of problem-based learning: A meta-analysis from the angle of assessment. *Review of Educational Research, 75,* 27–61.

Goldman, S. R., & Bisanz, G. L. (2002). Toward a functional analysis of scientific genres: Implications for understanding and learning processes. In J. Otero, J. A. Leon, & A. C. Graesser (Eds.), *The psychology of science text comprehension* (pp. 19–50). Mahwah, NJ: Erlbaum.

Goode, D. (2000). Creating a context for developmental English. *Teaching English in the Two-Year College, 27,* 270–277.

Greenleaf, C. L., Litman, C., Hanson, T. L., Rosen, R., Boscardin, C. K., Herman, J., & Jones, B. (2010). Integrating literacy and science in biology: Teaching and learning impacts of reading apprenticeship professional development. *American Educational Research Journal, 48,* 1–71.

Greeno, J. G. (2009). A theory bite on contextualizing, framing, and positioning: A companion to Son and Goldstone. *Cognition and Instruction, 27,* 269–275.

Grigg, W., Donahue, P., & Dion, G. (2007). *The nation's report card: 12th grade reading and mathematics* (NCES 2007-468). Washington, DC: National Center for Education Statistics.

Grubb, W. N., & Kraskouskas, E. (1992). *A time to every purpose: Integrating academic and occupational education in community colleges and technical institutes* (MDS-251). Berkeley: University of California at Berkeley, National Center for Research in Vocational Education.

Grubb, W. N., Worthen, H., Byrd, B., Webb, E., Badway, N., Case, C., & Villeneuve, J. C. (1999). *Honored but invisible: An inside look at teaching in community colleges.* New York, NY: Routledge.

Guthrie, J. T., Anderson, E., Alao, S., & Rinehart, J. (1999). Influences of concept-oriented reading instruction on strategy use and conceptual learning from text. *Elementary School Journal, 99,* 343–366.

Hattie, J., Biggs, J., & Purdie, N. (1996). Effects of learning skills interventions on student learning: A meta-analysis. *Review of Educational Research, 66,* 99–136.

Heller, R., & Greenleaf, C. L. (2007). *Literacy instruction in the content areas: Getting to the core of middle and high school improvement.* Washington, DC: Alliance for Excellent Education.

Hendricks, C. C. (2001). Teaching causal reasoning through cognitive apprenticeship: What are results from situated learning? *Journal of Educational Research, 94,* 302–311.

Higbee, J. L., Lundell, D., & Arendale, D. R. (Eds.). (2005). *The general college vision: Integrating intellectual growth, multicultural perspectives, and student development.* Minneapolis: General College and the Center for Research on Developmental Education and Urban Literacy, University of Minnesota-Twin Cities.

Jenkins, D., Zeidenberg, M., & Kienzl, G. (2009). *Educational outcomes of I-BEST, Washington State Community and Technical College System's Integrated Basic Education and Skills Training Program: Findings from a multivariate analysis* (CCRC Working Paper No. 16). New York, NY: Teachers College, Columbia University, Community College Research Center. Retrieved from http://ccrc.tc.columbia.edu/ContentByType.asp?t=1

Johnson, E. B. (2002). *Contextual teaching and learning: What it is and why it's here to stay.* Thousand Oaks, CA: Corwin.

Kalchik, S., & Oertle, K. M. (2010, September). *The theory and application of contextualized teaching and learning in relation to programs of study and career pathways. Transition highlights* (Issue 2). Retrieved from http://occrl.illinois.edu/files/Highlights/Highlight_09_2010.pdf

Karweit, N. (1998). Contextual learning: Review & synthesis. In A. M. Milne (Ed.), *Educational reform and vocational education* (pp. 53–84). Washington, DC: National Institute on Postsecondary Education, Libraries, and Lifelong Learning. (ERIC Document Reproduction Service No. ED421659)

Klein, P. D. (1999). Reopening inquiry into cognitive processes in writing-to-learn. *Educational Psychology Review, 11,* 203–270.

Kozeracki, C. (2005). Preparing faculty to meet the needs of developmental students. In C. A. Kozeracki (Ed.), *Responding to the challenges of developmental education* (New Directions for Community Colleges, No. 129, pp. 39–49). San Francisco, CA: Jossey-Bass.

Krajcik, J. S., & Sutherland, L. M. (2010). Supporting students in developing literacy in science. *Science, 328,* 456–459.

Lazar, M. K., Bean, R. M., & Van Horn, B. V. (1998). Linking the success of a basic skills program to workplace practices and productivity. *Journal of Adolescent & Adult Literacy, 41,* 352–362.

Lee, C. D., & Spratley, A. (2010). *Reading in the disciplines: The challenges of adolescent literacy.* New York, NY: Carnegie Corporation of New York.

Levin, H. M., & Calcagno, J. C. (2008). Remediation in the community college: An evaluator's perspective. *Community College Review, 35,* 181–207.

Levin, J. S., Cox, E. M., Cerven, C., & Haberler, Z. (2010). The recipe for promising practices in community colleges. *Community College Review, 38,* 31–58.

Martino, N. L., Norris, J., & Hoffman, P. (2001). Reading comprehension instruction: Effects of two types. *Journal of Developmental Education, 25,* 2–10.

Massey, D. D., & Heafner, T. L. (2004). Promoting reading comprehension in the social studies. *Journal of Adolescent and Adult Literacy, 48,* 26–40.

Mayer, R. E., & Wittrock, M. C. (1996). Problem-solving transfer. In D. C. Berliner & R. C. Calfee (Eds.), *Handbook of educational psychology* (pp. 47–62). New York, NY: Macmillan.

Mazzeo, C., Rab, S. Y., & Alssid, J. L. (2003). *Building bridges to college and careers: Contextualized basic skills programs at community colleges.* Brooklyn, NY: Workforce Strategy Center. Retrieved from http://www.workforcestrategy .org/images/pdfs/publications/Contextualized_basic_ed_report.pdf

McDermott, M. (2010). Using multimodal writing tasks in the science classroom. *The Science Teacher, 77,* 32–36.

McKenna, M. C., & Robinson, R. D. (2009). *Teaching through text: Reading and writing in the content areas* (5th ed.). Boston, MA: Pearson Education.

Mikulecky, L. (1994). *Literacy transfer: A review of the literature.* Philadelphia: National Center on Adult Literacy, University of Pennsylvania. Retrieved from http://citeseerx.ist.psu.edu/viewdoc/download?doi=10.1.1.20.6494&rep =repl&type=pdf

Mikulecky, L., & Lloyd, P. (1997). Evaluation of workplace literacy programs: A profile of effective instructional practices. *Journal of Literacy Research, 29,* 555–585.

Nash-Ditzel, S. (2010). Metacognitive reading strategies can improve self-regulation. *Journal of College Reading and Learning, 40,* 45–63.

National Council for Workforce Education & Jobs for the Future. (2010). *Breaking through: Contextualization toolkit.* Big Rapids, MI: Author. Retrieved from http://www.jff.org/sites/default/files/BT_toolkit_June7.pdf

National Governors Association and Council of Chief State School Officers. (2010). *Common core state standards: English language arts and literacy in history / social studies, science, and technical subjects.* Retrieved from http:// www.corestandards.org/assets/CCSSI_ELA%20Standards.pdf

Nokes, J. D. (2008). Aligning literacy practices in secondary history classes with research on learning. *Middle Grades Research Journal, 3*(3), 29–55.

Parr, B. A., Edwards. M. C., & Leising, J. G. (2008). Does a curriculum integration intervention to improve the mathematics achievement of students diminish their acquisition of technical competence? An experimental study in agricultural mechanics. *Journal of Agricultural Education, 49,* 61–71.

Pearson, P. D. (2010). Literacy and science: Each in the service of the other. *Science, 328,* 459–463.

Perin, D. (1997). Workplace literacy assessment. *Dyslexia, 3,* 190–200.

Perin, D. (2001). Academic-occupational integration as a reform strategy for the community college: Classroom perspectives. *Teachers College Record, 103,* 303–335.

Perin, D. (2005). Institutional decision making for increasing academic preparedness in community colleges. In C. A. Kozeracki (Ed.), *Responding to the challenges of developmental education* (New Directions for Community Colleges, No. 129, pp. 27–38). San Francisco, CA: Jossey-Bass.

Perin, D., & Charron, K. (2006). "Lights just click on every day": Academic preparedness and remediation in community colleges. In T. R. Bailey & V. S. Morest (Eds.), *Defending the community college equity agenda* (pp. 155–194). Baltimore, MD: Johns Hopkins Press.

Perin, D., & Hare, R. (2010). *A contextualized reading-writing intervention for community college students* (CCRC Brief No. 44). New York, NY: Community College Research Center, Teachers College, Columbia University. Retrieved from http://ccrc.tc.columbia.edu/Publication.asp?UID=788

Perkins, D. H., & Salomon, G. (1989). Are cognitive skills context-bound? *Educational Researcher, 18,* 16–25.

Prentice, C. M. (2001). ERIC review: Integrating academic and occupational instruction. *Community College Review, 29*(2), 80–93.

Radford, A. W., Belkner, L., Wheeless, S., & Shepherd, B. (2010). *Persistence and attainment of 2003–04 beginning postsecondary students: After six years.* Washington, DC: National Center for Educational Statistics. Retrieved from http://nces.ed.gov/pubsearch/pubsinfo.asp?pubid=2011151

Raelin, J. A. (2008). *Work-based learning: Bridging knowledge and action in the workplace.* San Francisco, CA: Jossey-Bass.

Reisman, A., & Wineburg, S. (2008). Teaching the skill of contextualizing in history. *Social Studies, 99,* 202–207.

Rutschow, E. Z., Richburg-Hayes, L., Brock, T., Orr, G., Cerna, O., Cullinan, D., & Martin, K. (2011). *Turning the tide: Five years of Achieving the Dream in community colleges.* New York, NY: Manpower Demonstration Research Corporation. Retrieved from http://www.mdrc.org/publications/578/full.pdf

Ryan, R. M., & Deci, E. L. (2000). Intrinsic and extrinsic motivation: Classic definitions and new directions. *Contemporary Educational Psychology, 25,* 54–67.

Salahu-Din, D., Persky, H., & Miller, J. (2008). *The nation's report card: Writing 2007* (NCES 2008-468). Washington, DC: National Center for Education Statistics, Institute of Education Sciences, U.S. Department of Education.

Shore, M., Shore, J., & Boggs, S. (2004). Allied health applications integrated into developmental mathematics using problem based learning. *Mathematics and Computer Education, 38,* 183–189.

Simpson, M. L., Hynd, C. R., Nist, S. L., & Burrell, K. I. (1997). College academic assistance programs and practices. *Educational Psychology Review, 9,* 39–87.

Simpson, M. L., & Nist, S. L. (2002). Encouraging active reading at the college level. In C. C. Block & M. Pressley (Eds.), *Comprehension instruction: Research-based practices* (pp. 365–381). New York, NY: Guilford.

Smagorinsky, P., & Smith, M. W. (1992). The nature of knowledge in composition and literary understanding: The question of specificity. *Review of Educational Research, 62,* 279–305.

Snyder, V. (2002). The effect of course-based reading strategy training on the reading comprehension skills of developmental college students. *Research and Teaching in Developmental Education, 18*(2), 37–41.

Son, J. Y., & Goldstone, R. L. (2009). Contextualization in perspective. *Cognition & Instruction, 27,* 51–89.

Song, B. (2006). Content-based ESL instruction: Long-term effects and outcomes. *English for Specific Purposes, 25,* 420–437.

Stahl, S. A., & Shanahan, C. (2004). Learning to think like a historian: Disciplinary knowledge through critical analysis of multiple documents. In T. L. Jetton & J. A. Dole (Eds.), *Adolescent literacy research and practice* (pp. 94–115). New York, NY: Guilford.

Sticht, T. G. (1995). *The military experience and workplace literacy: A review and synthesis for policy and practice.* Philadelphia, PA: National Center on Adult Literacy. (ERIC Document Reproduction Service No. ED380570)

Sticht, T. G. (2005). *Functional context education: Making learning relevant in the 21st century — Workshop participant's notebook.* Retrieved from http://www.nald.ca/library/research/fce/FCE.pdf

Sticht, T. G., Armstrong, W. A., Hickey, D. T., & Caylor, J. S. (1987). *Cast-off youth: Policy and training methods from the military experience.* New York, NY: Praeger.

Stone, J. R., III, Alfeld, C., Pearson, D., Lewis, M. V., & Jensen, S. (2006). *Building academic skills in context: Testing the value of enhanced math learning in CTE* (Final study). St. Paul, MN: National Research Center for Career and Technical Education. Retrieved from http://136.165.122.102/UserFiles/File/Math-in-CTE/MathLearningFinalStudy.pdf

Tai, E., & Rochford, R. A. (2007). Getting down to basics in Western civilization: It's about time. *Community College Journal of Research and Practice, 31,* 103–116.

Tilson, J. L., Castek, J., & Goss, M. (2010). Exploring the influence of science writing instruction on fourth graders' writing development. In R. T. Jimenez, V. J. Risko, M. K. Hundley, & D. W. Rowe (Eds.), *59th yearbook of the National Reading Conference* (pp. 117–134). Oak Creek, CA: National Reading Conference.

Vaughn, S., Martinez, L. R., Linan-Thompson, S., Reutebuch, C. K., Carlson, C. D., & Francis, D. J. (2009). Enhancing social studies vocabulary and comprehension for seventh-grade English language learners: Findings from two experimental studies. *Journal of Research on Educational Effectiveness, 2,* 297–324.

Washington State Board for Community and Technical Colleges. (2005). *I-BEST: A program integrating adult basic education and workforce training* (Research Report No. 05-2). Olympia, WA: Author.

Weinbaum, A., & Rogers, A. M. (1995). *Contextual learning: A critical aspect of school-to-work transition programs.* Washington, DC: Academy for Educational Development. (ERIC Document Reproduction Service No. 381666)

Weiss, A. J., Visher, M. G., & Wathington, H. (2010). *Learning communities for students in developmental reading: An impact study at Hillsborough Community College.* New York, NY: Columbia University, Teachers College, The National Center for Postsecondary Research.

Wisely, W. C. (2009). *Effectiveness of contextual approaches to developmental math in California community colleges* (Unpublished doctoral dissertation). University of the Pacific, Stockton, CA.

Building Bridges to Postsecondary Training for Low-Skill Adults: Outcomes of Washington State's I-BEST Program

Davis Jenkins, Matthew Zeidenberg, and Gregory Kienzl

Implemented in Washington State's community colleges and designed for low-skilled adults, the I-BEST program contextualizes basic skills into career and technical programs. In this article Jenkins, Zeidenberg, and Kienzl describe the program in detail and report the results of research on data from more than 31,000 students enrolled in it. The reported research indicates that those who participated in the I-BEST program performed better on many dimensions than nonparticipants.

Each year, community colleges, schools, and community organizations offer basic skills instruction to more than 2.5 million adults with limited skills and education. Such programs include Adult Basic Education (ABE) and GED preparation programs for individuals who do not have a high school credential and English-as-a-Second-Language (ESL) programs for persons with limited proficiency in English. Yet few of these students advance successfully to college-level education and training, even when they attend a basic skills program offered by a community college. Not doing so limits the potential of these individuals to secure jobs that pay family-supporting wages and that offer opportunities for career advancement. Integrated Basic Education and Skills Training, or I-BEST, is an innovative program created to address this problem.

First piloted in 2004–05, I-BEST was developed by the community and technical colleges in Washington State to increase the rate at which adult basic skills students enter and succeed in postsecondary occupational education and training. Under the I-BEST model, basic skills instructors and career-technical faculty jointly design and teach college-level occupational, or what in Washington State are called "workforce," courses for adult basic skills students. Instruction in basic skills is thereby integrated with instruction in college-level career-technical skills. This model challenges the conventional notion that basic skills instruction should be completed by students prior to starting college-level courses. The approach thus offers the potential to accelerate the transition of adult basic skills students into college programs.

This Brief, which summarizes a longer paper, presents findings from a CCRC study that investigated the outcomes of students who participated in the program. The study compared, over a two-year tracking period, the educational outcomes of I-BEST students with those of other basic skills students, including students who comprised a particularly apt comparison group—those non-I-BEST basic skills students who nonetheless enrolled in at least one workforce course in academic year 2006–07, the period of enrollment examined in the study. The analyses controlled for observed differences in background characteristics and enrollment patterns of students in the sample. We examined data on more than 31,000 basic skills students in Washington State, including nearly 900 I-BEST participants.

The Development of I-BEST

The design of I-BEST was motivated by research suggesting that teaching basic skills in the context of materials that are of interest to the student—sometimes called "contextual instruction"—can improve the learning of basic skills by adults. Under I-BEST, basic skills instruction is typically customized to a given workforce program For example, in an I-BEST nursing program, increased emphasis is placed on learning medical terms in addition to mastering everyday vocabulary used in all fields. If a student is having difficulty understanding technical material because of problems with English, the basic skills instructor is there to help. The theory is that student motivation and achievement will increase because students are able to immediately experience the usefulness of their basic skills education in learning technical skills and knowledge.

Both the basic skills instructor and the workforce instructor are required to be present in class for at least half of the total instructional time in an I-BEST course. Students receive college credit for the workforce portion of the program, but not for the basic skills instruction. While students may be referred to I-BEST programs by persons affiliated with a given college or by outside organizations, such as an employment center, participants often find out about I-BEST through word of mouth or by attending a non-I-BEST basic skills course (either ABE/GED or ESL).

Preliminary analyses of I-BEST program outcomes (which did not control for student characteristics) by researchers at the Washington State Board for Community and Technical Colleges (WSBCTC) found that participating students were substantially more likely than non-participating adult basic skills students to advance to college-level workforce programs and to reach the "tipping point" of having earned at least one year of credits and a credential. Reaching this point was correlated with a substantial earnings advantage among participants (Prince & Jenkins, 2005; WSBCTC, 2005, 2008). Based on these promising early results, the WSBCTC approved increased funding of programs using the I-BEST model. I-BEST courses receive 75 percent more funds per full-time-equivalent student than do regular basic skills courses to support the team teaching and added coordination involved in I-BEST programs.

With this enhanced funding, the program model has expanded from pilots at 5 colleges in 2004–05 to programs at all 34 community and technical colleges in the Washington State system. Nearly 140 I-BEST programs are currently offered in such fields as nurse assistant, early childhood education, and business technology. The WSBCTC requires that credits earned in I-BEST programs, which are typically a single quarter term in length (the Washington community and technical colleges operate on a quarter system), apply to certificate or degree programs that are part of a "career pathway," that is, programs that clearly connect to further education and career-path employment in the given field.

Data and Methods

The data used in this study were drawn from an administrative dataset shared with CCRC researchers by the WSBCTC on both I-BEST and non-I-BEST students who enrolled at any college in Washington State's community and technical college system at any time during the academic year 2006–07. We chose to study students who enrolled in 2006–07 because it was the first year that the program moved beyond the pilot phase and was in full operation. We restricted our study to those students who took a non-credit adult basic skills course (including, of course, the I-BEST students themselves) in that academic year. We did not include the many students who enrolled directly in programs designed to prepare for transfer to baccalaureate programs, because I-BEST programs exist only in occupational fields. We also restricted our study to students in the 24 colleges that offered I-BEST in 2006–07 (the program was expanded to all 34 colleges the following year).

The dataset contains information on the socioeconomic and demographic characteristics of each student in the sample, as well as transcript data, which we used to determine the number of credits completed and credentials earned. The transcript data enabled us to track students from the first quarter each student enrolled in the system through the end of academic year 2007–08, making it possible to control for any credits earned prior to 2006–07.

The study was designed to examine the effects of participation in I-BEST on the following educational outcomes over two years:

- Whether a student earned any college credits;

- The total number of college credits earned;

- The number of college vocational credits earned;

- Whether the student persisted into the following academic year;

- Whether the student earned a certificate or associate degree; and

- Whether the student achieved gains on basic skills tests.

For each of these outcomes, we first produced descriptive statistics comparing I-BEST students with the following two groups (the second is a subset of the first): all basic skills students not enrolled in I-BEST ("Non-I-BEST students") and those basic skills students not in I-BEST who took at least one workforce course during 2006–07 ("Non-I-BEST Workforce students").

We then performed regressions to compare outcomes between I-BEST students, the treatment group, and Non-I-BEST Workforce students, our comparison group (the full report also discusses findings for Non-I-BEST students who did not take a workforce course). In each case, we controlled for socioeconomic and demographic characteristics, enrollment intent and intensity, and previous schooling (all shown in Table 1, discussed below).

We considered the treatment in this study to be *enrollment* in I-BEST, rather than *completion* of an I-BEST program, because we wanted to view any program attrition effects as part of the program itself; that is, we wanted in our estimates of program effects to account for how successful I-BEST was at retaining students. Nevertheless, we were informed by WSBCTC staff that I-BEST programs have high retention rates.

In addition to regression analysis, we also estimated differences in student outcomes using another analytic method, propensity score matching (PSM), which matches treated subjects—in this case, students who enrolled in an I-BEST program—to selected untreated control subjects—in this case, basic skills students with similar background characteristics who did not enroll in I-BEST.

Although the two methods draw on different groups of students and therefore cannot be directly compared, we used both regression analysis and PSM to see how similar the results from the two methods would be and thus carry out an informal test of the robustness of our findings. For technical reasons described in the paper on which this Brief is based, we give more credence to the estimates of treatment effects produced by PSM than to the results of the regressions. Neither method allows us to correct for selection bias that could be caused by characteristics we do not observe or measure, however. Selection into I-BEST is not random; it may attract students who are more motivated than others with similar backgrounds and preparation for success in their education or careers.

Findings

We start by giving descriptive statistics on the I-BEST students, the Non-I-BEST students, and the Non-I-BEST Workforce students in our sample. We then present results of the regression and PSM analyses for each outcome. Standard errors for specific findings, found in the full report, are not shown here.

Table 1. Characteristics of Basic Skills Students, 2006–07

	I-BEST	All Non-I-BEST	Non-I-BEST Workforce
Number of students in program	896	30,182	1,355
Program Classification			
I-BEST student	100%	0.0%	0.0%
ABE/GED student	69.0%	36.0%	66.4%
ESL student	30.9%	63.8%	33.3%
Non-I-BEST Workforce student	0.0%	4.5%	100.0%
Social and Economic Characteristics			
Mean age	32.5	32.3	31.9
Female	64.8%	60.5%	69.2%
Hispanic	18.4%	38.3%	21.3%
Black, non-Hispanic	12.1%	6.9%	6.1%
Asian/Pacific Islander	12.3%	15.0%	12.4%
Single with dependent	22.2%	14.0%	22.8%
Married with dependent	27.8%	26.5%	24.1%
Disabled	7.1%	3.8%	11.0%
Estimated SES quintile (1 is highest, 5 is lowest)	3.6	3.5	3.5
Current Schooling Characteristics			
Intent is vocational (workforce training)	72.4%	22.7%	48.4%
Intent is academic (degree and/or transfer)	7.4%	9.1%	20.0%
Received aid	25.9%	2.1%	14.2%
Enrolled full time	67.1%	32.6%	49.0%
First enrolled in 1st quarter	30.1%	27.5%	40.0%
First enrolled in 2nd quarter	41.0%	33.1%	40.2%
First enrolled in 3rd quarter	18.5%	22.5%	15.6%
First enrolled in 4th quarter	10.4%	16.9%	4.2%
Previous Schooling Characteristics			
Mean college credits	13.9	0.9	8.8
Mean vocational credits	9.1	0.6	5.8
GED	12.7%	4.0%	10.0%
High school graduate	27.3%	16.9%	25.7%
Some college	10.4%	4.1%	7.5%
Certificate	3.7%	1.7%	3.4%
Associate degree	2.5%	1.8%	2.2%
Bachelor's degree	4.0%	4.6%	5.1%

Descriptive Characteristics

Overall, 896 I-BEST students were enrolled at 24 community or technical colleges in Washington State in academic year 2006–07. Of the 30,182 Non-I-BEST students in the sample, 1,356 also took a workforce course. Thus, like the I-BEST students, the latter enrolled in both basic skills and workforce coursework in 2006–07. However, unlike the I-BEST students, they did not necessarily take the coursework concurrently, and they did not take it as part of an integrated program designed to accelerate the transition from basic skills to college-level workforce programs. These Non-I-BEST Workforce students comprise the group that we believe is most comparable to the I-BEST group.

Table 1 shows the background characteristics that were used as control variables in the multivariate models. There are noteworthy similarities and differences between I-BEST students and the Non-I-BEST Workforce student subset. Both the I-BEST and the Non-I-BEST Workforce students were mainly ABE/GED students (as opposed to the Non-I-BEST students as a whole, who were predominantly ESL students). But Non-I-BEST Workforce students were more likely than I-BEST students to indicate upon entry that they intended to earn an academic credential or transfer to a four-year institution. Twenty percent of Non-I-BEST Workforce students indicated so, compared with seven percent of I-BEST students. Other differences of note are in the percentage of students who received financial aid and the percentage enrolled full time. In both cases, I-BEST students held an advantage over Non-I-BEST Workforce students in that they were more likely to receive aid and enroll full time. In terms of race/ethnicity, I-BEST students were more likely than Non-I-BEST Workforce students to be Black.

Earning College Credit

Using logistic regression analysis, we estimated that the probability of earning college credit for the I-BEST students was 34 percentage points higher than that for the Non-I-BEST Workforce students. The probability of earning college credit was 84 percent for I-BEST students, compared with 50 percent for Non-I-BEST Workforce students. There were no significant differences between the estimates for I-BEST students who started in ABE/GED and those who started in ESL. Both groups appear to have benefited similarly by enrolling in I-BEST.

Using PSM, we estimated that the average difference in the probability of earning college credit between I-BEST students and students in the matched comparison group was 23 percentage points. The probability for I-BEST students was 90 percent; it was 67 percent for the comparison group.

As previously mentioned, we cannot statistically compare the results of the regressions with those of the PSM analysis because each method takes a different approach to selecting appropriate comparison groups. However, the fact that these two different methods yield effect size estimates that are similar in magnitude increases our confidence in the results. PSM may give a more accurate estimate of the program's apparent effect on a given outcome.

Number of Credits Earned

Using OLS regression analysis, we estimated that I-BEST students earned an average of 45 quarter-term college credits, compared with 31 quarter-term credits for the Non-I-BEST Workforce students—a difference of 14 college credits. ABE/GED and ESL students in I-BEST earned 19 and 8 college credits more than those earned by Non-I-BEST Workforce students who were enrolled in ABE/GED and ESL, respectively.

With respect to college vocational credits (a subset of the college credits discussed above), we estimated that, on average, I-BEST students earned 40 vocational credits, while Non-I-BEST Workforce students earned 22 vocational credits—a difference of 18 vocational credits. ABE/GED I-BEST students earned 21 more vocational credits than the ABE/GED Non-I-BEST Workforce group. ESL I-BEST students earned 14 more credits than ESL Non-I-BEST Workforce students.

Using PSM, we estimated that the average number of college credits earned by I-BEST students was 52 credits, compared with an average of 34 credits for the matched comparison group—a difference of 18 college credits. An additional PSM estimate found that I-BEST students earned an average of 45 vocational credits, while the matched comparison group earned an average of 24 vocational credits—a difference of 21 vocational credits. Though not directly comparable, the regression and PSM estimates are of similar magnitude, indicating that the results are robust.

Persisting into 2007–08

We measured persistence into the second academic year, 2007–08, by examining whether a student had any transcript record in that year. By this definition, in order to have persisted, students must have completed, though not necessarily passed, a course in that year. We also considered students as having persisted if they earned an award in 2006–07, even if they did not have a transcript record in 2007–08, because these students experienced a successful outcome.

Using logistic regression, we estimated that I-BEST students had a probability of persisting that was 13 percentage points higher than Non-I-BEST Workforce students. We estimated that I-BEST students had an 80 percent probability of persisting into the second year (or completing a credential), compared with 67 percent for Non-I-BEST Workforce students. Among those enrolled in ABE/GED in both these groups, I-BEST students had a probability that was 12 percentage points higher. The corresponding difference in probability for ESL students was 15 percentage points.

Using PSM, we found that I-BEST students had a probability of persisting that was 17 percentage points higher than matched students. The I-BEST students had a 78 percent probability of persisting, compared with 61 percent for the matched students. Again, the results of the PSM model are similar to those of the regressions.

Earning an Award

To count in our analysis, awards may have been earned at any time within the two academic years of 2006–07 and 2007–08. It is important to note that virtually all of the awards earned by the students under study here were certificates (rather than associate degrees).

Our logistic regression results indicate that I-BEST students had a probability of earning an award that was 35 percentage points higher than that of Non-I-BEST Workforce students. We estimated that I-BEST students had a 51 percent probability of earning an award, compared with 16 percent for Non-I-BEST Workforce students. ABE/GED I-BEST students had a probability of earning an award that was 29 percentage points higher than ABE/GED Non-I-BEST Workforce students. For I-BEST and Non-I-BEST Workforce students enrolled in ESL, the respective difference was 47 percentage points.

Using PSM, we found that I-BEST students had a 55 percent probability of earning an award, compared with only 15 percent for the matched group—a 40 percentage point difference. The PSM estimates are similar to those from the regression analysis.

Achieving Gains on Basic Skills Tests

To make point gains on basic skills tests in our analysis, students needed to show a gain on any of the Comprehensive Adult Student Assessment Systems (CASAS) tests, whether in reading, listening, or math. Our logistic regression estimates indicate that, on average, I-BEST students had a probability of making CASAS point gains that was 13 percentage points higher than Non-I-BEST Workforce students. We estimated that the probability of achieving a CASAS test score gain was 60 percent for I-BEST students, compared with 47 percent for Non-I-BEST Workforce students. ABE/GED I-BEST students had, on average, a probability that was 12 percentage points higher than ABE/GED Non-I-BEST Workforce students. For I-BEST and Non-I-BEST Workforce students enrolled in ESL, the respective difference was 14 percentage points.

Using PSM, we found that I-BEST students had a probability of achieving a basic skills point gain that was 17 percentage points higher than matched Non-I-BEST students. The respective probabilities for these two groups were 62 and 45 percent. Once again, the PSM and regression estimates are similar.

Conclusion

Our findings show that students participating in I-BEST achieved better educational outcomes than did those non-participating basic skills students who nonetheless enrolled in at least one workforce course in the same academic year. Using regression analysis, we found that I-BEST students were more likely than Non-I-BEST Workforce students to continue into credit-bearing coursework and to earn credits that count toward a college credential. They were more likely to persist into the second year, to earn educational awards, and to show point gains in basic skills testing. On all of the outcomes we considered, I-BEST students did better than Non-I-BEST Workforce students. Moreover, the apparent gains in educational benefits were reaped by I-BEST students who enrolled in either ABE/GED or ESL.

We also found that I-BEST participants did better on all outcomes considered compared to a group of basic skills students who were matched to the I-BEST students using propensity score matching. Using PSM, the probability that I-BEST students earned at least one college credit over the two-year tracking period was 90 percent, while the probability for the matched students was 67 percent, a 23 percentage point difference. The probability of earning an occupational certificate was 55 percent for I-BEST students, compared with only 15 percent for the matched group.

While we cannot formally compare the results from the regression and propensity score matching analyses, the fact that the two methods produced similar results increases our confidence in the robustness of the findings. Both methods account for observed differences between the treated (I-BEST) and comparison groups, but neither can control for selection bias that may be due to unobserved differences between the groups. Some of these unobserved differences are likely related to the selection process, which we only partly understand. Thus, while the results indicate that participation in I-BEST is *correlated* with better educational outcomes over the two-year tracking period, it is important to note that they do not provide definitive evidence that the I-BEST program *caused* the superior outcomes. It could be that, because of the way students were selected into the program, those who participated were more motivated or had other characteristics not measured in this study that made them more likely to succeed.

CCRC plans to conduct further research to better understand the process by which students are selected into I-BEST. CCRC will also extend this study in at least three ways: first, by examining degree attainment and labor force outcomes of I-BEST students over a longer time period; second, by collecting financial data to estimate program cost-effectiveness; and third, by examining the practices of particular I-BEST programs that produce superior outcomes.

References

Prince, D. & Jenkins, D. (2005, April). *Building pathways to success for low-skill adult students: Lessons for community college policy and practice from a longitudinal student tracking study* (CCRC Brief No. 25). New York: Columbia University, Teachers College, Community College Research Center. Available at http://ccrc.tc.columbia.edu/Publication.asp?uid=288

WSBCTC [Washington State Board for Community and Technical Colleges]. (2005). *I-BEST: A program integrating adult basic education and workforce training.* Olympia, WA: Author. Retrieved from http://www.sbctc.ctc.edu/college/d_basicskills.aspx

WSBCTC. (2008). *Increasing student achievement for basic skills students* (Research Report No. 08-1). Olympia, WA: Author. Retrieved from http://www.sbctc.ctc.edu/college/education/resh_rpt_08_1_student_achieve_basic_skills.pdf

The Accelerated Learning Program: Throwing Open the Gates

Peter Adams, Sarah Gearhart, Robert Miller, and Anne Roberts

This article is generally considered to present the definitive discussion of a particular type of acceleration. Adams, Gearhart, Miller, and Rogers describe the well-known Accelerated Learning Program at the Community College of Baltimore County. They discuss the history that led the college to seek alternative methods of teaching developmental English, describe the evolution of the program, and identify current delivery strategies used.

Historical Context

In 2001, Mary Soliday, then at CUNY's City College, observed that in the early days of open admissions at the City University of New York, two groups favored basic writing courses for quite different reasons. The first group saw such courses as paths to success, courses that would help students who were weak in writing to conform to the conventions of the academy. The second group supported basic writing for quite a different reason, seeing it as a gate to keep unqualified students out of college-level courses and, thereby, maintain standards in those courses ("Ideologies" 57–58). Bruce Horner and Min-Zhan Lu have referred to these odd bedfellows as "the binary of political activism and academic excellence" (*Representing* 14).

In the 1990s, at what was then Essex Community College and is now the Community College of Baltimore County (CCBC), Peter Adams, then coordinator of the writing program, worried about the program. He recognized that an effective basic writing program might serve as a gate for students until they were ready to succeed in first-year composition and a path to college success as soon as they were ready. But he wanted to make sure that these developmental courses were more path than gate, leading students to success rather than barring them from it.

In Adams's first attempt to evaluate the program, he used data he had been compiling on an Apple IIe computer for four years. He had entered the placement results and grades in every writing course for students assessed since Fall of 1988. Using the 863 students who took the upper-level developmental writing course, ENGL 052, in academic year 1988–1989 as the cohort he would study, Adams calculated the pass rate for ENGL 052 as well as the pass rate for students who passed that course and took first-year composition (ENGL 101) within four years. Figures 1 and 2 display these data.

Figure 1. Success Rates for Students Who Took ENGL 052 in 1988–1989

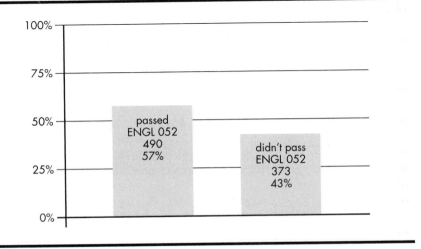

Figure 2. Success Rates for Students Who Took ENGL 101 after Passing ENGL 052 in 1988–1989

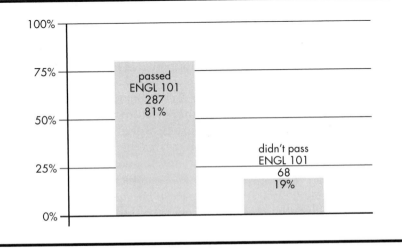

The pass rate of 57% in the developmental course didn't look too bad, and the whopping 81% pass rate in ENGL 101 was even higher than the rate for students placed directly into the college-level course. At first glance, it appeared that our basic writing course was doing a good job. In fact, developmental programs in writing, reading, and math have often pointed to such data as evidence that traditional approaches are working. As reassuring as these data looked, however, Adams worried that somehow they didn't tell the whole story, and when he undertook a more detailed, longitudinal study, he learned that his worry was justified.

Looking at success rates for one course at a time masks the true picture. When Adams looked at the longitudinal experience of students who attempted ENGL 052 and ENGL 101, he discovered an alarming situation. Two-thirds of the students who attempted ENGL 052 never passed ENGL 101. The problem was not that basic writers were attempting first-year composition and failing; the problem was that they were giving up before they ever reached that course, a fact hidden when he had simply looked at the pass rates for the small number of students who did make it into regular composition.

Figure 3 presents the number and percentage of students who passed each milestone during the four years from 1988 to 1992.

The students represented in Figure 3, like those in Figures 1 and 2, were followed for four years. When we say 57% passed ENGL 052, we mean they passed within four years, not necessarily the first time they attempted the course. A significant number took the course more than once before passing. When we say 43% didn't pass ENGL 052, we mean they didn't pass within four years; many of them attempted the course more than once.

Figure 3. Longitudinal Data on Students Who Took ENGL 052 in 1988–1989

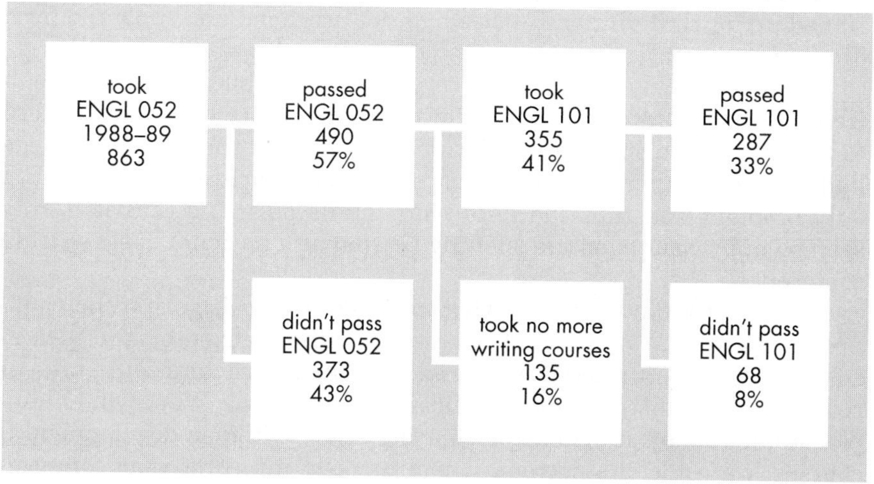

As Figure 3 reveals, instead of the 81% success rate that we saw in Figure 2, only about a third of students who began in ENGL 052 succeeded in passing ENGL 101. Our basic writing course was a path to success for only one-third of the students enrolled; for the other two-thirds, it appears to have been a locked gate.

We have come to conceptualize the situation represented in this chart as a pipeline that students must pass through to succeed. And we have concluded that the longer the pipeline, the more likely there will be "leakage" from it—in other words, the more likely students will drop out before passing first-year composition. Because the database we compiled in the early 1990s included data only for writing courses, we had no way of knowing whether these students dropped out of the college altogether, but we did know when they stopped taking writing courses. Further, since they could not achieve any degree or certificate at the college without passing ENGL 101, we knew that they didn't achieve any credential. Although our original intention in collecting these statistics was to help us enforce our placement system, we soon learned that it also helped us evaluate our writing program by allowing us to calculate the percentage of students who succeeded in passing each milestone in the program.

Then, in Fall of 1992, it became useful in another way. At that time, Peter Adams was chairing the Conference on Basic Writing (CBW), which led to his organizing the fourth national conference on basic writing, to be held at the University of Maryland in October of 1992. Things were moving along smoothly; David Bartholomae had agreed to give the keynote address, registrations were rolling in, and it looked like our carefully crafted budget was going to be adequate. And then, several weeks before the conference, Adams realized that he had a serious problem. Although the conference officially began on Friday morning, the organizers had planned an optional dinner on Thursday evening for those who arrived early . . . and more than a hundred people had signed up for that dinner. But we had not arranged nor budgeted for a dinner speaker.

Having already committed every cent in the budget, Adams realized that he would have to speak at the dinner since he couldn't afford to pay an outside speaker. He decided to report on the data his college had been collecting and analyzing on its basic writing students. The only problem was that the data were so discouraging that it hardly seemed appropriate for the opening session at a national basic writing conference.

For several days, Adams tried to think of a positive spin he could put on these data . . . without success. Finally, he fixed on the idea of suggesting some positive action basic writing instructors could take in response to the discouraging implications of the data. What would happen, Adams asked, if instead of isolating basic writers in developmental courses, we could mainstream them directly into first-year composition, while also providing appropriate support to help them succeed?

Most of Adams's talk that Thursday night was about how using a database to evaluate his college's writing program had revealed quite low success rates for the developmental program; only the last ten minutes or so were devoted to his very tentative idea that the success rate for basic writers might improve if they were "mainstreamed" into first-year composition. The lengthy and heated discussion that followed this talk was completely focused on the "mainstreaming" idea. Finally, with most of the audience still suffering from jet lag, the conference participants more or less agreed to disagree, and adjourned for the evening.

Adams knew the title of David Bartholomae's keynote address scheduled for the next morning, "The Tidy House: Basic Writing in the American Curriculum," but he had no idea what Bartholomae was actually going to talk about. As he sat in the audience listening, an odd feeling crept over him. He heard Bartholomae suggest that

> in the name of sympathy and empowerment, we have once again produced the "other" who is the incomplete version of ourselves, confirming existing patterns of power and authority, reproducing the hierarchies we had meant to question and overthrow, way back then in the 1970s. ("Tidy House" 18)

David Bartholomae, starting from a very different place, was arriving at a conclusion similar to the one suggested by Adams the evening before. At that point, Bartholomae and Adams were probably the only two people in the room who didn't think this coincidence had been carefully planned. The fact that articles representing their two talks ended up next to each other in the Spring 1993 issue of the *Journal of Basic Writing* (Bartholomae, "Tidy House"; Adams, "Basic Writing Reconsidered") only heightened everyone's assumption that they had conspired to question the essential nature of basic writing at a conference on basic writing. They hadn't, as they both insist to this day, despite the fact that few have ever believed them.

In the years since that 1992 conference, a number of institutions have adopted various versions of the mainstreaming approach that was suggested at the conference. Arizona State University, with leadership from Greg Glau, developed the well-known "stretch" model, which allows developmental students to be mainstreamed directly into first-year composition, but into a version that is "stretched out" over two semesters (*Stretch* at 10"). Quinnipiac University pioneered the "intensive" model, which has basic writers take a version of first-year composition that meets five hours a week instead of three (Segall 38–47). A few years later, Rhonda Grego and Nancy Thompson devised the "studio" approach at the University of South Carolina. In this model, students in first-year composition and sometimes other writing courses can also sign up for a one-hour-per-week studio section. There they meet with students from other classes to talk about "essays in progress" (6–14).

Many other schools developed variations on these approaches in the late 1990s and early 2000s. Our college was not one of these. Instead we endured a turbulent dozen or so years as three independent colleges were merged into one mega-college: the Community College of Baltimore County. In the process, fierce battles were fought, one chancellor received a vote of no confidence, tenure was abolished, and many faculty members devoted much of their energy to "aligning" the programs, courses, and policies of the three schools that had merged. By 2005, the worst of these struggles were over, and faculty were ready to return to more productive work. In the Fall of 2006, the English Department of the newly merged Community College of Baltimore County turned to the question of the low success rates in our basic writing courses.

In the meantime, many others were noticing the very low success rates for developmental programs nationwide. In a national study, Tom Bailey of the Community College Research Center at Columbia University found similarly alarming leakage in all developmental courses, including reading and math:

> How many students complete the sequences of developmental courses to which they are referred? The first conclusion to note is that many simply never enroll in developmental classes in the first place. In the Achieving the Dream sample, 21 percent of all students referred to developmental math education and 33 percent of students referred to developmental reading do not enroll in any developmental course within three years.
>
> Of those students referred to remediation, how many actually complete their full developmental sequences? Within three years of their initial assessment, about 42 percent of those referred to developmental reading in the Achieving the Dream sample complete their full sequence, but this accounts for two-thirds of those who actually *enroll* in at least one developmental reading course. These numbers are worse for math— only 31 percent of those referred to developmental math complete their sequence. (4–5)

In "Outcomes of Remediation," Hunter Boylan and Patrick Saxon have observed that "[a]n unknown number but perhaps as many as 40% of those taking remedial courses do not complete the courses, and consequently, do not complete remediation within one year." Reviewing large-scale studies from Minnesota, Maryland, and Texas, Boylan and Saxon conclude that "[t]he results of all these studies were fairly consistent. In summary, about 80% of those who completed remediation with a C or better passed their first college-level course in English or mathematics." Just as we at Essex Community College discovered when we began to look at longitudinal data, success rates for individual courses conceal a serious problem, for "[i]t should be noted . . . that not all of those who pass remedial courses actually took college-level courses in comparable subject areas. An Illinois study, for instance, reported that only 64% of those who completed remedial English and reading in the Fall of 1996 actually completed their first college-level courses in those subjects within a year."

So the problem we had discovered on the local level in 1992 appears to mirror similar problems nationally: too many students simply leak out of the pipeline of the required writing sequence.

Development of the Accelerated Learning Program

At an English Department meeting in January of 2007, several CCBC faculty members proposed that we pilot some form of mainstreaming to see if we could improve the success rates of our basic writing students. After considering several different models, we settled on what we now call the Accelerated Learning Program (ALP) as having the greatest potential. While we were not among the pioneering schools that developed mainstreaming approaches in the 1990s, we have benefited greatly from those programs. ALP has borrowed the best features of existing mainstreaming approaches, added some features from studios and learning communities, and developed several new features of our own.

Of course, the program we eventually developed reflected the realities of our existing approach to teaching writing. The writing sequence at CCBC includes two levels of basic writing and two levels of college composition. To graduate, students must pass any required basic writing courses and then pass two semesters of college composition, both of which are writing courses. Only the higher-level college composition course satisfies the composition graduation requirement when students transfer to most four-year schools.

Here's how ALP works. The program is available, on a voluntary basis, to all students whose placement indicates they need our upper-level basic writing course. Placement is determined at CCBC by the Accuplacer exam. Students may retest once and may also appeal by a writing sample. In addition, all sections of writing courses require students to write a diagnostic essay the first week of classes; when this essay indicates students should be in a different level course, they are advised, but not required, to move to that course.

A developmental student who volunteers for ALP registers directly for a designated section of ENGL 101, where he or she joins seven other developmental students and twelve students whose placement is ENGL 101. Apart from the inclusion of the eight ALP students, this is a regular, three-credit section of ENGL 101, meeting three hours a week for one semester. We think the fact that the basic writers are in a class with twelve students who are stronger writers, and perhaps more accomplished students, is an important feature of ALP because these 101-level students frequently serve as role models for the basic writers.

Equally important, we avoid the sometimes stigmatizing and often demoralizing effects of segregating basic writers into sections designated as just for them by fully integrating them into a college-level course and then providing additional support in the form of a second course. The eight developmental students in every ALP section of ENGL 101 also take what we call a companion course with the same instructor who teaches them in ENGL 101. In Maryland, state regulations bar the awarding of credit toward graduation for "remedial" courses; since this companion course is currently conceived of as a basic writing course (remedial, by the state's terminology), students may not receive credit for it. The companion course meets for three hours a week for one semester. In this class, which meets immediately after the 101 section, the instructor provides additional support to help the students succeed in composition. The class may begin with questions that arose in the earlier class. Other typical activities include brainstorming for the next essay in 101, reviewing drafts of a paper, or discussing common problems in finding a topic to write about. Frequently, instructors ask students to write short papers that will serve as scaffolding for the next essay or work with them on grammar or punctuation problems common to the group.

Gaining Administrative Support

After the English Department agreed it wanted to pilot ALP, meetings were set up with the Dean of Developmental Education and the Vice President for Instruction. At first, the Vice President declared the college simply could not afford to fund classes with only eight students, but a last-minute compromise was suggested: faculty could teach the companion course that met three hours a week with only eight students for two credits of load instead of three. The Vice President agreed, reluctantly. But would the faculty?

As it turns out, they did. After all, the companion course would have only eight students, and, while it would meet three hours a week, it would not really require a separate preparation. It's more like a workshop for the ENGL 101 class. Most importantly, as faculty began teaching the course, they found that ALP was often the most rewarding teaching they had ever done. As Sandra Grady, one of the earliest ALP instructors, declared at the end of the first semester, "That was the best teaching experience I've ever had," and Professor Grady has been teaching more than thirty years. All of us who have taught ALP courses have found having a class small enough so that we can get to know each student and pay attention to their individual needs provides a kind of satisfaction that is rarely possible with classes of twenty or more. Peter Adams, Robert Miller, and Anne Roberts, co-authors of this article, began teaching in that first semester, and Sarah Gearhart joined us in the second semester.

Results

As of the summer of 2009, the Community College of Baltimore County has offered thirty sections of ALP over two years to almost 240 students. The results, while preliminary, are extremely encouraging.

Figure 4. Success Rates of Students Who Took Traditional ENGL 052 in Fall 2007

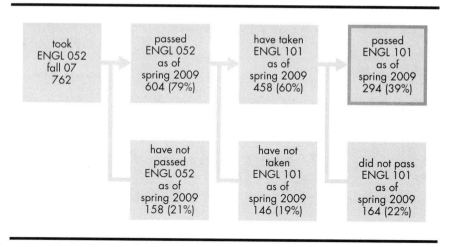

Figure 4 displays the results for a comparison group of students who took the *traditional* upper-level basic writing course in Fall of 2007. The data represent the results at the end of the Spring semester of 2009, so all of these students have had four semesters to pass their writing courses. Note that 21% of the original group have never passed ENGL 052. While it looks as though this group of students "failed" the course, in fact, many of them didn't actually "fail." For a variety of reasons, they simply gave up and stopped coming to class. Some became discouraged; others became overwhelmed. For some, events outside school demanded too much of them; for others, their personal lives required their attention. For these reasons, it would not be accurate to say that 21% failed. In addition, the 19% who passed ENGL 052 but didn't attempt ENGL 101 have clearly dropped out. This attrition rate of 40% is of great concern, as it was when we studied developmental students back in 1992.

Figure 5 presents the results for all the students who have taken ALP since the program began in Fall 2007, up to and including the Spring semester of 2009. While the first semester's cohort of 40 students has had four semesters to complete their writing courses, the remaining students have had fewer semesters. The most recent group, approximately 80 students who took ALP in Spring of 2009, has had only one semester. Despite this shorter time for most of the students, the ALP success rates are significantly higher and the drop-out rates significantly lower than for the comparison group. The boxes outlined in [dark gray] in Figures 4 and 5 show the success rates for the two groups.

Figure 5. Success Rates of Students Who Took ALP 052 from Fall 2007 to Spring 2008

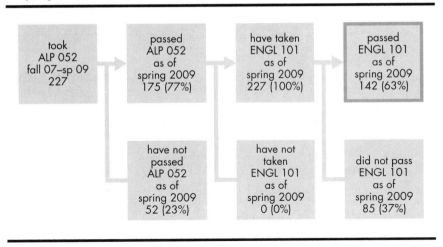

Why ALP Works

As we came to realize that ALP was producing striking improvement in student success, we began to speculate about why. What was it about ALP that contributed to those successes? We have identified eight features of ALP that we think are responsible for most of the gains in retention and success. Half of these are features we borrowed from earlier innovative programs.

Mainstreaming

Over the past fifteen years, a number of schools like Arizona State University, SUNY New Paltz, and City College (CUNY) have adopted models that mainstream basic writers into credit-bearing writing classes (see Glau; Rigolino and Freel; Soliday and Gleason). We think mainstreaming has a powerful psychological effect for basic writers. When students placed into basic writing are allowed to go immediately into first-year composition, their sense that they are excluded from the real college, that they are stigmatized as weak writers, and that they may not be "college material" is greatly reduced.

Cohort Learning

Each ALP student takes two courses, ENGL 101 and its companion course, in a cohort with seven other basic writers and the same instructor, an arrangement that owes much to the concept of learning communities. Vincent Tinto has argued that leaving college often "arises from isolation, specifically from the absence of sufficient contact between the individual [student] and other members of the social and academic communities of the college." He adds the observation that "membership in at least one supportive community, whatever its relationship to the center, may be sufficient to insure continued persistence" (55–61). As Faith Gabelnick and her co-authors have reported, learning communities, in which students take two or more courses with the same cohort of students, provide just such a community: "Learning community students value knowing other students in classes and realize an immediate sense of belonging" (67). Rebecca Mlynarczyk and Marcia Babbitt have observed similar results at Kingsborough Community College (71–89). In the ALP program, among the eight basic writers who spend six hours a week together in a cohort with the same instructor, we are finding similar increases in bonding and attachment to the college. The students begin to look out for each other in a variety of ways—calling to check on students who miss class, offering each other rides to campus, and, most importantly, helping each other to understand difficult concepts they encounter in their academic work.

Small Class Size

We have found the small class size of the companion course, only eight students, to be an essential feature of ALP. We arrived at the conclusion that the sections would have to be small by reading the work of Rhonda Grego and Nancy Thompson, who developed the concept of studios, "where a small group of students . . . meet frequently and regularly . . . to bring to the table the assignments they are working on for a writing course" (7). We knew we wanted the ALP students to comprise less than half the students in the 101 sections, where class size at our school is twenty, so we proposed a class size of eight for the companion course. We have concluded that many of the benefits of ALP derive from this small class size. Students are less prone to behavior problems when they are in a small group. The bonding mentioned earlier is more likely to occur. And the conversation can be focused on each individual's questions much more easily.

Contextual Learning

Both learning communities and studio courses credit some of their success to the fact that students are learning about writing in a meaningful context. Grego and Thompson point out that the conversations in studio sessions often explore the context for a writing assignment or for a teacher's comments on a student's essay (140–42). Similarly, learning communities, especially those that match a writing course with a "content course" such as history or psychology, tap into the advantages of contextual learning. The writing instruction seems more meaningful to the students because it is immediately applicable in the content course. In ALP, the ENGL 101 class provides a meaningful context for the work students do in the companion course. In more traditional basic writing classes, instructors frequently find themselves saying, "Now pay attention. This will be very helpful when you get to first-year composition." We don't have to say this in the ALP classes; our students are already in first-year composition. What we do in the companion course is immediately useful in the essays the students are writing in ENGL 101.

Acceleration

In the longitudinal studies we conducted, we discovered that many students never completed the sequence of required writing courses because they gave up at some point in the process. And the longer the course sequence, the more opportunities there are for such "giving up." Most startling to us was the nearly 20% of our students who actually passed the traditional basic writing course, but then gave up without ever even attempting ENGL 101. We have concluded that the longer the "pipeline" through which our basic writers must move before completing their writing sequence, the greater the chances they will give up and "leak" out of the pipeline. ALP shortens the pipeline for basic writers by allowing them to take their developmental writing and first-year composition courses in the same semester. This acceleration is one of the features we developed at the Community College of Baltimore County.

Heterogeneous Grouping

Another feature of ALP that was developed by CCBC is heterogeneous grouping. In most of the earlier mainstreaming models, basic writers were placed in first-year composition, but in sections populated only by other basic writers. Each group of eight ALP students takes ENGL 101 in a section with twelve 101-level writers who can serve as role models both for writing and for successful student behavior. We also find that the stigmatizing and demoralizing effects of placement in a course designed just for basic writers are greatly reduced by this feature.

Attention to Behavioral Issues

A third locally developed feature of ALP is our conscious and deliberate attention to behavioral issues. We believe that not understanding the kinds of behavior that lead to success in college is a major factor in some basic writers' lack of success. We work hard to help our students understand the type of behavior that will maximize their chances for success in college. For example, many of our basic writers have taken on more responsibilities than they can possibly fulfill. We ask students to create a timeline that accounts for everything they must do in a given week, an exercise that sometimes leads them to make changes in their lives to increase their chances for success. Some students discover they need to cut back on their hours at work; others realize that they have registered for too many courses.

Behavioral problems often result from attitudinal problems. In class we talk about what we call the "high school attitude" toward education: the attitude that it isn't "cool" to appear interested in class, to be seen taking notes or raising one's hand to answer a question. Using humor and sometimes even a little mockery, we lead students to realize that the "high school attitude" toward "coolness" isn't "cool" in college.

And then there are the recurring problems with cell phones and Facebook, with arriving late or falling asleep, with not buying the required text or not completing the required assignment. ALP instructors are aware that these kinds of issues will need more conscious attention, and the small class size makes such attention possible.

Attention to Life Problems

A fourth feature of ALP we developed at CCBC is to encourage instructors to pay deliberate attention to problems in the students' lives outside of school. Many students who give up on our courses do so, not because of any difficulty with the material in the course but, primarily, because of circumstances in their lives outside of college. They are evicted from their apartment, their children become ill, their boss insists they work more hours, they find themselves in abusive relationships, or they experience some other overwhelming life problem. ALP faculty recognize the need to address these life issues. They find time to ask students how their lives are going. They frequently refer students to sources of outside support for such concerns as financial aid, health issues, family problems, and legal problems. When several students in the same class have a similar problem, instead of sending them to see an advisor, we have the advisor visit the class. We have assembled a roster of resource people who are willing to visit our classes and work with students on life problems.

Costs

Regardless of its success rates, ALP may appear to be prohibitively expensive, as our Vice President for Instruction had initially thought. But careful analysis reveals that ALP actually costs less per *successful student* than more traditional approaches.

To see how this could be the case, consider a hypothetical group of 1,000 students who show up in September needing developmental writing. Under the traditional model, we would need to run 50 sections of basic writing to accommodate them (our class size for writing courses is 20). Since the actual cost of these 50 sections would vary depending on the salary levels of the instructors, we'll make this calculation in terms of faculty credit hours (FCHs). Since faculty are compensated with 3 FCHs for teaching our upper-level basic writing course, the cost for those 1,000 students would be 150 FCHs.

Because only 60% of students taking our traditional upper-level basic writing course ever take ENGL 101, we would need to accommodate just 600 students in ENGL 101, which would require 30 sections. At 3 FCHs per section, the ENGL 101 costs for 1,000 students would be 90 FCHs, and the total for ENGL 052 and 101 would be 240 FCHs.

To accommodate those same 1,000 students in an ALP program would require 125 sections (class size for the ALP classes is 8). Because of the small class size and because the companion course is not really a separate preparation, faculty receive 2, not 3, FCHs for a section of the companion course. The 125 sections would therefore cost the college 250 FCHs.

Since all 1,000 students would take ENGL 101, we would need 50 sections to accommodate all 1,000 students. At 3 FCHs per section, the 101 portion of the ALP program would cost 150 FCHs, and so the total cost for the ALP model would be 400 FCHs.

Before deciding which model is more expensive, however, it is not enough to consider just the costs; it is also necessary to consider the outcomes. Under the traditional model, 39%, or 390 students, will pass ENGL 101. Under ALP, 63%, or 630 students, will pass ENGL 101. As a result, the cost *per successful student* for the traditional model (390 students divided by 240 FCHs) would be 1.625 FCHs. For the ALP model, the cost (630 students divided by 400 FCHs) would be 1.575 FCHs per successful student. ALP actually costs less per successful student than the traditional model.

In sum, for basic writers, ALP doubles the success rate, halves the attrition rate, does it in half the time (one semester instead of two), and costs slightly less per successful student. When these data are presented to administrators, the case for adopting the ALP model is compelling.

Plans for the Future

ALP has produced very promising results. For each of the past four semesters, it has resulted in success rates at least double those for our traditional basic writing course. Having achieved these preliminary successes, our plans for the future include continued and expanded study of the program, improvements in the program to make it even more effective, scaling up of ALP at CCBC to 40 sections per semester in Fall 2011, and to approximately 70 sections per semester in Fall 2011, and dissemination of ALP to other colleges.

First, we want to insure the validity of our preliminary data, which has indicated such dramatic improvement in success rates for ALP students over students in the traditional program. We are concerned about two possible threats to the validity of that data: the possibility that students who volunteer for ALP are not representative of developmental writing students at CCBC, and the possibility of instructor bias in grading the ALP students in ENGL 101.

To address the possibility that students who volunteer for ALP are not a representative sample, we have formed a partnership with the Community College Research Center at Columbia University. CCRC is conducting multivariate analyses of the effects of participating in ALP on student pass rates in English 101 as well as on other measures, including rates of persistence and passing college-level courses in subjects other than English. This study will make use of "matched pairs," selecting a student who has taken the traditional ENGL 052 to be matched with an ALP student on eleven variables: race, gender, age, financial aid status, full- or part-time status, prior college credits, grades in prior college courses, placement scores, program, high school attended, and high school diploma status.

We are also concerned about the possibility of unconscious instructor bias in favor of the ALP students. The English Department has developed rubrics that describe a passing essay for the basic writing course and for ENGL 101. However, considering the close relationships that naturally develop between ALP faculty and the eight ALP students with whom they meet for six hours a week, it is possible that occasionally instructors unconsciously pass an ALP student in ENGL 101 whose performance was slightly below passing level. To investigate this possible bias, we will be following the ALP students into ENGL 102, the next course in the writing sequence, comparing their performance there with that of students who took traditional ENGL 052. ENGL 102 instructors will not have formed any kind of bond with the students and, in fact, will not even know that they were in ALP.

Also, we will be conducting a blind, holistic scoring of essays from ENGL 101 classes to compare the quality of the writing of ALP students who passed the course with the quality of the writing of 101-level students. If we determine through this study that some ALP students are being passed in ENGL 101 even though their performance is below the passing level, we will investigate other ways of making the pass/fail decision for these sections. We may, for example, decide to have final portfolios graded by someone other than the student's own instructor.

In addition to investigating any threats to the validity of our data on success rates of ALP students in ENGL 101, we will be investigating whether higher percentages of ALP students, compared to students who take the traditional basic writing course, continue to reach various milestones such as accumulating 15, 30, and 45 credits, one-year persistence, completion of certificate and degree programs, and successful transfer to four-year institutions.

Finally, we want to attempt to understand exactly what it is about ALP that leads to its successes and which features contribute most to the improved performance of ALP students. Using pre- and post-semester surveys, focus groups, and faculty reports, we will attempt to determine which of the eight features of ALP contribute most to student success.

We are fairly confident ALP works well in our context, so we look forward to learning if it works as well in at other colleges. To this end, we organized a conference on acceleration in June of 2009. Forty-one faculty from twenty-one different schools attended. After a spirited two-day conversation with lots of give and take and very good questions from participants, four schools agreed to pilot ALP on their campuses in the coming year: CUNY's Kingsborough Community College (New York), El Paso Community College (Texas), Patrick Henry Community College (Virginia), and Gateway Technical and Community College (Kentucky). We eagerly await their results. In addition, we are hopeful that other schools will adopt the ALP model in coming years. On June 23–25, 2010, we will be holding an expanded version of the Conference on Acceleration at CCBC.

ALP has benefited greatly from the work our colleagues at other institutions have done since that Conference on Basic Writing back in 1992. We have developed a model for developmental writing that shows great promise, and we are certain that others will improve on our model in coming years.

We are also convinced that this work is extremely important given the present climate for higher education. The country has begun to pay attention to basic writing and developmental education more broadly in ways both negative and positive. There is a growing realization that the programs we began so hopefully during those early days of open admissions have not performed nearly as well as we had hoped. Some would conclude from these low success rates that our budgets should be reduced or even that our programs should be eliminated. Susanmarie Harrington and Linda Adler-Kassner observe that we are working in "an educational environment in which basic writing and remedial programs are under attack" (8). Mary Soliday points out that "Outside the academy, critics of remediation waved the red flag of declining standards and literacy crisis to justify the need to downsize, privatize, and effectively restratify higher education. By blaming remedial programs for a constellation of educational woes, from budget crisis to low retention rates and falling standards, the critics of remediation practiced an effective politics of agency." That is, they attributed the blame for these growing problems to the developmental students and "the 'expensive' programs designed to meet their 'special' needs" (*Politics of Remediation* 106). In 2005, Bridget Terry Long, writing in *National CrossTalk*, observed that "this debate about the merits of investing in remediation, which has an estimated annual cost in the billions, has intensified in recent years. There are many questions about whether remediation should be offered in colleges at all." Long goes on to take a close look at how we determine the success of "remedial" programs and to demonstrate that with appropriate measures—comparing students with similar economic and educational backgrounds—remedial programs do indeed seem to help students do better in college.

Despite the positive implications of more nuanced research such as that conducted by Long, the criticism of basic writing programs is not likely to diminish in the near future. And in the field of basic writing itself the realization that many basic writing programs are falling short of the kind of results we had hoped for in the early days—a realization that first surfaced at the basic writing conference in Baltimore in 1992—is leading to the development of improved and innovative programs. In "Challenge and Opportunity: Rethinking the Role and Function of Developmental Education in the Community College," Tom Bailey notes that there has been "a dramatic expansion in experimentation with new approaches." Major funding agencies, both governmental and non-governmental, are beginning to see developmental education as an area of interest. However, if we are not able to improve our success rates, if we continue to serve as a gate, barring large numbers of students from receiving a college education, those who argue for a reduction or elimination of basic writing could prevail. That is why it is so important at this crucial time that we look for ways to make basic writing more effective. The very survival of our programs could be at stake. But there is an even more important reason for continuing to improve our effectiveness: the success of our programs is of life-changing importance to our students.

References

Adams, Peter. "Basic Writing Reconsidered." *Journal of Basic Writing* 12.1 (1993): 22–36. Print.

Bailey, Thomas. "Challenge and Opportunity: Rethinking the Role and Function of Developmental Education in the Community College." *New Directions for Community Colleges* (2009): 11–30. Web. 30 July 2009.

Bartholomae, David. "The Tidy House: Basic Writing in the American Curriculum." *Journal of Basic Writing* 12.1 (1993): 4–21. Print.

Boylan, Hunter R., and D. Patrick Saxon. "Outcomes of Remediation." League for Innovation. Web. 30 July 2009.

Gabelnick, Faith, Jean MacGregor, Roberta S. Matthews, and Barbara Leigh Smith. *Learning Communities: Creating Connections Among Students, Faculty, and Disciplines.* New Directions for Teaching and Learning. San Francisco: Jossey-Bass, 1990. Print.

Glau, Greg. "*Stretch* at 10: A Progress Report on Arizona State University's *Stretch Program*." *Journal of Basic Writing* 26.2 (2007): 30–48. Print.

Grego, Rhonda, and Nancy Thompson. *Teaching/Writing in Third Spaces.* Carbondale, IL: Southern Illinois UP, 2008. Print.

Harrington, Susanmarie, and Linda Adler-Kassner. "The Dilemma that Still Counts: Basic Writing at a Political Crossroads." *Journal of Basic Writing* 17.2 (1998): 3–24. Print.

Horner, Bruce, and Min-Zhan Lu. *Representing the "Other": Basic Writers and the Teaching of Basic Writing.* Urbana, IL: NCTE, 1999. Print.

Long, Bridget Terry. "The Remediation Debate: Are We Serving the Needs of Underprepared College Students?" *National CrossTalk.* The National Center for Public Policy and Higher Education, Fall 2005. Web. 20 Dec. 2009.

Mlynarczyk, Rebecca Williams, and Marcia Babbitt. "The Power of Academic Learning Communities." *Journal of Basic Writing* 21.1 (2002): 71–89. Print.

Rigolino, Rachel, and Penny Freel. "Re-Modeling Basic Writing." *Journal of Basic Writing* 26.2 (2007): 49–72. Print.

Segall, Mary T. "Embracing a Porcupine: Redesigning a Writing Program." *Journal of Basic Writing* 14.2 (1995): 38–47. Print.

Soliday, Mary. "Ideologies of Access and the Politics of Agency." *Mainstreaming Basic Writers: Politics and Pedagogies of Access.* Ed. Gerry McNenny and Sallyanne Fitzgerald. Mahwah, NJ: Erlbaum, 2001. 55–72. Print.

———. *The Politics of Remediation: Institutional and Student Needs in Higher Education.* Pittsburgh: U of Pittsburgh P, 2002. Print.

Soliday, Mary, and Barbara Gleason. "From Remediation to Enrichment: Evaluating a Mainstreaming Project." *Journal of Basic Writing* 16.1 (1997): 64–78. Print.

Tinto, Vincent. *Leaving College: Understanding the Causes and Cures of Student Attrition.* Chicago: U of Chicago P, 1986. Print.

Bridging the Gap: An Impact Study of Eight Developmental Summer Bridge Programs in Texas

Elisabeth A. Barnett, Rachel Hare Bork,
Alexander K. Mayer, Joshua Pretlow,
Heather D. Wathington, and Madeline Joy Weiss

Although summer bridge programs have been present in colleges and universities since at least the 1960s, this report represents the first large-scale empirical study of their efficacy. Elisabeth Barnett and her colleagues describe a project among eight Texas community colleges to implement and evaluate summer bridge programs as a means of facilitating transition to college. The summary addresses program designs and reports on their impact, suggesting that such programs have a modest positive effect.

Across the country, a growing number of recent high school graduates are participating in summer bridge programs. These programs provide accelerated and focused learning opportunities in order to help students acquire the knowledge and skills needed for college success. The state of Texas has given particular attention to summer programs as a way to increase students' college readiness. During the past several years, the Texas Higher Education Coordinating Board (THECB) has provided support to colleges establishing developmental summer bridge programs offering intensive remedial instruction in math, reading, and/or writing, along with an introduction to college. In contrast with traditional developmental education course sequences, which may span several semesters, the summer bridge programs were designed to help underprepared students build competencies over the course of several weeks before entering college.

While THECB funding for summer bridge programs has diminished, this type of program model remains popular in Texas and across the country. Nevertheless, little rigorous empirical research has been conducted on the effectiveness of summer bridge programs (Ackermann, 1990; Garcia, 1991; Myers & Drevlow, 1982; Santa Rita & Bacote, 1997). To address this gap in the research, in 2009 the National Center for Postsecondary Research (NCPR) launched an evaluation of summer bridge programs at eight sites in Texas to assess whether they reduce the need for developmental coursework upon fall matriculation and improve student outcomes in college.

The Developmental Summer Bridge Programs

The developmental summer bridge programs in this study were offered in the summer of 2009, primarily to recent high school graduates, at eight institutions of higher education—two open-admissions four-year institutions and six community colleges. Students attended the developmental summer bridge programs for three to six hours daily for four to five weeks and received instruction in at least one area of academic need—math, reading, or writing—and guidance in the "college knowledge" needed to navigate new academic terrain. All of the developmental summer bridge programs included four common features: accelerated instruction in math, reading, and/or writing; academic support; a college knowledge component; and the opportunity to earn a $400 stipend.[1]

The Research

The evaluation employed an experimental design to measure the effects of the programs on college enrollment and success. At each college, students who consented to participate in the study were randomly assigned to either a program group that was eligible to participate in a developmental summer bridge program or a control group that was eligible to use any services that the college provided other than the summer bridge programs. Random assignment creates two groups that are similar on all characteristics, including those that can be measured, such as age or academic attainment, and those that are more difficult to measure, such as motivation. This ensures that any differences in observed outcomes—called *impacts*—can be attributed to participation in the developmental summer bridge programs.

Eligible students who applied for admission into a developmental summer bridge program and agreed to participate in the study were included in the research sample. After consenting to participate and completing a baseline intake form, these students were randomly assigned to either the program group or the control group. About 60 percent of the students were assigned to the program group and given the opportunity to take one of the available slots in the summer bridge program (793 students), while about 40 percent were assigned to the control group and were able to participate in other college services but were not admitted to the program itself (525 students). Students in both groups consented to have their outcomes tracked for two full academic years.

NCPR collected and analyzed academic outcome data through the spring semester of 2011 for both program and control group students. This report presents the impact findings of the study, revealing whether the opportunity to participate in a summer bridge program influenced academic outcomes during the two years following participation. The primary outcomes tracked in this study were persistence, accumulation of credits, and progression through the developmental sequence and into students' first college-level math, reading, and writing courses.

Main Findings

After two years of follow-up, these are the main findings of this study:

- The programs had no effect on the average number of credits attempted or earned. Program group and control group students attempted the same number of credits (30.3). Students in the program group earned an average of 19.4 credits, and students in the control group earned an average of 19.9 credits; the difference in their outcomes is not statistically significant.

- The programs had an impact on first college-level course completion in math and writing that was evident in the year and a half following the program but no impact on first college-level course completion in reading during this same period. On average, students in the program group passed their first college-level math and writing courses at higher rates than students in the control group during this period. By the end of the two-year follow-up period, however, the differences between the two groups are no longer statistically significant.

- There is no evidence that the programs impacted persistence. During the two-year follow-up period, students in the program group enrolled in an average of 3.3 semesters, and students in the control group enrolled in an average of 3.4 semesters, a difference that is not statistically significant.

Program Costs

NCPR performed an analysis of the cost of the developmental summer bridge program. The sites varied in terms of program duration, intensity, and enrollment, and total costs to run the program during the summer of 2009 ranged from \$62,633 to \$296,033. Across the eight sites, per student costs ranged from \$835 to \$2,349. The average cost per student across all eight sites was \$1,319 (with a standard deviation of \$502).[2]

We also calculated the college-level credit accumulation that the developmental summer bridge programs would have had to produce in order to be cost effective on this outcome measure. Specifically, we considered how many additional college credits a developmental summer bridge program student would need to earn to justify the cost of the program. In order to do this, we assigned a monetary cost of \$338 to college credits earned, based on the typical cost of providing these credits in Texas.[3] The program group would have had to earn an additional 3.8 college-level credits on average for the program to justify its costs or "break even."

Implications

The findings in this report suggest that the developmental summer bridge programs contributed to positive outcomes in college-level course completion in math and writing that were evident during the first year and a half after program completion. However, the programs did not lead to increases in persistence or overall credit completion, raising the question of whether our theory of change and the changes in measured outcomes that we hypothesized were reasonable were too ambitious. It may be that we should not expect to find long-term impacts on credit accumulation and persistence from a short, intensive summer program. First-year developmental education students may need further support for greater impacts to be achieved.

In addition, our research suggests that accelerating students' completion of introductory college-level courses in math or English may not lead to the accumulation of more college credits overall. If the ultimate goal is college credential attainment, and credit accumulation indicates progress toward attaining a credential, improving academic preparedness through developmental summer bridge programs or other similar programs may not adequately promote attainment of this goal. Policymakers and practitioners concerned with college completion may want to consider approaches that go further in assisting students in ongoing credit accumulation and credential attainment.

Finally, our break-even cost analysis suggests that students in the developmental summer bridge programs would need to have earned an average of almost four additional college credits to justify the cost of the program (courses are typically worth three credits). Given that no impact on credit accumulation was found, college practitioners and policymakers may reasonably view the programs as expensive. Educators may want to consider if there are ways to reduce costs by embedding support programs such as these into the regular high school or college schedule.

Concluding Thoughts

Similar to other innovative developmental education programs that have been rigorously evaluated,[4] the developmental summer bridge programs studied here were found to have modest positive impacts in the short term. What is clear from this study and other developmental education research is that simple, short-term interventions yielding strong, long-term effects are difficult to find. With this in mind, we offer two suggestions for advancing the work of supporting underprepared students: (1) introducing new partnerships between high schools and colleges that reduce the need for remediation in college and (2) providing more support and transitional experiences to help students reach and sustain attainment goals. Because educational attainment is the result of a long process influenced by many factors, providing supports to students that span their years in high school and college may help them to develop the skills and knowledge required for postsecondary success.

Notes

1. For more information on the implementation of the programs, see Wathington et al. (2011).
2. Some costs may be interpreted as "start-up" costs, which are unlikely to be needed if the programs are run in subsequent years. If these costs are amortized over three years, then the average cost of the programs is reduced. In addition, this figure includes the student stipend of up to $400 per participant.
3. This is the average of the expenditure per credit across seven of the eight colleges based on Integrated Postsecondary Education Data System (IPEDS) data of expenditures per FTE (2008 data uprated to 2011 dollars). Expenditures per FTE are adjusted to capture expenditures per credit attempted. One college did not have available IPEDS data.
4. See, for example, findings from NCPR's Learning Communities Demonstration (Visher, Weiss, Weissman, Rudd, & Wathington, 2012).

References

Ackermann, S. P. (1990, April). *The benefits of summer bridge programs for underrepresented and low-income students.* Paper presented at the annual meeting of the American Education Research Association, Boston, MA.

Garcia, P. (1991). Summer bridge: Improving retention rates for underprepared students. *Journal of the Freshman Year Experience, 3*(2), 91–105.

Myers, C., & Drevlow, S. (1982, March). *Summer bridge program: A dropout intervention program for minority and low-income students at the University of California, San Diego.* Paper presented at the annual meeting of the American Education Research Association, New York, NY.

Santa Rita, E., & Bacote, J. B. (1997). The benefits of college discovery prefreshman summer program for minority and low-income students. *College Student Journal, 31*(2), 161–173.

Visher, M. G., Weiss, M. J., Weissman, E., Rudd, T., & Wathington, H. D. (with Teres, J., & Fong, K.). (2012). *The effects of learning communities for students in developmental education: A synthesis of findings from six colleges.* New York, NY: National Center for Postsecondary Research.

Wathington, H. D., Barnett, E. A., Weissman, E., Teres, J., Pretlow, J., & Nakanishi, A. (with Zeidenberg, M., Weiss, M. J., Black, A., Mitchell, C., & Watchen, J.). (2011). *Getting ready for college: An implementation and early impacts study of eight Texas developmental summer bridge programs.* New York, NY: National Center for Postsecondary Research.

Targeted Intervention for Developmental Education Students (T.I.D.E.S.)

Hunter R. Boylan

This article describes a systematic approach to assessment, placement, instruction, and support services based on improving placement through the use of noncognitive measures. It argues for increased use of noncognitive and student personal information to develop and implement individual learning plans for underprepared students. The article also includes an extensive list of noncognitive assessment instruments that may be used in developmental programs.

Each year over 2,000,000 students enroll in developmental education courses in U.S. colleges and universities (Saxon, Sullivan, Boylan, & Forrest, 2005). Most of these students are placed in developmental courses as a result of their scores on a single cognitive assessment instrument which is used as the basis for academic advising (Gerlaugh, Thompson, Boylan, & Davis, 2007). According to a recent report from the National Center for Education Statistics (2003), most colleges report that it takes students about a year to complete their developmental education requirements.

This means that at a time when the costs of participating in postsecondary education are increasing, a very large number of undergraduates must stay in school longer and pay more in order to complete developmental course requirements. Time in developmental education is well spent for many of these students. They complete their developmental courses quickly, and their participation enables them to develop the skills necessary for success in later college-level courses. For others, their time in developmental education is fraught with the frustration of either taking courses they do not really need or failing these courses and having to repeat them. It is possible, however, that an unknown number of the students taking these courses might either bypass them entirely or require more than coursework alone to be successful.

Students who score just under the cut score in a particular skill area might be able to bypass the developmental course in that subject, go directly into the college-level course in that subject, and be successful if they had the right kind of learning assistance services. Others at the lower end of the score distribution might need not only one or more developmental courses but also require a variety of additional learning assistance services in order to be successful. Unfortunately, conclusive research is not available regarding which students might profit from any particular combination of courses and services. A contributing factor is the lack of sufficient assessment data from enough sources to provide adequate advising information and appropriate placement for developmental students.

In U.S. colleges and universities, the assessment instruments used most widely to gather information for placement in developmental courses are ACCUPLACER™ and COMPASS® (Gerlaugh, Thompson, Boylan, & Davis, 2007). ACCUPLACER is published by the College Board and COMPASS is published by ACT. Both are computer-adaptive instruments which adjust the difficulty of follow-up questions based on students' responses to the previous question. This assessment technology is designed to provide an accurate measure of how much a given student knows about a particular area such as reading, English, or mathematics. Because such assessment instruments measure students' cognitive abilities, they are referred to as cognitive instruments.

As accurate as these instruments may be in assessing cognitive skills, however, they do not measure other factors that are equally important to student success. These factors include such things as attitude toward learning, motivation, autonomy, willingness to seek and accept help, desire to affiliate with peers or instructors, or willingness to expend effort on academic tasks (Sedlacek, 2004). These factors are generally referred to as noncognitive or affective characteristics because they measure how students feel or what they believe about themselves and learning (Bloom, 1976). Most college and university instructors would agree that these factors are as essential to success in college as are cognitive skills. In fact, Bloom (1976) estimates that at least 25% of how well a student performs in a particular course is related to affective factors. Sedlacek (2004) argues that the weaker a student's cognitive skills, the more important other affective factors in student success.

In addition to cognitive and affective factors, a variety of personal factors also influence students' likelihood of success in college. These factors would include information such as the number of hours students are employed per week, their eligibility for financial aid, the extent to which students have other adult responsibilities such as child care, or whether or not they are native speakers of English (Long, 2008; McCabe, 2003). Such factors influence the amount of time and attention students have available to attend courses, do homework, and study.

It is reasonable to assume that placement of developmental students could be improved if colleges and universities utilized multiple variables in assessing and advising their incoming students. In fact, Martha Maxwell (1997) has argued that colleges and universities should take a much greater and more varied amount of information into account when placing students into courses. McCabe (2003) argues that multiple variables such as cognitive and affective information should be used in the placement process for developmental students because they complement each other and allow the institution to view students holistically. However, a recent survey of community college developmental programs indicated that only 7% collect both cognitive and affective information on their students for placement purposes (Gerlaugh et al., 2007). A similar survey has not been conducted for universities; information regarding how many colleges and universities may use students' personal information to make placement decisions is also unavailable.

It is also reasonable to assume that advising and placement decisions could be improved if advisors were able to use a combination of cognitive, affective, and personal information about students to develop more integrated intervention plans for underprepared students. This is particularly true if these plans took advantage of and were based upon the variety of both developmental courses and learning assistance services available on their campuses (Muraskin & Lee, 2004).

This article proposes and describes an innovative model for using a combination of cognitive, affective, and personal information to target a variety of course-based and learning assistance–based interventions for developmental students. It is grounded in the theoretical work of several scholars of adult development and learning, most notably Arthur Chickering, Erik Erikson, and other more contemporary scholars. Most developmental theorists, for instance, argue that human beings develop as a result of some interaction between themselves and their environment and that the greater the variety of experiences within the environment the more development is likely to take place (Fischer, 1980; King & Kitchener, 1994). The model presented here expands the range of interventions and subsequent experiences of developmental students in a collegial environment.

In his classic work, *Education and Identity*, Chickering (1969) proposed that in order to be successful adults and/or college students it was necessary for individuals to develop in seven critical areas which he referred to as "vectors." Chickering proposed that academic coursework promoted individual development along many of these vectors and that experiences, such as belonging to clubs or participating in community service, promoted development in others.

Erikson (1968) postulated that the passage from youth to adulthood is marked by development of individual identity. In Erikson's view, this identity development is promoted through opportunities available in college to clarify interests, skills, and attitudes; experiment with different roles; make choices; experience achievement; overcome anxiety; and engage in reflection and introspection.

Both Chickering and Erikson agree that the college experience provides extremely fertile ground for individual development. The collegiate experience offers an array of coursework, interaction with peers and instructors, as well as extracurricular programs and opportunities that contribute to student academic and personal development. These experiences could be of great value to developmental students, who may be delayed in their individual development. Unfortunately, most postsecondary institutions have not organized their assessment, advising, and placement processes in such a way as to promote maximum individual development, either academic or personal. The model proposed here organizes the assessment, advising, and placement process in a manner designed to promote the greatest amount of development for at-risk and underprepared college students. It does this by guiding students to participate in a variety of interventions designed to promote cognitive and affective development along with practical, real-world support.

The model is referred to as Targeted Interventions for Developmental Education Students or "T.I.D.E.S." because it uses an expanded database—including cognitive, affective, and personal information—that enables academic advisors to specifically target appropriate interventions for students. Using this model, some students who currently place into developmental courses may be exempted from them whereas others may receive more intense and precisely focused interventions.

The T.I.D.E.S. Model

The basic method of T.I.D.E.S. is to gather a variety of assessment information to help academic advisors not only place students in courses but also place them in experiences that will either supplement or replace developmental courses. In order to implement the T.I.D.E.S. model several steps must be taken. These steps include the following:

- taking an inventory of available campus and community courses and services,

- developing student profiles to determine the types of services that might be helpful to students with various characteristics,

- assessing individual students' skills and characteristics,

- advising students using this assessment information to plan interventions,

- delivering targeted interventions according to the plan,

- monitoring students and evaluating their progress, and

- revising the targeted interventions as necessary (see Figure 1).

Figure 1. Diagram outlining various steps and details of the Targeted Interventions for Developmental Education Students model.

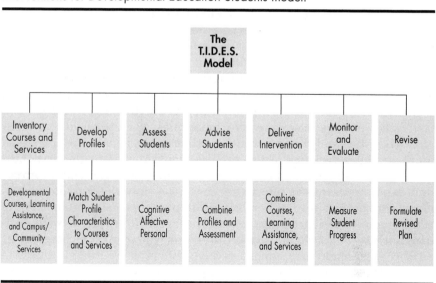

Taking Inventory

Several researchers have pointed out that the availability of comprehensive learning assistance and support services contributes to the success of underprepared college students (Kiemig, 1983; McCabe, 2000; Schwartz & Jenkins, 2007). The first step in the T.I.D.E.S. model, therefore, is to take an inventory of the courses, learning assistance, and other campus services available to students at a particular institution. This list might include such things as the number of levels and content of developmental courses and available services such as tutoring, counseling, Supplemental Instruction, learning communities, freshman seminars, student success courses, short-term workshops, and peer or professional mentoring.

This inventory might also include a more diverse or far-reaching range of campus or community services such as occupational assessment, child care, job counseling and placement, crisis intervention, or spiritual advising. In conducting this inventory, it is important to view the entire campus as well as community service agencies as potential providers of support for students, thus increasing the comprehensiveness of service options available to students.

Once this inventory has been completed, a list of courses and services available to students can be developed. It should describe the services and provide contact information that may be used by advisors and students. This list represents the available interventions that might be targeted to assist students on a particular campus and through local community service agencies. Developing this list and keeping it updated is critical to the success of the model because the list forms the basis for the provision of a comprehensive set of courses and services to students based on their individual characteristics.

Developing Student Profiles

Developing profiles of student types involves analyzing students' cognitive, affective, and personal characteristics and matching them to the available courses and services identified in the inventory process. Initially, this process would involve some guesswork regarding student characteristics and the interventions that might be appropriate based on these characteristics. These profiles would represent the first "best guesses" of developmental educators as to what combinations of courses and experiences might effectively meet the needs of individual students. The profiles would then be used to plan the best combinations of courses and experiences that might be targeted to students with various characteristics. Not only would students who score at various points on the assessment instrument receive different treatments but students with similar cognitive scores might also be assigned to very different courses and experiences depending on the affective characteristics of their profile. Consider the following examples.

Janice is an 18-year-old African-American student who recently graduated from high school with a 3.2 GPA. Her cognitive assessment indicates that she missed placing into college algebra (first college-level course at her community college) by five points. Her affective assessment indicates that she is highly motivated, seeks help willingly, and uses good study strategies. Her personal information indicates that she works only 10 hours a week, has no children, and is living at home with her parents. It might be that such a student could enroll in college algebra and be successful if she also had regular tutoring for college algebra.

Roberto is a 26-year-old Hispanic student who has just been released from active military service and is attending the local community college. He, too, missed the cut score for placement into college algebra by five points. His affective assessment indicates that he is highly motivated and well disciplined. His personal information indicates that he is married, has one child, and works 20 hours a week. Because he is well disciplined and motivated but has been out of high school for 8 years, it might be that he could take an "accelerated" 5-week developmental mathematics course online and obtain the preparation he needs rather than having to spend 16 weeks in developmental mathematics. A T.I.D.E.S. advisor might check Roberto's high school algebra grades to further inform his potential placement in an intensive algebra preparation section.

Joseph is a 22-year-old white student who dropped out of high school, went to work in a local textile mill when he was 18, and completed his GED when he was 19. He was laid off when the textile mill closed and has now returned to college to retrain. He, too, missed the cut score for placement into college algebra by five points. His affective assessment information indicates that he has low motivation, poor study skills, a negative attitude about education, and anxiety about returning to school. His personal information indicates that he is married, has three children, and is working part-time for 10 hours per week. It might be hypothesized that Joseph could best be placed in a developmental mathematics course in a learning community and receive regular counseling to facilitate his adjustment to college.

In order to implement the T.I.D.E.S. model, developmental educators and academic advisors would work together to use a series of profiles and hypothetical responses such as these as a guide to planning advisement and placement of students. Academic advisors would then use the combination of students' profiles and hypothetical responses as guidelines to place individual students into a variety of courses and experiences more accurately tailored to their academic needs and characteristics. Although no one has yet implemented this model in its entirety, research by Jenkins (2006) and Muraskin and Lee (2004) indicates that such planned advising and integrated interventions should contribute to improved academic performance on the part of underprepared students.

Assessing Students

Researchers in the field agree that mandatory assessment is a characteristic of successful developmental programs (McCabe, 2000; Morante, 1989; Roueche & Roueche, 1999). One of the keys to successfully implementing the T.I.D.E.S. model is strengthening the accuracy of assessment by using multiple variables to triangulate cognitive, affective, and personal; this approach yields a more meaningful and balanced student profile. Appropriate student profiles cannot be developed unless assessment activities include the collection of all three types of information.

Practically all colleges and universities in the United States conduct cognitive assessment of incoming students (National Center for Education Statistics, 2003). Many of these institutions also collect personal information about students as part of the assessment and advising process (Gerlaugh et al., 2007). As noted earlier, however, few also use affective measures in the assessment, advising, and placement process.

Fortunately, most of the computer-adaptive cognitive assessment instruments used by colleges and universities also allow institutions to include additional questions or instruments as part of the assessment battery. This feature permits institutions to gather additional affective and personal information during the initial assessment process in a cost-effective manner.

There are a variety of affective assessment measures available that might be included in the initial computerized assessment process. Most of these instruments are computer scored and would add only 30 to 45 minutes to the initial assessment process. Such measures provide information on a range of affective characteristics such as motivation, attitude toward learning, help-seeking behavior, autonomy, anxiety, desire for peer or instructor affiliation, self-efficacy, and/or willingness to expend effort on academic tasks.

Within the guidelines of students' right to privacy, additional personal information may be obtained from application information, questions included in the initial assessment process, or questions asked by academic advisors during the advising process. Through these methods, additional information on students—such as number of hours of employment, family responsibilities, or military status—can be obtained, and this information will increase the precision of the assessment process.

Advising Students

There is a substantial body of research and literature indicating that academic advising is essential to the success of developmental education activities (Boylan, 2002; Casazza & Silverman, 1996; Center for Student Success, 2007; Jenkins, 2006; Maxwell, 1997). Thoughtful and informed academic advising is critical to implementing the T.I.D.E.S. model. In order to implement it effectively, advisors must not only use their current knowledge about the institution's cognitive assessment instruments relative to required courses in a student's program of study, they must also become familiar with interpreting data from affective assessments while understanding the impact of students' personal characteristics on academic performance. This will require a considerable amount of retraining for academic advisors. They should, for instance, take the affective instruments themselves to understand the questions asked and how they are used to generate scores. They should also read the technical data for the cognitive and affective instruments they will use in order to develop a full understanding of what these scores mean and how they should be interpreted to students and in relation to the overall placement process.

In addition, advisors should know what information on students' personal characteristics is obtained and how it is obtained as well as the various ways in which this information might be interpreted. They should, for instance, be familiar with the limitations regarding accuracy of students' self-reported information and know what additional questions to ask during individual advising in order to validate and supplement this information. They should also know how to collect this information within the boundaries of students' privacy rights.

It is also essential that academic advisors know what courses are available to place students into; fortunately, advisors are expected to be among the most knowledgeable people in this regard on many campuses. In addition, they must be completely familiar with the various interventions available through campus learning assistance and support services in order to target these appropriately. Furthermore, they must also be aware of other campus and community resources such as day care, mental health counseling, or family services. For some students, an appropriate set of targeted interventions might also include participation in these types of services. For these reasons, it is vitally important that academic advisors be thoroughly involved in both taking inventory of campus and community services and in developing student profiles and integrating them with interventions.

Implementing this process will involve not only additional training but additional time and effort for academic advisors involved with T.I.D.E.S. The process requires that advisors combine data from a variety of sources to develop a plan for targeted interventions with individual students. This plan then forms the basis, or protocol, for the academic advising process.

Advisors must also be able to convince students that participating in this particular set of interventions is in their best interests. As research by Gerlaugh et al. (2007) indicates, recommended placement based on assessment is not necessarily mandatory at many colleges and universities. Furthermore, as Bailey, Jeong, and Cho (2008) have pointed out, even when placement is supposedly mandatory, a large number of underprepared students manage to avoid taking the courses into which placement assessments indicate they should be placed. Consequently, depending upon the policies of a particular institution, T.I.D.E.S. advisors will have to recommend, strongly encourage, or mandate that students participate in targeted interventions and work to ensure that these recommendations, encouragements, or mandates are followed by students.

Given the amount of training required and the time involved in targeting interventions based on cognitive, affective, and personal information, it may be advisable for larger institutions to begin by training a small number of advisors who work specifically with underprepared students. These advisors might then work with a specific subset of incoming students who are considered to be most at risk and provide them with targeted interventions. As more experience is gained in targeting interventions, the number of advisors to be trained and the number of students to be served might be increased.

Providing Interventions

Once a set of targeted interventions has been established for a particular student, it will also be necessary to insure that the student is able to take advantage of and follow through with them. Sometimes this may involve referring a student to other services and insuring that the referral is acted upon. This may require making appointments for students with other campus service providers and following up to make sure the appointments are kept. It may also require helping students develop schedules or time management programs that will enable them to fully participate in targeted interventions. Frequently, it may require monitoring students to insure that they actually participate in the targeted interventions recommended by an academic advisor. This process may be facilitated through the use of computerized databases and spreadsheets on student characteristics and interventions.

Boylan, who coined the term "academic intervention" (1980, p. 9), pointed out that successful intervention requires consistent follow-up monitoring of students subsequent to initial contact. Student monitoring, therefore, becomes an essential part of providing targeted interventions. Some sort of feedback system will be necessary to insure that students are actually participating in the interventions targeted for them. Such monitoring is a best practice in developmental education in any event and should be part of a comprehensive developmental program (Boylan, 2002; Center for Student Success, 2007; Continuous Quality Improvement Network, 2000).

This monitoring might be accomplished by academic advisors, by learning center personnel, by faculty teaching the courses that are part of the targeted intervention process, by peer mentors, or by a combination of professionals. Boylan (2002) and Boylan and Saxon (2005) report that student monitoring is a key component in promoting success for developmental students. Bordes and Aredondo (2005) further report that peer mentoring programs that monitor student classroom attendance as well as encourage their engagement with the institution are particularly effective for Hispanic students. Many other authors argue that various forms of peer and professional mentoring can have positive outcomes for all developmental students (Center for Student Success, 2007; Kuh, Kinzie, Schuh, & Whitt, 2005; McCabe, 2000).

Monitoring and Evaluating

In the T.I.D.E.S. model the bases for placing students in targeted interventions is a collection of profiles coordinated with interventions that are based on the informed judgment of developmental education professionals. Therefore careful monitoring and evaluation of student performance in targeted interventions is necessary to assess the efficacy of these informed judgments. Monitoring and evaluation will help to determine whether or not the profiles used to place students are accurate. If they are accurate, student performance in courses and retention will improve as well as students' attitudes, time-management, and other affective characteristics. If this improvement does not occur then the profiles used to place students in targeted interventions need to be revised. There will, no doubt, be a period of experimentation and trial and error involved in implementing the T.I.D.E.S. model, but such a period of experimentation and evaluation should accompany any change in the process of providing courses and services to underprepared students (Maxwell, 1997; McCabe, 2000).

It is recommended, therefore, that baseline data be established for student performance in courses and retention prior to implementing the model. This baseline data provides a standard of performance that may be used to measure the extent to which the T.I.D.E.S. model is contributing to student success. To accomplish this, data should be collected from the 3 years previous to T.I.D.E.S. implementation in the areas of:

- percentage of incoming students placed into developmental courses,
- student completion rates in developmental courses,
- student pass rates in developmental courses (C or better),
- first-semester retention for developmental students, and
- grades in the first college-level course in a particular subject following completion of the developmental education sequence in that subject.

The data from these areas over the past 3 years should be averaged to determine a baseline of student performance and retention. This examination will help determine if performance and retention will improve over the baseline performance data for students who have received targeted interventions.

Revising Profiles and Interventions

As students participate in the T.I.D.E.S. model, baseline quantitative information will become available on student performance. This data will help determine the interventions most likely to result in success for particular students.

Qualitative evaluation should also be collected as part of this process. Students participating in the T.I.D.E.S. model should be interviewed to gather qualitative data on the extent to which they considered the targeted interventions in which they participated to be helpful. Feedback from such interviews in combination with quantitative data will be useful in refining and modifying the profiles on which targeted interventions are based.

Advisors will initially be working with profiles regarding the combination of courses and services that is likely to work best for individual students. The evaluation process provides quantitative and qualitative data to evaluate, refine, and validate these profiles. It is unlikely that the evaluation process will validate all profiles and plans for targeted interventions. Those that are validated should be continued, and those that are not should be revised.

It is important to note that whatever initial set of profiles are developed to plan targeted interventions will, no doubt, have to be revised based on data and experience. In essence, profiles for students with particular characteristics and plans used for implementation of the T.I.D.E.S. model will be dynamic rather than static. These profiles and plans for targeted interventions will be revised and, through such revision and fine-tuning, new and accurate sets of integrated advising and intervention models will eventually be identified for most underprepared students at a particular institution. As a part of this revision process, campus and community resources and services should be monitored regularly to identify new services and delete those that may no longer be available.

Advantages and Disadvantages of the Model

Advantages

A primary advantage of the T.I.D.E.S. model is that it deliberately attempts to reduce the number of students taking developmental courses by placing as many students as possible directly into college-level courses with appropriate learning assistance and support services. For these students, the time spent in developmental courses is reduced. The time and resources saved on these students can then be reinvested into other students who require more comprehensive interventions.

Another advantage of the T.I.D.E.S. model is that it does not necessarily require that any new courses or services be added. The model takes advantage of courses and services that are already present. It should be noted, however, that the more comprehensive the available courses and services, the more sophisticated the possibilities for targeting interventions.

A very important advantage of this model is that it is based on activities already supported in the research and literature of the field as contributing to student success. Because of this it is unlikely that using this model will hinder student progress in developmental and college-level courses or increase attrition. In fact, it is quite possible that it will improve student performance and retention because, when properly implemented, it will insure that students' cognitive, affective, and personal characteristics are accommodated in a manner surpassing the current state of the art in developmental education.

The T.I.D.E.S. model is also advantageous in that it systematizes the interventions applied to help developmental students be successful. The author believes that many current models of developmental education are more or less random. Students are systematically placed in courses based on their cognitive skills, but the available learning assistance and other support services are usually accessed randomly by students. Some developmental students find their way to tutoring or study strategies courses or freshman seminars or learning communities, and some do not. The T.I.D.E.S. model insures that the students most in need of particular services receive them as part of an integrated package of assessment, advising, and intervention.

Disadvantages

Not all campuses will be able to implement the T.I.D.E.S. model. The model requires a comprehensive array of courses, learning assistance, and other support services. It also involves the use of community service resources which will be available to various degrees in different communities.

A further disadvantage of the model is that institutions and their students already invest a great deal of time and money in assessment. Implementing this model will require an increase in that investment on the part of the institution. The institution will have to purchase additional assessment instruments, and the administration of additional assessment will take additional time and expense. To a certain extent, the monetary investment can be reduced by using some of the most valid and reliable public domain affective assessment instruments.

Another disadvantage is that using more sources of information for advising and discussing more options with students will add to the amount of time that will be required for both students and advisors. This may require adding more advisors, starting the advising process earlier, or revising orientation procedures. However, it is also likely that, at some point after the model has been implemented and evaluated, time can be saved by establishing computerized formulas using assessment data and profiles to place students in targeted interventions and standardized procedures for monitoring participation.

To some extent these disadvantages might be balanced by increased student performance, retention, and satisfaction. All these, of course, will result in cost benefits for both the institution and its students. But it will, nevertheless, take time for this balance to become apparent. Furthermore, although eventual cost savings are likely to result from implementation of the T.I.D.E.S. model, this should not be the primary reason for using it.

Conclusion

As Robert McCabe (2003) argues, the number of underprepared students entering colleges and universities is unlikely to decrease in the foreseeable future. Postsecondary institutions must serve the students they have, not those they wish they had, and they must serve these students through some sort of developmental education. Acknowledging that the need for developmental education is likely to be present for some time, professionals have an obligation to search for ways to provide it in the most effective manner.

Bailey (2008) argues that, even for students with similar placement scores, different types of intervention may be required to prepare them for college-level work. The T.I.D.E.S. model provides for different types of intervention for students with different characteristics. It is grounded in research and provides a structure and a methodology that enables developmental education professionals to more accurately place students in courses and services and use these courses and services in a more systematic manner. The model requires revising assessment, advising, and placement procedures and targeting interventions to specific student characteristics rather than haphazardly assigning students to interventions. It is a model that not only requires but also acknowledges the informed professional judgment of well-trained developmental educators. Most importantly, however, is that it is a model that will save time in developmental courses for some students while ensuring that others receive the services and support most likely to contribute to their success.

References

Bailey, T. (2008). *Challenge and opportunity: Rethinking the role and function of developmental education in community college* (CCRC Working Paper No. 14). New York: Community College Research Center, Teachers College, Columbia University.

Bailey, T., Jeong, D., & Cho, S.-W. (2008). *Referral, enrollment, and completion of developmental education sequences in community colleges* (CCRC Working Paper No. 15). New York: Community College Research Center, Teachers College, Columbia University.

Bloom, B. (1976). *Human characteristics and school learning.* New York: McGraw-Hill.

Bordes, V., & Aredondo, P. (2005). Mentoring and 1st-year Latina/Chicano college students. *Journal of Hispanic Higher Education, 4*(2), 114–133.

Boylan, H. (1980). Academic intervention in developmental education. *Journal of Developmental & Remedial Education, 3*(1), 9–11.

Boylan, H. (2002). *What works: Research-based best practices in developmental education.* Boone, NC: Continuous Quality Improvement Network/National Center for Developmental Education.

Boylan, H., & Saxon, D. P. (2005). *Affirmation and discovery: A review of developmental education in Texas community colleges.* Austin, TX: Texas Association of Community Colleges.

Casazza, M., & Silverman, S. (1996). *Learning assistance and developmental education.* San Francisco: Jossey-Bass.

Center for Student Success. (2007). *Basic skills as a foundation for success in California community colleges.* Sacramento, CA: Center for Student Success, The Research and Planning Group of the California Community Colleges.

Continuous Quality Improvement Network/American Productivity and Quality Center. (2000). *Benchmarking best practices in developmental education.* Houston, TX: American Productivity and Quality Center.

Chickering, A. (1969). *Education and identity.* San Francisco: Jossey-Bass.

Erickson, E. (1968). *Identity, youth, and crisis.* New York: W. W. Norton & Co.

Fischer, K. (1980). A theory of cognitive development. *Psychological Review, 87*(6), 477–531.

Gerlaugh, K., Thompson, L., Boylan, H., & Davis, H. (2007). National study of developmental education II: Baseline data for community colleges. *Research in Developmental Education, 20*(4), 1–4.

Jenkins, D. (2006). *What community college management practices are effective in promoting student success? A study of high- and low-impact institutions.*

New York: Community College Research Center, Teachers College, Columbia University.

Kiemig, R. (1983). *Raising academic standards: A guide to learning improvement.* Washington, DC: Association for the Study of Higher Education.

King, P., & Kitchener, K. (1994). *Developing reflective judgment.* San Francisco: Jossey-Bass.

Kuh, G., Kinzie, J., Schuh, J., & Whitt, E. (2005). *Student success in college: Creating conditions that matter.* San Francisco: Jossey-Bass.

Long, B. (2008). *What is known about the impact of financial aid: Implications for policy.* New York: Columbia University, National Center for Postsecondary Research.

Maxwell, M. (1997). *Improving student learning skills.* Clearwater, FL: H & H Publishing.

McCabe, R. (2000). *No one to waste: A report to public decision makers and community college leaders.* Washington, DC: Community College Press.

McCabe, R. (2003). *Yes we can: A community college guide for developing America's underprepared.* Washington, DC: Community College Press.

Morante, E. (1989). Selecting tests and placing students. *Journal of Developmental Education, 13*(2), 2–4, 6.

Muraskin, L., & Lee, J. (2004). *Raising the graduation rates of low income college students.* Washington, DC: Pell Institute for the Study of Opportunity in Education.

National Center for Education Statistics. (2003). *Remedial education at degree-granting postsecondary institutions in Fall 2000.* Washington, DC: U.S. Department of Education.

Roueche, J., & Roueche, S. (1999). *High stakes, high performance: Making remediation work.* Washington, DC: Community College Press.

Saxon, D. P., Sullivan, M., Boylan, H., & Forrest, D. (2005). Developmental education facts, figures, and resources. *Research in Developmental Education, 19*(4), 1–4.

Sedlacek, W. (2004). *Beyond the big test: Noncognitive assessment in higher education.* San Francisco: Jossey-Bass.

Schwartz, W., & Jenkins, D. (2007). *Promising practices for community college developmental education.* New York: Community College Research Center, Teachers College, Columbia University.

Success Rates for Students Taking Compressed and Regular-Length Developmental Courses in the Community College

Caroline Q. Sheldon and Nathan R. Durdella

Although developmental programs have been using compressed courses for some time, this is the first article to look at how the length of compressed courses affects outcomes. Sheldon and Durdella report that although all participants in compressed courses were more likely to complete them than those enrolled in traditional developmental courses, there were differences in outcomes based on the length of the compressed courses. Furthermore, factors such as age, race, and gender appear to have little impact on course completion.

n recent years, developmental education in the community colleges has received much attention. Previous scholarship has focused on several themes related to student success in developmental education including the following: organizational and administrative practices, program components, staff or professional development, support services and counseling, and instructional practices (Center for Student Success, 2007). Within the instructional practices literature, scholarship has focused on learning theory, holistic development of developmental learners, culturally responsive instruction, and faculty cohort models (Center for Student Success, 2007). Further, research in this area has examined the effects of course sequencing and clustering courses, including the articulation of entry and exit skills among all courses within a sequence, alignment of comprehensive academic support mechanisms, and development of innovative learning communities (Center for Student Success, 2007).

To be sure, the prevalence of developmental education in the community colleges, the long-standing identity of community colleges as gateways to opportunity and baccalaureate attainment for students who have been historically excluded from higher education, and recently adopted accountability initiatives, such as those in the California Community Colleges, related to developmental education outcomes, makes student success and achievement in community college developmental education a high stakes issue. In California, only 51.3% of students succeed in basic skills courses (California Community College Chancellor's Office [CCCCO], 2009a), and 51.2% of developmental students advance to the next course level (CCCCO, 2009b). Nationally, the average number of community college developmental math courses offered was 3.6 (Lewis & Farris, 1996). And yet, in spite of scholarship that demonstrates a negative relationship between the length of time required for remediation and successful completion of a remediation program or course of study (Boylan & Bliss, 1997; Kangas & Ma, 1992a, b, c), there has been relatively little research about the relationship between the length of developmental education courses at community colleges and student success.

This study explored the relationship between course length and course success in community college developmental education courses. In so doing, the study elaborates our understanding of curriculum delivery strategies and their relationship to student success in developmental education courses. Specifically, this study explores the success rates and characteristics of community college students who succeed in developmental education courses of varying lengths.

Faculty and Student Perceptions of the Compressed Course Approach

Compressed courses (i.e., courses offered for the same number of units in less-than-full-term instruction) appear to benefit both faculty and students (Daniel, 2000). With respect to student and faculty perceptions of their experiences in compressed courses, Daniel reported that students in an intensive English program indicated a higher level of motivation in compressed courses when compared to their counterparts in traditional-term courses. Further, Daniel reported that students believed that compressed courses allowed for more time for student-faculty interaction but less time to complete assignments. Carley (2002) concluded that the majority of students in his single institution study preferred meeting two days per week for fewer weeks.

While students who enrolled in compressed courses generally perceived a positive experienced, Daniel (2000) reported that faculty felt that compressed courses allowed for more in-depth discussions and experiential activities. Rosen, Howell, and Johnson (1982) found that instructors of compressed courses in accounting perceived greater effectiveness under the conditions. Beachler (2003) also found that over a third of faculty surveyed in a single institution study reported that students were more successful and less likely to withdraw from classes in compressed versus regular-length courses. By contrast, Beachler reported that 40% of faculty in her study reported that the compressed-course format adversely affects students' levels of anxiety and stress. Rosen et al. (1982) confirm this finding in their evaluation of compressed formats in accounting courses. They found that students in compressed courses perceived stress under the conditions. Still, faculty who teach in compressed courses in the summer generally felt that they were able to establish rapport with students more quickly (Kretovics, Crowe, & Hyun, 2005). With respect to student performance in compressed courses offered in the summer, Kretovics et al. found that faculty whom they surveyed reported that students are more focused on learning outcomes, participate more in class discussions, and attend class more regularly.

Student Performance in Compressed Courses

While studies demonstrate that both faculty and students perceive aspects of compressed course formats positively, research demonstrates that course length affects student performance (Geltner & Logan, 2001; van Scyoc & Gleason, 1993). In fact, van Scyoc and Gleason observed that students enrolled in compressed courses scored better on tests than students enrolled in traditional semester-length courses, with one notable exception. Van Scyoc and Gleason noted that the effect of course length seemed to disappear when knowledge retention was measured. These findings appear to support research that has observed that students who enroll in short-term, time-intensive courses perform on par with or better than students enrolled in semester-length courses.

While the notion of offering accelerated or compressed courses to developmental education students may seem counterintuitive, there is evidence indicating the viability of the concept. The study most relevant to the discussion of student success in compressed-format courses at community colleges was conducted at Santa Monica Community College (Geltner & Logan, 2001). The authors examined successful course completion, or the percentage of students passing courses with a grade of C or better, and withdrawal rates for native students enrolled in compressed-format courses and compared them with the success and withdrawal rates of native students enrolled in regular-length classes. Native students were identified as continuing students not transferred to the college from another institution. University students enrolled in one summer school course at the college were excluded from the analysis. Grades received were aggregated across variables based upon the length of the course. Assuming that instructors with higher than average grade distributions were not overrepresented in the compressed scheduling format, the effect of grading variation by instructor should have been removed as a factor influencing success rates.

In Geltner and Logan's study, analyses of success rates by department revealed that with the exception of two subject areas, successful course completion rates were higher for courses offered in compressed formats than in traditional semester-length courses. In general, shorter course length corresponded to higher successful course completion rates. For example, in math, those courses offered in the 6-week compressed format had successful course completion rates of 67% compared to 61% for courses compressed in an 8-week time period and 52% for the regular-length 16-week course. Withdrawal rates were 17% for the 6-week course, 21% for the 8-week course, and 26% for the 16-week course.

The authors also observed the same relationship between course length and success rates when controlling for demographic characteristics such as age and ethnicity and for student performance characteristics such as cumulative grade point average and student probationary status. While the authors note that better students tended to enroll in the compressed courses, even those students with lower cumulative grade point average or probationary status achieved higher success rates in aggregate than their counterparts enrolled in traditional-length courses. Forty percent of probationary students enrolled in 6-week courses successfully completed them compared to 33% of those enrolled in 8-week courses, and only 23% of probationary students enrolled in 16-week classes. The same general pattern of higher success rates for compressed courses was observed for all ethnic and age groups.

Remediation, Student Achievement, and Compressed Courses

As primary providers of developmental education, community colleges have accommodated increased demand for developmental education services by extending their curriculum to serve a greater variety of student preparedness levels. The most recent study on the subject from the National Center for Education Statistics (Lewis & Farris, 1996) documents that community colleges, on average, offer a greater number of developmental courses than other higher education institutions, a trend particularly apparent in math (Lewis & Farris, 1996). In fall 1995, the average number of developmental mathematics courses offered in the community colleges was 3.6 compared to 2.0 for public four-year universities (Lewis & Farris, 1996).

Extension of the developmental math curriculum in the community colleges, although appropriate in terms of accommodating disparate levels of preparation, may exacerbate the problem associated with the length of time required for successful remediation and the achievement of college level skills.

Even though a negative relationship between the length of time for remediation, student persistence, and college success is well documented (Boylan & Bliss, 1997; Kangas & Ma, 1992a, b, c), current scheduling practices and curriculum structures within community colleges often demand that seriously deficient students who desire to transfer successfully complete three to four developmental courses in each subject area, often over a period of two or more years, before even attempting transferable courses in English and mathematics. In their efforts to accommodate various levels of preparation by extending the developmental curriculum, community colleges may have unintentionally imposed an institutional barrier to transfer.

Although Geltner and Logan's study addresses the overall success rates of community college students enrolled in compressed courses, it does not specifically address the performance of students enrolled in developmental classes offered in the compressed format. It is also unclear whether the compressed math and English courses in the Santa Monica study contain an overrepresentation of transfer-level courses. Because of the limitations of the Santa Monica study and the lack of published research in the area of developmental courses offered in a compressed format, this study of community college students enrolled in compressed developmental math, English, and reading courses was conducted in order to assess whether a relationship between course length and course success exists.

Research Questions and Hypotheses

This study addressed two fundamental questions: Is there an educational benefit to community college students when developmental courses are offered in a compressed format? And, if so, what is the nature of the benefit? That is to say, are there any observable differences in benefits based upon a student's age, gender, or ethnicity? If there is no relationship between developmental course length and success in developmental courses, we would expect the following hypotheses to hold true:

H1: There is no statistical or practical difference in success rates for students taking compressed or regular-length developmental English, reading, or math courses.

H2: There is no statistical or practical difference in success rates for students taking compressed or regular-length developmental English, reading, or math courses when social or academic characteristics such as ethnicity, gender, age, or cumulative grade point average are controlled.

Method

Data Source and Analytic Approach

The data for this study are drawn from historical enrollment records of a large, suburban community college with a large percentage of historically underrepresented students. The population of interest for this study was native or continuing community college students who enrolled in at least one developmental English, reading, or math course offered in either a compressed or regular-length format. To identify the population of interest, student enrollment records for spring 1998 through fall 2001 were extracted from the college's database, compiled, and aggregated by type of course. Courses in the database are identified as basic skills, vocational, or transfer. Courses categorized as basic skills represent developmental education courses.

In an attempt to control for variation in success rates that might be attributed to university students enrolling in developmental education courses at the local community college, students categorized as new to college or transfers from other colleges were excluded from the analysis. Only those records for students enrolled in courses designated as developmental were included in the study, and only those students identified as native or continuing students were included in the study. Additionally, an attempt was made to control for variation in success rates that might be attributable to high school concurrent enrollees. As a result, students below the age of 17 were also excluded from the analysis.

A total of 21,165 enrollment records were examined. Of those included in the study, 3,360 enrollment records were for students enrolled in compressed developmental courses and 17,805 were for students enrolled in regular-length courses. For the purpose of this study, compressed courses are defined as those courses offered for the same amount of units in less than 15 weeks; regular-length courses are defined as those courses offered in the standard 15-to-18 week format. During the period under study, these compressed courses were offered in 6- and 8-week formats. Table 1 presents the distribution of enrollment records by course type and length.

In this investigation, the goal was to explore the nature of the relationship between success in developmental courses and course length.

Table 1. Percent Distribution of Students in Developmental Education Courses, Spring 1998 to Fall 2001

Course	5–6 Week Course	8–9 Week Course	15–18 Week Course
English 20	28.67	32.39	20.38
Math 20	35.43	6.58	25.64
Math 40	0.00	60.70	29.60
Reading 42	5.90	0.00	4.48
Reading 43	19.82	0.25	13.91
Reading 54	10.10	0.08	6.04

Note. The total number of students is 21,165 for all classes and 4,636 for English 20; 5,410 for Math 20; 6,000 for Math 40; 926 for Reading 42; 2,907 for Reading 43; and 1,286 in Reading 54.

Due to the exploratory nature of the study and the structure and availability of the data contained in the database, the analytic approach to the data was largely descriptive and employed the following analytic techniques: contingency tables, chi-square analysis, and percent difference. (Percent difference was selected as the means of assessing the potential strength of association between the variables because of the limitations associated with using Cramer's *V* when large sample sizes are present. As well, Lambda was also deemed inappropriate due to percent differences larger than 5% and consistency in the mode for the dependent and independent variables.) The data were first examined to assess whether any significant differences based on academic and social characteristics were present for compressed versus regular-length course enrollees. Next, the data were analyzed to determine whether evidence of a relationship between course length and course success was present. Finally, the data were examined to assess the relationship between course length and course success when social and academic characteristics were controlled.

Variables and Their Indicators

The data source provides a number of institutional and student-level variables previously demonstrated to be related to student success in courses. For the purpose of this study, course success in developmental education courses is theorized to be related to course length even when type of course and academic and social background characteristics are controlled.

DEPENDENT VARIABLE

The dependent variable for this study is the success rate of students enrolled in developmental courses. It is constructed as the percentage of students who received a grade of A, B, C, or CR divided by the total number of students attempting the course and receiving a final grade disposition in the course, inclusive of course withdrawals.

INDEPENDENT VARIABLES

Independent variables include type of course and several academic and social background characteristics such as age, gender, ethnicity, and cumulative grade point average. Type of course includes the three areas of offerings for developmental education at the community college where the study was conducted—English, mathematics, and reading. For English, only one course, English 20, Basic Writing, was examined because it was the only developmental English course offered in both a compressed and regular-length format. English 20 is considered to reflect students with English skills two levels below college level. In math, Math 20, Basic Mathematics, and Math 40, Survey of Mathematics, were examined. These courses are designed for students three and two levels below college level math skills, respectively. In reading, three courses were examined: Reading 42, Reading Access for College Students; Reading 43, Basic Reading Skills; and Reading 54, Developmental Reading. These courses are for students with skill levels, respectively, three levels, two levels, and one level below college level.

Age is reflective of the student's age at the time of taking the developmental course. It is constructed dichotomously as traditional versus nontraditional age students. Traditional age students are defined as those below the age of 25, while nontraditional are defined as those 25 years of age and above. Ethnicities are categorized as follows: Asian and Pacific Islanders (including students identifying as Filipino), African American, Latino, White, and Other (including Native American, and students who did not indicate their ethnicity). Cumulative grade point average is also constructed dichotomously; categories include students with cumulative grade point averages below 2.0 and those with grade point averages at or above 2.0.

Results

Students Enrolling in Compressed and Regular-Length Courses

Table 2 presents the distribution of enrollment records by social and academic background characteristics. As is illustrated in Table 2, Asian and Pacific Islander students are slightly overrepresented in compressed courses compared to their overall representation in the study while Latino students are slightly underrepresented. These differences were statistically and practically significant (X^2 = 456.652, α = .000, df = 5). Students aged 25 and older were also slightly overrepresented (X^2 = 24.888, α = .000, df = 1) as were students with cumulative grade point averages 2.0 and above (X^2 = 29.606, α = .000, df = 1).

Table 2. Percent Distribution of Enrollment by Course Length
and Background Characteristics

Characteristic	Compressed Course	Regular-Length Course
Gender	$x^2 = 2.232^*$	
Male	33.10	34.43
Female	66.90	65.57
Ethnicity	$x^2 = 456.652^{**}$	
Asian/Pacific Islander	14.11	7.46
African American	10.54	8.82
Latino	50.83	57.12
White	4.20	7.09
Other	20.33	19.50
Age	$x^2 = 24.888^{**}$	
Below 25	68.87	73.06
25 and older	31.13	26.94
GPA	$x^2 = 29.606^{**}$	
Below 2.0	26.28	30.98
2.0 and above	73.72	69.02

Note. The total number of students is 21,165 for gender, ethnicity, age, and GPA.
$^*\alpha = .328.$
$^{**}\alpha \leq .000.$

Success Rates in Compressed versus Regular Length Courses

When an analysis of success rates in compressed and regular-length developmental courses was performed, a pattern of higher successful course completion rates for compressed developmental courses was observed across each of the departments under study. Table 3 presents the results of success rates by department. Of the three departments studied, the highest successful course completion rates occurred in courses offered in the 8-week format. (Only four students took a reading course offered in the 8-week format; success rates for reading are for 6-week format classes.) Among 8-week format courses, English had the highest successful completion rate at approximately 87%. In examining success rates for courses offered in the 6-week format, reading had the highest success rate. Nearly 77% of students attempting a compressed reading course successfully completed that course compared to approximately 76% for English and 58% for math. As is indicated in Table 3, these differences were both statistically and practically significant.

An examination of success rates by course for English, reading, and math reveals that students enrolling in compressed-format courses were more likely to succeed. Indeed, a clear pattern of students who

Table 3. Success Rates by Department and Course Length

Department and Success	5–6 Week Course	8–9 Week Course	15–18 Week Course
English	$x^2 = 195.175*$		
Percent successful	75.80	86.90	56.70
Math	$x^2 = 69.553*$		
Percent successful	57.91	65.35	51.15
Reading	$x^2 = 52.9591*$		
Percent successful	77.68		66.30

Note. The total number of students in English is 4,636; in math 11,410; and in reading 5,115.
*$\alpha = .000$.

were more likely to successfully complete compressed-course formats than students enrolled in regular-length courses was observed. Table 4 presents the success rates by course of students enrolled in compressed-format courses compared to those enrolled in regular-length courses. Among compressed math courses, Math 40, Survey of Mathematics, had a higher successful course completion rate than Math 20, Basic

Table 4. Success Rates by Course and Course Length

Course and Success	5–6 Week Course	8–9 Week Course	15–18 Week Course
English			
English 20	$x^2 = 195.175*$		
Percent successful	75.80	86.90	56.70
Math			
Math 20	$x^2 = 23.804*$		
Percent successful	57.91	49.37	48.38
Math 40	$x^2 = 47.344*$		
Percent successful		67.08	53.56
Reading			
Reading 42	$x^2 = 15.072**$		
Percent successful	80.62		63.11
Reading 43	$x^2 = 21.165*$		
Percent successful	75.00		63.53
Reading 54	$x^2 = 17.557*$		
Percent successful	81.19		66.82

Note. The total number of students in English 20 is 4,636; in Math 20, 5,410; in Math 40, 6,000; in Reading 42, 926; in Reading 43, 2,904; and in Reading 54, 1,285.
*$\alpha \leq .000$.
**$\alpha \leq .001$.

Math. The success rate for Math 40 in the 8-week compressed format was 67% compared to 49% for Math 20 offered in the 8-week format. Reading 54, Developmental Reading, and Reading 42, had the highest successful course completion rates among the three developmental reading courses offered in compressed form. The successful course completion rates for compressed reading courses offered in the 6-week format were approximately 81% for Reading 54 and Reading 42 compared to 75% for Reading 43, Basic Reading Skills.

When controlling for social and academic background characteristics, success rates by course length were examined. Table 5 presents the distribution of success rates by selected social and academic background characteristics for students enrolled in developmental courses. With the exception of gender, a statistically and practically significant pattern of higher success rates in compressed-format courses was observed across all social and academic background characteristics. Students, irrespective of age, gender, and ethnicity, were more likely to successfully complete developmental courses offered in a compressed format than their counterparts enrolled in regular-length developmental education courses. This pattern was observed for students of all ethnic backgrounds, categories of age, as well as for students with

Table 5. Success Rates by Course Length and a Set of Social and Academic Background Characteristics

Characteristics and Success	5–6 Week Course	8–9 Week Course	15–18 Week Course
Gender	$x^2 = 1.348*$		
Male	69.13	69.19	51.92
Female	71.98	74.12	57.34
Ethnicity	$x^2 = 214.667**$		
Asian/Pacific Islander	77.78	87.75	62.20
African American	53.78	58.91	42.78
Latino	71.28	70.52	55.79
White	62.79	78.18	61.12
Other	72.22	69.96	55.70
Age	$x^2 = 10.785***$		
Below 25	66.29	71.57	52.78
25 and over	78.82	74.29	62.80
GPA	$x^2 = 77.554**$		
Below 2.0	54.45	122.51	38.09
2.0 and over	76.91	77.42	63.28

Note. The total number of students is 21,165 for gender, ethnicity, age, and GPA.
$*\alpha = .510$.
$**\alpha \leq .000$.
$***\alpha \leq .005$.

cumulative grade point averages above and below 2.0. With respect to gender, a similar pattern was observed without statistical but with practical significance. That is, women experienced higher course success rates when both 6- and 8-week compressed classes were compared to their counterparts in 15-week classes.

Although success rates for women and men enrolled in compressed-format courses exceeded corresponding rates for regular-session courses, women were more likely to be successful in compressed courses than men. For women enrolled in compressed developmental education courses, the success rate was about 73% compared to a success rate of 67% for men enrolled in compressed developmental courses. Higher success rates for women were also observed in regular-length session courses.

Higher success rates in compressed developmental courses also were observed for all of the major ethnic groups at the college. Asian and Pacific Islander students enrolled in compressed developmental courses had the highest successful course completion rates (82%), followed by Latino students (71%), White students (69%), and African American students (56%). A nearly identical pattern was observed for regular-length developmental courses with one notable difference. In regular-length courses, slightly higher success rates were observed for White students compared to Latino students. In compressed developmental courses, the success rate for Latino students was 71.0% compared to 69% for White students. Success rates for Latino and White students enrolled in regular-length developmental courses were 56% and 61% respectively (see Table 5).

Students of all age groups performed better in compressed developmental courses than did students enrolled in regular-length courses. Students aged 25 years and above had a success rate of 77% in compressed courses compared to 63% for their counterparts enrolled in regular-length courses. Traditional age students followed the same pattern. The success rate for traditional age students in compressed courses was 68% compared to 53% for their counterparts enrolled in the regular-length courses. However, nontraditional age students (those aged 25 and older) were more likely to succeed than traditional students (those ages 17 to 24 years) in compressed format courses. The success rate for nontraditional students was 77% compared to 68% for traditional students.

Students with cumulative grade point averages below 2.00 performed better in compressed-format courses than their counterparts enrolled in regular-length courses. Among students with cumulative grade point averages below 2.00, approximately 54% successfully completed compressed courses compared to approximately 38% successfully completing regular-length courses. Students with grade point averages above 2.00 also fared better in compressed courses. The success rate for students with grade point averages above 2.00 enrolled in compressed basic skills courses was nearly 77% compared to 63% for their counterparts enrolled in the equivalent courses offered during the regular session.

Discussion and Conclusion

Evaluation of Research Questions and Hypotheses

The results of this study clearly demonstrate that for students enrolled at this particular community college, developmental course length is associated with statistically and practically significant differences in course success in developmental education courses, and these differences are consistently observed across all categories of age, gender, and ethnicity. With regard to the research questions and hypotheses, the results of this study provide evidence that there is a benefit to offering community college developmental education courses in a compressed format, and the benefit extends to all categories of students.

Implications for Practice and Future Research

The results of this study offer key insights for the practice of developmental education in the community college and future research in this area. With regard to the practice of developmental education in the community college, it is imperative that practitioners understand that the notion that developmental students need more time (i.e., longer courses offered over a greater number of weeks) to master developmental material may be faulty. This study demonstrates that developmental students are quite capable of successfully assimilating course material in a shorter amount of time when the material is presented in a more intense, compressed format. Practitioners at the community college may want to reconsider the way that they offer developmental courses so that the achievement and progress of students through the developmental education curriculum can be maximized.

Experimenting with offering developmental courses in a compressed format also affords community colleges the opportunity to further examine developmental students' progress and achievement through a sequence of developmental education courses. Specifically, are students who take a sequence of compressed developmental courses better able to retain material and progress through the developmental curriculum than those students who take a sequence of developmental courses offered in a more traditional format? While this study demonstrates the efficacy of compressed developmental education offerings for community college students enrolled in one course, it does not address the efficacy of offering a sequence of compressed developmental education courses. Future research in this area is crucial for practitioners faced with making instructional policy decisions with respect to their developmental education programs. Such research is important to support community colleges in successfully developing innovative and effective programs and services that increase developmental students' achievement and progress toward educational goals.

It should be noted that while this study demonstrates that course length is associated with success in one developmental course, it does not illuminate the elements of compressed courses that may play a substantive role in developmental student success nor does it address the role of student motivation and commitment in course success. For example, does the intensity of compressed courses offer community college students more opportunities for getting to know one another and, thus, facilitate the creation of informal learning communities among students who might not ordinarily participate in such experiences? Or do compressed courses simply reduce opportunities for students' life experiences, such as family and work responsibilities, to interfere with successful course completion?

This study does not examine the relationship between motivation and commitment and successful course completion. For example, are higher successful course completion rates in compressed courses a reflection of a higher degree of commitment and motivation on the part of students? Is there a possibility that higher success rates would still be observed after the effects of motivation and commitment are accounted for? All of these issues need to be further examined in order to more fully understand the efficacy and benefits of offering a compressed developmental education program for community college students. Future research should attempt to discover the nature of the relationship between curriculum delivery strategy and student attitudes and behavior.

This study represents an exploration into the efficacy of a different curriculum delivery strategy for community college developmental education students: offering developmental education courses in a compressed format. It reveals that there is a relationship between successful course completion in developmental education courses and course format. It adds to the practice of education by proposing further exploration of alternative curriculum delivery strategies for community college developmental education programs that are based upon developing and offering curriculum in ways that are demonstrated to have empirically based positive outcomes for students. Further research should be conducted to more adequately assess the efficacy of compressed developmental education courses and programs for community college students.

References

Beachler, J. (2003). *Results of the alternative calendar survey: A survey of faculty, classified staff and administrators at California community colleges that have moved from an 18-week semester to a compressed calendar.* (ERIC Document Reproduction Service No. ED479971)

Boylan, H. R., Bonham, B. S., & Bliss, L. B. (1997, Spring). Program components and their relationship to student performance. *Journal of Developmental Education, 20*(3), 2–7.

California Community College Chancellor's Office. (2009a). *Data mart.* Retrieved January 29, 2009, from http://www.cccco.edu/mis/onlinestat

California Community College Chancellor's Office. (2009b). *Focus on results: Accountability reporting for the California community colleges.* Retrieved February 1, 2009, from http://www.cccco.edu/Portals/4/TRIS/research/ARCC/arcc_2009_ final.pdf

Carley, M. (2002). *Community college compressed calendars: Results of a student survey and a faculty survey.* (ERIC Document Reproduction Service No. ED466740).

Center for Student Success, Research and Planning Group for California Community Colleges. (2007). *Basic skills as a foundation for student success in California community colleges.* Retrieved December 2, 2008, from http://www.eric.ed.gov/ERICDocs/data/ericdocs2sql/content_storage_01/0000019b/80/28/07/ef.pdf

Daniel, E. L. (2000, June). A review of time-shortened courses across disciplines. *College Student Journal, 34*(2), 298–309.

Geltner, P., & Logan, R. (2001). *The influence of term length on student success.* (ERIC Document Reproduction Service No. ED455858)

Kangas, J., & Ma, T. (1992a). *Persistence of fall 1988 ENGL 330 / 335 students through transfer level English (1A) over four academic years (fall 1988–spring 1992).* Research Report #267. (ERIC Document Reproduction Service No. ED383361)

Kangas, J., & Ma, T. (1992b). *Persistence of fall 1988 ENGL 321 & ENGL 322 students through transfer level English (1A) over four academic years (fall 1988–spring 1992).* Research Report #268. (ERIC Document Reproduction Service No. ED383362)

Kangas, J., & Ma, T. (1992c). *Persistence of fall 1988 Math 310, Math 12 & Math 13 students through transfer level math over four academic years (fall 1988–spring 1992).* Research Report #269. (ERIC Document Reproduction Service No. ED383363)

Kretovics, M. A., Crowe, A. R., & Hyun, E. (2005). A study of faculty perceptions of summer compressed course teaching. *Innovative Higher Education, 30*(1), 37–51.

Lewis, L., & Farris, E. (1996). *Remedial education at higher education institutions in fall 1995* (NCES 97-584). Washington, DC: U.S. Department of Education, National Center for Education Statistics.

Rosen, L. S., Howell, W. C., & Johnson, T. (1982, April). An evaluation of the compressed-format for instruction in accounting. *The Accounting Review, 57*(2), 403–413.

van Scyoc, L. J., & Gleason, J. (1993). Traditional or intensive course lengths? A comparison of outcomes in economics learning. *The Journal of Economics Education, 24*(1), 15–22.

Developmental Mathematics: Challenges, Promising Practices, and Recent Initiatives

Barbara S. Bonham and Hunter R. Boylan

Developmental math represents one of the major barriers to completion for underprepared students. In recent years, scholars, professional associations, and practitioners have developed a number of innovations in methodology and curricula to address the high noncompletion rates in developmental math. This article is the first to describe the major innovations in teaching developmental math as well as revising the developmental math curriculum.

There is considerable public debate about the underpreparedness of students entering colleges today and the efficacy of responses to this underpreparedness. There are a large number of students who place into developmental courses, particularly mathematics, and are prevented from achieving their educational goals because they never complete these courses. Developmental mathematics as a barrier to educational opportunity represents a serious concern for the students as well as higher education policy makers.

Sierpinska, Bobos, and Knipping (2008) discuss the sources of numerous frustrations expressed by students in a university-level prerequisite mathematics course. Examples include the irrelevance of course material, disinterest by faculty teaching courses, a lack of support from the college, and a lack of understanding from their instructors.

Developmental mathematics program, including courses and related support services, ostensibly exist on college campuses to help students achieve their goals. Yet, in many cases, they have become road blocks to students' success. Courses which were originally designed to promote student academic achievement now often serve as barriers to that achievement. In a summary of data from the U.S. Department of Education, Noel-Levitz (2006) reports,

> In all of higher education, including four-year institutions, there is no harder course to pass than one in developmental mathematics. Basic Algebra, in fact, receives top billing in a report from the U.S. Department of Education on the highest failure and withdrawal rates for postsecondary courses. (p. 2)

Drawing on the research of Bailey, Jenkins, and Leinbach (2005), Epper and Baker (2009) state, "The challenge of raising math skills is further compounded by the fact that students who test into remedial math coursework are disproportionately minority and disproportionately first-generation, two characteristics of at-risk students" (p. 3).

According to the most recent National Center for Education Statistics (NCES) study in this area entitled *Remedial Education at Degree Granting Postsecondary Institutions* (Parsad & Lewis, 2003), approximately three-fourths of the colleges and universities in the U.S. that enrolled freshmen offered at least one developmental course. Of those that offered developmental mathematics, 60% offered between 2 and 4 courses, with an average of 2.5 courses. The average for public two-year colleges was 3.4 courses. This means that a student placing in the lowest level of developmental mathematics at a community college must take approximately 10 hours of mathematics courses before even having an opportunity to attempt college-level mathematics. The same NCES study reports that mathematics was the developmental course most likely offered by colleges and universities, with 72% reporting offering at least one developmental mathematics course (68% offered developmental writing courses and 56% offered developmental reading courses). Seventy-two percent of the developmental mathematics courses are offered in the traditional academic department rather than in a developmental education department. These courses usually (73–78%) receive only institutional, not degree, credit. The courses may, therefore, be used to qualify for financial aid but do not usually count toward graduation.

In a special report on community colleges, the NCES (Provasnik & Planty, 2008) reported that, for the 2006–2007 term, there were 1,045 community colleges in the United States enrolling 6.2 million students or 35% of all students enrolled in postsecondary institutions. Nearly 75% of students entering two-year colleges must take one or more developmental mathematics courses (Noel-Levitz, 2006). In Fall 2000, the proportion of entering freshmen who were enrolled in remedial courses was larger for mathematics (22%) than for writing (14%) or for reading (11%) (Parsad & Lewis, 2003). According to Lutzer, Rodi, Kirkman, and Maxwell (2007), the results from the 2005 survey by the Conference Board of Mathematical Sciences revealed enrollment in precollege mathematics courses accounted for 56% of total mathematics and statistics enrollment in two-year institutions.

For many students entering college these courses have become a frightening obstacle. For some students, it prolongs their time at colleges, requires them to take and retake these courses, and results in eventual failure or withdrawal. Furthermore, a significant number of college students never enroll in the developmental mathematics courses into which they place. Based on data from the Achieving the Dream sample, Bailey (2009) reported that about one-fifth of all students in that sample who needed to take developmental mathematics courses did not enroll in a single one of these courses over a 3-year period.

Completion of the Developmental Math Sequence

Unfortunately not many of those who do enroll complete the full sequence of recommended developmental mathematics courses. In a statewide study including a sampling of two-year and four-year colleges, the completion rate for the full sequence of developmental courses was the lowest in mathematics at 21% (Schiel & Sawyer, 2002). In a much larger and more controlled national study drawing on college transcript data from the National Educational Longitudinal Study (NELS) Attewell, Lavin, Domina, and Levey (p. 153 in this book) report that only 30% of students pass all of the developmental mathematics courses in which they enroll. The NELS is based on a 1988 representative cohort of 8th graders who went on to college and for whom data was tracked up to 2006 in this study. The math sequence completion difference between these studies may be influenced by two important factors: (a) the exclusion of any students who return to college many years after leaving high school from the longitudinal database and (b) the use of a national representative sample compared with a smaller, statewide, nonrandom sample.

Although developmental mathematics courses have proven to be an obstacle for many students, research reflects that students who passed their developmental mathematics course requirements were as successful in subsequent mathematics courses as those who were not required to take developmental mathematics courses (Bahr, 2008). Similar findings were reported in a statewide study conducted by ACT involving students from both two-year and four-year colleges (Schiel & Sawyer, 2002). Results from this study indicated that developmental mathematics courses were effective for those who completed them. Unfortunately only 21% of the students in this study completed their developmental mathematics coursework.

Fortunately, all of the attention focused on developmental mathematics programs at two- and four-year colleges has resulted in a major shift in the content, organization, and delivery of some of these programs. Stuart (2009) reports that colleges are changing from simply providing access to students who are underprepared for college-level courses to a more rigorous involvement, including study of and development of courses and services to meet the very diverse demographic backgrounds of students. He notes, "more and more colleges and universities are ditching the old stigma associated with remedial education and reinventing their remedial and retention programs" (Stuart, 2009, p. 14). In the last decade, there has been an increase in the application and use of research-based best instructional practices in developmental mathematics programs and in the use of innovative approaches to teaching and learning. Early results are revealing significant improvements in students' success. These are discussed in the following sections which outline successful teaching practices used in developmental mathematics, appropriate delivery models, efforts to address affective factors, expanded professional development, new partnerships, and promising innovative initiatives.

Teaching Strategies

Successful programs utilize multiple teaching and learning strategies (Boylan, 2002; Epper & Baker, 2009; Massachusetts Community Colleges Executive Office, 2006) to improve students' success in developmental mathematics. A report published by the OVAE (Office of Vocational and Adult Education; Golfin, Jordan, Hull, & Ruffin, 2005) focused on developmental mathematics instruction and provided recommendations for promising practices emerging from their literature review. These included greater use of technology as a supplement in classroom instruction, integration of classroom and lab instruction, offering students a variety of delivery formats, project-based instruction, proper student assessment and placement, integration of counseling for students, and professional development for faculty.

Other reports and studies have identified the successful application and use of varied teaching techniques as strategies to improve students' success and retention in developmental mathematics. Examples of these include: mastery learning (Boggs, Shore, & Shore, 2004; Rotman, 1982); attention to affective factors (Hammerman & Goldberg, 2003; Taylor & Galligan, 2006); mentoring programs (Sperling & Massachusetts Community College, 2009; Visher, Butcher, & Cerna, 2010); integration of math study skills and learning strategies (Acee, 2009; Nolting, 1997); supplemental instruction (Blanc, DeBuhr, & Martin, 1983; Martin & Arendale, 1994; Peacock, 2008; Phelps & Evans, 2006); active learning, including cooperative and collaborative learning approaches (Barkley, Cross, & Major, 2005; Davidson & Kroll, 1991); contextual learning (Crawford, 2001); problem solving and modeling (AMATYC, 2006; Ashwin, 2003); integrated classroom activities, laboratory activities, and learning centers (Boylan, 2002; Perin, p. 93 in this book).

Delivery Models

In an overview of current practices Epper and Baker (2009) identified a number of special projects being implemented in community colleges over the last 5 years. For example, Foothills College in California has implemented a program titled Math My Way. This program focused on intensity of instruction (additional time on task and an emphasis on mastery) while utilizing self-paced delivery and technology (ALEKS software), Supplemental Instruction, tutoring, and classes held on consecutive days. Results reveal a 20% higher success rate in college-level math for program completers. Other projects described in the report by Epper and Baker are course redesign projects supported by The National Center for Academic Transformation (NCAT). Jarmon (2009a) commented in a presentation that "Course redesign is a process of re-designing whole courses (rather than individual classes or sections) to achieve better learning outcomes at a lower cost by taking advantage of capabilities of information technology." Course redesign can involve a whole course, as is the case at Cleveland State Technical College in Tennessee, or focus on competencies needed for specific programs or courses, such as the program at Jackson State College in Tennessee. The former is referred to as the "emporium model" and the latter as the "linked workshop model" (Jarmon, 2009b).

There are a variety of redesign models that have recently emerged. These include supplemental, replacement, emporium, fully online, buf-fet, and linked workshops (Jarmon, 2009b). Different approaches have been taken in the redesign of the curriculum in developmental math-ematics. According to Lucas and McCormick (2007), some have accel-erated it, some slowed it down, and some attempted to decrease the number of topics.

Examples of courses recommended as targets for redesign are those with high withdrawal/failure rates, those drawing from students with inconsistent preparation, those having difficulty getting qualified adjuncts, or those from which students have difficulty in subsequent classes. Course redesign is not specifically targeted to developmental mathematics alone. For instance, the redesign project using the Math Emporium model at Virginia Tech and the University of Alabama are for higher levels of mathematics. Course redesign promotes the use of multiple teaching approaches rather than a single method. Many of these approaches are supported by research or have been identified as promising practices in developmental mathematics. These research-based or promising practices include mastery learning, active learning, individualized assistance, modularization, or personalized assistance (such as Structured Learning Assistance, frequent feedback, or the use of laboratories rather than classrooms). In these approaches technol-ogy is utilized where it is most appropriate, on homework, quizzes, and exams, for example. Tutorials are delivered through computer-based instruction supplemented by small-group instruction and test reviews. This approach fosters greater student engagement with the material as well as with each other.

One of the major advantages of the project is that it encourages the use of multiple approaches to teaching developmental mathematics. Students actually learn math by doing math rather than spending time listening to someone talk about doing math. The major disadvan-tage can be an overreliance on the technology to deliver all instruction with little or no intervention, even when students are experiencing dif-ficulty. In a discussion of lessons learned regarding course redesign one caution noted was, "don't necessarily redesign around technology . . . always consider students' needs and skills when choosing the online tools" (Foreign Language Resource Center, 2009, p. 1). Additional rec-ommendations regarding course redesign from colleges involved in the process include the following: (a) establish clear goals, learning outcomes, and assessment methods; (b) insure that the project is faculty driven with strong administrative support; (c) choose carefully what can be done most effectively online; (d) develop a conceptual framework to guide the process; (e) build institution-wide support; and (f) deliver a good orientation for students (Foreign Language Resource Center, 2009; Search, 2009). The Tennessee Board of Regents has committed to a redesign initiative in developmental mathematics and English. This initiative involves 9 universities and 13 community colleges (NCAT, 2009).

Affective Factors

The affective domain is frequently an untapped area in attempts to promote students' achievement and retention in developmental mathematics programs. Yet research dating back to the early 1980s has revealed the importance of its relationship to students' success in mathematics (Schoenfeld, 1983). In the last decade increased attention has been given to this relationship, particularly by researchers in the area of educational psychology as well as educators in the field of mathematics education (Muis, 2004). The importance of the relationship between the cognitive and affective factors influencing students' success in developmental mathematics cannot be ignored. Bandura's (1997) work in the area of social cognitive theory maintains that it is the students' beliefs about the value of the learning experience, their expectations of success, and their enjoyment of it that will motivate them to engage material actively and persist in spite of initial failures.

Research supports the relationship between attitude toward mathematics and achievement in mathematics (De Corte, Verschaffel, & Depaepe, 2008; Ma & Xu, 2004; Muis, 2004). Ma and Xu (2004) found a reciprocal relationship between every attitudinal measure used in this study and mathematics achievement. This is a significant study contributing valuable information regarding the relationship between students' attitudes and achievement.

In addition to the relationship between attitude toward mathematics and students' success, research findings also reveal the impact of other affective factors including low self-efficacy and confidence in ability to do mathematics, test anxiety, and math anxiety (Bates, 2007; Bonham, 2008; Hall & Ponton, 2005; Higbee & Thomas, 1999; Rodriguez, 2002; Tobias, 1993). These affective variables can become barriers to students' success and have a "negative and inhibitory impact on learning and performance in mathematics" (De Corte, Verschaffel, & Depaepe, 2008, p. 25).

This is a rich area of information for educators designing developmental mathematics courses and one that should definitely not be ignored by anyone attempting to improve student performance in developmental mathematics. Students, faculty, and support staff need to understand the influence of affective factors on students' success and retention in developmental mathematics. They should be familiar with and employ strategies to help alleviate mathematics anxiety, build self-confidence, and maximize student learning in mathematics.

Another important point is that collaborative efforts among students result in a higher degree of accomplishment by all participants; students help each other and in doing so build a supportive community. This raises their performance level as well as their belief in their ability to do well in mathematics (Barkley, Cross, & Major, 2005; Davidson & Kroll, 1991). Galbraith and Jones (2006) discuss the use of team learning in which students act as teaching assistants. The use of learning groups also contributes to the development of trust and cooperation among the students as well as with the instructor. DePree (1998) has found that small-group instruction significantly increases math confidence for historically underrepresented groups such as female, Hispanic-American, and Native-American students.

Writing—such as journal, error analysis, and student-developed word problems—can also enhance learning in mathematics; it can improve students' understanding of mathematics as well as their attitudes and beliefs about mathematics. Research reveals that it is an effective strategy for minority students and for students with learning disabilities (Loud, 1999; Pugalee, 1997). However, as Meier and Rishel (1998) point out, these student writing assignments must be carefully designed in order to successfully foster student learning and engagement. Without a connection to the class material, a writing assignment will be less engaging to students and unlikely to increase student understanding or attitude toward mathematics.

An effective way to reduce math anxiety is to create a safe learning environment in which students feel comfortable expressing themselves without fear or ridicule. Use of the following strategies can foster a safe environment and create a sense of belongingness: discuss classroom etiquette, use icebreakers or group warm-up activities, teach relaxation techniques, and use affective assessment instruments to help students understand their attitudes toward learning (Bonham, 2008; Levine-Brown, Bonham, Saxon, & Boylan, 2008; Saxon, Levine-Brown, & Boylan, 2008).

Based on the findings of Peskoff (2000) and Nolting (2002), a list of strategies for coping with and helping to alleviate mathematics anxiety are listed in *Beyond Crossroads* (AMATYC, 2006). Information for actions to be taken by faculty and departments are also delineated. These include recommendations for workshops on study skills, math anxiety, and multiple assessment use.

Professional Development

"As mathematics teaching changes across the world, faculty teaching developmental mathematics courses must rethink both what should be taught and how it should be taught" (Mathematical Association of

America, 2010, p. 1). The implications of that statement affect recruitment and hiring, professional development, and curriculum review and revision in the area of developmental mathematics. Many educators teaching developmental mathematics are highly qualified in the discipline of mathematics. However, they may have limited coursework or formal training in developmental education, college teaching, student learning, or the application of varied teaching strategies. Those who have been teaching developmental mathematics can attest to the fact that it differs substantially from teaching more advanced college-level math courses. New faculty may question why these students are in college or why these courses are being taught at the college level. According to the AMATYC standard on professionalism (2006), developmental mathematics educators need specialized preparation in the following areas: developmental mathematics, technical mathematics, teaching preparation, intensive math background, and statistics knowledge. These guidelines are recommended for use in recruitment, hiring, orientation, and mentoring diverse mathematics faculty.

According to Boylan (2002), training and professional development is a priority in the most successful developmental programs. Faculty and staff working with developmental students are supported and encouraged to attend conferences, training institutes, and graduate courses. Those who participate in such activities are encouraged to share what they have learned with their colleagues in formal and informal settings. It is important to realize that a sustained and intensive series of professional development activities are much more effective than "one shot" professional development workshops (Boylan, 2002).

Partnerships

Improving the percentage of students who are prepared for college-level mathematics involves a complex set of issues related to learning, assessment, curriculum, teaching, and professionalism. Mathematics educators at all levels (PK–16 including Adult Basic Skills) need to build public understanding and support for the changes in mathematics education. Building partnerships with Adult Basic Education programs, ESOL, high schools, other colleges, business and industry, as well as with the local community agencies is recommended by the major associations in the field of mathematics as well as by many national projects (ACHIEVE, 2004; Adelman, 2006; AMATYC, 2006; Boylan, 2002). These collaborative efforts can promote the alignment of exit and entrance requirements. Such efforts can also create partnerships with faculty in other disciplines to integrate mathematics across the curriculum and with business and industry to ensure that necessary employee skills and strategies are included in mathematics courses and programs.

Special Projects Focused on Developmental Mathematics

There have been a number of recent improvement projects sponsored by major associations in mathematics and national organizations. These have provided information to guide the design and development of effective learning environments for developmental mathematics.

The American Mathematical Association of Two-Year Colleges has been very focused recently on developmental mathematics projects. In past years their two publications, *Crossroads in Mathematics* and *Beyond Crossroads in Mathematics*, have contributed significantly to establishing mathematics standards and guidelines for the first 2 years of college. The first document, *Crossroads in Mathematics*, published in 1995,

> emphasized desired modes of student thinking and guidelines for selecting content and instructional strategies. The purposes of the second standards document, *Beyond Crossroads*, was to renew and extend the goals, principles, and standards set for in *Crossroads* and to continue the call for implementation . . . with an additional set of standards which focus on student learning and the learning environment, assessment of student learning, curriculum and program development, instruction, and professionalism. (AMATYC, 2006, p. 1)

Recent activities supported by AMATYC include the Syllabus Project, which provides on-line posting and sharing of course syllabi for different levels of developmental math courses. Also available are links to organizations and resources.

Some of the most current activities include the AMATYC's partnership with Monterrey Institute for Technology and Education (MITE). MITE, with a 5 million dollar grant from Bill and Melinda Gates, which will combine the four courses required in most remedial math sequences. Using preassessments and multiple learning approaches, MITE hopes to create coursework that can be customized to each individual student's needs.

The Carnegie Foundation for the Advancement of Teaching has undertaken a project to make "mathematics a gateway not a gatekeeper course" (Bryk & Triesman, 2010). The authors note that redesigning the curriculum content is necessary but not sufficient to stem the crises of failure and noncompletion in developmental mathematics. They also argue that there needs to be an integrated academic support system as well. "We need to strengthen the connections of students to successful peers, to their institutions, and to pathways to occupations and education" (Bryk & Triesman, 2010, p. 20). Carnegie's development of a statistics pathway de-emphasizes algebra and focuses on real-life, workforce oriented, mathematics tasks. This model may help solve the problems for a large number of community college students needing developmental mathematics courses. This pathway is designed to fulfill math requirements for many occupations and to help students become more academically successful. The project team has already met with community college leaders and members of mathematics and national education groups. They are working in collaboration with Achieving the Dream and the California Community College System's Basic Skills Initiative (Boroch et al., 2007). The groundwork for this project began in the Summer of 2010 when community college teams met with designers, researchers, and practitioners to begin the design and development of resources and assessments for the pathway.

Conclusion

It is unfortunate that developmental courses, once envisioned as a gateway to educational opportunity, have become barriers to that opportunity for many students. Although those who pass developmental courses tend to do well in college, an unacceptable number fail to complete these courses. This is most true in developmental mathematics.

Fortunately, there is a great deal of research to identify promising practices that may improve the quality of developmental mathematics instruction. There are also a number of projects being undertaken to redesign the content and improve the delivery of developmental mathematics courses. For these efforts to be successful it will be necessary for professional associations, foundations, policy makers, and developmental mathematics instructors to collaborate in changing the way developmental mathematics courses are structured, taught, and delivered. This will be neither an easy nor a short-term process. However, it is a process that must be undertaken if educational opportunity is to remain a reality in U.S. postsecondary education. We can no longer deny our weakest and poorest citizens the opportunity to obtain a college credential simply because we are unable to teach them how to factor polynomials.

References

Acee, T. (2009). Strategic learning and college readiness: An interview with Claire Ellen Weinstein. *Journal of Developmental Education, 33*(1), 20–26. Retrieved from Education Research Complete database.

ACHIEVE. (2004). Ready or not. Creating a high school diploma that counts. *American diploma project.* Retrieved from http://www.achieve.org/ReadyorNot

Adelman, C. (2006). *The toolbox revisited: Paths to degree completion from high school through college.* Washington, DC: U.S. Department of Education. Institute of Education Sciences.

AMATYC. (1995). *Crossroads in mathematics: Standards for introductory college mathematics before calculus.* Memphis, TN: Author.

AMATYC. (2006). *Beyond crossroads: Implementing mathematics standards in the first two years of college.* Memphis, TN: Author.

Ashwin, P. (2003). Peer support: Relations between the context, process, and outcomes for students who are supported. *Instructional Science, 31,* 159–173.

Bahr, P. (2008). Does mathematics remediation work?: A comparative analysis of academic attainment among community college students. *Research in Higher Education, 49*(5), 420–450. doi:10.1007/511162-008-9089-4

Bailey, T. (2009, Spring). Challenges and opportunity: Rethinking the role and function of developmental education in community colleges. In *New Directions in Community Colleges, 145. Policies and practices to improve student preparation and success* (pp. 11–30). Wilmington, DE: Wiley Periodicals, Inc.

Bailey, T., Jenkins, D., & Leinbach, T. (2005, January). *Community college low-income and minority student completion study: Descriptive statistics from the 1992 high school cohort.* New York, NY: Community College Research Center, Columbia University.

Bandura, A. (1997). *Self-efficacy: The exercise of self-control.* New York, NY: W. H. Freeman and Company.

Barkley, E. F., Cross, K. P., & Major, C. H. (2005). *Collaborative learning techniques: A handbook for college faculty.* San Francisco, CA: Jossey-Bass.

Bates, V. (2007). The impact of preparedness, self-efficacy, and math anxiety on the success of African American males in developmental mathematics at a community college. *Dissertation Abstracts International Section A, 68.* Retrieved from PsycINFO database.

Blanc, R., DeBuhr, L., & Martin, D. (1983). Breaking the attrition cycle: The effects of Supplemental Instruction on undergraduate performance and attrition. *Journal of Higher Education, 54*(1), 80–90.

Boggs, S., Shore, M., & Shore, J. (2004). Using e-learning platforms for master learning in developmental mathematics courses. *Mathematics & Computer Education, 38*(2), 213–220. Retrieved from Education Research Complete database.

Bonham, B. S. (2008, May). *Affective barriers to success in pre-college mathematics.* Keynote address delivered at the Quantitative Literacy Conference, Emory & Henry College, Emory, VA.

Boroch, D., Fillipot, I., Hope, L., Johnstone, R., Mery, P., Serban, A. . . . Gabriner, R. S. (2007). *Basic skills as a foundation for student success in California community colleges, Part 1: Review of literature and effective practices.* Sacramento, CA: Research and Planning Group of the California Community Colleges, Center for Student Success.

Boylan, H. R. (2002). *What works: Research-based best practices in developmental education.* Boone, NC: Continuous Quality Improvement Network/National Center for Developmental Education.

Bryk, A., & Treisman, U. (2010, April 18). Make math a gateway, not a gatekeeper. *Chronicle of Higher Education, 56*(32), B19–B20. Retrieved from Academic Search Complete database.

Crawford, M. (2001). *Teaching contextually: Research, rationale, and techniques for improving student motivation and achievement in mathematics and science.* Waco, TX: CCI Publishing Inc. Retrieved from http://www.cord.org/uploadedfiles/Teaching%20Contextually%20%28Crawford%29.pdf

Davidson, N., & Kroll, D. (1991). An overview of research on cooperative learning related to mathematics. *Journal for Research in Mathematics Education, 22,* 362–365.

DeCorte, F., Verschaffel, L., & Depaepe, F. (2008). Unraveling the relationship between students' mathematics-related beliefs and the classroom culture. *European Psychologist, 13*(1), 24–36. doi:10.1027/1016-9040.13.1.24

DePree, J. (1998, Fall). Small-group instruction: Impact on basic algebra students. *Journal of Developmental Education, 22*(1), 2–4, 6.

Epper, R., & Baker, E. (2009). *Technology solutions for developmental mathematics: An overview of current and emerging practices.* Report funded by William and Flora Hewlett Foundation and Bill and Melinda Gates Foundation. Retrieved from http://www.gatesfoundation.org/learning/Documents/technology-solutions-for-developmental-math-jan-2009.pdf

Foreign Language Resource Center. (2009). *What we have learned about course redesign.* Retrieved from http://www.thencat.org/RedesignAlliance/UNCCH_Workshop_Slides/UNCCH%20Lessons%20Learned%20111309.pdf

Galbraith, M., & Jones, M. (2006). The art and science of teaching developmental mathematics: Building perspective through dialogue. *Journal of Developmental Education, 30*(2), 20–27. Retrieved from Academic Search Complete database.

Golfin, P., Jordan, W., Hull, D., & Ruffin, M. (2005). *Strengthening mathematics skills at the postsecondary level: Literature review and analysis.* Washington, DC: U.S. Department of Education, Office of Vocational and Adult Education. Retrieved from ERIC database. (ED494241)

Hall, J., & Ponton, M. (2005). Mathematics self-efficacy of college freshmen. *Journal of Developmental Education, 28*(3), 26–33. Retrieved from Education Research Complete database.

Hammerman, N., & Goldberg, R. (2003). Strategies for developmental mathematics at the college level. *Mathematics & Computer Education, 37*(1), 79–95. Retrieved from Education Research Complete database.

Higbee, J., & Thomas, P. (1999). Affective and cognitive factors related to mathematics achievement. *Journal of Developmental Education, 23*(1), 8–15.

Jarmon, C. (2009a, November). *Getting started on course redesign.* Conference presented in Chapel Hill, NC. Retrieved from http://www.thencat.org/RedesignAlliance/UNC-CH%20Event%20Agenda.pdf

Jarmon, C. (2009b, October). *Redesigning developmental mathematics.* Presentation at the National Center for Academic Transformation conference on Increasing Student Success in Developmental Mathematics, Nashville, TN. Retrieved from http://thencat.org/RedesignAlliance/TBR_Workshop_Slides/Jarmon%20Dev%20Math%20101609.pdf

Levine-Brown, P., Bonham, B. S., Saxon, D. P., & Boylan, H. R. (2008). *Affective assessment for developmental students, Part 2. 22*(2), 1–4.

Loud, B. J. (1999). Effects of journal writing on attitudes, beliefs, and achievement of students in college mathematics courses. *Dissertation Abstracts International: Section: A. 60*(3), 0680.

Lucas, M. S., & McCormick, N. J. (2007). Redesigning mathematics curriculum for underprepared college students. *The Journal of Effective Teaching, 7*(2), 36–50. Retrieved from http://www.uncwil.edu/cte/et/articles/Vol7_2/Volume0702.pdf#page=41

Lutzer, D., Rodi, S., Kirkman, E., & Maxwell, J. (2007). *Statistical abstract of undergraduate programs in the mathematical sciences in the United States.* Providence, RI: American Mathematical Society. Retrieved from http://www.ams.org/profession/data/cbms-survey/cbms2005

Ma, X., & Xu, J. (2004). Determining the causal ordering between attitude toward mathematics and achievement in mathematics. *American Journal of Education, 119*(3), 256–280. Retrieved from Education Research Complete database.

Martin, D., & Arendale, D. (1994). Supplemental Instruction: Increasing achievement and retention. *New Directions in Teaching and Learning, 60*(4), 1–91.

Massachusetts Community College Executive Office (MACCEO). (2006). *100% math initiative: Building a foundation for student success in developmental math.* Boston, MA: Author.

Mathematical Association of America. (2010). *Teaching developmental mathematics.* Retrieved from http://www.maa/org/l_and_l/developmental/dm.html

Meier, J., & Rischel, T. (1998). Writing in the teaching and learning of mathematics. *Mathematical Association of America Notes, 48.* New York, NY: Cambridge University Press.

Muis, K. R. (2004). Personal epistemology and mathematics: A critical review and synthesis of research. *Review of Educational Research, 74, 317–377.*

National Center for Academic Transformation (NCAT). (2009, October). *Increasing student success in developmental mathematics.* Conference presented in Nashville, TN. Retrieved from http://www.thencat.org/RedesignAlliance/TBR%20Dev%20Math%2010_16%20Agenda.pdf

Noel-Levitz, Inc. (2006). *Student success in developmental math: Strategies to overcome barriers to retention.* Iowa City, IA: Noel-Levitz. Retrieved from https://www.noellevitz.com/NR/rdonlyres/B4148B72.C135-4AD4-A04C-2l66821C872C/o/ENABLEMATH_paper_0706indd.pdf

Nolting, P. (1997). Develop study skills rather than avoiding mathematics courses. *Disability Compliance for Higher Education, 3*(4).

Nolting, P. (2002). *Winning at math.* Brandenton, FL: Academic Success Press, Inc.

Parsad, B., & Lewis, L. (2003). *Remedial education at degree-granting postsecondary institutions in Fall, 2000* (NCES 2004-010). Washington, DC: U.S. Department of Education, National Center for Education Statistics. Retrieved from http://nces.ed.gov/pubs2004/2004010.pdf

Peacock, M. (2008). A program evaluation of supplemental instruction for developmental mathematics at a community college in Virginia. *Dissertation Abstracts International Section A, 69.* Retrieved from PsycINFO database.

Peskoff, F. (2000). *Mathematics anxiety and the adult student: An analysis of successful coping strategies.* Snow Cap, NC: Peppercorn Books. Retrieved from ERIC database.

Phelps, J., & Evans, R. (2006). Supplemental instruction in developmental mathematics. *Community College Enterprise, 12*(1), 21–37. Retrieved from Education Research Complete database, http://findarticles.com/p/articles/mi_qa4057/is_200604/ai_n17171706/pg_2/?tag=content.col1

Provasnik, S., & Planty, M. (2008). *Community colleges: Special supplement to The Condition of Education 2008* (NCES 2008-033). Washington, DC: National Center for Education Statistics, Institute of Education Sciences, U.S. Department of Education. Retrieved from http://nces.ed.gov/programs/coe/2008/analysis/2008033.pdf

Pugalee, D. (April, 1997). Connecting writing to the mathematics curriculum. *Mathematics Teacher, 90, 308–310.*

Rodriguez, L. (2002). Improving services to developmental mathematics students by understanding the concept of self-efficacy. *Research in Developmental Education, 17*(2), 1–4.

Rotman, J. (1982). *Developmental mathematics and the Lansing Community College Math Lab.* Retrieved from ERIC database. (ED224542)

Saxon, D. P., Levine-Brown, P., & Boylan, H. R. (2008). Affective assessment for developmental students, part 1. *Research in Developmental Education, 22*(1), 1–4.

Schiel, J., & Sawyer, R. (2002). *Using posttesting to show the effectiveness of developmental/remedial courses* (ACT Research Report No. 2000-3). Iowa City, IA: ACT, Inc. Retrieved from http://www.act.org/research/briefs/2002-3/html

Schoenfeld, A. H. (1983). Beyond the purely cognitive: Belief systems, social cognition, and metacognitions as driving forces in intellectual performance. *Cognitive Science, 7*, 329–363.

Search, S. (2009, November). *Case study: Tallahassee Community College.* Presentation at the NCAT Getting Started with Course Redesign conference, Chapel Hill, NC.

Sierpinska, A., Bobos, G., & Knipping, C. (2008). Sources of students' frustration in pre-university level, prerequisite mathematics courses. *Instructional Science, 36*(4), 289–320. doi:10.1007/s11251-007-9033-6

Sperling, C. (2009). *The Massachusetts Community Colleges developmental education best policy and practice audit: Final report.* Retrieved from ERIC database. (ED506649)

Stuart, R. (2009). Reinventing remedial education. *Diverse Issues in Higher Education, 26*(18), 14–17. Retrieved from Education Research Complete database.

Taylor, J., & Galligan, L. (2006). Mathematics for maths anxious tertiary students: Integrating the cognitive and affective domains using interactive multimedia. *Literacy & Numeracy Studies, 15*(1), 23–43. Retrieved from Education Research Complete database.

Tobias, S. (1993). *Overcoming math anxiety.* New York, NY: W. W. Norton & Company.

Visher, M., Butcher, K., & Cerna, O. (2010, February). *Guiding developmental math students to campus services: An impact evaluation of the Beacon Program at South Texas College.* New York, NY: MDRC. Retrieved from http://www.mdrc.org/publications/540/overview.html

Cloud Computing and Developmental Education

Douglas R. Holschuh and David C. Caverly

The use of technology in developmental education has expanded rapidly in the twenty-first century. The following brief Techtalk columns from the Journal of Developmental Education *describe some of the most current uses of technology in our field. They not only describe available technologies but also point out ways in which developmental educators can use them. In "Cloud Computing and Developmental Education," Holschuh and Caverly explain how cloud technology can promote collaboration and communication among students and faculty without the requirement of specialized software. In "Second Life and Developmental Education," Burgess and Caverly discuss the potential applications of virtual worlds to developmental instruction. Finally, in "Mobile Learning and Access," Caverly, Ward, and Caverly address the issue of mobile phone use in the classroom and suggest that rather than being an annoyance, mobile phones can also contribute to learning.*

The Advent of Cloud Computing

The history of personal computing could be summed up as a race to provide larger and larger amounts of data storage that can be manipulated at faster and faster speeds in smaller and smaller devices. Over the years, data has moved from floppy disks to hard drives to USB thumb drives and most recently to solid-state RAM drives. Likewise, computers downsized from the desktop to the laptop and even smaller with netbooks like the HP Mini and tablet computers like the new Apple iPad. This idea has had a strong impact in changing the way users work, play, and socialize.

Concurrently, the computer network that used to link only college campuses, businesses, and government agencies began to spread as well, and it eventually made its way to individual computers. Personal computers began to connect to this larger network, the Internet, through wired connections like phone modems and cable modems and then through wireless connections, which facilitated the move to smaller, more mobile computers. Over the past decade and a half, these personal machines, with their local data storage and processing power, have merged with the Internet, and a computer infrastructure was created where it is often difficult to discern where the individual computer ends and the network begins.

Both of these ideas, shrinking computing devices and increasing network access, have converged in recent years to bring us handheld mobile devices like iPhones, smartphones, and tablet computers that connect to the Internet over always-on cellular connections. Now the network really is everywhere, or at least everywhere there is a cell-phone signal.

Cloud computing is the natural extension of this always-on connection, and it posits a view of computing in which all data and all the applications to create and manipulate that data exist in the "cloud"; that is, on the Internet in various online services. If you are putting your photos on Flickr (www.flickr.com), writing documents using Google Docs (docs.google.com), posting your thoughts to a blog, collaborating with coworkers in a wiki, socializing with Facebook (www.facebook.com), or tweeting from your phone using Twitter (www.twitter.com). you are already using the cloud (although true cloud computing would see all computing, not just some, occurring in this manner).

To access the cloud, all that is needed is an Internet connection and a way to view the Internet, most likely a web browser or other "app" that connects to the Internet. With cloud computing, it no longer matters what local hardware (laptop, desktop, smartphone, netbook) or what operating system (Windows, Mac OS X, Linux) is being used. It is a view of computing that supersedes any past battle in the personal computing world, whether that battle was Windows versus Macs, Netscape versus Microsoft, or proprietary software versus open-source software. With cloud computing, none of these divisions matter; data and applications are available everywhere. As John Gage at Sun Microsystems said years ago, "The network is the computer" (PCWorld, 2009). The choice of how to access that network is up to the individual.

Implications of Cloud Computing

So, what does this mean for developmental students and educators? The first, and perhaps most important, element when addressing issues inherent to the digital divide is lowered costs, both for software and hardware. Why pay for Microsoft Office when you can use the free, web-based office suites offered by Google or Zoho (www.zoho.com) or even Microsoft itself (which will begin offering a browser-based version of their Office applications with the release of Office 2010)? If all you need to do is resize a photo, why pay for Adobe Photoshop, when you can use Adobe's Photoshop Online (www.photoshop.com)? Why use Endnote when you can keep track of references in Zotero (www.zotero.org), a free plug-in for the Firefox browser that works with both Microsoft Office and the free, open-source OpenOffice (www.openoffice.org)?

Additionally, it is not just applications that are being offered for free, but data storage as well. With cloud computing, instead of saving everything to large local hard drives, faculty and students can instead save everything they create in these services to the services themselves. Presentations created in Zoho can be stored in your account directly on Zoho's web site; photos uploaded from cameras can be stored directly on photo-sharing services like Flickr or Smugmug (www.smugmug.com). Because the applications and the data are stored on the web, they can be accessed with far smaller and often far cheaper devices than ever before. A netbook—a small, inexpensive (from $250 to $500), low-powered laptop with limited storage capacities—is just as useful as the fastest desktop computer. Even a smartphone can be powerful enough to access many of these cloud services. In fact, data can be seamlessly shared between any number of devices without the hassle of transferring the documents from one device to another. From the office, from a campus computer lab, from a coffee shop, or from a park, the latest version of a document or project is always online and always available.

This constant availability also lends itself to the sharing of both documents and document creation over the Internet. If several students are collaborating to coedit a document (Caverly & Ward, 2008), they can do that by all logging into Google Docs and working on the same document instead of passing a Word file over a USB drive or email. Wikis, such as PBworks (www.pbworks.com), Wikispaces (www.wikispaces.com), or the one built into most campus learning management systems, are another powerful tool for coediting documents, allowing multiple users to edit the same documents while keeping the latest version (as well as a chronology of revisions) on the web at all times. These web applications eliminate the need for faculty and students to have specific software to edit the document (and the hassle of converting from one file format to another). The only software everyone needs is a free web browser like Firefox, Safari, or Internet Explorer.

Potential Drawbacks to Cloud Computing

Of course, no technology is without its negatives, and with cloud computing perhaps the greatest drawback is the very real possibility that students and faculty will not be able to be online everywhere and at all times. The network is close to ubiquitous, but holes exist, more so as you leave major metropolitan areas and college campuses. Even if the Internet is available, there is always the possibility of a service being down, and large companies like Google (Raphael, 2009) and Facebook (McCarthy, 2009a) have had major outages in the past year, leaving users of their services without access for short periods of time. There is also the danger that one of these services will lose data, although it is far more likely that an individual computer user will lose data than, say, Google, with their multiple servers and consistent backups.

There are also security, privacy, and ownership issues when it comes to using an online service, and it is important to know how the service provider will both protect and use customer data. For example, Google targets Gmail users with advertising based on the content of their e-mails. They are not actually reading these e-mails, but Google does aggregate the data to help provide the ads that allow them to offer the service for free (Google, 2010). Ownership of uploaded data can also be an issue (i.e., do online service providers own your data in any way?), and large services like Facebook have struggled to devise good content-rights terms for the data posted to their service (McCarthy, 2009b). If students or faculty are to use any of these services for their personal use or, more importantly, for campus use, it is essential to know how these issues will be handled.

Conclusion

Cloud computing offers many possibilities to developmental educators for its use, whether for communicating with students through social networking services like Facebook, sending out updates via Twitter, providing online tutoring, or having students collaborate on their writing using a wiki. Many students are already well versed in this world of online applications, and they are already using them to create and store their data. The more educators can leverage this to their advantage, the better. In addition, it opens up a world of low-cost computing to a larger socioeconomic population of students. Cloud computing may really be computing for the masses, offering the very latest in technology while leveling the playing field more than ever before.

References

Caverly, D. C., & Ward. A. (2008). Techtalk: Wikis and collaborative knowledge construction. *Journal of Developmental Education*, *32*(2), 36–37.

Google. (2010). Ads in Gmail. Retrieved from http://mailgoogle.com/support/bin/answer.py?hl=en&answer=6603

McCarthy, C. (2009a). Facebook database outage cut off about 150,000. *Cnet News*. Retrieved from http://news.cnet.com/8301-13577_3-10373349-36.html

McCarthy, C. (2009b). Facebook faces furor over content rights. *CNN.com*. Retrieved from http://www.cnn.com/2009/TECH/02/17/facebook.terms.service/index.html

PCWorld. (2009). Sun's history in pictures. *PCWorld*. Retrieved from http://www.pcworld.com/businesscenter/article/163933/suns_history_in_pictures.html

Raphael. J. R. (2009). Gmail outage marks sixth downtime in eight months. *PCWorld*. Retrieved from http://www.pcworld.com/article/160153/gmail_outage_marks_sixth_downtime_in_eight_months.html

Second Life and Developmental Education

Melissa L. Burgess and David C. Caverly

In our previous two columns, we discussed the potential for using blogs and wikis with developmental education (DE) students. Another Web 2.0 technology, virtual environments like *Second Life*, provides a virtual world where residents create avatars (three-dimensional [3-D] self-representations) and navigate around an online environment (Caverly, Peterson, Delaney, & Starks-Martin, 2009). Other virtual environments comparable to *Second Life* have emerged (Virtual Environments Info Group, 2007).

Second Life differs from asynchronous blogs and wikis because the 3-D interface allows users to immerse themselves into synchronous interactivity. Information can be disseminated through video, note cards, e-mail, simulations, mapping, bodily actions, or text-based conversation histories. Avatars can discuss this information using text-based chatting (thus creating a downloadable history) or through a voice tool (requiring a microphone and speakers). Communicating synchronously through avatars provides the opportunity for greater social interactivity which is a vital factor when developing a community of inquiry within online or hybrid DE courses or learning support (Garrison, 1985; Peterson & Caverly, 2006).

From a MMOG to a MUVE

Second Life grew out of Massively Multiplayer Online Games (MMOG) of the 1970s such as *Dungeons and Dragons* (Wikipedia Foundation Inc., 2009a) and more currently *World of Warcraft* (Wikipedia Foundation Inc., 2009b). Emerging as *Linden World* in 2002, it allowed users, by invitation only, to create avatars known as "primitars" (Rymaszewski, Wagner, Wallace, Winters, Ondrejka, & Batsone-Cunningham, 2006), gawky robots made of prims (objects). *Second Life* was envisioned not as another game but as a new "country" where users (i.e., avatars) could explore and interact. In 2003 *Second Life* became publically available, which allowed *Second Life* to gain users and become a Massive Multi-user Virtual Environment (MUVE).

At the time of this writing, approximately 1.4 million users log into *Second Life* regularly. Activities in *Second Life* have grown from gaming to simulations, collaborations, and explorations that mirror real-world learning environments. The potential for *Second Life* for teaching and learning holds great promise for constructivist learning among DE students.

Second Life in Higher Education

With *Second Life* tools for creating and scripting, immersion into these social, collaborative spaces serves as fertile ground in higher education. There are more than 200 higher education institutions with an active presence in *Second Life*, sharing virtual tours of their campuses, instructional activities in a variety of disciplines, and educational experiences (Rymaszewski et al., 2006). The *Second Life* Educators (SLED) listserv has more than 3,900 members sharing discussions on best practices, conferences, workshops, and courses within *Second Life*. Examples of how *Second Life* is being used for instruction in higher education can also be found (Kay & FitzGerald, 2009; Mengel, Simonds, & Houck, 2009; xxArete2XX, 2009).

Second Life in Developmental Education

Second Life can simulate a highly engaging, problem-solving, collaborative, immersive learning environment for DE students, particularly if the pedagogy involves cognitive, social, and teaching presence (Garrison, Anderson, & Archer, 2000; Peterson & Caverly, 2006). *Second Life* teaching activities could provide the type of online instruction environment millennial students desire (Howe & Strauss, 2000), thereby appealing to DE students and the strategies they are developing (i.e., self-regulation, engagement, reading, and writing).

For example, a virtual environment for effective math group tutoring might be created in a campus's *Second Life* learning center between a tutor's avatar and several DE students' avatars as the tutor teaches them how to solve functions with two unknowns. The tutor's avatar could begin by showing math examples in business or engineering (i.e., the cognitive presence's triggering event), discussing solutions (i.e., exploration), modeling procedures for solving two functions (i.e., integration), and asking the students to solve other functions (i.e., resolution). *Second Life* can provide a social presence as both tutor and DE students' avatars interact in a risk-free emotional environment, allow for open communication, and work together collaboratively. *Second Life* demands synchronous teaching presence as the tutor's avatar delivers instruction by defining the topics and allowing the DE students' avatars to share their understanding through discussion. Whether *Second Life* provides a better technological delivery mechanism than traditional online math tutoring through the addition of the avatar is a research question; still, the potential is great.

Similarly, DE student avatars could attend a simulated biology class they are unable to take due to institutional prerequisites, compare their lecture and lab notes with a Supplemental Instruction Leader's lab notes, and consequently be better prepared to take the class in the future. Other DE student avatars could attend a blocked American history class, read and annotate the textbook and primary source materials, compare their notes with each other and with the Supplemental Instruction Leader's notes, and collaboratively prepare and take a virtual test. All three of these virtual environment scenarios provide technological scaffolding to accommodate time and distance demands of many DE students as well as provide sound instruction through a cognitive, social, and teaching presence.

Thus far, one pilot study conducted in a developmental reading *Second Life* classroom at Sam Houston State University might provide some direction for DE and virtual environments (Burgess, personal communication, March 4, 2009). Delaney and Caverly (2008) found some success in another study which taught concepts of schema theory and metacognition to preservice teacher education graduate students.

Potential for Virtual Environments

Developmental educators are facing a sharp turning point with regard to Web 2.0 technologies and the ways in which they can be utilized in DE classrooms. This prompts the need for further exploration and research. Examples of questions to investigate this goal might include: What new literacy skills (Leu, Kinzer, Coiro, & Cammack, 2004) do our DE students actually have, and what do they need? How can educators capitalize and build on these new literacy skills using Web 2.0 technologies? How must educators align individual views of learning environments to accommodate and nurture these new literacies with instruction that responds to the unique opportunities they offer? And, most importantly, what affordances are there, if any, for DE students with these new literacies?

Conclusion

Taking steps toward the discovery of Web 2.0 technologies will advance conversations on this front, thereby enabling an informed direction and application regarding this pedagogical/paradigmatic shift. We invite the DE teaching and learning community to further this important dialogue by joining DE organizations (i.e., College Reading and Learning Association [CRLA], National Association for Developmental Education [NADE]) and their respective technology special interest groups. Engaging in ongoing professional conversations on Web 2.0 and other technologies will help to advance knowledge to reflect the teaching and learning needs of 21st century DE students.

References

Caverly, D. C., Peterson, C. L., Delaney, C. J., & Starks-Martin, G. (2009). Technology integration. In R. F. Flippo & D. C. Caverly (Eds.), *Handbook of college reading and study strategy research* (2nd ed., pp. 314–350). New York: Routledge.

Delaney, C., & Caverly, D. C. (2008, April). *Its a wonderful Second Life. Or is it?: An exploratory study of constructivist learning in a virtual world.* Invited paper presented at the College of Education Faculty Research Colloquium, Texas State University-San Marcos.

Garrison, D. R. (1985). Three generations of technological innovations in distance education. *Distance Education, 6*(2), 235–241.

Garrison, D. R., Anderson, T., & Archer, W. (2000). Critical inquiry in a text-based environment: Computer conferencing in higher education. *The Internet and Higher Education, 2*(2/3), 87–105.

Howe, N., & Strauss, W. (2000). *Millennials rising: The next great generation.* New York: Vintage.

Kay, J., & FitzGerald, S. (2009). Second Life *in education.* Retrieved March 20, 2009, from http://sleducation.wikispaces.com/educationaluses

Leu, J. D. J., Kinzer, C. K., Coiro, J. L., & Cammack, D. W. (2004). Toward a theory of new literacies emerging from the Internet and other information and communication technologies. In R. B. Ruddell & N. Unrau (Eds.), *Theoretical models and processes of reading* (5th ed., pp. 1570–1630). Newark, DE: International Reading Association. Retrieved March 20, 2009, from http://www.readingonline.org/newliteracies/leu/

Mengel, M. A., Simonds, R., & Houck, R. (2009). Educational uses of *Second Life* [video]. *YouTube.* Retrieved March 22, 2009, from http://www.youtube.com/watch?v=qOFU90UF2HA

Peterson, C. L., & Caverly, D. C. (2006). Techtalk: What students need to know about online discussion forums. *Journal of Developmental Education, 29*(3), 40–41.

Rymaszewski, M., Wagner, J. A., Wallace, M., Winters, C., Ondrejka, C., & Batsone-Cunningham, B. (2006). Second Life: *The official guide* (2nd ed.). Indianapolis, IN: Wiley.

Virtual Environments Info Group. (2007). *Virtual worlds comparison chart.* Author. Retrieved March 5, 2009, from http://www.virtualenvironments.info/virtual-worlds-comparison-chart

Wikipedia Foundation Inc. (2009a). *Dungeons & dragons.* Retrieved March 20, 2009, from http://en.wikipedia.org/wiki/Dungeons_%26_Dragons

Wikipedia Foundation Inc. (2009b). *World of warcraft.* Retrieved March 20, 2009, from http://en.wikipedia.org/wiki/World_of_Warcraft

xxArete2XX. (2009). Education in *Second Life*: Explore the possibilities [video]. *YouTube*. Retrieved March 22, 2009, from http://www.youtube.com/watch?v = TMGR9q43dag

Mobile Learning and Access

David C. Caverly, Anne R. Ward, and Michael J. Caverly

As any college professor will attest, mobile phones are ubiquitous on college campuses. Although many students have access to this technology in their purses and pockets, hands-on accessibility to technology does not guarantee digital literacy. There are two levels of a digital divide: a first level as a divide in access to hardware, software, and broadband Internet connections and a second level as a divide in knowledge in digital literacy on how to use this technology (Caverly, Peterson, Delaney, & Starks-Martin, 2009).

Mobile Learning

Morgan Stanley (2008) reports 60% of the world's population has access to a mobile phone, though this is somewhat misleading as there are more mobile phones in Italy than there are people (Wikipedia Foundation Inc., 2009b). Mobile phones have replaced desktop or laptop computers as the primary means of wireless Internet access for English-speaking Hispanics (68%) and African Americans (65%) in the U.S., far outpacing Whites (33%), many of whom choose to use laptops (Horrigan, 2009). Anderson and Rainie (2008) project by 2020 mobile phones will be the primary connection device for the Internet.

Despite the increasing hands-on accessibility of these powerful mobile devices, most college professors dissuade their use and consider them to be distractions. Students' phones are often collected before a test, and often students are removed from class if they are "googling" a term used by the professor. This disconnect between out-of-school literacy skills (i.e., critical literacy skills; Pawan & Honeyford, 2009) and in-school literacy tasks (i.e., academic literacy) has generated reports of boredom and low motivation among many students (Prensky, 2009).

However, in classrooms that include a blending of critical literacy skills with academic literacy tasks, a different picture emerged. For example, Thortan and Houser (as cited in Zhang, 2008) found 71% of Japanese college students preferred the use of text messages to e-mail and 93% saw value in receiving English lessons sent to their mobile phones. Misono and Akahori (2008) reported that using text messaging with a secret word provided during class was an efficient means of taking attendance in a large lecture hall. Hartnell-Young and Heym (2008) demonstrated effective uses with secondary school students completing social-constructivist learning projects in which mobile phones were used for timing experiments, sharing files, photographing scientific apparati, conversing via text message, syncing calendars, creating narrative movies, using the Global Positioning System (GPS) to identify locations, and transferring files from home to school. Uffendell, Hefferen, and Finnigan (2009) found three uses of mobile phones effective for college students with disabilities. A mobile phone's GPS with speech aided students' mobility, text messaging with speech improved the delivery of messages from the college, and the Mobile Daisy Player (V. 2.2; codefactory, 2009) read e-books to students.

Repurposing Mobile Phones

As more students acquire 3G (third generation, Internet capable) phones, more applications to developmental education will emerge. In the meantime, GPS capabilities in 3G mobile phones can facilitate a campus orientation through a mobile WebQuest (Bottentuit, Coutinho, & Sternaldt, 2006). Students could be asked to explore the support programs on campus, create scenarios when a student would need these supports, and send their assignment as an attachment to a text message. Basic text messaging capabilities could be used to ask students to reflect on what they are learning. Text messages could act as "exit slips," comments providing feedback for the instructor. Such reflections could require application-level understanding as students consider in their own words how strategies can be applied to a given discipline as compared to the knowledge-level questions typically resulting from the use of clickers (Fies & Marshall, 2008). The Internet accessibility of 3G phones could allow students to search for real-world examples of concepts and procedures, paste these into a text document, and forward these to another student to verify.

At this time, there are over 60,000 apps (software applications) for 3G mobile phones. For example, a free app, myHomework (V. 2.0; Rigoneri, 2009), allows students to keep track of homework, classes, projects, and tests. Google Mobile app (V. 0.3; Google Inc., 2009), also free, allows students to search Google using voice input. Documents to Go® (V. 1.1; DataViz Inc., 2009), a $5 app, allows students to upload Microsoft Word or Excel files and edit them on their phones wherever they are. iSign lite (V. 1.0; Basil, 2008) provides an avatar signing words chosen from a list, allowing students to communicate with other students with hearing impairments.

Other apps might take more creativity to integrate into developmental education but show promise. For example, a free app, The Extraordinaries (V. 1.0, Colker, Rigby, Ahjua, Mendosa, Freitas, & Zak, 2009), sends microvolunteering opportunities for community service to students' phones. These service opportunities include reporting GPS locations of potholes to a local government agency, translating a nonprofit's website into a foreign language, tagging images for the Smithsonian, or providing citizen journalism much like what happened during the protests over the recent Iranian presidential election (Wikipedia Foundation Inc., 2009a).

Augmented reality (AR) is also emerging through video-capable mobile phones. AR research has demonstrated over the last 5 years how three-dimensional images can be seen from two-dimensional bar code markers (National Center for Supercomputing Applications, 2008). Mixed reality book: Earth structure (Larngear Technology, 2008) depicts a three-dimensional textbook. This summer, AR has been adopted for 3G phones, allowing information to be embedded into a video image (Joos2322, 2009).

Conclusion

Developmental educators might look to mobile phones as a potential resource or classroom learning tool rather than as a classroom distracter. Mobile phones can be used as a platform to build on critical literacy skills for academic literacy tasks. Their potential is only as good as our creativity.

References

Anderson, J. Q., & Rainie, L. (2008). *The future of the Internet III.* Washington, DC: Pew Internet & American Life Project. Retrieved from http://www.elon.edu/e-web/predictions/expertsurveys/2008survey/default.xhtml

Basil, A. (2008). iSign lite (Version 1.0) [3G phone app]. Retrieved from http://idev2.com/iSign/iSign.html

Bottentuit, J. B., Jr., Coutinho, C., & Sternaldt, D. (2006). *M-learning and webquest: The new technologies as pedagogical resource.* Retrieved from http://repositorium.sdum.uminho.pt/handle/1822/6380

Caverly, D. C., Peterson, C. L., Delaney, C. J., & Starks-Martin, G. (2009). Technology integration. In R. F. Flippo & D. C. Caverly (Eds.), *Handbook of college reading and study strategy research* (2nd ed., pp. 314–350). New York: Routledge.

codefactory. (2009). Mobile daisy player (Version 2.2) [3G phone app]. Retrieved from http://www.codefactory.es/en/products.asp?id=268

Colker, J., Rigby, B., Ahjua, S., Mendosa, K., Freitas, N., & Zak, D. (2009). The extraordinaries (Version 1.0) [3G phone app]. Retrieved from http://www.theextraordinaries.org/

DataViz Inc. (2009). Documents to go® (Version 1.1) [3G phone app]. Retrieved from http://www.dataviz.com/iphone

Fies, C., & Marshall, J. (2008). The C3 framework: Evaluating classroom response system interactions in university classrooms. *Journal of Science Education & Technology, 17*(5), 483–499. doi:10.1007/s10956-008-9116-4

Google Inc. (2009). Googlemobile app (Version 0.3) [3G phone app]. Retrieved from http://www.google.com/mobile/products/search.html#p=default

Hartnell-Young, E., & Heym, N. (2008). *How mobile phones help learning in secondary schools.* Nottingham, UK: University of Nottingham. Retrieved from http://partners.becta.org.uk/index.php?catcode=_re_rp_02&rid=15482&section=rh

Horrigan, J. (2009). *Wireless Internet use*. Washington, DC: Pew Internet & American Life Project. Retrieved from http://www.pewinternet.org/Reports/2009/12-Wireless-Internet-Use.aspx

Joos2322. (2009). Wikitude AR travel guide (Part 2) [Video file]. Retrieved from http://www.youtube.com/watch?v=tpaJBu4BEuA

Larngear Technology. (2008). Mixed reality book: Earth structure [Video file]. Retrieved from http://www.youtube.com/watch?v=1RuZY1NfJ3k

Misono, T., & Akahori, K. (2008. September). *The potential for utilizing mobile phones as a study aid for university lectures*. Paper presented at the 4th International Conference on Research in Access and Developmental Education, San Juan, PR. Retrieved from http://www.ncde.appstate.edu/researchconf3.htm

Morgan Stanley. (2008). Technology / Internet trends — presentation from Web 2.0 summit. Retrieved from http://www.morganstanley.com/institutional/techresearch/internet_trends.html

National Center for Supercomputing Applications. (2008). *Augmented reality: Enhancing learning and teaching with inexpensive 3D imagery*. Urbana-Champaign: University of Illinois at Urbana-Champaign. Retrieved from https://netfiles.uiuc.edu/a-craig/www/AR/

Pawan, F., & Honeyford, M. (2009). Academic literacy. In R. F. Flippo & D. C. Caverly (Eds.), *Handbook of college reading and study strategy research* (2nd ed., pp. 26–46). New York: Routledge.

Prensky, M. (2009). H. Sapiens digital: From digital immigrants and digital natives to digital wisdom. *Journal of Online Learning, 5*(3). Retrieved from http://www.innovateonline.info/index.php?view=article&id=705&action=login

Rigoneri, R. (2009). myHomework (Version 2.0). Retrieved from http://www.myhomework.rigoneri.com/

Uffendell, M., Hefferan, M., & Finnigan, M. (2009). *RNIB college learners get smart with their mobile phones*. Retrieved from http://partners.becta.org.uk/index.php?section=rh&catcode=_re_rp_02&rid=16842

Wikipedia Foundation Inc. (2009a). *Citizen journalism* [web page]. Retrieved from http://en.wikipedia.org/wiki/Citizen_journalism

Wikipedia Foundation Inc. (2009b). *List of countries by number of mobile phones in use*. Retrieved from http://en.wikipedia.org/wiki/List_of_countries_by_number_of_mobile_phones_in_use#cite_note-2

Zhang, K. (2008). Ubiquitous technology for language learning: The u-Japan movement in higher education. *Journal of Computing in Higher Education, 20*(2), 81–91.

Chapter 3 Questions for Further Reflection

1. Are there any commonalities among the various "innovations" suggested in this chapter to improve developmental education?

2. Which innovations are truly "new" and which are simply modifications of techniques we have been using for years?

3. What are some ways you and your colleagues can use noncognitive assessment to improve the quality of developmental education activities on your campus?

4. Many successful programs serve relatively few students. How can these programs be "scaled up" so that larger numbers of underprepared students can benefit from them? Other than funding, what are the barriers to scaling up innovations at your institution?

5. How does the organizational structure on your campus promote the implementation of innovation in developmental education? How does it inhibit the implementation of innovation?

6. How has reading the material in this book changed your thinking about the way developmental education is delivered on your campus?

Organizations and Resources

Association for the Tutoring Profession (myatp.org)
This professional association works primarily with tutors in colleges and universities, although private and public school tutors also participate. It holds an annual conference, trains and certifies tutors, and provides a code of ethics for the tutoring profession. It also publishes an online journal for tutors and tutor trainers.

Bill and Melinda Gates Foundation (gatesfoundation.org)
Currently the wealthiest global foundation, it funds projects to improve health, reduce poverty, and enhance education all over the world. Among its North American initiatives, the Gates Foundation funds several higher education projects to bring innovation to scale and use technology to enhance developmental education. It also funds other organizations such as Complete College America and the National Center for Academic Transformation.

College Reading and Learning Association (crla.net)
This professional association addresses the needs of learning assistance and developmental education professionals through publications, conferences, and professional development. It conducts an annual conference, publishes the *Journal of College Reading and Learning* along with a variety of reports, and offers certification for tutoring and mentoring programs.

Complete College America (completecollege.org)
Established in 2009, this nonprofit organization, funded by a variety of foundations, attempts to influence state policy affecting student completion, particularly in community colleges. It developed and maintains its own database and uses that database to generate a variety of reports on student completion.

Community College Research Center (ccrc.tc.columbia.edu)
This organization conducted a large number of highly influential studies on various aspects of developmental education in community colleges between 2007 and 2012. Although the funding for this center has expired, all of its studies are available for review on the center's Web site.

Council of Learning Assistance and Developmental Education Associations (cladea.net)

The council includes representatives from the major professional associations in the field (ATP, CRLA, NADE, NCDE, and NCLCA). Its purpose is to provide a unified voice addressing critical issues in the field and to coordinate and promote member association activities. It also recognizes outstanding individual contributions to the field by electing Fellows of the Council.

Education Commission of the States (ecs.org)

This nonprofit organization was founded in the 1960s to enhance public education through information sharing among state policy makers. Among its programs are Getting Past Go, an initiative funded by the Lumina Foundation to develop policies and strategies to reform developmental education and improve college completion rates.

Learning Support Centers in Higher Education (lsche.net)

This open educational resource network supports learning assistance centers in postsecondary education. It features a variety of resources for learning assistance professionals including definitions, bibliographies, articles, reports, sample syllabi, program descriptions, and a calendar of events in the field.

LRNASST (teachingcenter.ufl.edu/lrnasst.html)

This is the open forum for learning assistance professionals to post comments, questions, and resources, and to engage in discussions of relevant professional issues. Thousands of learning assistance and developmental education professionals from the United States and around the world currently participate in LRNASST.

MDRC (mdrc.org)

MDRC is a nonprofit, nonpartisan, social research organization that has focused some of its efforts on developmental education in the past several years. MDRC's most noted work in the field has been on the scientific study of learning communities, summer bridge programs, and innovations designed to accelerate student completion in general and in developmental courses in particular. MDRC also studies the scaling up of innovations in developmental education.

National Association for Developmental Education (nade.net)

This is the largest professional association in the field. It publishes the *NADE Digest* and offers the *Journal of Developmental Education* as a membership benefit. It also sponsors regional and national conferences, supports research in the field, provides certification for developmental programs, and offers a variety of professional development benefits to members.

National Center for Academic Transformation (thencat.org)

This nonprofit organization promotes information technology to revise and enhance learning environments. It has been one of the primary advocates and consultants in the developmental education curriculum redesign movement. The center claims that institutions using its methodology have experienced dramatic reduction in costs while improving outcomes.

National Center for Developmental Education (ncde.appstat.edu)

The center is a nonprofit organization housed at Appalachian State University. It publishes the *Journal of Developmental Education* and *Research in Developmental Education*, hosts the Kellogg Institute for the Training and Certification of Developmental Educators, does contract research, maintains a resource library on developmental education, and provides resources to professionals in the field.

National College Learning Center Association (nclca.org)

This professional association is devoted exclusively to those working in college and university learning assistance programs. It provides learning center leadership certification, publishes the *Learning Assistance Review*, and holds an annual national conference. It also provides conference proceedings, an extensive learning center bibliography, and a resource directory for members.

Recommended Readings

Adelman, C. (2006, February). *The toolbox revisited: Paths to degree completion from high school through college.* Washington, DC: U.S. Department of Education.

Aghion, P., Boustan, L., Hoxby, C., & Vandenbussche, J. (2009, March). *The causal impact of education on economic growth: Evidence from the U.S.* Boston, MA: Center for Education Policy Research, Harvard University.

American College Testing. (2013). *The condition of college and career readiness 2013.* Iowa City: ACT.

Arendale, D. (2010). Access at the crossroads: Learning assistance in higher education. *ASHE Higher Education Report, 35*(6). San Francisco, CA: Jossey-Bass.

Boroch, D., Hope, L., Gabriner, L., Smith, B., Mery, P., Asera, R., & Johnstone, R. (2010). *Student success in community colleges: A practical guide to developmental education.* San Francisco, CA: Jossey-Bass.

Boylan, H. (2002). *What works: Research-based best practices in developmental education.* Boone, NC: Continuous Quality Improvement Network/National Center for Developmental Education.

Carnavale, A., & Rose, S. (2011). *The undereducated American.* Washington, DC: Center on Education and the Workforce, Georgetown University.

Casazza, M., & Silverman, S. (1996). Learning assistance and developmental education. San Francisco, CA: Jossey-Bass.

Clark-Thayer, S., & Putnam Cole, L. (2009). *NADE self-evaluation guides: Best practice in academic support programs.* Clearwater, FL: H & H Publishing.

Collins, M. (2009, June). *Setting up success in developmental education: How state policies can help community colleges improve student success outcomes.* Boston, MA: Jobs for the Future.

Hughes, K., & Scott-Clayton, J. (2011). Assessing developmental assessment in community colleges. *Community College Review, 39*(4), 327–351.

Jenkins, D., & Weiss, M. (2011, September). *Charting pathways to completion for low-income community college students* (CCRC Working Paper #34). New York, NY: Community College Research Center, Teachers College, Columbia University.

Karp, M. (2011). *Toward a new understanding of non-academic support: Four mechanisms encouraging positive student outcomes in the community college.* (CCRC Working Paper #28). New York, NY: Community College Research Center, Teachers College, Columbia University.

Keimig, R. T. (1983). *Raising academic standards: A guide to learning improvement.* Washington, DC: Association for the Study of Higher Education/Educational Resource Information Center.

Martin, D., & Arendale, D. (2004). *Supplemental instruction: Increasing achievement and retention.* San Francisco: CA: Jossey-Bass.

Maxwell, M. (1997). *Improving student learning skills.* Clearwater, FL: H & H Publishing.

McAbe, R. (2003). *Yes we can: A community college guide for developing America's underprepared.* Washington, DC: American Association of Community Colleges.

Melguiso, T., Hagedorn, L., & Cypers, S. (2008). Remedial/developmental education and the cost of community college transfer: A Los Angeles County sample. *The Review of Higher Education, 31*(4), 401–431.

Price, D., & Roberts, B. (2009). Improving student success by strengthening developmental education in community colleges: The role of state policy. *The working poor families project policy brief, Winter 2008–2009.* Boston, MA: Jobs for the Future.

Prince, M. (2004). Does active learning work: A review of the research. *Journal of Engineering Education, 39*(3), 223–231.

Roueche, J., & Roueche, S. (1999). *High stakes, high performance: Making remediation work.* Washington, DC: American Association of Community Colleges.

Rutschow, E., Richburg-Hayes, L., Brock, T., Orr, G., Cerna, O., Cullinan, D., Reid Kerrigan, M., Jenkins, D., Gooden, S., & Martin, K. (2011, January). *Turning the tide: Five years of Achieving the Dream in community colleges.* New York, NY: MDRC.

Simpson, M., Stahl, N., & Francis, M. (2004). Reading and learning strategies: Recommendations for the 21st century. *Journal of Developmental Education, 28*(2), 2–4, 6–8, 10–12, 14, 16.

Smith Jaggers, S. (2011). *Online learning: Does it help low-income and underprepared students?* (CCRC Working paper #26). New York, NY: Community College Research Center, Teachers College, Columbia University.

Stahl, N. A., & King, J. R. (2009). "A history of college reading." In R. F. Flippo & D. C. Caverly (Eds.), *Handbook of college reading and study strategy research* (2nd ed.). New York, NY: Routledge/Taylor and Francis.

Tinto, V. (1985). *Leaving college: The causes and cures of student attrition.* Chicago, IL: University of Chicago Press.

Tinto, V. (2012). *Completing college: Rethinking institutional action.* Chicago, IL: University of Chicago Press.

Visher, M., Schneider, E., Wathington, H., & Collado, H. (2010, March). *Scaling up learning communities: The experience of six community colleges.* New York, NY: National Center for Postsecondary Research.

White, W. (2004). The physical environment of learning support centers. *The Learning Assistance Review, 9*(1), 17–27.

About the Editors

Hunter R. Boylan is the Director of the National Center for Developmental Education and a Professor of Higher Education at Appalachian State University in Boone, NC. He is a member of the Editorial Boards of the *Journal of Developmental Education*, the *International Journal of Education and Development*, and the *Journal of Teaching and Learning* and serves on the Advisory Boards of the Carnegie Foundation Statway Project, the National Center for Postsecondary Research, and the National Association for Developmental Education (NADE). He is the former Chair of the Council of Learning Assistance and Developmental Education Associations, a Past President of NADE, a previous Technical Assistant for the Gates Foundation Developmental Education Initiative, and the original Director of the nation's first Doctoral Program in Developmental Education at Grambling State University. He has received the NADE award for "Outstanding Leadership" and the association's "Outstanding Research" Award is named after him as are the research scholarships of the Association for the Tutoring Profession and the National College Learning Center Association. He is the author or co-author of seven books and over 100 research articles, book chapters, and monographs.

Barbara S. Bonham is a professor of Higher Education at Appalachian State University. She also serves as Senior Researcher for the National Center for Developmental Education and a faculty member for the Kellogg Institute. She had served as Coordinator of the Higher Education Graduate Program for 10 years. Her teaching background includes twelve years in the field of developmental education at Bloomsburg University as a math instructor, lab coordinator, tutorial supervisor, and assistant to the Director in a Student Services Program (TRIO). She has over forty years of teaching experience overall. She has served as consultant to numerous two-year and four-year colleges in the area of developmental education, particularly mathematics, as well as a program reviewer and evaluator for Title III, Title V, FIPSE, Achieving the Dream projects and technical assistant for the Developmental Education Initiative. Her extensive list of state, national, and international keynote addresses, workshops, technical reports, and presentations reflect her broad areas of research and expertise. These include college teaching and learning, adult development, instructional design, culturally responsive learning environments, program planning, promising practices in developmental education, developmental mathematics, non-western approaches to adult learning, and educational systems in other countries. Her recent scholarly leave in New Zealand provided an opportunity to conduct an in-depth study of the models used for developmental education known as bridging programs and support services.

Acknowledgments (*continued from p. ii*)

Peter Adams, Sarah Gearhart, Robert Miller, and Anne Roberts, "The Accelerated Learning Program: Throwing Open the Gates" from the *Journal of Basic Writing*, Fall 2009, 28:2: pp. 50–69. Reprinted by permission of the publisher.

David R. Arendale, "History of Learning Assistance in U.S. Postsecondary Education," from ACCESS AT THE CROSSROADS (ASHE Higher Education Report, 35(6) 23–54. Copyright © 2010 by Wiley Periodicals, Inc. Reproduced with permission of John Wiley & Sons, Inc.

Paul A. Attewell, David E. Lavin, Thurston Domina, and Tania Levey, "New Evidence on College Remediation" from *The Journal of Higher Education*, vol. 77, No. 5, Sept./Oct. 2008. Copyright © 2008 by The Ohio State University Press. Reproduced with permission.

Thomas Bailey, Dong Wook Jeong, and Sung-Woo Cho, "Referral, Enrollment, and Completion in Developmental Education Sequences in Community Colleges" is reprinted from the *Economics of Education Review*, copyright © 2010 by Elsevier. Reprinted with permission of Elsevier.

Elisabeth Barnett et al., "Bridging the Gap: An Impact Study of Eight Developmental Summer Bridge Programs in Texas" the Executive Summary pp. 1–5 by the National Center for Postsecondary Research, a partnership of CCRC, MDRC, Curry School of Education at the University of Virginia; and faculty at Harvard University. Used with permission of the National Center for Postsecondary Research.

Barbara S. Bonham and Hunter R. Boylan, "Developmental Mathematics: Challenges, Promising Practices, and Recent Initiatives" from Journal of *Developmental Education* 34(3) 2–10 (2011). Published by The National Center for Developmental Education, Appalachian State University, Boone, NC 28608. Reprinted with permission of the publisher.

Hunter R. Boylan, "Targeted Intervention for Developmental Education Students (T.I.D.E.S)," from the *Journal of Developmental Education*, 32(3) 14–18 (2009). Published by The National Center for Developmental Education, Appalachian State University, Boone, NC 28608. Reprinted with permission of the publisher.

Hunter R. Boylan and William G. White, Jr., "Educating All the Nation's People: The Historical Roots of Developmental Education" from *Research in Developmental Education* 4(4) 1–4 (1987). Published by The National Center for Developmental Education, Appalachian State University, Boone, NC 28608. Reprinted with permission of the publisher.

Ellen Brier, "Bridging the Academic Preparation Gap: An Historical View" from the *Journal of Developmental Education*, 8(1), 2–5 (1984). Published by The National Center for Developmental Education, Appalachian State University, Boone, NC 28608. Reprinted with permission of the publisher.

Melissa L. Burgess and David C. Caverly, "Techtalk: 'Second Life' and Developmental Education" from the *Journal of Developmental Education*, 32(3), 42–43. Published by the National Center for Developmental Education, Appalachian State University, Boone, NC 28608. Reprinted with permission of the publisher.

David C. Caverly and Anne R. Ward, "Techtalk: Mobile Learning and Access" from the *Journal of Developmental Education*, 33(1), 38–39. Published by the National Center for Developmental Education, Appalachian State University, Boone, NC 28608. Reprinted with permission of the publisher.

Nikki Edgecombe, "Accelerating the Academic Achievement of Students Referred to Developmental Education" from *CCRC Working Paper* No. 30, Feb. 2011. Used with the permission of the Community College Research Center, Teachers College, Columbia University.

Robert A. Frost, Stephen L. Strom, JoAnna Downey, Deanna D. Schultz, and Teresa A. Holland, "Enhancing Student Learning with Academic and Student Affairs Collaboration" from *Community College Enterprise*, vol. 16, #1, pp. 35–51, Spring 2010. Reprinted with permission from The Community College Enterprise.

386

Douglas R. Holschuh and David C. Caverly, "Techtalk: Cloud Computing and Developmental Education" from the *Journal of Developmental Education*, 33(3) 38–39, Spring 2010. Published by the National Center for Developmental Education, Appalachian State University, Boone, NC 28608. Reprinted with permission of the publisher.

Davis Jenkins, Matthew Zeidenberg, and Gregory Kienzl, "Building Bridges to Postsecondary Training for Low-Skill Adults: Outcomes of Washington State's I-BEST Program," *CCRC Brief* No. 42, May 2009. Used with permission of the Community College Research Center, Teachers College, Columbia University. For updates on this research see "Contextualized College Transition Strategies for Adult Basic Skills Students: Learning from Washington State's I-BEST Program Model," http://ccrc.tc .columbia.edu/publications/i-best-program-final-phase-report.html and "Washington State's Integrated Basic Education and Skills Training Program (I-BEST): New Evidence of Effectiveness," http://ccrc.tc.columbia.edu/publications/i-best-new-evidence .html.

Jamie P. Merisotis and Ronald A. Phipps, "Remedial Education in Colleges and Universities: What's Really Going on?" from *The Review of Higher Education* 24:1 (2000), 67–85. Copyright © 2000 by the Association for the Study of Higher Education. Reprinted with permission of Johns Hopkins University Press.

Delores Perin, "Remediation Beyond Developmental Education: The Use of Learning Assistance Centers to Increase Academic Preparedness in Community Colleges" from *Community College Journal of Research & Practice*, vol. 28, #7, Aug. 2004, reprinted by permission of the publisher, Taylor & Francis Ltd, http://www.tandf.co.uk/journals.

Delores Perin, "Facilitating Student Learning Through Contextualization: A Review of Evidence" from *Community College Review*, vol. 39, #3 (July 2011). Copyright © 2011 by North Carolina State University. Reprinted by permission of SAGE Publications.

Elizabeth Zachry Rutschow and Emily Schneider, from "Unlocking the Gate: What We Know About Improving Developmental Education" from *MDRC Report*, June 2011. Reprinted by permission of the publisher.

Susan Scrivener and Erin Coghlan, "Opening Doors to Student Success: A Synthesis of Findings from an Evaluation at Six Community Colleges" from *MDRC Paper*, March 11, 2012. Reprinted by permission of the publisher.

Caroline Q. Sheldon and Nathan R. Durdella, "Success Rates for Students Taking Compressed and Regular Length Developmental Courses in the Community College" from *Community College Journal of Research and Practice*, vol. 34, #1–2, reprinted by permission of the publisher, Taylor & Francis Ltd, http://www.tandf.co.uk/journals.

William G. White, Nara Martirosyan, and Reuben Wanjohi, "Preparatory Programs in Nineteenth Century Midwest Land Grant Colleges (Part 1)," from *Research in Developmental Education* 23(1), 2009. Published by The National Center for Developmental Education, Appalachian State University, Boone, NC 28608. Reprinted with permission of the publisher.